W9-ABI-492

PLOTS OF ENLIGHTENMENT

*Education and the Novel
in Eighteenth-Century England*

Plots of Enlightenment

EDUCATION AND THE NOVEL

IN EIGHTEENTH-CENTURY ENGLAND

Richard A. Barney

STANFORD UNIVERSITY PRESS

Stanford, California

Stanford University Press
Stanford, California
© 1999 by the Board of Trustees of the
Leland Stanford Junior University
Printed in the United States of America
CIP data appear at the end of the book

For Edie, who has always been there

Acknowledgments

Writing a book about education has been a process of learning constantly, and from many people. At the University of Virginia, where this book got its start, Ralph Cohen's rigorously philosophical mind provided arduous grounds for conceptualizing its framework; Martin Battestin, Douglas Patey, Michael Levenson, and Patricia Meyer Spacks were acute readers of the earliest drafts; and Leo Damrosch, James Turner, and Pat Gill offered helpful suggestions and moral support along the way. My only regret is that Irvin Ehrenpreis did not live long enough to offer more insights than he did, or to see the book reach its final destination.

In its later stages, this project received an enormous intellectual boost from John Bender, Carol Flynn, Eve Bannet, and Hunter Cadzow; Michael McKeon's dauntingly generous contributions may be incalculable. I have also benefited from Ron Schleifer's shrewd advice, Bob Markley's advocacy, Lenny Davis's expansiveness (sometimes late at night), Bill Warner's consistent interest, Lorna Clymer's keen intelligence (with a twist), Michael Bérubé's help with the title, Helen Tartar's patience, and Dan Cottom's acuity, combined with friendly prodding to get this thing done. James Thompson, Alex Petit, Steve Pincus, Margaret Ezell, and Kristina Straub have offered various excellent suggestions, all appreciated. And then there has been the invaluable mix of discernment and outlandish humor from the mind of Rick Barr.

I am equally grateful for the support I have had, sometimes intellectual, sometimes emotional, sometimes constitutional, from a number of other people, including John Ireland, Rebeca Itzkowich, Del Kolve, Mac Thigpen, John Lavier, Rajani Sudan, Gayle

Cadzow, Gene Enrico, Sherry Enrico, Mike Lee, and Bob Davis. The same goes for my family members, who can now rest in declaring that it is finished. A second-string of unwitting supporters also materialized in the likes of The Pretender, Tristram, Tijon, Kimet, Bruno, Zsa Zsa, and Rusty. Julia's companionate reflections came along at just the right time.

I am thankful for fellowships from the American Society for Eighteenth-Century Studies, the South Central Modern Language Association, the Huntington Library, and the Clark Library, which enabled me to write chapter 1, substantially revise chapter 3, and revise several others, including chapter 2. Closer to home, I have benefited immensely from grants from the Oklahoma Foundation for the Humanities, the University of Oklahoma Research Council, and the University of Oklahoma College of Arts and Sciences, all of which helped me write chapter 5, review the entire manuscript, find engravings, and generate an index. I thank these institutions for their assistance.

I have appreciated the help of the special collections staff at several institutions, including the British Museum, the University of California at Los Angeles, the University of California at Santa Barbara, Columbia University, Southern Methodist University, and Rutgers University; the same is true for the Folger, Newberry, Clark, Huntington, and British Libraries, as well as for the Library Company of Philadelphia. John Bidwell, during his tenure at the Clark Library, deserves particular thanks for his erudite generosity. I also thank the British Library, the British Museum, the Newberry Library, the Huntington Library, and the Clark Library for granting permission to publish the illustrations.

Sections of the introduction and chapter 1 appeared as "Subjectivity, the Novel, and the *Bildung* Blocks of Critical Theory," *Genre* 26 (1993): 359–76. I am grateful to the journal for giving me permission to use that material here.

R.A.B.

Contents

Illustrations

PLOTS OF ENLIGHTENMENT

INTRODUCTION

~~

Early Modern Identity and the Rise of Improvisational Fictions

> Because the habitus is an endless capacity to engender products—
> thoughts, perceptions, expressions, actions—whose limits are set
> by the historically and socially situated conditions of its produc-
> tion, the conditioned and conditional freedom it secures is as re-
> mote from a creation of unpredictable novelty as it is from a sim-
> ple mechanical reproduction of the initial conditionings.
>
> —Pierre Bourdieu, *Outline of a Theory of Practice*

Tristram Shandy must have been exaggerating, as usual, when
he claimed that a bad education nearly deprived him of his man-
hood. But predictably, he also meant every word. Readers of Laurence Sterne's novel will probably remember the strangely comical
moment when, as a boy, Tristram clambers up to the sill of an open
window, only to have its sash suddenly fall and nearly sever his sexual organ—the emblem, as we know from the rest of the book, of
Tristram's obsessive interest in the potent symbolism of everything
from noses to narrative digressions. Tristram momentarily blames
Susannah, the chambermaid, for not warning him of the potential
danger, but he focuses primarily on his father's ineffectual attention
to educating him properly. The problem both in this case and many
others, reports Tristram, is "the slow progress my father made in his

Tristra-pædia; at which . . . he was three years and something more, indefatigably at work, and at last, had scarce compleated, by his own reckoning, one half of his undertaking: the misfortune was, that I was all that time totally neglected . . . and what was almost as bad, by the very delay, the first part of the work, upon which my father had spent the most of his pains, was rendered entirely useless,— every day a page or two became of no consequence."[1] The latter part of Mr. Shandy's opus proves equally unserviceable, since it is eccentric, teeming with omissions both fundamental and trivial. But given this particular trauma, Tristram takes things into his own hands, deciding to formulate, with characteristically ironic bravado, some rules of education himself. Of the "remarkable chapter in the *Tristrapædia* . . . *upon sash-windows*," he reports, "I wrote the chapter myself" (307). At this point, however, the situation has become hopelessly entangled: Tristram's development, though hilariously amusing, has been grotesquely misshapen by his father's faulty pedagogy, which in turn is now infected by Tristram's idiosyncratic personality and whimsy.

In its own peculiar way, this episode captures several important issues this book will explore regarding the relevance of philosophy, education, and gender to the eighteenth-century novel's shape and history. In fact, its very strangeness helps illustrate the two main arguments of this study: first, educational theory during the late seventeenth and early eighteenth centuries formed an indispensable source for the English novel's narrative form and its often contradictory representation of individuals' social identity; and second, in understanding the early novel's pedagogical agenda, we can trace the outlines of a crucial fictional antecedent to the later development of the subgenre called the *novel of education*, or *Bildungsroman*. Both of these arguments place the emphasis of this book on English novelists' first experiments with pedagogical ideas during the early and mid-eighteenth century, before the novel acquired its full-blown status, by the turn of the nineteenth century, as a genre distinctly qualified to edify readers via the fictionalized maturation of its protagonists. The first half of the eighteenth century, therefore, proves decisive for understanding how the foundation was initially laid for what later could often be taken for granted—the novel's philosophical, social, and literary credentials as a book of virtues. In the first section of this chapter, I will consider the first claim about the early novel's pedagogical indebtedness, before turning in the second section to discuss the relevance of the novel of education.

Epistemology, Social Discipline, and the Rise of the Novel

At the very least, *Tristram Shandy* offers itself as a kind of cautionary metacritical tale about how both successful socialization and coherent novelistic discourse depend on an effective organization of epistemology by pedagogy. Tristram's development as a youth is propelled—fitfully, even convulsively—by the haphazard coincidence of stimuli around him, a fact reflected by Tristram's digressive, agitated narrative delivery. But that phenomenon relies on more than mere personal eccentricity: it demonstrates Tristram's thorough familiarity with John Locke's argument in *An Essay concerning Human Understanding* (1690) that knowledge is formed by the contingent association of ideas—what Tristram calls the "strange combination of ideas" which, among other things, explains his fascination with time because his mother happened to be thinking about a clock when he was conceived.[2] Tristram's mishap with the window sash further underscores this point: an empiricist epistemology must have something else in order to organize novelistic storytelling as we usually find it in the early modern period, and that something else is the practical implementation of an educational model.

This is an important point given that in studies of the eighteenth-century novel and its origins, epistemology has often served as the key rubric under which critics have labored, and in those terms, Locke's *Essay* has been assigned a signal historical role in influencing the work of later writers and novelists. The emphasis on epistemology has significantly marked the work of scholars such as Ian Watt, Eric Rothstein, Ira Konigsberg, Eve Tavor, and Michael McKeon, to name only a few.[3] Their discussions have proven heuristically powerful in laying out the broad empiricist contours of the eighteenth-century novel, particularly in terms of its newly conceived realistic form, its "modern" depiction of character psychology, and its employment of a secularized, skeptical perspective on both discourse and human perception.[4] But at least two difficulties have persisted in making such connections: first, the problem of offering a plausible link between Locke's abstract philosophical principles—so apparently remote from anything resembling "literary" methods—and the formal innovations of the novel; and second, having established such a linkage, solving the puzzle of exactly what kind of narrative form is implied by Locke's description of the formation of knowledge. Both questions, I will argue, can be productively examined in terms of the theory, practice, and contextual politics of early modern educational programs. Furthermore, early modern pedagogical texts—such as Locke's *Some Thoughts concerning Education* (1693), Mary Astell's *A Serious Proposal to the Ladies* (1694, pt. 1; 1697, pt. 2), Judith Drake's *An Essay in Defence of the Female Sex* (1696), or François Fénelon's *Instructions for the Education of a Daughter* (1708)—provide a more palpable historical explanation than previously offered for the narrative practice of both male and female novelists during the period.

Describing the relation between Locke's *Essay* and the novel inevitably invokes the problem of the relation between philosophy and "literature." Two tacks can be taken to solve this dilemma, both of which are useful, although ultimately, they at best tell only part of the early novel's story. The first approach is to point out the tremendous popularity and influence of Locke's ideas, a strategy that portrays the transition from philosophy to the novel in terms of cause and effect, in a process often characterized as a social "climate" so thoroughly saturated by Lockean principles that it cannot help producing the precipitate of Lockean fictions based on the accumulation of experience and gradual organization of knowledge.[5] This atmospheric description helps capture the extraordinary degree to which the popular media of British culture—including newspapers, occasional essays, and sermons—disseminated Locke's concepts, but put this way, the connection between Locke and later novelists nonetheless remains foggy. Furthermore, although this characterization can persuasively indicate a conceptual continuity between Locke's arguments and novel writing, it is unable to describe the discursive transformations that took place in moving from one generic mode to the other. While the attempt to describe such a change may inevitably rely on metaphorical linkages, climatological or otherwise, the connection can be made more concrete and historically specific.

A second way to approach Locke's philosophy and the novel is to treat them as analogous discursive formations produced by much larger, even glacial, historical changes, such as the emergence of "realist" criteria for judging writing of all kinds, or the development of an individualistic, bourgeois description of human identity and social relations. In these terms, large-scale shifts in England's social consciousness can be viewed as having formed comparable, though distinct, features of both philosophy and fiction, a description that can also incorporate in its explanation the significant impact Locke had on specific novelists.[6] But despite its versatility and sophistication, this approach also risks taking for granted a generic distinction that during the eighteenth century was still only in the making—as when Ian Watt, one exemplar of this perspective, summarily remarks that "philosophy is one thing and literature is another."[7] I shall be working by contrast from the historical premise that during much of the early modern period, the two disciplines were still incompletely distinguished from one another and therefore intimately informed each other's development, even as the ground was being laid for their ultimate disjunction by the late 1700s. This means the pedagogical orientation of both epistemology and the novel during the early eighteenth century can be credited to a generic instability resulting from the gradual separation of "philosophy" from "literature" as we now understand them.

As a part of this historical process, educational writing was also emerging as a distinct generic form (with a host of identifiable subgenres), at times being perceived as a specialized application of epistemology in the broadest sense. But it was significantly protean in its conventions and aspirations, reflecting an often indeterminate generic standing between philosophical and "literary" treatments of instruction or socialization. This scenario forms part of what Michael McKeon describes as a widespread "destabilization of generic categories" during the seventeenth and eighteenth centuries, when the ability to adjudicate between truth and fiction became complicated, if not obscured, resulting in the difference between "romance" and "history" becoming severely problematic. He further links this generic mutation to a larger destabilization of social categories, initiated by the "progressive" attack on the aristocratic ideology of virtue and its supposedly inherent linkage with social rank. By the 1740s, McKeon argues, the novel achieves (relative) generic stability and unambiguous recognition by forming a successful "conflation" of the issues regarding truth and virtue in its storytelling.[8] This account becomes further nuanced in the context of contemporaneous pedagogical theory, because it represents a substantially earlier attempt to achieve such a combination, given that education is precisely the place where epistemology and social theory converge during the last decades of the seventeenth century and the first two decades of the eighteenth century. Since this period's educational writing explicitly treats epistemology and theories about socialization as twin branches of a larger, naturalized system of acculturation, it provides a crucial antecedent for considering the novel's similar goals in instructing its readers.[9]

In treating philosophy and literature as gradually emerging categories during the early Enlightenment, I will also examine the ways in which philosophy itself was often transformed and—in specific, material terms—rewritten in the development of novelistic writing. It will therefore be useful to draw on what could be called recent "textualist" approaches to Locke's philosophy, particularly John Richetti's and Paul de Man's analyses of the *Essay concerning Human Understanding* in terms of narrative patterns and literary devices such as metaphor, since they offer suggestive ways to consider the encroachment of early modern philosophy on fiction and the other way around. The difficulty, however, lies in the fact that a textualist framework has so far produced two extremes: for de Man, it locates a fundamental failure of philosophy to control its linguistic medium, while for Richetti, it explains how philosophical writers can in fact redeem their arguments from the threat of inconsistency or even incoherence. De Man argues that Locke's essay succumbs to the unreliable, even arbitrary, modulations of its own metaphorical language despite Locke's best efforts to expel or control them, in the end exhibiting a sinuous discussion that undercuts his goals of rigorously proper knowledge and reliable truth. "From the recognition of language as trope," de Man asserts, "one is led to the telling of a tale"—though here Locke's recognition is implicit at best, and the tale a metastory about how philosophy's dream of establishing first principles and solid foundations is frustrated and indelibly fractured.[10] Richetti, by contrast, contends that empiricist philosophers from Locke to Hume employ rhetorical devices of "dramatic setting, implicit narrativity, persona, and other *supervising* 'scenic' tendencies" as a kind of discursive damage control.[11] In the *Essay*, he argues, Locke negotiates his way through the uncertainties of unreliable perceptions and their analysis by "narration": "naming that avoids mere labels, an active and continuously reflexive literary manner" that introduces its own kind of epistemological slippage while finally enabling Locke to control and manipulate the empiricist project to its successful conclusion.[12]

De Man's and Richetti's conclusions about the *Essay* are emphatically at odds with each other, but there is no compelling reason for having to choose between the extremes of philosophy as magnificent failure and philosophy as problematic but assured success. Beyond de Man's view of the *Essay* as a genre that implodes under the pressure of its linguistic form, and Richetti's view of it as a new "comic, quasi-novelistic document" (111) that nonetheless remains steadfastly philosophical, is a third possibility: considering Locke's work an exemplary instance in seventeenth- and early eighteenth-century writing of *generic displacement*—a metaphorical opening or rupture in philosophical discourse that does not derail philosophical writing but indicates instead the ways by which other, less lofty, nonliterary genres such as educational discourse could be even more readily transformed by the implementation of literary modes. The phenomenon de Man and Richetti describe can be attributed to the late seventeenth and early eighteenth centuries' installment of unprecedented, sharp distinctions between kinds of discourses, including "true history" and romance, and philosophical and "literary" genres. That same process inevitably produced residual traces of those "foreign" genres that had earlier been part of a more loosely conceived generic category. But it is also true that in the midst of this categorical instability, there were some discourses such as educational writing that registered a restless and aggressive appropriation of other modes in the interest of pragmatic effectiveness. As such, educational writing exhibits an analogous function to the novel's, and in the process contributes to the novel's strategies for contending with similar problems concerning the prospect of human sociability. The process of narrative is crucial to both forms, in other words, because it can bridge similar gaps in the attempt to formulate a sound ideology of English citizenship. Thus early modern educational writing can be considered a kind of discursive way station both thematically and formally between Enlightenment epistemology and the emerging novel.

If we turn again to Tristram Shandy's bizarre childhood experience, its lesson about the relative merits of epistemology versus education in organizing early modern fiction invokes the historically contentious relation between two distinctly poststructuralist approaches to the Enlightenment's representation of individual identity. The first, based particularly on the work of Jacques Derrida and Paul de Man, could be called *deconstructive*, and the second, based on Michel Foucault's analyses, has emphasized the powerful role of socioinstitutional disciplines and their affiliated discourses. Derrida and de Man have argued that the Enlightenment's aim to grasp universal reason or calculable sociopolitical identity is inevitably compromised by the machinations of discourse, whether they appear in the linguistic form of figural language, or the more general form of *différance*, or undecidability. For these deconstructors, fully coherent personal identity, or a national citizenship completely consistent with Nature, for instance, is never accomplished, its realization always postponed. As critics have sometimes pointed out, Sterne's novel represents an uncannily familiar version of postmodern displacement in its play on everything from the indeterminacy of linguistic reference to the instability of Tristram's ego boundaries. And yet, as I have already suggested, episodes like the one about the faulty window sash also conjure the need for an overarching pedagogical or social apparatus by which to reimagine Tristram's hapless development. This suggests that, at least in the context of early modern fiction, one needs to reappraise de Man's concept of pedagogy as the central trope by which to conceive a form of communication that would successfully resist the temptations of authoritarian claims for metaphysical truth. As a form of noncoercive, impersonal, even unpredictable knowledge, pedagogy can perform that service because, he says, "teaching is not primarily an intersubjective relationship between people but a cognitive process in which self and other are only tangentially and contiguously involved."[13] It is important to insist, however, that the idea of teaching as a cognitively contingent process should not lead to overlooking the ways by which that very condition can produce the impetus for social orchestration or institutional intervention. Hence in the first two chapters of this book, I will consider how the often indeterminate tropes used in Enlightenment writing about education—including figures of speech regarding medicine, horticulture, the theater, or political empire—consistently point to the ineluctable empowerment or privilege of the educator (as metaphorical doctor, gardener, stage director, or even monarch) in the pedagogical situation. The example of educationalists such as Locke, Astell, Drake, and others suggests that, given an inevitable conceptual or philosophical uncertainty about the relation between human beings' individual prerogative and their potential reformability, the project of teaching students desirable social values can only succeed given the more or less arbitrary assertion of authority, which at a particular historical moment springs from contingencies such as economic class, social rank, gender, and age.[14]

Even given the singularity of Tristram's response to the window sash episode, his insistence that the *Tristra-pædia* include sections on things such as chamber pots and windows reflects precisely the exhaustively systematic documentation of the socializing process that by the mid-eighteenth century was becoming increasingly linked to the implementation of disciplinary institutions as described by Foucault. With that in mind, I aim to establish a provisional alliance between a deconstructive and a disciplinary approach to individual subjectivity in order to consider how what is undecidable can have a decisive relation to what is culturally practical. This does not mean imagining a synthesis of perspectives, but instead considering how a sociocultural agenda can intervene in the constitution of indeterminate subjectivity, and how in turn the prospect of discontinuity modifies a tendency in Foucault's work to perceive the disciplinary process as virtually totalizing.[15]

In his own way, Foucault has often insisted on the discontinuities that conventional historiography ignores in establishing coherent selfhood at the center of a seamless historical narrative. In the *Archaeology of Knowledge*, he argues:

> [C]ontinuous history is the indispensable correlative of the founding function of the subject: the guarantee that everything that has eluded him may be restored to him; the certainty that time will disperse nothing without restoring it in a reconstituted unity; the promise that one day the subject—in the form of historical consciousness—will once again be able to appropriate, to bring back under his sway, all those things that are kept at a distance by difference, and find in them what might be called his abode.[16]

At key moments in his work on the disciplines, however, Foucault appears to reinvest the principles of continuity and self-presence in the advent of what he calls "complete institutions." In describing, for instance, the institution of eighteenth-century medical practice, he writes:

> This enclosed, segmented space, observed at every point, in which the individuals are inserted in a fixed place, in which the slightest movements are supervised, in which all events are recorded, in which an uninterrupted work of writing links the centre and periphery, in which power is exercised without division, according to a continuous hierarchical figure, in which each individual is constantly located, examined and distributed among the living beings, the sick and the dead—all this constitutes a compact model of the disciplinary mechanism.[17]

By this account, the self is the construct, rather than the stable center, of the social edifice, but now the institution of discipline itself acquires a kind of self-coherence by which it can survey all actions, order all experience, and chart all positions via "an uninterrupted work of writing." This characterization is in keeping with the kind of (pan)optimism expressed by Jeremy Bentham in describing the function of the Panopticon, which serves as the central model for Foucault's analysis. It therefore accurately represents the aggressive ideal—the dark dream—of the disciplinary project. But it also tends to conflate the "ideal" functions of the disciplines and their affiliated discourses with their specific applications in the historical constitution of early modern citizens.[18]

Scholars of the early modern novel drawing on Foucault's work have contended with the Panopticon's monolithic interpretive shadow by invoking, at least momentarily, contending principles such as social resistance, carnivalesque disruption, or the stratified conditions of gender relations. And yet the result has nonetheless been a similar emphasis on thoroughgoing disciplinary power, which can be attributed at least partly to using the modern prison as either explicit model—as in John Bender's exploration of the "penitentiary idea"—or as implicit metaphor—as in Nancy Armstrong's explanation of women's power of surveillance in the newly conceived bourgeois household.[19] In exploring the relation of educational theory to the emergence of the novel, I will examine the similar methods that both educational institutions and penitentiaries adopted during the eighteenth century, including the use of covert supervision and the implementation of meticulous scheduling and testing in the process of (re)shaping individual behavior. At a certain level of sociohistorical analysis, comparing these modes of institutionalization makes good sense, because as Foucault points out, the reinvention of the prison system during the Enlightenment was premised precisely on incorporating educational methods in the aim to reform, rather than merely detain, inmates. In other ways, however, a wholesale interpretation of the novel's pedagogical legacy using a penitential grid can conceal or at least distort the very real distinctions that should be noted concerning the role of early modern educational thought in shaping contemporaneous fiction. It may well be, in other words, that Westerners have lived in the prison house of discipline since at least the advent of the Enlightenment, but it is crucial to distinguish the various degrees to which hegemony or social control has been implemented in the specific disciplinary institutions inflected by variables such as class, rank, and function.

When we consider the revisionist proposals of educational theorists during the late seventeenth and early eighteenth centuries, we find, in fact, that the proposals are united in the common goal of reducing a sense of prisonlike austerity in the schooling of middle- and upper-class pupils. For some, like Locke, that goal could be achieved by emphasizing the use of private tutors, while for others, like Mary Astell, it could be realized in establishing a private retreat for women that would institute a pedagogical policy of gentle encouragement and disciplinary ease. But even granting the new penitentiary's stress on reform rather than punishment, there is a crucial distinction between using the prison, rather than the school, as a basis for modeling the formation of early modern citizens: this difference is the prison's inevitable creation of its inmates' constantly tangible *confinement* or lack of mobility—in short, the painful deprivation of their liberty, one of the watchwords of early modern educationalists' aim to form self-reliant individuals. No matter how gentle its methods, clandestine its techniques, or indirect its procedures, the penitentiary could not successfully induce its inmates to forget they were incarcerated, let alone imagine they were in any sense "free." It could well be, of course, that the sense of freedom early modern educators intended to foster was illusory, only the appearance of choice in the process of indoctrinating students all the more powerfully in normative behavior. And yet, as a component repeatedly stressed as a new requirement in the education of children, individual liberty needs to be taken seriously as part of the matrix of "modern" subjectivity, which during the eighteenth century was becoming increasingly conceived as part of a system of civil rights for individual citizens.

Approaching the discipline of early eighteenth-century education this way means revising Foucault's description of the period's various articulations of individual autonomy or private rights, which he considers mainly as a discursive mask covering the reality of hegemonic disciplinary institutions. In *Discipline and Punish*, he concludes that "the general juridical form that guaranteed a system of rights that were egalitarian in principle was supported by these tiny, everyday, physical mechanisms, by all those systems of micropower that are essentially non-egalitarian and asymmetrical that we call the disciplines. . . . The real, corporal disciplines constituted the foundation of the formal, juridical liberties."[20] This description contains two strongly "materialist" claims. The first one is that human subjectivity becomes exclusively the product of disciplinary practices, rather than an identity based on self-possessed rationality, an idea often identified as the humanist legacy of the Enlightenment. The second is that despite its crucial contribution to forming modern subjectivity, "discourse" in the broadest sense remains secondary to what Foucault describes as discipline's more "real" edifice or "foundation." I want to revise this picture in two ways: first, by viewing the discourses about rights and the institutions of discipline as more or less equally competing components in the articulation of early modern identity; and second, by considering both written discourse and material institutions during the period as having internalized a dual emphasis on egalitarianism and hegemony in the attempt to define individual citizenship.

In these terms, the eighteenth-century English novel is heavily influenced by the aim in contemporaneous educational writing to negotiate a provisional alliance between the contending values of individual autonomy and social discipline. During the novel's early stages, in fact, the increased emphasis on either of these principles immediately invokes—or provokes—the other's importance as a salutary antidote. In this context, the novel does not merely issue a promise of freedom that is secondary to, and also undermined by, the specific educational practices of the period; it performs instead what Pierre Bourdieu and Jean-Claude Passeron call "pedagogic action," which, being "always objectively situated between the two unattainable poles of pure force and pure reason," reproduces a system of cultural values in the population—in the case of novels, in readers—via the mechanism of a naturalized "symbolic effect."[21] As one part of this effect, the novel also has the crucial role of both anticipating and shaping eighteenth-century educational practice while locating as well the gaps or fissures inherent in a cultural logic intent on fostering constrained personal liberty.

From this perspective the gap between personal prerogative and social control forms two competing constructions of individual identity. Put another way, it creates the opposing poles of what can be imagined as a sociopolitical continuum given the mediation of a national education. That mediation could be articulated in Lockean terms as the reconciliation of individual rights and political responsibility, or in republican terms as the harnessing of personal ability (*virtù*) to public citizenship. In either case, I will approach the idea of autonomous individuality as one social construction bumping up against or contending with another, while recognizing that this encounter could often be articulated in the vocabulary of inherent human nature pitted against social restriction. Even during the Enlightenment, however, authors were attuned to the constructedness of presumably natural individuality. Bernard Mandeville, for example, as a social critic and satirist who insisted on the unavoidable transgressiveness of individual agency, briefly invoked the notion of natural human impulses in order to explain it, before emphasizing an entirely different—and emphatically social—set of metaphors. As he put it:

> Every Person is to be consider'd as an entire Individual, a wonderful Machine endued with Thought and a Will independent from any thing visible from without. . . . a necessitous Being, that is Subject to Hunger and Thirst, and has many Passions to gratify, and at the same time a vast Compound, a lesser World, with a Sovreignty, and Court of Judicature within, that has a private Welfare and Preservation of its own to mind, altogether abstract from the Good of the Publick.[22]

Viewed this way, the individual may be self-enclosed, but he or she is also a composite of natural, judiciary, and political elements that determine his or her self-definition. Aside from the instincts for self-preservation, therefore, the self is defined as a self-governing entity precisely to the degree to which it appropriates and redeploys, in miniature, the armature of civil and political organization.

Still, the opposition perceived by Mandeville and many of his contemporaries between individual autonomy and social conformity was an extreme, bifurcated version of the Enlightenment's general definition of selfhood in terms of what Pierre Bourdieu calls the *habitus*, the "systems of durable, transposable *dispositions*" that constitute socialized individuals by invoking both personal initiative and social conditioning.[23] For Bourdieu, the point is to avoid conceiving subjectivity as either the outcome of "unpredictable novelty" or "creative free will" (95, 73)—the axiom of existentialism, as well as, to some extent, of humanism—or as "an epiphenomenon of hypostatized structure" (84)—the tendency in structuralist accounts and, I would add, in many New Historicist characterizations of disciplined selfhood. Instead, he argues, individuals are shaped by the habitus's network of "structured structures predisposed to function as structuring structures, that is, as principles of the generation and structuring of practices and representations which can be objectively 'regulated' and 'regular' without in any way being the product of obedience to rules, [and] objectively adapted to their goals without presupposing a conscious aiming at ends" (72). Although here Bourdieu downplays the role of individual intent, it nonetheless plays a key part in determining the daily experience of one's social identity, because Bourdieu perceives a crucial gap between disposition and its enactment, or the habitus's structure and its actual practice. The habitus, he argues, must operate on the principle of "regulated improvisation," by which individuals must actively work to adapt an internalized system of social codes to the specific, contingent circumstances in which they always find themselves.

Another way to explain this phenomenon is to recall Judith Butler's analysis of how human subjectivity is constructed by social acculturation. Despite the clear differences between her deconstructive approach and Bourdieu's sociological interpretation, both finally concur that an individual's identity always sustains some measure of indeterminacy that must be mediated by the performance of that identity. For Butler, that indeterminacy occurs because subjectivity's construction by social codes does not mean it is completely calculated by them. She argues, "the subject is not *determined* by the rules through which it is generated because signification is *not a founding act, but rather a regulated process of repetition*" which individuals can alter by initiating some kind of "variation on that repetition."[24] Butler's explanation of performed social identity helps pinpoint exactly how, from Bourdieu's perspective, the gap between the habitus and its application might be breached and how, in the process, individuals can have an active hand in modifying both the implementation and even the structure of the habitus. I would argue further that the relation between individual disposition and its realization in specific circumstances in many ways follows the logic Derrida finds in the relation between "theory" and "practice," or more specifically in the dynamics of the supplement, which works to compensate for a lack or deficiency in a larger network while also producing an excess that can potentially divert the system's original orientation. Hence in Bourdieu's account, while the aim is to "regulate" the habitus's implementation, the process of improvisation is supplementary because it inevitably introduces an element of unpredictability or displacement, or both. If, by Butler's view, an individual's improvisations can generate significant changes in the social system, even to the point of producing "performative subversions,"[25] then there is equally the chance that an individual's most subversive designs will not create the intended result given a particular set of adverse or unforeseen historical circumstances. By the same token, even the most assiduous attempts to adhere to the habitus's structure can, given the right cultural conditions, result in a notable deviation from the original structure. Taking this approach means tracing the complex—and, at times, necessarily indeterminate—interaction of disciplinary inculcation, individual agency, and the historical conditions that set the stage for improvisational performance.

This book argues that during the late seventeenth and early eighteenth centuries, both educational writers and novelists introduced in England a new sense of "modern" identity by portraying it as the formation of improvisational subjectivity. Telling the story of the novel's rise this way means drawing out the historical assumptions that are only implicit in Bourdieu's characterization of the social habitus, but can be discerned more clearly in his explanation of how education forms improvised identity. In *Reproduction in Education, Society and Culture*, Bourdieu and Passeron describe how improvisational disposition is inculcated using a "'soft approach,'" which includes employing "non-directive methods, 'invisible pedagogy', dialogue, participation, [and] 'human relations'"; it therefore sharply contrasts the "'strong arm'" techniques of imposed authority and strict didacticism, which create a more rigid form of identity.[26] Although generally, Bourdieu and Passeron intend to offer a theoretical account of "soft" pedagogical methods that spans Western history from the classical period to the late twentieth century, their comments also occasionally suggest that such methods became predominant during the early modern era, especially given the transition from feudalism to bourgeois democracy.[27] In this sense, a historical interpretation of the habitus approximates Foucault's account of the modern disciplines' rise during the same period.

In exploring the connections, however, between educational writing and the novel's self-definition as a genre seriously intent on educating readers, as well as delighting or enticing them, I will not focus mainly on the role of conduct books, as scholars such as Nancy Armstrong have done in emphasizing a strongly Foucauldian view of early modern fiction. Instead, while keeping in mind the broad range of genres constituting the general category of educational discourse—including conduct and courtesy books, sermons, guide books, and tracts—I will discuss primarily the role of what I have been calling "educational theory," those early modern works that drew substantially on philosophical, sociological, or psychological premises in telling teachers how to teach students successfully. In contrast to authors of conduct books, who addressed young or adult readers directly in prescribing a model of virtuous behavior, the authors of educational theory were more attuned to the inherent difficulties of a pedagogical project that purported to be neither rule governed nor unruly, and that claimed to sponsor both individual freedom and social restraint at the same time. Rather than assume that "correct" social identity could be construed as a largely formulaic inventory of exhortations and prohibitions, these writers stressed that not only identity but also the educational process itself was a matter of improvising on a set of ideal goals for citizenship. Of course, conduct books did have their own ambiguities, as in their crediting readers with self-determination while also insisting that they readily submit to their literary authority. But since conduct books have tended to create the impression of forming an exhaustively disciplined personal identity (as in Armstrong's interpretation),[28] and since they were historically only one part of the eighteenth century's educational milieu, I will study their role in the context of work by Astell, Locke, Drake, Fénelon, and others, who considered the moral codes promulgated by conduct books to be the general standard for educating the middle and upper classes, while also emphasizing that they were to be inculcated using indirect or "liberal" methods.

In confronting directly the uncertainties endemic to the process of forming improvisational identity, early modern pedagogical theory imagines education as performing the key ideological function of naturalizing as much as possible the virtues desirable in English citizens. As Bourdieu describes it, the habitus is "history turned into nature," thereby constituting a domain of collective cultural assumptions that Bourdieu calls *doxa*.[29] But he also suggests that this naturalizing transaction can be complete only under the most ideal circumstances: "in the extreme case, that is to say, when there is a quasi-perfect correspondence between the objective order and the subjective principles of organization (as in ancient societies) the natural and social world appears as self-evident. This experience we shall call *doxa*" (164). In this scenario, the realm of doxa is distinct from the domain of disputed opinion, which includes the "confrontation of competing discourses" on a scale ranging from the orthodox to the heterodox.[30] But in societies other than what Bourdieu calls "mythico-ritual system[s]" (165), in the transactions, that is, of less ideal—one could also say "modern"—societies, the distinction between the conscious and unconscious spheres is less strictly definable. The material of doxa periodically slips back into the sphere of social orthodoxy, which in turn attempts to legitimate itself by still more efforts to naturalize its agenda. (This might be called the paradox of doxa.) Thus active individual agency often plays a more important role in improvising on the habitus than Bourdieu's account might initially suggest.

Within this framework, the role of ideology, particularly at the moment of its original installation by education, is to *approximate* doxa as much as possible.[31] Especially in light of Enlightenment educational theory, ideology's task of instilling doxa in students is therefore always tenuous and only partially successful. Given the two levels at which a crucial gap persists—first, in the general lack of correspondence between the natural and social order, and second, in the difference between the habitus and individuals' implementation of it—I will explore in both educational writing and the novel the specific, textual means by which early modern authors attempt to mediate among those discontinuities. The provisional solution, I argue in chapters 1 and 2, is to deploy narrative metaphors that can form a credible sequence of educational "events" or improvisations. That process can be found in the tropes drawn from dramatic performance, while the aim to naturalize students' education appears especially in the use of horticultural and medical metaphors. The trope of empire, moreover, especially in the context of women authors, offers an incisive way to consider both the powers and limitations of individual agency: on the one hand, appropriating the idea of empire could suggest for educators and novelists alike the potential of improvisation to generate cultural change, but on the other hand, it could indicate with equal weight the degree to which individuals can be subjugated to the hegemony of a larger sociopolitical schema. Hence I have chosen to concentrate my efforts particularly on educationalists such as Mary Astell, as well as on novelists such as Daniel Defoe, Charlotte Lennox, and Eliza Haywood, all who examine the relevance of "empire" to the prospect of self-determination and enlightenment.

Whatever its specific form, the figural representation of improvisational subjectivity is a fiction in the broadest and narrowest senses: it must be deliberately assembled from the cultural assumptions at hand, and as a process of gradual instruction, it takes the form of an ongoing story. Since this fictional representation, moreover, can accommodate a variety of social perspectives, this study considers how eighteenth-century novels occupy distinct positions along the imagined continuum between autonomy and constraint. It treats the novel as a popular new form uniquely situated to represent that pedagogical continuum because more than any of its literary predecessors, it could assimilate and transform other generic forms in the process of instructive storytelling. As an expansive, "modern" genre offering an unprecedented ability to depict a comprehensive picture of English national identity, the novel also enacts the dual imperatives of the educational process most strik-

ingly by frequently appropriating—and influencing in turn—the
narrative experiments emerging in traditional educational writing.
In the context of eighteenth-century educators' increasingly
explicit aim to construct a national identity for their pupils, the potential of individual improvisation to resist, alter, or perhaps even
transform the status quo is particularly important when we consider
the role of gender in shaping the educational agendas of both men
and women educators or novelists. Recalling once again Tristram
Shandy's peculiar mishap, for instance, it is clear that in his case
gender plays a crucial part of his agitation about his lack of instruction. Though he declares that his injury was "nothing,—I did not
lose two drops of blood by it,"[32] the reader learns later that *something* has clearly happened to his precious bodily member, since af-
terward his father begins a lengthy discussion about circumcision
by remarking, "this *Tristram* of ours, I find, comes very hardly by all
his religious rites" (308). As further evidence of his male anxiety,
Tristram fiercely blames Susannah, the chambermaid, for his accident, before turning his attention to his father's pedagogical fail-
ings. On the one hand, he alleges feminine carelessness is the cause
for his injury, while on the other, he compensates for an unspecified loss of physical prowess by asserting a greater potency than his
father's regarding educational insight. In the end, Tristram's combined fixation and denial indicate that by his lights, a poor education threatens to deprive him—if only in piecemeal fashion—not
only of his masculinity but also of his identity as a male at the most
fundamentally anatomical level. As an unplanned rite of initiation,
Tristram's accident has inducted him into a life of chronically *un-
regulated improvisations: thereafter, an extraordinary male paranoia
manifests itself both in his persistently tentative sense of ego boundaries and in the palpable lack of direct narrative thrust in the novel
as a whole.

Though extreme, Tristram's case suggests an intimate tie between education and gender that is all the more important in considering those women educationalists and novelists intent on imagining new social possibilities for their female peers under the auspices of pedagogical reform. Whether they stressed the importance
of religious knowledge, moral understanding, or familiarity with

the literary tradition, authors such as Mary Astell, Judith Drake, Lady Mary Chudleigh, and Damaris Masham wrote with confidence that, without venturing to overturn entirely the traditional English conventions regarding the roles of the sexes, they could make women's social prerogatives substantially more equitable through a better education for them. In charting the important differences in female writers' conception of human nature and its pedagogical formation, however, my aim is to avoid treating their work as a discursive tradition that is virtually self-contained, or at least largely detached from the work by men on the same subject.

Until most recently, the tendency of historical studies of the eighteenth-century English novel has been to characterize it as being constituted by two separate traditions organized by gender—even if that pattern has emerged only implicitly in the selection of works scholars have chosen to discuss. When we consider some of the most influential scholarship published during the past fifteen years—including, for example, Lennard Davis's *Factual Fictions*, Jane Spencer's *The Rise of the Woman Novelist*, Dale Spender's *Mothers of the Novel*, Nancy Armstrong's *Desire and Domestic Fiction*, John Bender's *Imagining the Penitentiary*, Michael McKeon's *The Origins of the English Novel*, or Janet Todd's *The Sign of Angellica*—we find that critics have focused predominantly on fiction by either male or female authors.[33] In feminist work, to be sure, there has been the need to account for the context of a male tradition against which a distinct female literary tradition is usually strongly contrasted. To a great extent, that approach has been the result of the very real need, especially when it comes to early modern female authors, to recover a legacy of primary texts by women who, after receiving perhaps some attention during the nineteenth and early twentieth centuries, had fallen out of view until the 1970s and 80s. But we have yet to articulate a broadly based description of early modern culture that would provide for a thorough engagement with the complex continuities and discontinuities among the works of men *and* women novelists.

This is not to argue that, given particular historical contexts, scholars may not have good reason for focusing exclusively on the fictional work of either male or female novelists during the Enlightenment. Instead, it is to concur with Margaret Ezell's observation that the inclination to perceive a sharp distinction between a male and female literary tradition is a phenomenon related to a nineteenth-century view of literature that has persisted in the twentieth century. In *Writing Women's Literary History*, Ezell points out that during the seventeenth and eighteenth centuries, neither readers nor critics judged women's texts by standards considered exclusively or uniformly feminine—in the sense of either a unified female aesthetic, or a universal foundation of female experience.[34] Instead, a kind of literary androgyny—the combined features of "feminine" piety and "masculine" strength of wit or style—was often the standard of measurement by which male authors evaluated the work of their female counterparts, and vice versa. During the 1600s, Ezell explains, a literary culture constituted in part by the circulation of unpublished manuscripts was particularly inclined to include women in a definition of generalized authorship. It would not be until the later eighteenth century, after the institution of a full-blown literary marketplace, and hence the development of women authors' more controversial role as public literary figures, that the sense of distinctly gendered literary traditions would begin to surface.[35]

In the context of this emerging distinction between men's and women's work, I want to relate, without conflating, the pedagogical arguments of men and women writers during the seventeenth and early eighteenth centuries in the interest of considering similar patterns in the fiction by male and female novelists. This book argues, in fact, that during this period both male and female educationalists were formulating a similar model of improvisational identity, although that model would also be significantly inflected by women's interest in revising the traditional views of how to reshape female "nature," and it would be similarly altered later by novelists such as Lennox and Haywood. To some extent, then, the vocabulary of "feminism" will apply, although there would not emerge in English letters a comprehensive argument for women's rights, for instance, until the end of the eighteenth century with the work of Mary Hays and Mary Wollstonecraft. Nonetheless, the work by educationalists such as Mary Astell and Judith Drake, on the one side, and the novels by authors such as Lennox and Haywood, on the other, form a crucial part of feminism's history because these women began to imagine the category of gender as a separate, semiautonomous cultural category by applying the contemporaneous arguments attacking a traditional social hierarchy based on rank to an analysis of the condition of middle- and upperclass women. And the fundamental premise of this project was that those women should be able to enlarge their share of the social franchise by way of better education and intellectual self-improvement.

In tracing the historical connections among the works of male and female educationalists who contributed to the shape of early modern fiction, I will focus particularly on Locke's *Some Thoughts concerning Education* as a text that, for several reasons, provides a useful place for conducting an exemplary textualist reading of what is at stake in Locke and his contemporaries' conception of improvisational education. During the eighteenth century, the *Education* was read at least as widely as the *Essay*, acquiring some of its prestige from that earlier famous work, but in the end establishing its own terrain with a readership that cut across the barriers of gender, educational background, and even class. By 1800, the *Education* had appeared in more than twenty-five English editions, and during the first decades of the 1700s, it was translated into French, German, Italian, and Dutch.[36] It appealed to a much broader readership than Locke's book on human understanding, since it did not require sophisticated learning and had immediate applications to England's pressing concern to foster social tolerance, form civil solidarity, and marshal the nation's human resources for better productivity. By Margaret Ezell's account, Locke's work inaugurated a new phase in English letters by making education a topic not only for learned treatises but also "polite" literature and popular journalism.[37] To cite only a few instances of the *Education*'s popularity: Leibniz declared it a much better work than Locke's *Essay*; Lord Chesterfield strongly recommended Locke's pedagogical ideals both to his son and his peers; Eustace Budgell's series in the *Spectator* and George Osborne in the *London Journal* popularized the *Education*'s principles; and in the sequel to Richardson's famed first novel, an au-

thority on virtue no less than Pamela herself spends a lengthy portion of the book evaluating Locke's pedagogical principles in her
characteristically exhaustive fashion.

Locke's educational treatise, in short, stirred an animated exploration of pedagogical ideals, family relations, and social values
that lasted well into the late eighteenth century; it became a cultural touchstone for discussions that spanned elite and popular genres, philosophical and practical concerns, theological, psychological, and political issues. Still, despite Jay Fliegelman's claim that the
Education's "influence on eighteenth-century English literature can
hardly be overemphasized,"[38] I will not be characterizing the entire
body of the period's pedagogical or fictional writing as strictly
Lockean. To be sure, the *Education* is an ideal site for excavating the
links between pedagogical theory and the novel not because it is
the *only* source for the novel's educational pedigree or aspirations,
but because it is a text that draws on a full range of empiricist arguments that were strongly influential for the next century; as such,
the *Education* is strategically situated for examining how eighteenth-century educational writing becomes an overdetermined
genre—a form drawing on the precepts and conventions of philosophical discourse while at the same time placing them under the
pressures of a new narrative format. Although women educationalists such as Astell, Drake, and Masham were familiar with Locke's
work, they were also acutely aware of the masculinist implications
of his ideas. At the very least, they sometimes reformulated and re-
deployed his concepts for their own feminist purposes; on many
other occasions, they drew on very different pedagogical, literary,
or philosophical sources for their own arguments. Hence the *Education* will at times offer a problematic case of exemplary pedagogical thinking. Before focusing our attention on the relation between Locke's educational work and that of his contemporaries,
however, I will consider its significance for a subgenre of the novel
that has long been a fixture of canonical scholarship: the *Bildungsroman*, or, translated literally, the novel of formation.

The Novel of Education and Pedagogical Emplotment

In addition to advancing a new perspective on the early modern novel's construction of socialized individuality, this study proposes to explore the contribution of eighteenth-century educational discourse to the so-called *novel of education*. In other words, the British novel of education can be considered exactly that: not only as a genre that treats the themes of individual identity and maturation but also as a literary offshoot—even a discursive aberration—of educational theory. Traditionally, critics of the British *Bildungsroman* have concentrated on the familiar canon of nineteenth-century works such as Dickens's *Great Expectations* or *David Copperfield*, Brontë's *Jane Eyre*, Eliot's *Mill on the Floss*, Meredith's *The Ordeal of Richard Feverel*, and Samuel Butler's *The Way of All Flesh*. Within this framework, the British genre is often characterized as an Anglicized extension of the German *Bildungsroman* as it was rendered by Goethe in *Wilhelm Meisters Lehrjahre* and later transplanted by Carlyle in his translation of Goethe's work in 1824 (as *Wilhelm Meister's Apprenticeship*). And Carlyle's later publication of *Sartor Resartus* (1833)—an autobiographical work drawing heavily from his imbibing Goethe's work—then serves as the first fictional adaptation in England of the German genre that had originated as early as 1766–67 with Wieland's *Geschichte des Agathon*.[39]

Though instructive, this approach to literary history overlooks several important links of influence and borrowing that occurred during the eighteenth century, particularly Goethe's reliance on philosophical discussions of education by writers such as Kant and Rousseau—writers who in turn were heavily indebted to the epistemological and pedagogical theories of John Locke. The main point, however, is not to claim that the British novel of education must have emerged from indigenous British sources, since for some time literary historians of English literature have said so, if only as a passing remark. It is instead to offer a detailed historical account of the genre's earliest beginnings by tracing them through the conventions of eighteenth-century educational writing. In examining women authors of the *Bildungsroman* in late eighteenth- and nineteenth-century Britain, Susan Fraiman has pointed out that the representation of female development offered by Frances Burney, Jane Austen, and Charlotte Brontë had significant roots in the model of self-divided female identity articulated in late eighteenth-century conduct books (I will come back to that idea in a moment).[40] With that in mind, I argue two things: first, examining the formal and thematic significance of Locke's *Education* can trace one strand of the sinuous thread of influence in the *Bildungsroman*'s emergence in Europe; and second, studying the educational treatises by women that preceded the conduct books in Fraiman's analysis indicates that, when taken as a whole, the work of both male and female educationalists forms the key source for a nascent, experimental version of the British novel of education during the early eighteenth century. In short, this study argues that the nineteenth-century British *Bildungsroman* has profound conceptual roots in early modern educational theory and that it is also indebted to the dynamics of narrative form implicit in the texts by Locke, Astell, Stephen Penton, and others.

Given my emphasis on *education* as key to understanding this type of novel, I must also address the issue of terminology, because given the German penchant for taxonomic distinctions, the *Bildungsroman* proper is usually immediately distinguished from its variants, particularly the *Entwicklungsroman* and the *Erziehungsroman*. The definition of the *Bildungsroman* hinges on describing the key term *Bildung*, which has historically been designated as a holistic cultural identity resulting from self-cultivation. Susanne Howe, for instance, one of the first English-language critics of the genre, defines the *Bildungsroman* as the "novel of all-around development or self-culture" with "a more or less conscious attempt on the part of the hero to integrate his powers, to cultivate himself by his experience."[41] For its part, the *Entwicklungsroman* demarcates a more general terrain: according to Martin Swales, it marks "any novel having one central figure whose experiences and whose changing self occupy a role of structural primacy within the fiction." The *Erziehungsroman*, by contrast, describes a more circumscribed work, one "explicitly (and narrowly) pedagogic in the sense that it is concerned with a certain set of values to be acquired, of lessons to be learned."[42]

As these definitions suggest, the categorization of these sub-genres is not critically neutral, for scholars consistently valorize the *Bildungsroman* as the form most capacious and compact at the same time. Rather than focused on the merely "technical" aspects of education and rather than only broadly concerned with a nebulous pattern of experience, the *Bildungsroman* presents a culturally specific and philosophically expansive narrative of self-formation. For Swales, for example, it "implies the generality of a culture, the clustering of values by which the individual grows and evolves" (14). Franco Moretti makes explicit what is often only implicit for Swales and other critics in making this claim: that the *Bildungsroman* effectively forges a synthesis of the *Entwicklungsroman*'s "subjective unfolding of an individuality" and the *Erziehungsroman*'s "portrayal of an objective process, observed from the standpoint of the educator."[43]

The idea that the *Bildungsroman* combines the best of both worlds—generically or conceptually—is in fact part of the legacy of Wilhelm Dilthey's influential formulation of the genre at the turn of the twentieth century in *Das Erlebnis und die Dichtung* (*Poetry and Experience*), first published in 1906. In that work, Dilthey describes the *Bildungsroman* as a form that is complexly ambidextrous—one focusing emphatically on the individual's inner consciousness while also finally encompassing the entirety of human nature. He writes:

[T]he *Bildungsroman* is distinguished from all previous biographical compositions in that it intentionally and artistically depicts that which is universally human in such a life-course. The *Bildungsroman* is closely associated with the new developmental psychology established by Leibniz, with the idea of a natural education in conformity with the inner development of the psyche. . . . The *Bildungsroman* is also associated with the ideal of humanity with which Lessing and Herder inspired their contemporaries. A lawlike development is discerned in the individual's life; each of its levels has intrinsic value and is at the same time the basis for a higher level. Life's dissonances and conflicts appear as necessary transitions to be withstood by the individual on his way towards maturity and harmony. The "greatest happiness of earth's children" [wrote Goethe] is "personality," as a unified and permanent form of human existence.[44]

By this characterization, the *Bildungsroman* captures both psychological individuality and existential generality, the peculiarity of specific personality and the universality of human nature in the broadest sense.

Dilthey's description no doubt draws on the Hegelian idea of the *concrete universal*—the articulation of the ideal dialectic relation of the particular and the general. It also reflects the symbolic logic of *Aufhebung*, which defines the ability to absorb and transcend constitutive parts in forming an integral, organic whole.[45] More importantly, his arguments rely implicitly or explicitly on the precepts of European Romanticism. This makes sound critical sense for the purposes of sketching out the historical context for the *Bildungsroman*'s appearance on the literary scene during the late eighteenth and early nineteenth centuries. When Dilthey speaks, for example, of the genre's portrayal of a "natural education" whose "lawlike development" culminates in "that which is universally human," one is reminded of Wordsworth's declaration in the "Preface" to the *Lyrical Ballads* that his exploration of the human imagination would trace "the primary laws of our nature."[46] Dilthey accounts further for the *Bildungsroman*'s psychological orientation by pointing to the cultural and political environment that contributed to the recognizable responses associated with Romanticism. He attributes it to Germany's late eighteenth-century "interest in inner culture":

> [T]hese *Bildungsromane* gave expression to the individualism of a culture whose sphere of interest was limited to private life. The governmental authority of the civil service and the military in the small and middle-sized German states confronted the young generation of writers as alien. But these young people were delighted and enraptured by what poets had discovered about the world of the individual and his self-development. Today's reader of Jean Paul's *Flegeljahre* . . . or *Titan* in which everything about the contemporary German *Bildungsroman* is epitomized, will find the aura of a past world, the transfiguration of existence in the dawn of life, an infinite investment of feeling in a restricted existence, the obscure, wistful, power of ideals of German youths eager to declare war on an antiquated world in all its life forms.[47]

Though admittedly brief, Dilthey's account of the cultural context for the *Bildungsroman*'s emergence has suggestive historical value in delineating the ethos of self-cultivation at the turn of the nineteenth century. But his methodology, as much as his historical description, is heavily "Romantic": Dilthey's critical apparatus thoroughly endorses the ideal of individual selfhood's ultimate dilation to encompass the entirety of the outside world—the goal of an organic unity of the human and natural order. Those values are reflected in his assertion that genuine poetry "restores the totality of lived experience" (106).

While less philosophically Germanic, the views of more recent critics of the *Bildungsroman* also draw on Romantic values—whether they appear in the form of Moretti's identification of "interiority" as one of the genre's key features, or in Jerome Hamilton Buckley's more pragmatic discussion of authors' "powerful personal vision" in portraying spiritual apprenticeship.[48] Like Dilthey, they too participate in rehearsing what Jerome McGann has called the "Romantic ideology."[49] That ideology encompasses not only assumptions about interiority and organic selfhood but also, perhaps more fundamentally, the apparently endemic opposition between self and society or system. By the time of the Romantics, the distinction between self and society may have seemed natural, but much like the difference between philosophy and literature during the eighteenth century, that distinction emerged only gradually, from the epistemological, political, and pedagogical debates (among others) during the period, as well as from the implementation of new medical, educational, and legal institutions. The language of self versus system may be one of the most invisible—and intractable—tropes that persists in post-Romantic scholarship, but it is my aim to offer in its place a historical account of how educational theory—and thereafter, the novel—helped bring that contentious concept into being by articulating the elements of improvisational identity.

When it comes to novels of education written by women, there is one last sense in which the "romantic" has constituted a limited perspective, since the rituals including courtship, love, and

marriage have often been considered the chief matrix within which
female heroines arrive at personal and social maturity. That form of
female socialization, however, does not produce the kind of organic
selfhood Dilthey describes, because as Susan Fraiman suggests, a
critical investment in the ideas of mastery and coherent self-image
as the *Bildungsroman*'s raison d'être has its roots in a specifically masculine model of development; for both women and their fictional
counterparts, she argues, acquiring a sense of self during the eighteenth and nineteenth centuries is fundamentally bifurcated into
two opposing narratives of self-consolidation *and* deformation, the
second of which entails "a loss of authority, an abandonment of
goals."[50] Hence the achievement of romantic love for women is by
no means "Romantic" in the grander sense, since it can mean both
fulfillment and painful self-negation. In the context of an improvisational description of identity, this dual story line takes a somewhat
different shape, because in the performance of the habitus, women's
maturation follows a mediated trajectory rarely split into two entirely opposed patterns. But as I will show in chapter 5 regarding
both Haywood's *History of Miss Betsy Thoughtless* (1751) and
Lennox's *The Female Quixote* (1752), the heroines' improvisations
on traditional femininity confirm Fraiman's remark that the female
Bildungsroman can evoke a "degree of rude and rebellious agency
within a complex set of constraints" (xi).

Pinpointing the legacy of Romanticism—with regard to or-
ganicism or gender—in critics' arguments about the novel of education by no means denigrates their usefulness, but it does suggest
why the *Bildungsroman* has been heralded as superior to (or at least
more formally complex than) the *Entwicklungsroman* and *Erziehungsroman*. It also indicates why that orientation succeeds in hard-
ening a taxonomic distinction that in turn discourages the consideration of substantial historical and generic change in the *Bildungsroman* and its related counterparts. In order, therefore, to
consider the earlier roots of the English *Bildungsroman*, this study
will take a substantially different tack in approaching this genre as a
discursive and cultural form. Rather than establishing a new set of
definitive generic features, my purpose will be to trace mutable
outlines and follow structural mutations in the theoretical and "lit-

erary" educational texts by Locke and other writers. And instead of considering the pedagogical work of Locke or his contemporaries as the integral, all-determining "origin" of the early English novel of education, I will treat it in Edward Said's sense as a "beginning"—as a decisive point of departure in the historical development of the form and as a provisional launching point for the critical narrative I will be telling.[51] In similar fashion, my account of the genre's history aims to resist perhaps the most seductive teleological metaphor that frequently characterizes discussions of the novel of growing up: the trope of the novel as a form evolving to organic "maturity," much like its protagonists. The success of that resistance remains open to scrutiny, but my goal is to treat the eventual narrativization of educational writing in the form of the novel as a *non*organic process, and as only one of many other developments in pedagogical discourse during the eighteenth century which do not culminate in "literary" consolidation, but instead spread themselves across a broad spectrum of philosophical, theological, and popular media.

In arguing that the English *Bildungsroman* and its variants emerge from Enlightenment educational discourse, I will be using the term *novel of education* not in the traditionally limited sense of the *Erziehungsroman*, which is putatively limited to a narrow, or "technical," aspect of lesson learning, but with the understanding that the tremendous historical transformation of educational writing from the seventeenth to the nineteenth century repeatedly violates and reformulates such strict generic categories. In fact, as I argue in the first three chapters, the concept of education sponsored by both male and female early modern educationalists extends far beyond mere institutional technique, investing its ultimate operation in the daily life experience of consciousness. That idea indicates the crucial ideological weight attached to an individual's maturation by experience of the world, and it also suggests the way in which later "Romantic" portrayals of intently private development may share similar goals for establishing protagonists'—and readers'—social conformity.

While remembering that conduct books, in conjunction with the novel, formed a new sense of personal interiority for men and

women in the eighteenth century, I will also stress the concern of
early modern educationalists with the unveiling or "exteriorization" of personal interiority in the course of educating pupils. Despite Locke's insistence, for example, on a student's individual freedoms and imminent political rights, and despite the appealing
rugged individualism of fictional characters such as Robinson Crusoe or Arabella, the texts I consider treat individual interiority
more as a problem to be contained than as terrain to be enthusias-
tically explored and ultimately celebrated. Instead, Locke, Astell,
Defoe, and Haywood approach individual development from a decidedly external point of view, keeping a constant eye on the social
and institutional implications of the exfoliation of selfhood. The
point is to establish access to the convolutions of individual motive
and identity, although that channel of communication between interiority and exteriority is never entirely stable. In these authors'
work one sees instead a constant juggling of contrary agendas: the
hallmark of improvisational subjectivity and its fictional representation is their rehearsal of the competing agendas of individual interiority versus disciplinary surveillance with the aim of containing
them—without complete resolution—within the parameters of
narrative emplotment. It is here, as Eve Sedgwick notes, that ideology
and narrative converge:

> It is important that ideology . . . is always at least implicitly narrative,
> and that, in order for the reweaving of ideology to be truly invisible,
> the narrative is necessarily chiasmic in structure: that is, that the sub-
> ject of the beginning of the narrative is different from the subject at
> the end, and that the two subjects cross each other in a rhetorical fig-
> ure that conceals their discontinuity.[52]

Pedagogical process as ideological "plot" therefore takes on several
related meanings. It is first of all the distribution of educational
events and stages of development in a temporal sequence designed
to mediate between individuality and conformity. Second, "plot"
designates the pedagogical sphere of a metaphorical garden plot, a
favorite eighteenth-century textual construct combining the essential operations of Nature with the salutary application of human artifice. In complicating this natural/artificial register, pedagogical
plot also takes on the connotations of a secret plan or cunning strat-

agem, for in the ideal scenario the pupil remains unaware of the tutor's educational method. Hence a student's development—and as a corollary, the reader's perception of that process—is valorized by "natural" sequence, as well as orchestrated by social or "artificial" correctives. There is also a fourth ambience to the term *plot*: given the emotional, intellectual, and social power of clandestine pedagogy to mold an individual's identity, it is hard not to perceive at times an implicit menace or even violence in the administration of such pedagogical "plotting."

Given the complexity of instructional emplotment, one of this book's chief aims is to capture an expansive sense of how the novel of education emerged as part of a diverse network of nonliterary discourses, institutional practices, and national trends in Enlightenment England. My argument, therefore, stresses the cultural history of early modern educational ideas at least as much as it traces the novel's strict literary history. The first three chapters are devoted to considering a broad range of elements—including educational treatises, plays, illustrations, innovative school programs, and new "scientific" theories of personal identity—that shaped and were in turn shaped by the novel's form and content. The last two chapters then focus on particular novels that form exemplary moments in the novel of education's earliest history. Chapter 1, entitled "Lockean Education, Narrative Metaphor, and the Inflections of Gender," examines several aspects of pedagogical plotting in the work of Locke and his contemporary educationalists. In tracing the dynamics of these authors' frequent metaphors for the process of educating students—including gardening and medicine—I discuss how they articulate for both male and female authors a naturalized approach to forming human disposition, while the women stress a distinct sense of female self-determination by employing the trope of pedagogical "empire." In chapter 2, "Theatrical Education and the Thickening of Plot," I turn to discuss the metaphor of pedagogy as dramatic performance, considering how in Locke's *Education*, it produces—in conjunction with his other natural metaphors—a structural deformation of Locke's otherwise straightforward adherence to the conventions of philosophical writing, an alteration that produces in effect a sinuous, storylike presentation of

Locke's argument. Given the additional association of theatricality with feminine disposition, this narrative pattern outlines the more literary treatments of educational process in eighteenth-century fiction, including the debate about women's putative volatility and moral vulnerability.

This scenario provides a conceptual backdrop from which to survey the educational interests of novelists including Henry Fielding, Mary Davys, François Fénelon, and Delarivière Manley, while also defining a new sense in which female novelists could pursue a "progressive" agenda.

Before turning to fictional adaptations of educational writing, chapter 3, "Pedagogical Politics and the Idea of Public Privacy," explores the social, political, and institutional implications of improvisational education, beginning with Locke's proposal for poor children's working schools, a plan later adopted and modified by organizations such as the Society for Promoting Christian Knowledge. These new educational institutions provide a historical setting for the emerging fictionalization of educational discourse. And they play an important role in a three-part affiliation of republican, liberal, and Christian perspectives, converging in frequently uneasy fashion to define private identity in terms that could also be made eminently public. To that end, several kinds of related cultural practices—including William Hogarth's satiric engravings about moral apprenticeship and John Lavater's pious agenda for physiognomical analysis—serve to help ensure the individual's scrutability and the success of larger economic and political norms. As evidence of the institutional improvisations also possible within the context of pedagogical discipline, Mary Astell's description in *A Serious Proposal to the Ladies* of an educational retreat for women illustrates that alternative views on gender and class could generate significant alternatives to pervasive educational surveillance.

Taken together, the next two chapters sketch out the novel of education's literary history during the first half of the eighteenth century by offering exemplary readings of fiction by three novelists, one male and two female, who implement the educational process in contrasting ways. Chapter 4, entitled "*Robinson Crusoe*, Education, and Schizophrenic Narrative," treats Defoe's work as one of the first successful consolidations of the novel of education's generic form, which serves as a point of comparison with the later work of female novelists at midcentury. Focusing first on Defoe's fictional experimentation in his earlier conduct book *The Family Instructor* (1715), I discuss how his combination of improvisational and Puritan premises in that work applies to the novel's amalgamation of spiritual autobiography and the early modern pedagogical stress on cumulative learning. In chapter 5, "Romancing the Home: *The Female Quixote*, *Betsy Thoughtless*, and the Dream of Feminine Empire," I turn to consider how Charlotte Lennox and Eliza Haywood explore in different ways women's potential for seizing the sense of pedagogical empire proposed by educationalists such as Mary Astell. Their protagonists, as autodidacts who initially attempt to master everyone around them, provide an implicit critique of Crusoe's imperial ambitions on his island as they learn the value of self-limitation, especially as women. But while Lennox documents the apparent failure of Arabella to establish a sense of romantic, even quasi-feminist, self-determination, her text implies an alternative model of female identity that Haywood applies explicitly in portraying the mature Betsy as having an ironic perspective on the "performance" of desirable femininity. The difference lies in these authors' distinct conceptions of what kind of genuine improvisation might be available for upper-class, mid-eighteenth-century English women, although ultimately, the model adopted by Haywood proves the more influential one for the novel of education by women in the latter half of the century.

Finally, the Marxian imperative "always historicize" provides a compelling rationale for tracing the sociohistorical significance of the English novel of education's development as a genre. In investigating the analogical and historical links between early modern educationalists' concept of pedagogical supervision, its adaptation in charity schools, and the related patterns of narrative emplotment, I describe a cultural context for the novel of education in England that sharply contrasts the one Dilthey describes in Germany. Rather than a literary discourse surfacing amidst the clamor of youthful alienation from contemporary society, the English novel emerges from a widespread social directive to negotiate successful civic and political organization—to find natural and human-made mechanisms by which to reconcile individuality to conformity. That distinct cultural purpose characterizes the English novel of education as a genre concerned not only with representing that process of socialization in a protagonist's development but also with implementing narrative strategies that can approach the similar goal of edifying readers. It is a form intent on presenting the gradual exfoliation of personal identity for public and "readerly" scrutiny—with the further goal of inculcating such norms in readers themselves.

CHAPTER ONE

*Lockean Education, Narrative Metaphor,
and the Inflections of Gender*

> The right Management of Children, and the carrying it in a due
> Mean betwixt a rigorous Severity, on the one Side, and too slack
> a Hand, on the other, is a nice Point.
>
> —John Clarke, *An Essay upon the Education of Youth*

> Since God has given Women as well as Men intelligent Souls,
> why should they be forbidden to improve them?
>
> —Mary Astell, *A Serious Proposal to the Ladies*

By the evidence of the Enlightenment, advocating a new pedagogical program inevitably depended on asserting, or at least assuming, a continuous social circuit leading from the one to the
many, or from the particular to the universal. In his dedication to
Some Thoughts concerning Education, for instance, Locke draws on this
rationale when he suggests that the apparent narrowness of his concern with a "Gentleman's Calling" in fact extends to the entire social domain. "If those of that Rank are by their Education once set
right," he explains, "they will quickly bring all the rest into Order"—and that "rest" reaches to the "Welfare and Prosperity of the
Nation," which "so much depends" on sound education.[1] This
claim reflects Locke's focus on the class, gender, and geographical
setting he considers most important, giving priority to the educa-

tion of the sons of landed gentry. Once established, however, that pedagogical nexus can presumably extend its instructive network to include the lower classes, the nobility, and the weaker sex—those young women otherwise largely absent from Locke's discussion.

In effect, Locke considers his primary concern with boys to be generalized easily to the level of universal principles of human nature and pedagogy, remarking that "where the Difference of Sex requires different Treatment, 'twill be no hard matter to distinguish" (sec. 6)—although this is a distinction that, in the end, he lets fall into silence.[2] While attempting to obviate sexual difference, however, Locke's discussion is ultimately couched in terms largely masculine and directed toward the creation of the "Man of Business."[3] This scenario suggests that despite Locke's own inclinations, one should remain attuned to the crucial differences, the cumulative or resistant dissonances, inhabiting his gentrified and masculinized pedagogical program. Even Locke's "Man of Business," in fact, is a less composed or self-coherent individual than he might seem at first: he emerges as a composite of disparate perspectives on human subjectivity, which are alternately secular and Christian, individualist and conformist. This chapter therefore focuses extensively on the linguistic and literary mechanisms, grouped together under the heading of "narrative metaphors," by which Locke sets out to bridge the gaps among his various educational points of departure, and which not only undergird an ideology of the "free" individual but also shape a particular way of telling the story of that person's education.

The problem of gender and generalization has further implications regarding the inherent difficulties in making an historical argument by way of exemplarity. This chapter argues that Locke's *Education* played a dual role in the history of early modern educational thought: first, his treatise consolidated many of the pedagogical innovations proposed since the mid-seventeenth century by authors such as Comenius, Bathsua Makin, and Jean Gailhard; second, it was exemplary of a new turn in educational theory from the late seventeenth to the early eighteenth century, as represented by Fénelon, Mary Astell, John Essex, and others. This approach permits a detailed consideration of the discursive strategies by which authors such as Locke construct a new kind of self-reliant, yet culturally conformed, English individual. I will also aim to establish a complex sense of the *Education*'s context, particularly regarding the degree to which contemporary female writers on education formed a gendered perspective distinct from Locke's putatively universal principles concerning pedagogy's psychological, social, or moral dimensions. The primary purpose will be to consider how a shared pedagogical sense of "supervised" individuality, as well as a distinct sense of women's need for "masculine" forms of knowledge or assertiveness, provides an underlying narrative logic for fictional treatments of acculturation by male and female novelists during the early eighteenth century. I will begin by considering first the general contours of Locke's pedagogical program.

Virtue, Prohibition, and the Snares of Authority

In the *Education*, Locke draws on the *Essay*'s rejection of innate ideas to describe the young child as "white Paper, or Wax," a general blankness "to be moulded and fashioned as one pleases" (sec. 216). That description—coupled with his similar mention in the *Essay* of the mind initially as a "white Paper, void of all Characters," but to be "engraven" by experience[4]—suggests that education is a kind of social writing, which scripts the text of the child's personality and attributes toward desirable ends. Locke proceeds to form a hierarchy of educational aims, distinguishing, on a graduated scale, their pedagogical range of applicability across the social spectrum of class and gender. The four aims he emphasizes, in descending order of importance, are Virtue, Wisdom, Breeding, and Learning. The first goal, virtue, Locke calls "the hard and valuable part to be aimed at in Education" (sec. 70); it is composed of universal moral standards of conduct. Chief among those standards is self-denial, which Locke calls "the great Principle and Foundation of all Vertue and Worth" (sec. 33), for it is the key to a child's restrained enjoyment of liberty at the onset of adulthood. For its part, wisdom defines the ability to perceive clearly, discern accurately, and choose prudently. As an ability cultivated in the later stages of childhood and concerned with the ways of the world, it provides the necessary implement for making moral virtue truly efficacious.

The conduit for both virtue and wisdom proves to be breeding, and Locke insists on its importance: "Breeding is that, which sets a Gloss upon all his other good qualities, and renders them useful to him. . . . Without good Breeding his other Accomplishments make him pass but for Proud, Conceited, Vain, or Foolish" (sec. 93). The skills of civility, carriage, and graciousness, therefore, as the measure of high social rank, are key to exercising the fundamental values of virtue and wisdom. Finally comes learning, since Locke demotes the importance that was usually given to the accumulation of facts or literate skills, whether they come in the form of languages, sciences, disciplines, and histories, or reading, computation, and argumentation. He contends that even if important knowledge is neglected until late in a child's development, that deficiency, unlike a lack of morality, can be quickly remedied.

Within the outlines of this four-part schema, Locke describes how to establish in children a form of what Pierre Bourdieu calls a social habitus, a system of "durable, transposable *dispositions*" that function "without in any way being the product of obedience to rules."[5] In their theoretical account of how education produces the habitus, Bourdieu and Jean-Claude Passeron explain that it is the result of "pedagogic work," a form of inculcation that works "without resorting to external repression or, in particular, physical coercion."[6] But at the same time, as Bourdieu is quick to point out, children's bodies are still key to the process of learning disposition—as in absorbing the cultural valences of physical gesture (breeding) or even the inhabiting of domestic space—since the habitus operates ideologically at both the conscious and unconscious levels.[7] In the *Education*, this pedagogical dynamic becomes manifest when, given his stress in the *Essay* on the essential role of sensory reception and mental reflection, Locke makes firsthand experience the crux of a child's learning process. Accompanying that emphasis is his frequent description of educating a child by "gentle and insensible Degrees,"[8] a procedure that abandons using a plethora of prescriptive rules or injunctions and, more surprisingly, any kind of initial prohibition (sec. 85). As in the *Essay*, Locke puts experience before understanding: on the one hand, neither memorized factual information nor ethical rules of conduct will prove compelling for a child until each is substantiated first by the improvisations of trial and error; on the other hand, a child could be introduced prematurely to various vices if supplied with a series of "untimely Prohibitions" (sec. 85). And because the approach Locke describes requires thorough planning and meticulous individual attention, he recommends drawing on the skills of a private tutor, an arrangement that also avoids the corrupting influence of public schools.

A second hallmark of Locke's pedagogical program, despite spending more than thirty-three sections on the caring for a child's health, diet, and exercise, is his aim to shift part of the emphasis from the body to the mind as the chief means by which to motivate children to moral conformity. After limiting corporal punishment to a method of last resort because it can permanently harden a child's sensibility, Locke substitutes the more effective tool of "Reputation"—using praise and blame to bend a child's behavior in a desirable direction. Drawing on a child's inherent "Pleasure in being esteemed, and valued" (sec. 57), this approach not only displaces the infliction of bodily pain with the more direct manipulation of the mind but also installs a crucial social consciousness that will restrain his conduct when a child comes of age.

That strategy for preparing a child's social cooperativeness is enhanced by Locke's endorsement of the inculcation of habits, which, as a subtle form of bodily manipulation, can supply reliable youthful behavior in the face of an undeveloped memory and an absence of rules. Although they are emphatically nonrational responses, habits, produced by "repeated Practice, and the same Action done over and over again" (sec. 66), can support rational activity while a child's reasoning powers remain immature. As Locke puts it, "Habits . . . , being once established, operate of themselves easily and naturally, without the Assistance of the Memory" (sec. 66). The full value of automatic reflex becomes clearer in Locke's summary of the creation of self-denial: "the Principle of all Vertue and Excellency lies in a Power of denying our selves the Satisfaction of our own Desires, where Reason does not authorize them. This Power is to be got and improved by Custom, made easy and familiar by an *early* Practice" (sec. 38). This passage recalls Locke's wrestling in the *Essay* with the problem of desire's intransigent relation to rational consideration, including the challenge of having desire "raised proportionably" to the will's determination of the greater good.[9] Here, however, in contrast to his uncertainty in the *Essay*, Locke offers the strong solution of inculcating habits, which in effect can *educate desire* to mesh with rational choice.

Ideally, then, Locke's "Custom" is the prime mechanism in forming a pupil's habitus, since it promises ultimately to combine the operations of the body with the rationality of the mind in an ideological disposition that is both partially self-aware and partly unreflective.[10] But Locke's proposals for avoiding prescription, virtually eliminating bodily punishment, and fostering habits also pose some logical inconsistencies that are linked to other, more general difficulties in his educational program. In the first place, his design suggests that human rationality be undergirded by the decidedly *non*rational device of formed habit. Both reason and habit are putatively "natural," the first inherently, the second by virtue of acquired spontaneity, but the problem may lie, as it also does in the *Second Treatise*, in the nature of Nature itself.

In the course of Locke's pedagogical discussion, for instance, the child's tabula rasa turns out to be not quite as blank as it first seemed. In addition to Locke's acknowledgment that children have "Original Tempers" of personality, because "God has stampt certain Characters upon Men's Minds,"[11] there turn out to be inherent, self-promoting passions or drives common to all humanity, including the love of power and dominion, "the first Original of most vicious Habits, that are ordinary and natural" (sec. 103). If that is not complication enough, then Locke also attributes some childhood behavior to the condition of being "the Sons of *Adam*" (sec. 132; also sec. 139), invoking, though only momentarily, the Christian view of corrupt human nature. If education's role is to "write" social virtues onto the self's text, then the process appears now to deal less with a straightforward first draft than a kind of human palimpsest, in which initial drives, personal proclivities, and spiritual deficiencies must be written over or *re*written for the purposes of maturation. But even in that event, the faint traces of previous inclinations can always reassert themselves and become visible. In those terms, perhaps even Locke's estimate that nine-tenths of individual character can be formed by instruction (see sec. 1) is overly optimistic.

This ambivalence about children's—and ultimately, human—nature seems to produce a similarly divided pedagogical response, since Locke endorses both candid honesty with children and deceptive stratagems. With regard to children's frequent questions, for example, Locke charges that "they *never* receive *Deceitful* and *Eluding Answers*. They easily perceive when they are slighted, or deceived; and quickly learn the Trick of Neglect, Dissimulation and Falshood, which they observe others to make use of " (sec. 120). He similarly inveighs against keeping an older boy "hood-wink'd" by making him assume that the world is entirely benevolent or free of vice (sec. 94). By contrast, consider this injunction: "cheat him into it if you can" (sec. 155). In this case, regarding ways to induce children to learn how to read and enjoy it, Locke stresses "Contrivances" and "Baits" as the means to trick them into something their uncooperative selves might otherwise resist (secs. 150, 156). Here and elsewhere, when Locke recommends that children be "cozen'd into . . . Knowledge,"[12] his motives are perfectly well intentioned, but his methods are nonetheless susceptible to the danger he has already cautioned against: that from deception, children deception learn.

Given the dual prospect of a child's blank, malleable self and a self-interested, wayward one—not to mention the sheer practicality of using what works—Locke's double approach makes good sense. But the possibility of a dual human nature soon introduces the related question of parental power: Should parents exert dominating stringency over children's renegade or Adamic potential, or should they relax into a casual leniency that only occasionally intercedes, especially by means of rational explanation, in their children's natural development? It is a dilemma reflected in Bourdieu and Passeron's remark that pedagogy is "always objectively situated between the two unattainable poles of pure force and pure reason."[13] Unlike his discussion of this issue in the *Second Treatise*, Locke's approach here seems to be to pose several extremes, trying in the meantime to find a satisfactory balance. The first kind of parents that come under fire in the *Education*, for instance, are those who are indulgent, exercising virtually no adult prerogative.[14] But Locke is equally concerned with excessive strictness, claiming that it will inevitably cow children into depressive lethargy and, more important, seriously undermine their preparation for the freedoms of adult life. And that is aside from the fact that even as children, they "have as much a Mind to shew that they are free, . . . that they are absolute and independent, as any of the proudest of your grown Men" (sec. 73).

Still, Locke maintains, parents should establish their authority early as children's "Lords" and "Absolute Governors" (sec. 41), later softening that capacity with liberality and friendship. He sums up this bifurcated pedagogical approach best when he writes:

> [I]f the *Mind* be curbed, and *humbled* too much in Children; if their *Spirits* be abased and *broken* much, by too strict an Hand over them, they lose all their Vigor and Industry, and are in a worse State than the former. For extravagant young Fellows, that have Liveliness and Spirit, come sometimes to be set right. . . . But *dejected Minds*, timorous and tame, and *low Spirits*, are hardly ever to be raised, and very seldom attain to any thing. To avoid the Danger, that is on either hand, is the great Art; and he that has found a way, how to keep up a Child's Spirit, easy, active and free; and yet, at the same time, to restrain him to things that are uneasy to him; he, I say, that knows how to reconcile these seeming Contradictions, has, in my Opinion, got the true Secret of Education. (sec. 46)

These contradictions are clearly more than "seeming," and that is why their effective negotiation marks the "true Secret" Locke so highly praises. To understand what is finally at stake here, we can turn briefly to some remarks Locke made in a letter in 1693 to William Molyneux, in which he comments on the puzzle of divine omnipotence and human self-determination, for Locke's concern with parental power encapsulates on a smaller scale the same mind-wrenching paradox. To Molyneux's observation that there were "contradictions" in the first edition of the *Essay*'s discussion of liberty, Locke replies:

> I do not wonder to find you think my discourse about liberty a little too fine spun. . . . I own freely to you the weakness of my understanding, that though it be unquestionable that there is omnipotence and omniscience in God our maker, and I cannot have a clearer perception of any thing than that I am free, yet I cannot make freedom in man consistent with omnipotence and omniscience in God, though I am as fully perswaded of both as of any truths I most firmly assent to. And therefore I have long since given off the consideration of that question, resolving all into this short conclusion, That if it be possible for God to make a free agent, then man is free, though I see not the way of it.[15]

Whether or not he had "long since" given up on resolving divine omnipotence by 1693, Locke certainly contended with a different form of this problem in deciding the relationship between adults and children while writing the *Education* (from about 1684 to 1690). Though by no means as all-encompassing as divine power, adult authority nonetheless poses a thorny situation. Even in the laudable case of attempting to protect a child from physical harm, an adult's interdiction or preventive measures will seem an arbitrary exercise of power to the child, who by default has no understanding of the particular danger at hand. As Frances Ferguson astutely summarizes this scenario, "an education that seems legitimate to both student and teacher may be no education at all, for the understanding that a student must have to recognize the legitimacy of his teacher's authority would involve his already knowing what is being taught. In other words, freedom and education make competing claims when there is any imbalance between what the teacher knows and what the pupil knows."[16] Ferguson concludes that in confronting the competing claims of freedom and education, Locke "chooses both" by emphasizing in the *Second Treatise* that after a child has reached adult maturity, his parents no longer have the prerogative to command his obedience. But as Locke himself recognized, this premise goes only so far in resolving the problem. While there is certainly the question whether acquiring a socially sanctioned disposition would undermine a young adult's ability to exercise genuine liberty, in the *Education* Locke remains concerned about mustering power during the pedagogical process itself, since it determines so much about a child's future role as propertied individual and citizen. The challenge would be how to negotiate between the equally tenable needs for autonomy and for acculturation.

The Modernization of Learning and the Prerogatives of Gender

Locke's ambivalence about exercising pedagogical power is linked in part to the larger issue of the *Education*'s dual relation to traditional seventeenth-century views about education's goals and procedures. In the first place, Locke echoed many of the period's already entrenched views about pedagogy by underscoring the priority of Christian virtue, the importance of breeding and proper comportment for the upper classes, and the effectiveness of instilling in pupils the reflex of genuine self-denial. These similarities have led J. Paul Hunter to remark that "Locke was in fact uttering mostly commonplaces" from the guide tradition since at least the 1640s.[17] On the face of it, then, his educational program would have seemed a matter of common sense to earlier writers on education such as Richard Brathwaite, Jean Gailhard, Obadiah Walker, Hannah Woolley, Bathsua Makin, or even John Milton.

But there are two other aspects of Locke's treatise that helped generate a significant difference in the way education would be imagined in the decades after the Revolution of 1688, and that difference often impinged on how pedagogical authority was portrayed. In effect, the *Education* proved to help consolidate several earlier, though generally scattered, innovative proposals about how to teach children more effectively, while it also described a number of concepts embodying a new sense of pedagogy shared by many of his contemporaries. To view his work this way is to avoid one of two extreme positions often taken by critics and historians of Locke's work. We can consider the *Education* as more than a compact rehearsal of received cultural wisdom, as Hunter does, and as less than a single-handed revolution in pedagogical thinking, as Jay

Fliegelman or Nathan Tarcov tend to do (for very different reasons),[18] in order to explore how Locke's work was part of a complex, piecemeal, and often subtle shift in England's perspective on
the educational process.

While Locke does not explicitly cite them, there are several
notable precedents in the earlier seventeenth century for his proposals concerning an incremental, empirically based, and gentle
pedagogy. Charles Webster credits Francis Bacon's *Advancement of
Learning* (1605) with initiating in England an increasing pedagogical interest in studying Nature and its operations as the source of
practicable human knowledge, rather than maintaining what Bacon
viewed as humanism's excessive commitment to classical authors,
protracted language study, and fascination with rhetorical ornateness for its own sake.[19] As an example of this development, which
was often spurred by Puritan reformist zeal, Gerrard Winstanley
would declare later in the century that young people should "learn
the inward knowledg[e] of things which are, and find out the secrets of Nature," on the assumption that "To know the secrets of
nature, is to know the Works of God."[20] As an enthusiast for Bacon's scientific outlook, Czech educationalist John Comenius also
helped shape English ideas, especially during the Interregnum, by
advocating a pedagogical program founded on "nature as our
guide," which included the use of inductive, graduated instruction
suited to children's psychological capacities and empirical experience.[21] His reforms in the teaching of foreign languages (mainly
Latin)—which stressed a simplified order of instruction and drew
on children's understanding of their native tongue—were particularly influential in England, where his *Janua linguarum reserata* and
Orbis sensualium pictus were issued in multiple editions from the
1630s until the end of the century.[22] Comenius's general pedagogical aim, as he explained in *A Reformation of Schooles* (1642), was to
streamline the "study of learning" so that it "was but a pleasant
paines-taking, or serious recreation" for students.[23] For Samuel
Hartlib and several of his contemporaries, Comenius's ideas were
especially compelling. In his *A Light to Grammar, and All other Arts
and Sciences* (1641), for instance, Hezekiah Woodward draws on
Comenius's work to advocate an educational approach based on the

stimulation and elevation of the senses, explaining that with this method, a pupil "shall doe his work *playing*, and play *working*."[24] Even Milton, who by contrast was no enthusiast for Comenius's views, acknowledged the empirical imperative when he remarked in *Of Education* (1644) that "our understanding cannot in this body found it selfe but on sensible things."[25]

These educational concepts clearly anticipated those Locke would discuss in his treatise several decades later. But there were several reasons why the pedagogical innovations proposed or inspired by Comenius did not take complete hold on English soil, and why it would not be until much later, especially not until after 1688, that similar empiricist ideas would change English educational thought. Although Comenius went to London at Hartlib's invitation from 1641 to 1642, with the plan of implementing his educational philosophy of "Pansophia," or universal knowledge, in a system of schools built across the nation, his visit was cut short because of a lack of funds to get started and the rumblings of civil war.[26] Although several of his shorter treatises or textbooks were published in England during the 1640s and 50s, largely by Hartlib's sponsorship, Comenius's most comprehensive account of his educational theory, the *Didactica Magna* (1657), never reached a more popular audience in England because it was not translated (from Latin) into English until the late nineteenth century.[27] Even if it had been translated during the seventeenth century, however, that text's genuinely radical claims for the time—that the state should sponsor the same practical, nonscholastic learning for children of both genders and from all social ranks—would probably not have gained substantive popular support. As it was, none of Comenius's English admirers who were literate in Latin voiced approval of the *Didactica*'s egalitarian agenda, although perhaps the Interregnum's Puritan ethos prevented Hartlib and others from attacking it outright.

It would, in any case, be true that after the Restoration, the Puritan advocacy even for Comenius's less controversial views was an implicit though palpable liability. After 1660, some of the new principles regarding pedagogical sequencing and empirical experience continued to make headway, but many authors on education persisted in drawing on the conventions of rote memorization and rule-governed didacticism. In addition, conduct and courtesy book standbys such as Obadiah Walker's *Of Education* (1673), Jean Gailhard's *The Compleat Gentleman* (1678), Hannah Woolley's *The Gentlewomans Companion* (1673), and the frequently reissued editions of Richard Brathwaite's *The English Gentleman* (1st ed., 1630) and *The English Gentlewoman* (1st ed., 1631) helped stress the nation's renewed sense of cultural hegemony according to both rank and gender. Although Milton's tract on education had been published several years before Charles II's return to the throne, his position suggests a version of the Restoration's educational viewpoint, since he had assimilated the notion of graduated instruction via the senses while retaining an investment in more traditional ideas of learning. Admittedly, his commitment to humanist letters had less appeal during the 1670s and 80s, but elite learning for the upper-class gentlemen remained a standard. After religious piety and morality, for instance, Jean Gailhard made "*Erudition,* or learning" the goal of gentlemanly training; Obadiah Walker took "*Science* and *Speculative Learning*" as a given as well, devoting the first chapter of his book, as the title indicated, to what was "*Necessary to Learning. 1. Capacity. 2. Instruction. 3. Exercise and Practise.*"[28]

Milton's outlook therefore seems to mark an important juncture in England's shift during the seventeenth century to a more "modern," empirically based version of educational theory and practice. Nancy Armstrong and Leonard Tennenhouse have argued that during Milton's career, "the English Revolution produced a revolution in his writing," because his later poetry, notably *Paradise Lost,* "mounted a critique, however inadvertently, of the entire universe of meaning that a humanist education had prepared Milton to reproduce." For them, Milton's epic poem in particular—published more than twenty years after *Of Education*—introduced a turning point in English culture from a model of subjectivity based on aristocratic privilege to one based on a form of authorial literacy and intellectual labor.[29] That development would also hinge, however, on a further turn after the Revolution of 1688, when educationalists such as Locke, Mary Astell, Damaris Masham, and François Fénelon began to describe the individual as an agent formed by a composite disposition of habitual reflex and rational reflection—

formed, that is, by a modern sense of habitus.[30] Ultimately, Locke's
demotion of "learning" to a last priority not only demonstrated
contempt for scholasticism but also dealt a further blow to the idea
of learning as a mark of aristocratic privilege. But more was at stake
than the content of education, because the predominant approach
to instruction for all social ranks until the end of the seventeenth
century was based on the model of apprenticeship. In his treatise on
education, Walker succinctly captures this traditional view when he
writes:

> There is but one way and manner of learning, be the subject what
> ever it will. In *manuall Arts* the Master first sheweth his Apprentice,
> what he is to do; next works it himself in his presence, and gives him
> rules, and then sets him to work. The same is the way of breeding a
> *Gentleman*, or a *Scholar*. The Educator prescribeth his *end*, gives him
> *rules* and *precepts*, presents him *examples* and *patterns*; and then *sets him
> to act* according to what was before taught him.[31]

Even in Comenius's concept of graduated learning, the teacher-
pupil relationship was often portrayed as a didactic, face-to-face encounter, as depicted in an illustration of his *Orbis pictus* (fig. 1),
where the master raises his hand, forefinger extended, driving
home his exhortation to wisdom.

By contrast, without completely rejecting the device of direct
instruction, Locke and his contemporaries set out to displace the
model of apprenticeship-like prescription and rule observation by
endorsing the inculcation of moral habits by way of "insensible degrees." The importance of habits had of course long been accepted
in seventeenth-century educational thought, although earlier in the
century the stress was usually on combating *bad* habits, especially by
ready punishment, rather than on generating a beneficial complex
of habits—what Mary Astell and others would call "habitude"—
that formed a holistic orientation to virtue and sociability.[32] In *An
Essay in Defence of the Female Sex* (1696), for instance, Judith Drake
argues that men regularly need the company of educated women in
order to gain a collection of essential social skills such as "*Compla-
cence, Gallantry, Good Humour, Invention,* and . . . the *Art of Insinuation,*" since "Assiduity and constant Practice will contract such
Habits, as will make any thing easie and familiar, even to the worst

The Mafter and the Boy. | *Magifter & Puer.*

Figure 1. John Amos Comenius, *Orbis sensualium pictus*, 1659; London, 1672. In this moment of direct instruction, a master invites a potential pupil to learn wisdom. Courtesy William Andrews Clark Memorial Library, University of California, Los Angeles.

contriv'd Disposition. . . . This is the great advantage Men reap by our [women's] Society."[33] Astell remarks that "without a right habitude and temper of mind, we are not capable of Felicity," though she proposes a form of salutary, and temporary, retreat: for her, women should form a habitus by way of "*Religious Retirement*" on the model of a Protestant monastery (hence habitude approaches religious, even Catholic, habit).[34] For his part, in a chapter entitled "The First Foundations of Education" in *Instructions for the Education of a Daughter* (1707), Fénelon argues that habituation has the advantage of having prelinguistic "insensible Consequences" in facilitating young girls' instruction, since it can teach them good behavior even before they know the words to describe it. He concludes a little later: "the first Habits are still the most durable" in a young woman's later years.[35] During the early and mid-eighteenth century, beneficial habituation would be cited repeatedly as an essential part of pedagogical procedure.[36] The new emphasis spurred Fénelon to devote an entire chapter of his famous treatise on female education to the subject of "*Indirect Instructions*," which encapsulated the pedagogical principles also endorsed by Locke and others. He urged a gentle approach without "set Lessons, and Remonstrances" or the use of "dry and absolute Authority." Instead, adults should teach their daughters by working to "mix Instruction with their Sport; so that Wisdom may not be discover'd to them but by Intervals, and with a smiling Countenance."[37] The consensus of other authors was that this was the right approach. It squared with Chévremont's declared resistance to "an *Art of Teaching by Rules*," as it did with Solomon Lowe's new system for learning Latin, which was so streamlined, he claimed, that a student "will gain knowledge and use of everything, before he is aware."[38] And it also supported Damaris Masham's contention that children's education was properly a woman's "Province in that division of Cares of Humane Life, which ought to be made between a Man and his Wife. For that softness, gentleness and tenderness, natural to the Female Sex, renders them much more capable than Men are of such an insinuating Condescention to the Capacities of young Children, as is necessary in the Instruction and Government of them insensibly to form their early Inclinations."[39]

In effect, the method of indirect pedagogy inaugurates a significant shift in English educational protocol, not because it is entirely original, given some of the proposals offered earlier by Comenius's English adherents in the 1640s, but because as a program shared by many other educationalists, it synthesized a range of ideas into a powerful model for teaching the populace. Strikingly, in his *Light to Grammar* (1641), Woodward defines a pedagogical concept he calls "precognition," which is notably similar to Fénelon's or Masham's. He describes his approach as the

> *anticipation* of the understanding, that is, a stealing upon it, and catching of it, unfolding unto it, that the childe *knowes not* by that *medium* or meanes he *knew before*; or, It is that whereby I slip into a childs understanding before he be aware; so as a child shall have done his task,

before he shall suspect that any was imposed: this is done by *Precognition*; for it conveyes a *light* into the understanding, which the child hath lighted at his owne candle.[40]

As powerful as this concept was, however, it would never be mentioned by anyone writing about education later in the century. It would not be until fifty years later that another version of precognitive pedagogy would gather widespread cultural impetus.

Part of the reason for that cultural momentum was certainly Locke's prestige as philosopher and educationalist, which was combined with Fénelon's considerable influence in the early eighteenth century. Authors on education such as Judith Drake, John Clarke, and Wetenhall Wilkes explicitly cited Locke's *Essay* or the *Education* as key to understanding good teaching,[41] and even when they did not invoke his work directly, these and other writers drew on a distinctly Lockean description of empirical or epistemological process. Astell's claim that women need to make a temporary retreat from society, for instance, in the interest of educating themselves, is based on the distinction Locke makes between sensation and reflection. Those women who remain in society will continue to be distracted from higher thoughts, she explains, because

> they must necessarily push aside all other Objects, and the Mind being prepossess'd and gratefully entertain'd with those pleasing perceptions which external objects occasion, takes up with them as its only Good, is not at leisure to taste those delights which arise from a Reflection on it self, nor to receive the *Ideas* which such a Reflection conveys, and consequently forms all its Notions by such *Ideas* only as sensation has furnish'd it with.[42]

Fénelon also had an important impact on England's concept of educating women, particularly in the form of *Instructions for the Education of a Daughter*, first published in France in 1687 and later translated and issued in several English editions during the late seventeenth and early eighteenth centuries. Several of his other shorter works on education—such as devotions for children—were often appended to his treatise or collected in a separate volume, such as one called *The Characters and Properties of True Charity Display'd* (1752), where Fénelon's and Locke's legacies intersect. On the title page of a section of the text called *Some Serious Reflections on the Melancholy Consequences Which too naturally attend the Neglect of Parents*, the translators placed an epigraph attributed to Locke regarding the importance of habit formation.[43] But it is the first section of the book entitled *The Accomplish'd Governess*—a text frequently anthologized in other English publications from the early 1700s—that indicates that by the mid-eighteenth century, the proposals outlined by Fénelon, Locke, and others were already thought of as a fully codifiable educational program.[44] In effect, the text reduces things to a list of descriptive guidelines for adults (ironically, a list of rules for a process prohibiting rules). For example:

> Rule 1. Be sure to study her *Constitution* and *Genius*.
>
> 2. Follow *Nature*, and proceed easily and patiently. . . .
>
> 9. Never use any little *dissembling* Arts, to persuade her to any Thing you would have her do. . . .
>
> 16. Put *Questions* yourself to her, as it were, in *Play*, and encourage her to *answer* you. . . .
>
> 18. Insinuate into her the *Principles* of *Politeness*, and true *Modesty*, but especially Christian *Humility*. . . .
>
> 30. Study well the *Rules* of *indirect Instruction*, and apply them properly on every Occasion.
>
> 31. Acquaint her, in the most pleasant and insinuating Manner, with the *Sacred History*; nor let it seem her *Lesson* but her *Recreation*.
>
> 32. Instil[l], in like Manner, into her the *Principles* of true *Religion*, according to her Capacity, in the most familiar and diverting Way.[45]

As if to demonstrate that by 1750, these kind of instructions were so much a standard that they could be usefully inverted, Benjamin Bourn, in *A Sure Guide to Hell . . . Containing Directions . . . To Parents in the Education of their Children*, offers a quasi-satiric nightmare version of sound pedagogical procedure. As the putative author of this text, Satan offers advice on how to insure the damnation of children: his council includes avoiding the inculcation of self-denial, beating children for petty matters in order to instill dread, making pupils hate Scripture by having them learn it by rote, and encouraging their childish vices in order "to build . . . vicious Habits."[46] In short, Bourn engages in a massive form of reverse psychology, with tongue in cheek, in order to reinforce the educational status quo.

By midcentury the pedagogical order I have been describing was more than a mere concept but also less than a paradigm—if by paradigm, we are to understand Foucault's idea of an *episteme* constituting the total reorganization of cultural knowledge.[47] In relying on that premise Dorothea von Mucke, for instance, has persuasively argued that during the mid-1700s continental linguistic theory contributed to a widespread model of covert instruction, especially in Rousseau.[48] But despite her claim that this development was an exhaustive European paradigm, the evidence in England, at least, suggests otherwise. In the case of the apprenticeship model for education, it would be displaced by the turn of the eighteenth century, but not eliminated, becoming an increasingly residual cultural formation, while the precognitive version became dominant.[49] More importantly, while making a significant contribution to the pedagogy of indirection, the female educationalists during the 1690s—particularly Astell and Masham—posed a significant dissenting challenge to several of its masculinist assumptions or applications.

Part of the problem was that the description of humanity's profound malleability in early childhood, especially as it was described by Locke and Fénelon, became attached to women as a permanent feature even in adulthood. If by their account, children were predictably changeful or easily distracted, then in many male educators' opinion women suffered chronically by nature from a similar affliction. According to Fénelon, women "have a natural flexibleness, so as to be able to act any part," a constitution that easily leads to "Irresolution and Inconstancy." And the women who succumb to those quandaries, he concludes, "no sooner have a Design, but they presently change it: They lay a great many Foundations, but they never finish the Building: They say not *I desire*; but, *I could desire*: they deliberate, but never resolve. Their Motion is not Progressive, but Circular: They advance no more, than the Person who walks in a Labyrinth."[50] It is by this rationale that women, much more than children, would serve as the Enlightenment emblem of dangerous indecision or lack of fortitude.

In response to this kind of characterization, Judith Drake, for instance, argues that the related attribute of "levity"—defined as "an unsteddy Humor that makes men like and dislike, seek and reject frequently the same things upon slender or no Reasons"—was common to both men *and* women as children. She explains further that given their greater exposure to the world of social manners, young women had the advantage over men in developing sound judgment sooner.[51] Other authors such as Astell and Masham acknowledged women's sometimes deplorable inconstancy, although they attributed it mainly to a faulty upbringing, as in Astell's remarks earlier that an environment of sensory distractions prevents women from elevating their minds.[52] At the heart of this debate are the exact terms by which a modern habitus for women should be constituted, since it is precisely the lack of self-awareness in habitual behavior that disturbs Drake, Astell, and Masham, who aim to improve women's lot in English society. In other words, if the habitus is a complex disposition composed of both unconscious reflex and rational capacity, then these authors find that women are handicapped by the culture's inclination to make them creatures mainly of the first element and only barely of the second. Even with regard to men's education, of course, there would be uncertainty about where the line should be drawn between reflex and reflection. At times, Locke seems to suggest an ideal scenario where a student's entire collection of habits would become subject to rational understanding. But as he sometimes indicated, it was more likely that a great deal of one's ideological disposition would remain buried in the comfort of familiar behavior.

For Astell, however, that possibility threatens women's ability to become complete human beings. Women, she argues, have become too absorbed into a superficial and mechanical orientation to their lives: "such an unthinking way of living, when like Machin[e]s we are condemn'd every day to repent the impertinencies of the day before; shortens our Views, contracts our Minds, exposes [us] to a thousand practical Errors."[53] The same prospect alarms Masham, because it could affect the crucial issue of women's Christian faith, which is her main concern. "In regard of what Religion exacts," she comments, women are told "that they must *Be-lieve* and *Do* such and such things . . . ; but they are not put upon searching the Scriptures for themselves, to see whether, or no, these things are so."[54] Hence both Astell and Masham attack what Bourdieu and Passeron call the habitus's key component of "durability"—its propensity to perpetuate itself in automatic reflex. And their weapon for this attack is to emphasize women's capacity—and urgent need—to use their reason. Astell hopes to inspire a new woman who "cleaves to Piety, because 'tis her Wisdom, her Interest, her Joy, not because she has been accustom'd to it."[55] For Masham, the goal is to produce a woman with a full understanding of her faith, who is therefore immune to the temptations of irreverence, superficiality, or dogmatism.

Taking this tack meant first that women needed to make the case for their natural capacity for rational thinking, and here, Locke's empiricist ideas would in fact help their cause. In implicitly invoking his language in the *Essay*, for example, Judith Drake argues for mental parity between men and women: "learned Men maintain . . . that all Souls are equal, and alike, and that consequently there is no such distinction, as Male and Female Souls; that there are no innate *Idea's*, but that all the Notions we have, are deriv'd from our External Senses, either immediately, or by Reflection."[56] This argument would also lead, however, to a serious disagreement with Locke's views on learning. While Drake, Astell, and others readily acknowledged that virtue was the paramount issue, their interest in spurring women's rationality produced a powerful stress on gaining at least some degree of learned knowledge, which they knew was a key form of cultural capital.[57] As Mary More put it in "The Womans Right," the problem was "the want of learning, and the same education in women, that men have, which makes them [women] lose their right."[58] In Chudleigh's *The Ladies Defence* (1701), her spokesperson Melissa would concur:

> 'Tis hard we should be by the Men despis'd,
> Yet kept from knowing what wou'd make us priz'd:
> Debarr'd from Knowledge, banished from the Schools,
> And with the utmost Industry bred Fools.
> Laugh'd out of Reason, jested out of Sense,
> And nothing left but Native Innocence:

Then told we are incapable of Wit,
And only for the meanest Drudgeries fit.[59]

As a man of the university, Locke may have been able to demote learning's importance all too quickly, but for women, it was too important to be so summarily dismissed. Just how *much* learning was appropriate for women, however, would be a hotly debated issue. In 1673, Bathsua Makin reconstructed a brief history of women's literary, mathematical, and philosophical accomplishments since antiquity, arguing to reinstate women's place among respected intellectuals. But later, female educationalists were generally less ambitious in their claims. Drake considered anything approaching scholastic learning to be highly unsuitable, especially given her interest in promoting polite social relations among the sexes. While Astell is generally vague about the curriculum at her "*Academical*" retreat, she does say her students will not "pretend to be walking Libraries," but confine themselves to the English language and to "a competent Knowle[d]ge of the Books of GOD, Nature I mean and the Holy Scriptures." She even assures men, "We will not vie with them in thumbing over Authors," in the attempt to "overtop them."[60]

Perhaps the most interesting case about female learning is Damaris Masham's, since her views appear in the context of directly answering Locke's *Education*. The daughter of Cambridge Platonist Ralph Cudworth and Locke's longtime friend, Masham was widely believed to have coauthored with him a book entitled *A Discourse Concerning the Love of God* (1696), which defended the *Essay* against charges of irreligion.[61] In 1705, she published *Occasional Thoughts in Reference to a Vertuous or Christian Life*, which is less an attempt to apply Locke's views to women, than it is a response to his having overlooked their particular educational needs. In citing Locke's "excellent *Treatise of Education*," Masham comments that "he shews how early and how great a Watchfulness and Prudence are requisite to the forming the Mind of a Child to Vertue; and whoso shall read what he has writ on that Subject, will, it is very likely, think that few Mothers are qualify'd for such an undertaking as this: But that they are not so is the Fault which should be amended."[62] Without explicitly blaming Locke for contributing to this "fault," Masham points to the problem in an earlier passage: the "improvement of the Understanding by useful Knowledge . . . is commonly very little thought of in reference to one whole Sex" (7)—namely, women.[63] Masham therefore argues that women, as much as men, need to study the tenets of Christian faith, most of all because as prospective mothers, they have the crucial social—indeed, national—responsibility of training children of both sexes in virtue during the first years of their lives. As noted earlier, she attributes this role to the dispensation of nature, which designates women the task of teaching at home. Masham stresses that this education in faith is limited to the practical, since she says women should not aspire to theologians' learned command of technical theological argument. On this crucial point, however, Masham's text misspeaks her. In refuting anticipated critics of her proposal, Masham writes that they will claim she wants women to "have the Science of Doctors, and be well skill'd in Theological Disputes and Controversies; than the Study of which I suppose there could scarce be found for them a more useful Employment" (165). In the errata for the book, this passage is corrected to read: a "more *useless* Employment." The corrected version, then, reverses the earlier sense, agreeing with Masham's original point. But this apparently slight discrepancy suggests a much greater, though largely implicit, contradiction in her discourse: the desire to assert women's capacity and right to an intellectual domain usually reserved to men, and the impulse to maintain women's more traditional place in the domestic sphere. It is a conflict made all the more difficult given Masham's reputation at the time as one of the most learned persons—man or woman—in England.[64]

This point brings us back to Locke's concern with pedagogical power, because despite their important differences, the male and female authors on education share the problem—with important variations—of how to reconcile what seem to be opposed versions of subjectivity: a sovereign, autonomous self and one fully conformed—or at least readily conformable—to social mores. The prospect of women's personal sovereignty certainly compels Masham, who writes that women need "liberty of Action" in order to choose genuine spirituality; it would mean they should be "left at liberty to believe, or not believe, according to what, upon examination, appears to them to be the sense of the Scriptures" (11, 44). Astell argues more generally that women can and should acquire the status of a "Voluntary Agent," whose reason enables her to choose actions based upon independent judgment.[65] This is a new emphasis in early modern educational thinking about women as well as men, and it is an important part of the turn of cultural and political events around 1688. If it is true that with the arrival of the Restoration more traditional gender roles became reestablished in England,[66] then by the time of the Glorious Revolution, there was a sense of new possibilities. For women that sense was generated in part by new professional opportunities as stage actresses and writers, notably represented by Aphra Behn's spectacular success. In political terms, moreover, given the terms of contractual monarchy, installed with William of Orange's taking the throne, an English citizen's civic responsibility depended less on automatic obedience to royal decree and more on a self-conducted evaluation of the monarch's obligation to serve the kingdom. In that context, gently shaping individuals' social disposition made a good fit with a form of citizenship turned more sharply toward the national interest at large.[67]

This enlarged sense of personal prerogative, however, would also confront the inevitable requirements of authority, whether social or spiritual. In a passage that bracingly recalls Locke's dilemma, Astell captures this double perspective:

> We are conscious of our own Liberty, who ever denies it denies that he is capable of Rewards and Punishments, degrades his Nature and makes himself but a more curious piece of Mechanism; and none but Atheists will call in question the Providence of GOD, or deny that he Governs *All*, even the most Free of all his Creatures. But who can reconcile me these?[68]

Astell's answer to that question is that no one can, that in this world one can rely only on faith in the divine order of things. But the quandary would remain, and at its worst it would produce a sense of not only a torn self but also of two distinguishable selves. In his *Letter of Genteel and Moral Advice*, Wetenhall Wilkes described that kind of duality to his niece this way:

You are further to consider yourself, (first) as a reasonable Creature, capable of becoming yourself either happy or miserable: and (secondly) as a sociable Being, capable of contributing to the Happiness or Misery of others. Suitable to this double Capacity, upon Examination you will find yourself furnished with two Principles of Action: First, with Self-love to render you wakeful to your own personal Interest; and in the next place, with Benevolence to dispose you for giving your utmost Assistance to all engaged in the same Pursuit.[69]

On the face of it, one's rational self would be the reason that educators like Locke can imagine treating children with the utmost respect or even leniency, and yet, given the example of women writers considered here, it is also possible that one's self-possessed rationality is precisely the ground on which to resist or challenge the social inequities imposed by educational norms. In short, the modern sense of habitus could not completely eliminate for men or women the uncertainties about how or when pedagogical authority should be enforced. But there would be useful ways—both practical and discursive—by which to negotiate that difficult terrain. Locke's *Education* offers an informative example of how that could be done.

Supervisory Education and the Regulation of Nature

Locke's response to the competing requirements of freedom and pedagogical control is once more to invoke the aid of Nature, though this time accompanied by the salutary assistance of human agency. That response distinguishes itself in the metaphor of husbandry or gardening, a trope saturating the *Education*'s pages from first to last. Locke constantly speaks of "good Husbandry," planting "seeds" of moral virtue, cultivating good habits, weeding out vices, and reaping the benefits of good behavior.[70] Accompanying this dialect are repeated references to the "favourable *Seasons of Aptitude and Inclination*" (sec. 74), which should guide the tutor in introducing new information or tasks.[71]

At first sight, to be sure, referring to the "root" of selfishness or to "weeding" out undesirable traits appears relatively casual or unremarkable. But the accumulated weight of their use—particularly in passages that pack an entire range of gardening terminology tightly together—invigorates what might otherwise seem the deadest of metaphors. It is particularly arresting, for instance, when Locke writes that if parents or tutors "are fain to come to the Plough and the Harrow, the Spade and the Pick-ax," in order to eliminate children's early errors, then they "must go deep to come at the Roots; and all the Force, Skill, and Diligence we can use, is scarce enough to cleanse the vitiated Seed-Plat overgrown with Weeds, and restore us the hopes of Fruits, to reward our Pains in season" (sec. 84). After moments like this, one cannot help taking notice of the most casual mention of vices "taking root" or tutors "weeding out" self-interest. Aside from its prominence, this language is pedagogically significant because it harbors two distinct attitudes toward natural agency: on the one hand, it celebrates spontaneous vitality and "natural" growth, while on the other it recognizes that the same spontaneity has an inherent tendency to produce noxious faults and, in the end, dangerous social evils. The compensating advantage of the analogy of husbandry, however, is that nature becomes satisfactorily *domesticated*, its impulses safely harnessed so education can take advantage of its native powers.

A second trope that serves a similar function appears in Locke's slightly less frequent reliance on the language of medical doctoring to describe correcting children's moral faults. If by reducing the importance of physical punishment, Locke's impulse has been partly to replace the body with the mind as the chief instrument to induce obedience, then that move has also endowed the mind with the bodily aura of substance, material function, and vulnerability to disease. A "lazy, listless Humour," for example, "is the proper state of one Sick, and out of order in his Health" (sec. 208). In language that recalls his discussion of human irrationality in the *Essay*, moreover, Locke describes childish inattentiveness as a "Contagion, that Poisons the Mind" (sec. 37) and stubborn willfulness as a "natural Infirmity" that, in being "help'd towards an Amendment," can also produce the occasional "Relapse" (sec. 80). A tutor or parent must therefore proceed like a pedagogical physician, ever alert to a moral "Distemper" or "Disease," and ever ready to "work . . . the Cure" or prescribe the appropriate "Remedy."[72] And such action must be taken cautiously, for it can make natural defects even worse: "If *Severity* carried to the highest Pitch does prevail, and works a Cure upon the present unruly Distemper, it is often by bringing in the room of it, a worse and more dangerous Disease, by breaking the Mind" (sec. 51). Like the Lockean metaphor of husbandry, this physiological approach embodies a double attitude toward nature, since here it is not only the source of degenerative childhood maladies but also the mechanism that will complete the healing spell after an adult's intercession. Still, the terminology of disease and the body has more ominous resonance than the language of gardening, even drastic "uprooting" or "ploughing," and it therefore captures Locke's gravest misgivings about letting nature take its course. Strangely, however, these two tropes not only mesh to turn the same pedagogical wheel, but on occasion can become ambiguously entangled or mutually blurred. The word *cure* is apparently the catalyst, since at one point in adjacent sections Locke seems to use it in two different senses, the first suggesting the final step of "curing" fruits or vegetables after harvest, and the second designating the more common sense of defeating disease. Childish faults, he first remarks, "should be . . . left only to Time and Imitation, and riper Years to cure" (sec. 63). He then describes instilling in children good habits, commenting that "having this way cured in your Child any Fault, it is cured for ever; And thus one by one you may weed them out all, and plant what Habits you please" (sec. 64). His first remark may in fact be using "cure" in the medical sense, but in that case, *both* passages employ a wildly mixed metaphor of some kind of medical husbandry or horticultural medicine. But sanitizing Locke's metaphorical excess here would in fact miss its significance. The point is that these two tropes synchronize to propel Locke's pedagogical program and, ultimately, are *structurally identical* in their application to the problems of dualistic human nature and freedom versus authority.

A key to both the medical and horticultural figures of speech is their ability to contend with potentially disabling contradictions by focusing on the usefulness of *process*. Recall Locke's words in the preceding paragraph, when he claims that the "Faults *of their Age, rather than of the Children themselves*" should be removed by leaving children "only to Time and Imitation, and riper Years to cure" (sec. 63; my emphasis). This comment represents Locke's most optimistic outlook, since time itself will administer the appropriate remedy, but it also underscores his strategy to negotiate between the contradictory demands of freedom and control, for instance, by committing them to an *alternating temporal process*—in other words, a narrative that can accommodate more dexterously his opposing educational agendas.

Perhaps the best way to consider this strategy is to look at a passage where Locke discusses an education that has misfired:

> *Affectation* is not, I confess, an early Fault of Childhood, or the Product of untaught Nature; it is of that sort of Weeds, which grow not in the wild uncultivated Waste, but in Garden-Plots, under the Negligent Hand, or Unskilful Care of a Gardener. Management and Instruction, and some Sense of the Necessity of Breeding, are requisite to make any one capable of *Affectation*, which endeavours to correct Natural Defects, and has always the Laudable Aim of Pleasing, though it always misses it; and the more it labours to put on Gracefulness, the farther it is from it. For this Reason it is the more carefully to be watched, because it is the proper Fault of . . . a perverted Education. (sec. 66)

Besides censoring the artificiality of affected breeding as the product of poor instruction, this passage suggests Locke's larger tactic for solving the dilemma concerning when adult intercession should be imposed and when it should not. By characterizing affectation as something "the more carefully to be *watched*," Locke makes the initial tutorial or parental role essentially passive, thereby momentarily guarding against the adult "negligent Hand," which actually has been too much involved in the child's development. Watching carefully is thus the educator's first responsibility, and it is only after observing a child's mistakes or faults that he (like the father) "should interpose his Authority and Commands" (sec. 85).

Locke's discussion of sound education is in fact permeated by the language of tutorial "observation" or scrutiny; it should come as no surprise that he attributes so much importance and power to that activity, given the epistemological privilege he assigns in the *Essay* to "seeing" as the "most instructive of our Senses," a claim reinforced in that text by his repeated referral to "light" as the measure of authentic rationality or "visible certain Truth."[73] In the *Education*, "observation" connotes a range of meanings, most importantly the literal act of watching, wisely evaluating a child's behavior, and, as a corollary, putting into practice Lockean pedagogical guidelines. As Locke puts it, his program, "if observed" by the teacher, will effectively enable comportment to "be carefully watched in young People," and the tutor thereafter to "judge . . . the Temper, Inclination and weak side of his Pupil."[74]

Careful observation and appraisal, in turn, provide the opportunity for interceding in a student's development and bringing it to satisfactory fruition. This sequence forms a pattern I call *Observation, Intervention, and Resolution*, represented as follows:

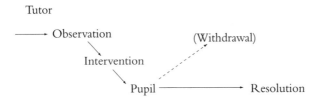

This scheme constitutes Locke's pedagogical solution to the competing demands of freedom and control, in part by virtually removing the tutor's presence as a figure of authority or power. Locke's observational language frequently establishes what is a kind of virtual space for adult supervision: to describe children's learning as always proceeding "*under the Eye* and Direction of the Tutor," or of other adults "who have the *Over-sight* of their Education," suggests a physical position elevated and removed by virtue of its mature potency (a spatial arrangement also indicated by the sketch above).[75] That suggestion becomes explicit on those occasions when Locke cautions: "though you have your Eyes upon him, to watch what he does with the time which he has at his own disposal, yet you must not let him perceive, that you, or any body else, do so. For that may hinder him from following his own Inclination" (sec. 125; see also sec. 102). In other words, this subterfuge will allow the child to learn in what seems spontaneous fashion, without even the awareness that he has been put to the task of learning.[76] And furthermore, it constructs the entire overarching *structure* for "cozening" children into knowledge, the agenda for "indirect" or "insinuating" instruction we have already witnessed. This education by stealth—which I will call *supervisory*, or *observant*, education—exhibits several earmarks of the "disciplinary" procedures Foucault describes as emerging during the Enlightenment, including the elements of surveillance and de-emphasized punishment.[77] But this point demarcates a crucial juncture in articulating the distinctive features of supervisory pedagogy, because while this model shares some similar features with Foucault's explanation of the role of surveillance in reforming individuals, there are also some important differences that produce a substantially different paradigm for "modern" socialization than the one Foucault offers. The most telling difference emerges concerning Foucault's description of surveillance as the fundamental organizing center—both theoretically and in institutional practice—for the entire range of disciplinary effects that include the key process of internalization. As he writes in *Discipline and Punish*, discipline "presupposes a mechanism that coerces by means of observation; an apparatus in which the techniques that make it possible to see induce effects of power" (170–71). In the supervisory model, by contrast, even an idealized, Jeremy Bentham-style surveillance does not have sufficient power to constitute the effects of human subjectivity as thoroughly as Foucault imagines, even when that surveillance is combined with Foucault's description of the individual's psychic internalization of disciplinary principles (including self-surveillance) and his explanation of the carefully planned social scenario modeled on a spatial arrangement—or "architecture"—of sociopolitical organization. A supervisory approach indicates instead that pedagogical observation as a form of power is only partially effective, requiring at some point a more active assertion of authority—the educational or institutional analogue of "improvisation" in Bourdieu's sense of putting the structures of the habitus into practice. Put another way, in this kind of supervision, intervention does more than "accompany" or "follow" observation, because at some point observation must reach the limit of its ability or even fail—it requires some form of intervention as a necessary supplement to the educational process.

By the same token, just as pedagogical power is never so sufficiently housed at the level of surveillance that it cannot proceed without specific moments of active mediation, the implementation of supervision I am describing is never so pervasive or totalized (in Foucault's sense of "total" institutions) that students cannot or will not need to improvise in the process of their own, individual enactments of the habitus. In other words, the "errors" Locke intends to correct after they have inevitably occurred are in fact the recurring evidence that, no matter how thoroughgoing a tutor's pedagogical observation or staging of the pedagogical scenario, students will always generate variations on the principles of desirable norms, variations often functioning as transgressions against the system of norms whose structure is nonetheless increasingly undergirding the students' social disposition in the first place. In other words, the process of supervisory education is one that stages the complementary and often competing acts of improvisation by the tutor, on the one hand, and those by the individual pupil, on the other, while at the same time aiming to "regulate" that exchange in the interest of (re)producing ideological normalcy in that student.

For Locke, while the tutor's interventions should be orchestrated whenever possible to be indirect or at least hardly perceptible by the pupil, these efforts are always a form of direct action from the perspective of the pedagogue. Probably the best example of this fact is Locke's story about getting a child to want to read, because it is a story that encapsulates in miniature the general observation-intervention-resolution pattern. He writes:

> I remember being at a Friend's House, whose younger Son, a Child in Coats, was not easily *brought* to his Book (being taught *to read* at home by his Mother)[.] I advised to try another way, than requiring it of him as his Duty; we therefore, in a Discourse on purpose amongst ourselves, in his hearing, but without taking any notice of him, declared, That it was the Privilege and Advantage of Heirs and Elder Brothers, to be Scholars; that this made them fine Gentlemen, and beloved by every body: And that for Younger Brothers, 'twas a Favour to admit them to Breeding; to be taught to *Read* and *Write*, was more than came to their share; they might be ignorant Bumpkins and Clowns, if they pleased. This so wrought upon the Child, that afterwards he desired to be taught; would come himself to his Mother to *learn*. . . . I doubt not but some way like this might be

taken with other Children; and when Their Tempers are found, some Thoughts be instilled into them, that might set them upon desiring of *Learning* themselves, and make them seek it, as another sort of Play or Recreation.[78]

The ineffectuality of prescription, the gentle use of authority, the child's all-important perception of independence, and making study into a form of play—all of these are captured in this pedagogical success story. What this narrative also illustrates is how supervisory education can induce a child to internalize the ideological structure of patrilinear power in English society. Here, the boy becomes motivated to improve himself by accepting the premise that usually only the eldest sons have the prerogative of a full-blown education, which is tied, ultimately, to inheriting the family's estate. As for Locke's pedagogical argument, supervisory education provides the ground-level structure (or skeleton) for Locke's gardening and medical terminology: if like his friend, other adults monitored children's weeds and promptly pulled them, or, alternately, if they examined children carefully for telltale symptoms and applied effective remedies, then they too could enjoy (or reap) the same heartening benefits.

As a design to accommodate a host of epistemological, practical, and social imperatives, Locke's strategy of supervisory education is probably best characterized as a scheme of "both/and." Though in some respects Locke must certainly plan to balance parts of his education program, such as his insistence that children be as free as possible and that parents have a sturdy upper hand, it is clear too that his task is more than merely stabilizing the thrust of two equally "good" aims. In addition to the opposition of honesty and deception in teaching children, for instance, there is the larger collision of the natural and the humanly artificial, which are themselves further fractured by self-division. A child's desire for freedom, for example, motivated by the spontaneity of the natural state, can prove itself to be deceptive, for as Locke frequently notes, it is also the source of potentially crippling moral disabilities. And adult authority, for its part, though supposedly administering the offices of rational, civil conduct, seems compelled to apply intricate ruses and, worse, to distort natural processes by a "perverted Education" in affectation. That is why a simple rapprochement remains unfeasible: Locke must persist in including both power *and* liberty, naturalness and artificiality, forthrightness and stratagem.

The task of implementing the both/and mandate falls to the dexterous management of narrative—here, Locke's invention of an observant education that is acutely *ambi*dextrous. In effect, the sequence of observation-intervention-resolution constitutes a pedagogical narrative unit, whose repetition forms the cycles of gradual learning, much like Locke's description of how habit is acquired: by "the same Action done over and over again." This narrative pattern also recalls the general contours of Locke's speculative history, in the *Second Treatise*, concerning humanity's eventual entry into fully political society. In that account, the passage from the state of nature to that of civil society is portrayed as a movement from an essentially pleasant, unambitious existence, which is then troubled by the dubious introduction of absolute monarchy and money, to the establishment of broad civil protections and the balance of powers. In large terms, it is a story beginning with natural spontaneity, shaken by human excess—particularly greed for power or property—and ending with mature civil community. It is, in other words, the communal version of what goes on for a Lockean pupil, though also with some crucial differences. In similar fashion, the student begins with ostensive liberty, then commits some excessive error or fault, and is finally brought within the boundaries of civil conduct. His development is further similar to that of the historical group's in that Locke characterizes most childish faults as the consequence of the "first Original of most vicious Habits"—the "love of Dominion" (secs. 103, 104)—which manifests itself in various forms of overextending one's legitimate claim to possessions, adult attention, or other prerogatives.

The telling difference, however, is in the quality of the process. For Locke's quasi-political populace, the political maturing process is brutishly slow and painful: though God is no doubt witness to their trials, they must rely on being "instructed" by experience, or "taught" by the "Covetousness or Ambition" of political officeholders.[79] Before reaching the civil state, the population must endure the prolonged trials of an era "very unsafe, very unsecure," and "full of fears and continual dangers" (sec. 123). By contrast,

Locke's student can exult in a particularly calm environment, protected from severe calamity by the observant role of his tutor. And unlike the historical account, Locke's educational narrative proceeds under the auspices of an ingenious superstructure that can fluidly accommodate what in the *Second Treatise* remain dangling inconsistencies. Locke's pedagogue has learned the lessons of a more arduous precedent.

Of course, even with the tensile strengths of supervisory education, there is still no real prospect for dead-set routine, practically speaking or theoretically. With the benefits of extreme flexibility come the uncertainties of relative instability. If tutors are charged with the "Over-sight" of their pupil's education, then it is surely possible that that term could reassume its usual denotation of "error" or "omission," thereby undermining the confident authority originally designated. As Locke comments in the *Education* about parents' frequent mistakes with leniency: "These are Oversights usually committed, by those who seem to take the greatest Care of their Children's Education."[80] Careful scrutiny, considered intervention, may not suffice. If, on the one hand, children's folly counts among the "Faults of their Age, . . . [to] be left only to Time and Imitation, and riper Years to cure," then on the other hand, there is always the initially innocuous "Self-love . . . which from small Beginnings in Pins and Cherry-stones, will, if let alone, grow up to higher Frauds, and be in danger to end at last in down-right harden'd Dishonesty" (secs. 63, 110). The natural metaphor continues to sprout ever-greener ambiguities, and even a diligent tutorial scrutiny may miss the symptoms of a genuinely serious ailment.

In effect, these practical uncertainties suggest a pedagogical project that never really musters the kind of rigorous systematization Foucault ascribes to the disciplinary program of Jeremy Bentham's imagined institution of the Panopticon. For despite being able to instill students with an effective gentrified and patrilineal ideology, Locke's program houses its own internal inconsistencies which are endemic to any ideological construction of social identity. In this sense, his treatise illustrates Foucault's remark in *The History of Sexuality* that "discourse can be both an instrument and an effect of power, but also a hindrance, a stumbling-block, a point of resistance."[81] But as Foucault notes elsewhere, producing such an apparent "failure" of an ideology or disciplinary institution, as in the case of "delinquency," is in fact the occasion for ever more vigorous attempts to reassert that same social regimen.[82]

The ambiguities in Locke's educational plan are linked further to a theological indeterminacy similar to that in the *Second Treatise*, where Locke's historical account seems to have substantially secularized the portrayal of human origins and development while also retaining elements of the Christian view on original sin. In the new environment of his supervised educational garden, Locke apparently proposes to rewrite the story of Eden by eliminating prohibition, diluting the consequences of error, and, as in the *Second Treatise*, representing the child's development as an inspiring natural ascension into the realm of mature rationality and civil status. But here too, Locke resurrects the daunting prospect that youthful human nature is fundamentally flawed and dangerous, the liability of being "the Sons of *Adam*."[83] One's impression is often that Locke's revisionist perspective is the stronger one, but in keeping with the complexity of observant education's structure, both secularly Edenic *and* scripturally Adamic elements compose the story of Lockean education. The advent of the Fall lurks disturbingly behind the scenes of readily molding the pliant "Wax" of a malleable childhood. It is an ambivalence equally applicable to the claims made by Locke's contemporary educationalists.

Natural Mediation and the Trope of Feminine Empire

In the decades before the Revolution of 1688, the metaphors of gardening and medicine were not uncommon in the educational treatises or conduct books written by both men and women. In 1631, for instance, Richard Brathwaite remarked that a child's "*Native seeds* of *goodnesse* . . . would grow ranke and wilde, unless they were by seasonable *instruction ripened*." Some forty years later, Hannah Woolley lamented "the great negligence of Parents, in letting the fertile ground of their Daughters lie fallow."[84] Medicinal descriptions also made an appearance, though less frequently. Brathwaite cautioned his readers about the "dangerous phrenzy" of an overly excited fancy, which could "infect your *heart*." In warning against a related danger of telling children strange tales about ghosts or witches, Obadiah Walker claimed such stories "are to the mind what a Feaver is the body, filling the Soul with preternatural, irregular conceits."[85]

In some cases, as with Obadiah Walker, using these educational tropes indicated a perception similar to Locke's regarding Nature's dual nature. But in many other instances, educationalists drew on its metaphoric resources as though it were an untroubled authority. There could be several reasons for this strategy. Richard Brathwaite expressed the conviction that gentility was produced by natural— and by implication, aristocratic—bloodlines: "there are *native Seeds of goodnesse sowne*," he claimed, "*in generous bloods by lineall succession*."[86] Comenius sought an even more remote origin in order to establish Nature as a unitary standard: "by the word *nature* we mean, not the corruption which has laid hold of all men since the Fall . . . , but our first and original condition, to which, as a starting point, we must be recalled."[87] For his part, Hezekiah Woodward asserted Nature's reliability by whimsical analogue: in his educational program, he claimed to "*follow Nature all along, keeping pace with her, which is constant, not* Grashopper-like, *hopping, and leaping, now up, then downe againe presently*."[88]

By contrast, educational writers after 1688, including Locke, employ the language of horticulture and medicine more frequently than did their predecessors, and with a new semantic valence. Mary Astell strikes a familiar note about Nature's mixed qualities when she remarks:

> Nature as bad as it is, and as much as it is complain'd of, is so far improveable by the grace of GOD, upon our honest and hearty endeavours, that if we are not wanting to our selves, we may all in *some*, tho not in an *equal* measure, be instruments of his Glory.[89]

That observation feeds several elaborate horticultural tropes, such as when she comments on women's natural abilities, despite men's lack of assistance:

> The Soil is rich and would, if well cultivated, produce a noble Harvest, if then the Unskilful Managers *not only permit, but incourage* noxious Weeds, tho' we shall suffer by their Neglect, yet they ought

not in justice to blame any but themselves, if they reap the Fruit of their own Folly.[90]

Like Astell, authors writing on education during the early eighteenth century draw on similar horticultural terminology, in which errors are both inherent (therefore "permitted") in human nature and produced ("encouraged") by adult supervision.[91]

The language of disease and cure was perhaps even more widespread from the 1690s to the mid-eighteenth century and was used especially by those authors who perceived the nation to be at risk from a poorly educated populace. In 1705, Masham claimed that because "inveterate Maladies are difficultly cur'd," lingering immoral propensities in England were threatening to undermine "those Civil and Religious Liberties" that had been gained with the Revolution in 1688.[92] Much later, with equally broad national concerns in *British Education* (1756), Thomas Sheridan would argue that "symptoms in a state are sure prognosticks of approaching ruin; and its end cannot be far off unless prevented by adequate remedies. As the disease arises from an universal corruption of manners, it can be cured only by a general reformation." In prescribing his own course of pedagogical reform, Sheridan draws explicitly on the work of "two eminent physicians"—Milton and Locke—whose educational treatises, he asserts, have been the only ones "of any note" to strike "at the root of the disease" or to describe "a course of lenitives" for England's recovery.[93]

For some writers, employing this kind of medical or horticultural imagery registered a self-conscious double gesture similar to Locke's, in tracing both a secular and Christian view of human development. Fénelon, for instance, while recommending the gentle approach of "indirect instruction," which relies on assuming a benevolent disposition in children, also remarks, "Man is born in the Corruption of Sin, his Body being vexed with a contagious Disease."[94] Other authors, of course, such as Masham, Astell, or Richard Peers, vigorously proclaimed a Christian perspective on humanity's inherent corruption. Unlike Locke, they did not need the aid of Catharine Trotter, who defended him against the charge that he held a "Socinian" view of Scripture that discounted the idea of innate human depravity.[95] But however staunchly these educationalists may have asserted their Christian orthodoxy, there remained the fact that the new program of instruction by "insinuation" produced a substantial softening of, if not a resistance to, the Christian standard regarding human identity. And in that sense, like Locke himself, his contemporaries employed the language of medicine or gardening with notable ambivalence.

This shared vocabulary suggests, then, that Locke's supervisory schema of observation, intervention, and resolution articulates a commonly shared, implicitly narrative logic in his contemporaries' educational proposals. As further evidence of that connection, the language of "watching" also frequently appears in educational treatises from the 1690s onward. In *A Serious Proposal to the Ladies*, for example, Astell invokes the familiar image of the watchful physician when she describes the tutors in her religious retreat as "Watching over their [students'] souls with tenderness and prudence; applying fitting Medicines with sweetness & affability. Sagacious in discovering the very approaches of a fault, wise in preventing, and charitable in bearing with all pityable Infirmities."[96] Similarly, Masham refers to adults as "watchful inspectors" of children; and John Clarke claims "it is the Business of *Education* to watch over" the early stages of children's mental vulnerability.[97]

A few of these authors also go so far as to describe a "fictional" orchestration of a child's educational experience. An enthusiast for Lockean pedagogical method, Clarke espouses a weak version of this strategy when he recommends pretending there are virtually no rules of grammar when beginning to teach students Latin. For his part, Fénelon comes the closest when he describes the following approach to a girl's education: "it may be now and then needful to spur her forward discreetly with some kind of Contempt and Reproaches; which you must not do your self. But it must be done by an inferiour Person, such for instance as another Child, and without your seeming to know anything of it."[98] But significantly, there are no similar descriptions in the work by women authors, suggesting that perceptions of gender turn the application of supervisory education in a different direction. Astell is a case in point, since she stresses having virtue "wisely insinuated" in her students via the ministrations of friendship, rather than the covert manipulations Locke or Fénelon describe. She describes genuine friendship as a form of moral empowerment, since it is "without doubt, the best

Instructor to teach us our duty to our Neighbour, and a most excellent Monitor to excite us to make payment as far as our power will reach." But this kind of friendship also produces a miniaturized and more dispersed form of supervisory instruction. As Astell puts it, nothing "shou'd hinder them [women] from ent[e]ring into an holy combination to watch over each other for Good, to advise, encourage and direct, and to observe the minutest fault in order to its amendment."[99]

In Astell's educational system, there can be a smooth transition from instruction administered by an authorized tutor to that shaped by two women's mutual inspection, to a genuine form of self-examination and discipline. That sequence certainly corresponds to the process of internalization required for creating children's habitus regardless of gender. But Astell's emphasis on the *self*-motivation of her readers or prospective students indicates another place where gender produces a notable difference in educational description. If for Astell as well as for her male contemporaries, medical and horticultural terminology helps mediate between the competing agendas of two selves—one naturally his or her own subject, the other subjected to (masculinist) social norms—then the trope of empire building suggests a distinctly feminine form of pedagogical mediation and cultural appropriation. In the first pages of *A Serious Proposal to the Ladies*, Astell first employs this metaphor when she exhorts her female readers to be "so true to your Interest as not to lessen your Empire, and depreciate your Charms." Shortly after, the political theme becomes more explicit when she tells her readers: "We will . . . enquire what it is that stops your flight, that keeps you groveling here below, like *Domitian* catching Flies, when you should be busied in obtaining Empires."[100]

This is a complex rhetorical move, since Astell is comparing women unfavorably to Domitian, the last Roman Caesar famous for amusing himself in private retirement with catching flies and killing them with a sharp knife, rather than attending to the affairs of state.[101] The analogy gives Astell a powerful way to disparage the useless employments that she claims have traditionally occupied women's time. It enables her, for instance, to substitute self-achieved "empire" for the illusory attractions of "conquest" or amatory intrigue, a danger often mentioned by other women writing about education. Hence the metaphor of empire promotes a form of salutary female boldness or even aggression by which women can determine their fate. Unlike the tropes of gardening or medicine, this metaphor assumes the perspective of the pupil herself as powerful *auto*didact, suggesting that her efforts will succeed even to the point of exceeding the spoils usually associated with colonial enterprise. As Astell tells her female readers, her aim is to "procure you such Ornaments as all the Treasures of the *Indies* are not able to purchase" (4). The values of colonial empire, in fact, were often invoked by women educationalists as a way to advance the cause of female prerogative. Two decades before Astell, Bathsua Makin had attempted to shame English men into better attitudes toward women by remarking, "Doubtless this under-breeding of Women began amongst Heathen and Barbarous People; it continues with the *Indians*, where they make their Women meer slaves, and wear them out in drudgery" (22–23). The implication, of course, was that as a more civilized nation, England should treat its women comparably better, giving them the substantial education appropriate not only to their natural capacities but also to their standing as European citizens. At the turn of the century, Mary Chudleigh makes a similar move by attacking the prospect of husbands "introducing *Persion* Customs" into English marriages, since those customs made women little more than servile subordinates.[102]

Women can claim their empire, Astell tells her readers, by overthrowing men's "Tyranny in Ignorance and Folly, since it is in your Power to regain your Freedom, if you please but t'endeavour it."[103] This assertion of female power certainly counters Fénelon's portrayal of women's vulnerable or "soft" femininity, which is vividly captured in the frontispiece to his *Instructions for the Education of a Daughter* (fig. 2). In the engraving's left-hand corner is a female figure, who, mirror in hand, represents Fénelon's prospective pupil

FIGURE 2 (facing page). Frontispiece to François de Salignac de la Mothe-Fénelon, *Instructions for the Education of a Daughter*, 1707. The woman in the lower-left corner is being saved from the arrows of two cupid figures by Wisdom, who points in the direction in which a subdued male figure representing temptation must exit. Courtesy The Huntington Library, San Marino, California.

WISDOM *is the* Principal *Thing.* Solom.

Printed for I. Bowyer at the Rose y. Corner of S.t Pauls Church Yard
in Ludgate street. E. K. inven. M. V.t Gucht sculp

as a woman in danger of the "conquest" of two cupid figures aiming at her with bow and arrow. Meanwhile, she is surrounded by the activity of other figures who save her from corruption: a small figure subdues the representative of temptation with a pike, and Wisdom points in the direction of temptation's imminent exit while holding a scroll bearing the title of Fénelon's treatise. For Astell, by contrast, women can and must seize the implements of virtuous warfare for themselves. In the battle against vice, she explains, women's religious education will enable them to "disarm it of *Custom*, the only thing that recommends it, bravely win its strongest Fort, and turn its own Cannon against it self."[104]

Of course, the vocabulary of empire would also seem to insert women into the traditionally masculine stronghold of the public sphere, and on this point, Astell substantially qualifies her revisionary zeal. As she explains, "the true end of all our Prayers and external Observances, is . . . to obtain for us the Empire of our Passions." Hence her religious retreat will produce a woman whose "Heroic Soul is too great to ambition any Empire but that of her own Breast."[105] This emendation is rhetorically complex. It brings women back within the domestic and personal domain, allowing Astell to assure men that she intends to leave their legal and political authority intact. But it also harbors an implicit agenda of appropriating for women the forms of public—even "heroic"—life while disparaging full access to those forms as spiritually debilitating:

> The Men therefore may still enjoy their Prerogatives for us, we mean not to intrench on any of their Lawful Privileges. . . . They may busy their heads with Affairs of State, and spend their Time and Strength in recommending themselves to an uncertain Master, or a more giddy Multitude, our only endeavour shall be to be absolute Monarchs in our own Bosoms. They shall still if they please dispute about Religion, let 'em only give us leave to Understand and Practice it. And whilst they have unrival'd the Glory of speaking as *many* Languages as *Babel* afforded, we only desire to express our selves Pertinently and Judiciously in *One*.[106]

In effect, Astell's trope of feminine empire occupies a middle ground between "feminist" ambition and traditional gender norms. It advances the campaign to improve women's lot while attempting to assuage the anxiety—for both sexes—that such innovations would inevitably agitate. What is more, it embodies the dual gesture of dissent and conformity characteristic of women educationalists writing during the late seventeenth and early eighteenth centuries, among them Woolley, Makin, Masham, Drake, and Chudleigh. In Chudleigh's *The Ladies Defence*, for example, after having boldly asserted women's right to learning, Melissa concedes: "The Tyrant Man may still possess the Throne: / 'Tis in our Minds that we wou'd Rule alone. / Those unseen Empires give us leave to sway, / And to our reason private Homage pay" (18).

Finally, then, female educational writers would share with their male counterparts a common interest in promoting a "modern" English disposition, which could describe both male and female habitude and which would ideally combine rational reflection and habitual reflex, as well as autonomous self-determination and social cooperativeness. They would also therefore share an investment in the gentler methods of precognitive, supervisory instruction, whose metaphoric constitution in terms of horticulture and medicine could accommodate a palpably divided sense of natural process or cultural authority. This double logic, however, would take a very different course given the inequitable conditions women such as Astell, Drake, and others perceived in England's postrevolutionary goal of providing its citizens with enlarged, if not liberal, opportunities. They knew that women like themselves deserved a fully "rational" education that would inevitably encroach on male prerogative—and that is precisely what the trope of feminine empire was meant to capture. And yet, in contrast to later women writers such as Mary Hays or Mary Wollstonecraft, they refrained from embarking on an all-out campaign for political equality. Still, it must be said that this difference is less a mark of lamentably weak determination in Astell, Masham, or any other earlier women educationalists, than it is a consequence of the far more restricted sociohistorical context in which those women lived and wrote during the late seventeenth and early eighteenth centuries. Their apparently cautious improvisations regarding female learning were both substantial and decisive while also conditioned by Astell's conservative political views or Masham's intent to emphasize religious piety.

This dual sense of female empire—verging on the domain of public male privilege, while transmuting that incursion into the language of private sovereignty—will be especially important later, when evaluating the pedagogical implications of women's fiction, particularly Charlotte Lennox's *Female Quixote*. But first, in the next chapter, we need to consider one last metaphor pertinent both to Locke's *Education* and other educationalists' work—the theater—which illuminates the more literary dimensions of supervisory education and its fictional applications.

CHAPTER TWO

Theatrical Education and the Thickening of Plot

Would it not be an insufferable thing for a learned Professor . . .
[to be] in an instant overturned by an upstart Novelist?

—Locke, *Essay concerning Human Understanding*

If the project of supervisory education implies an improvised, sometimes slippery, narrative about the negotiation between the habitus and its individualized applications by students, then it also corresponds to notably "literary" experiments or mutations in the writing of educational discourse itself. In this chapter, I examine how the characterization of education as a form of theatrical performance combines with the tropes of medicine and gardening in producing a storylike quality in Locke's *Education*. This process, moreover, induces a deviation from the conventions of expository prose or philosophical description that suggests the ways other educational texts during the late seventeenth and early eighteenth centuries would focus on the issue of "dramatic" personality while sometimes also exploring the use of narrative formats in appealing to readers.

81

The trope of dramaticality has further significance for the novel's engagement with educational ideas, since the theater was often associated with the disruptive power of "novelty" in individual behavior, especially when it came to describing women, who were imagined as having an intimate affinity both with plays and their counterpart in real life—superficial or excessively passionate behavior. In this context, I will examine toward the end of this chapter the general literary and cultural scene in which early eighteenth-century novelists explored the relation between education and virtue, particularly with regard to gender. In effect, the degree to which novelists contributed to the history of the novel of education depended strikingly on the extent to which they subscribed to a model of improvisational development: that criterion distinguishes the fictional practice of authors such as Samuel Richardson and Delarivière Manley, who did not, from that of authors such as Daniel Defoe or Eliza Haywood, who did. But even among those who adopted the idea of improvised identity, they also adapted its features to very different conceptions of how sexual purity served as an emblem of personal development, particularly in the characterization of men versus women. The issue of whether virtue was primarily to be preserved or acquired remained a divisive one.

Literary Conceits and the Theater of Educational Writing

In Locke's *Education*, the narrative pattern set by supervisory education not only forms the backbone of his pedagogical theory but also informs the way he writes his treatise. Locke's discussion is noticeably crosshatched by a substantial number of narrative examples or inset stories that illustrate his points, and of those relating directly to a student's progress, almost all of them are structured along the lines of the observation-intervention-resolution paradigm.[1] Locke's prose exhibits remarkable fluidity in incorporating his various interests and points. Although earlier he had drawn on examples in both the *Essay* and the *Second Treatise*, in the *Education*, he adduces many more narrative examples and more frequently explores their details, maneuvering deftly back and forth between abstract discussion and the supportive stories he provides. Locke's style is almost conversational at times, including an occasional use of the familiar "you" to address the reader, partially the result, no doubt, of the fact that the treatise was originally a series of personal letters to his friend Edward Clarke. Beyond this, the organization of the treatise ultimately turns out to be extremely loose-jointed: although like his other works, it is set up according to particular topics (for instance, "Reputation," "Manners," "Company," "Obstinacy") as well as numbered sections, the *Education* routinely proceeds in circular fashion, returning to issues or proposals already talked about in order to emend or supplement them, sometimes at length.

As if to emphasize the work's informality, at one point Locke goes so far as to claim, "now I am by chance fallen on [the] Subject" of Bible reading. In another instance, after devoting a lengthy section to tutors, he almost sounds like an apologetic Shandean narrator: "But to return to our Method again" (secs. 159, 95). The fluidity of his procedure is accentuated on those occasions when he blurs the distinction between a theoretical description, a hypothetical (narrative) example, and an actual story. After declaring the relative unimportance of teaching a child the "*Languages* and *Sciences*," Locke asserts that teaching Latin is extremely easy, surmising: "his Mother may teach it him her self, if she will but spend two or three hours in a day with him. . . . For she need but buy a *Latin* Testament. . . . And when she understands the Evangelists in *Latin*, let her, in the same manner, read *Aesop's Fables*." What at first seemed conjectural advice, however, turns out to be true fact: "I do not mention this, as an Imagination of what I fansie may do, but as of a thing I have known done" (sec. 177). It is a surprising sleight of hand that shifts from fact to fiction and back again, suggesting the plastic strategy of a supervising tutor.

There are several clues, in fact, linking this strategy to Locke's self-conceived role of educating his less enlightened readers. He sets up his own pedagogical expertise, for example, against common practice, which includes the ominous agency of "Instructors to Vice" (sec. 37). In other instances, directly addressing his readers, Locke stresses that he "cannot too often inculcate" in them various principles of his educational theory (sec. 107; see also 148). But the most telling evidence appears a few pages into the *Education*, when Locke begins to consider the paramount aim of instilling virtuous habits in children. His opening remarks point to his own supervisory role as writer/teacher:

> [T]he great Principle and Foundation of all Vertue and Worth, is placed in this, That a Man is able to *deny himself* his own Desires. . . . The great Mistake I have observed in People's breeding their Children has been, that this has not been taken Care enough of in its *due Season*; That the Mind has not been made obedient to Discipline, and pliant to Reason, when at first it was most tender, and most easy to be bowed. . . . Parents think they may safely enough indulge their little Irregularities, and make themselves Sport with that pretty Perverseness, which they think well enough becomes that innocent Age. But to a fond Parent, that would not have his Child corrected for a perverse Trick, but excused it, saying, it was a small Matter; [it should be] replied, Ay, but Custom is a great one. (sec. 34)

Readers witness in this passage—and in the *Education* as a whole—Locke's deliberate intervention in the usual course of parents' educational policy, an intervention that comes only after he has already carefully "observed" its misguided trajectory. This tactic proves to be the hallmark of Locke's approach, for he often attacks received wisdom about instructing children—even suggesting that his criticisms constitute "a little Satyr" (sec. 37)—by offering as a substitute, as he does here, his own principles couched in the seasonal metaphors of educational husbandry.

In intervening to change what he considers the ruling educational dogma of the day—including the reliance on learning by rote, prohibition, frequent corporal punishment, and classical "learning"—Locke nonetheless seems to follow his own advice of introducing new instruction as delicately or even as indirectly as possible. Rather than announce the truth of his pedagogical convictions, Locke frequently opts for gentle, sometimes tenuous suggestions. He often says he is "apt to think" particular educational methods useful, or that another "may" be the best choice, or that he "imagines" what will be the desirable result.[2] The strongest assertion is routinely articulated "I doubt not" (sec. 148); and the opportunities for instructing readers sometimes appear as an appeal for permission: "give me leave here to inculcate again . . . " (sec. 148; see also 159).

In pursuing this persona of the companionable tutor, who softens his lessons as much as possible by disarming disguises, Locke also employs a form of indirect dialogue, by which he places questions or objections in his readers' mouths before proceeding to answer them. In one of the longer interjections, after Locke has recommended keeping children at home rather than in public schools, we hear: "you will be ready to say, What shall I do with my Son? If I keep him always at home, he will be in danger to be my young Master; and if I send him abroad, how is it possible to keep him from the contagion of Rudeness and Vice, which is so every where in fashion? In my house, he will perhaps be more innocent, but more ignorant too of the World: Wanting there change of Company, and being used constantly to the same Faces, he will, when he comes abroad, be a sheepish or conceited Creature."[3] How does Locke begin his answer? "I confess, both sides have their Inconveniences."

This exchange, like the others, is notable for how it extends Locke's educational principle of freedom and tutorial gentleness to a device of rhetorical usefulness. If we are the student-readers at this juncture, speaking what is putatively our mind, then Locke has allowed us to challenge his authorial and pedagogical authority in the interest of gaining additional insight. Entertaining a spontaneous outburst fits his agenda for an education based on the twists and turns of natural experience, however inconvenient they may first appear. Furthermore, not only is Locke's reply paradigmatically respectful but he also manages to guide his interlocutors—imperceptibly, behind the scenes—to the extent of placing in their questions his *own* diction of "contagion," which he then will accurately diagnose and explain. The technique of dialogue supplies a method of tutorial conversation able to naturalize Locke's intervention in England's pedagogical business as usual.

Since the mode of dialogue also connotes a larger aesthetic context in which it might operate—namely, the theater—it provides an inroad to another part of Locke's discursive implementation of supervisory educational principles. The *Education*'s first dramatic reference can be found in what initially seems a casual analogy in Locke's dedication: "the early Corruption of Youth is now become so general a Complaint, that he cannot be thought wholly impertinent, who brings the Consideration of this Matter *on the Stage*, and offers something, if it be but to excite others, or afford Matter of Correction" (111–12; my emphasis). Like his other tropes of medicine and gardening, this apparently inert metaphor becomes charged with the salient function of housing Locke's supervisory program. When Locke discusses how a youth should be introduced to the ways of the world, for instance, he invokes distinctly theatrical language: "The Scene should be gently open'd, and his Entrance made step by step, and the Dangers pointed out that attend him from the several Degrees, Tempers, Designs, and Clubs of Men. He should be prepared to be shock'd by some, and caress'd by others. . . . He should be instructed . . . where he should let them see, and when dissemble the Knowledge of them, and their aims and workings" (sec. 94). The student is neither patient nor plant, but an actor who can be safely directed by the tutor in all the world's stage, even to the extent of knowing when to "dissemble" his understanding of it.

This scenario is another version of the observation-intervention-resolution pattern, although in this case there are important differences from its previous manifestation in terms of medicine and husbandry. In the Lockean amphitheater, where pedagogical rule-giving is taboo, the pupil/actor must proceed, painfully enough, with *no idea* what his lines are. He must constantly respond to pedagogical props or other players who enter the scene, which more often than not both serve as the tutor's stage directions and provide the student with a gradually accumulating sense of his role. On occasion, there might be reason for direct counsel with the director, but to a great extent, the child must serve as his own naive audience, since ideally he should be unaware that the spontaneity of this theatrical education is in fact an illusion. This metaphor carries with it the greatest sense of artifice in the Lockean canon of tropes, but it too aspires to naturalness in the child's obliviousness, initially at least, to the art of pedagogical blocking.

Even should the child glance past the stage lights and perceive

the gaze of his tutor along with the contrivance of his role, Locke
remains assured that the educational show can go on undeterred.
As he puts it: "the peculiar *Physiognomy of the Mind* is most discern-
able in Children, before Art and Cunning have taught them to hide
their Deformities, and conceal their ill Inclinations under a dissembled out-side. . . . And if you carefully observe the Characters of his
Mind, now in the first Scenes of his Life, you will ever after be able
to judge which way his Thoughts lean, and what he aims at, even
hereafter, when, as he grows up, the Plot thickens, and he puts on
several Shapes to act it" (secs. 101–2). This passage is saturated with
theatrical allusions, not only in the more obvious mentions of
"scenes" and "acting," or in what seems a punning reference to
"art," but also in the phrase "the Plot thickens": the first use of that
phrase listed by the *Oxford English Dictionary* comes from Buckingham's play *The Rehearsal* (1672), in which one of the characters remarks in act 3, "Ay, now the plot thickens very much upon us."[4]
Whether or not Locke has this contemporary play in mind, it is
striking that the tutor's directorial role is strengthened by the techniques of (putative) science—here, the "Physiognomy of the
Mind," a turn of phrase suggesting not only the study of facial features to determine a person's character but also the ability thereby
to penetrate to the innermost recesses of the human brain (an issue
I will take up in chapter 3). Should the pupil decide to chance his
own interpretation of his role, he apparently faces a formidable collaboration of scientistic and artistic countermeasures.

But if we return now to Locke's dramatic self-description at
the outset of the treatise, there may be reason to question such a
confidently rendered scenario. Recall that he wants to bring "the
Consideration of this Matter on the Stage, and offer . . . something,
if it be but to excite others, or afford Matter of Correction"; this
first of all suggests bringing education front and center in the nation's agenda for self-improvement. But the theatrical mode also introduces the excessiveness of spectacle, for Locke seems willing to
settle for merely "exciting" his readers, although educating them
about corrective measures is also his intent. That distinction invokes
the familiar goal of instructing as well as entertaining one's audience, though Locke indicates here that only one part of that dual

aim may suffice. Even given that possibility, would the *Education* excite its readers by impressing them with the inventiveness of its proposals, or might it not also agitate them with the scandal of his extremely nontraditional, and sometimes non-Christian, views? Put another way, could Locke's ambition to overhaul English educational practice upstage itself by the distractions of melodramatic revisionism?

This kind of uncertainty is apparently endemic to the tropes of staging, cultivating, or diagnosing the education of children—it is, in other words, part and parcel of the makeup of supervisory education and its attending narrative form. In those terms, both Locke's inset stories and his own prose in general become constituted by narrative contours of observant education, including all its elastic strengths and inevitable ambiguities. This suggests, furthermore, that the metaphorical story lines plotting out Locke's discourse in the *Education* introduce a significant deviation from his rational philosophical program as set out in the *Essay* and the *Second Treatise*, thereby "thickening" and complicating it at the same time that they enable its deployment as pedagogical practice. Although John Richetti is justified in claiming that in the *Essay* Locke often uses "dramatic setting, implicit narrativity, persona, and other supervising 'scenic' tendencies,"[5] his analysis would also indicate that the *Education*'s explicit and thoroughly structural employment of supervisory narrative form constitutes a radically different kind of text. Unlike his occasional strategy in the *Essay*, Locke's garden "plot" in the *Education* encompasses an entire discursive territory.

One way to understand how Locke's supervisory metaphors effect such a change is to turn briefly to the *Essay*'s discussion of correct linguistic and rational procedure for discovering reliable truths. In describing how ideas should be connected or juxtaposed in the enlargement of knowledge, Locke makes a crucial distinction between the nature of analogy and metaphor or "conceit." For the purpose of constructing reliable probable knowledge, analogy, "the great Rule of Probability," is the only choice, since it will *relate without conflating* the ideas being considered.[6] Analogy provides this essential function because it is the instrument of judgment, whose operation Locke defines as "the putting *Ideas* together, or separating them from one another in the Mind, when their certain Agreement or Disagreement is not perceived, but *presumed* to be so" (4.14.4). Metaphor, by contrast, is the agent of wit or fancy, and Locke declaims its inferiority when comparing it to the results of judgment:

> For *Wit* lying most in the assemblage of *Ideas*, and putting those together with quickness and variety, wherein can be found any resemblance or congruity, thereby to make up pleasant Pictures, and agreeable Visions in Fancy: *Judgment*, on the contrary, lies quite on the other side, in separating carefully, one from another, *Ideas*, wherein can be found the least difference, thereby to avoid being misled by Similitude, and affinity to take one thing for another. This is a way of proceeding quite contrary to Metaphor and Allusion, wherein, for the most part, lies that entertainment and pleasantry of Wit. (2.11.2)

The consequence of this contrast is to award analogy the distinction of being the proper tool, conceptually or linguistically, for the advancement of philosophy, while metaphor is relegated to the status of a troublesome imposter intruding on rigorous rational thinking, or a casual device suitable for the lower generic aspirations of the "literary" arts of poetry or other "entertaining" writing. Making this distinction relies on the discriminating language of depth and surface: the sound application of syllogisms, for instance, should "discover a Fallacy hid in a rhetorical Flourish, or cunningly wrapp'd up in a smooth Period; and stripping an Absurdity of the Cover of Wit, . . . shew it in its naked Deformity."[7] And as a further black mark against metaphor's dubious usefulness, Locke asserts that enthusiasm "ris[es] from the Conceits of a warmed or over-weening Brain" (4.19.7), thus linking in one punning blow human irrationality to linguistic disorderliness.[8]

Clearly Locke's sinuous plotline in the *Education* qualifies for his definition of metaphorical maneuverability, but I would argue that it is not a matter of choosing metaphor pure and simple, but of an ineluctable textual slide from analogy to conceit. This conclusion, moreover, has significant consequences in an attempt to determine the *Education*'s metaphysical and generic status—whether or not it qualifies, in other words, as a genuinely philosophical text.

Commentators have disagreed on this point. John Yolton, on the
one hand, asserts that "'philosophy of education' is too sophisticated a label" for the treatise, because Locke worked from "general
conceptual frameworks," which were often unstated or less rigorous, rather than a set of systematic premises.[9] On the other hand,
James Axtell remarks that although the *Education* was written essentially for the purposes of instructing landed gentlemen, who
composed only 4 to 5 percent of the entire English population,
Locke's fundamental principles concerning habituation, esteem,
example, corporal punishment, and so forth form an authentically
universal pedagogical program.[10] Pierre Coste, the first to translate
the *Education* into French in 1695, agrees: "It is certain that this
Work was particularly designed for the education of Gentlemen:
but this does not prevent its serving also for the education of all
sorts of Children, of whatever class they are: for if you except that
which the Author says about Exercises that a young Gentleman
ought to learn, nearly all the rules that he gives, are universal."[11]

Coste's remark suggests that in fact the *Education* is a kind of
mixed work—in his view, a philosophical proposal with an overlay
of more local concerns. Locke seems to corroborate this idea when
he stops approximately two-thirds through the treatise to conclude
what he terms "the general Method of Educating a young Gentleman"—the part of his discussion devoted particularly to the fundamental issues of moral virtue and wisdom. In the last portion of the
Education, Locke then turns to "descend to a more particular Consideration" of gentlemanly instruction, including preparing boys
for their future role as head and executor of an inherited estate. It is
only at that point that Locke claims to employ "the popular Use"
of words such as *virtue, wisdom, breeding,* or *learning,* thereby signaling less concern with philosophical rigor.

If the *Education* is in fact a discursively hybrid text—part philosophy and part something else—then there can be no simple way
to designate its status. It may be helpful, however, to recall Locke's
remark early in the *Essay* that philosophy is "*nothing but the true
Knowledge of Things*" (Epistle 10), not in order to balloon the definition of philosophy so that its boundaries impinge on any text at-
testing its own truth-value, but in order to be reminded that Locke

would generally have required the *same linguistic protocols* for his epistemological, political, and pedagogical theories. At the end of the *Education*, he apparently softened his usual standard of using the precision of analogical terms determined by strict judgment. But in the first part of the treatise, where I have concentrated my analysis of his supervisory narratives, he would certainly have preferred maintaining the more exacting procedures.

The fact is, however, that given the complex of competing aims and mutually resistant assumptions I have already described in his educational program, there seems to be little opportunity for clean distinctions, plain linkages, or relations that remain stably intact—all these the criteria for analogy's workplace. Instead, Locke's pedagogy is the key situation for the operation of what he calls "conceit," which establishes fluid connections among disparate or colliding elements. Locke may want his medicinal, gardening, and theatrical tropes to function as genuine analogies and therefore be discardable after they have served their purpose, leaving behind the pristine clarity of indigenous ideas. But the evidence suggests instead that supervisory education and its subtending tropes are ultimately inextricable. The ambition of making education natural, sin-free, and rationally independent while also contrived, redemptive, and restrained by habit—that ambition can articulate itself only in language like that of the garden, clinic, or theater.

I have often characterized the function of these tropes as pedagogical problem-solvers, whose very elasticity and complexity could enable Locke's project to proceed. In that sense, such metaphors resemble what Fredric Jameson calls a "strategy of containment": a formal or textual mechanism that performs the dual task of masking the inconsistencies in a particular sociopolitical ideology while simultaneously empowering that ideology to do its work.[12] Locke's proposal for supervisory education operates similarly because its installation of the hidden, observing tutor provides the means by which the need for social and finally political authority is both affirmed and denied. In chapter 3, I will return to the political work this arrangement can muster. For the moment, however, I want to contrast that portrait with a view of supervisory tropes as dysfunctional or at least unpredictable textual components. That perspective draws on Paul de Man's analysis of the *Essay*, particularly his argument that despite Locke's attempt to restrict the deleterious potential of metaphorical language, his philosophical project for reliable linguistic meaning and referentiality is not only contaminated but also fundamentally constituted by elusive tropological movements.[13] Despite de Man's suspicion of metaphysical assumptions, however, his own discussion seems to approach philosophical ambition, since his aim in analyzing the *Essay* is to demonstrate that it is one more exemplary instance of the linguistic dilemma in philosophy from at least the Enlightenment to the twentieth century. The machinations of language thus become a nearly universal standard by which to decide that philosophy is as "literary" as literature, or vice versa.

Rather than treat metaphorical indeterminacy as the site for philosophical failure, I would like to approach it instead in decidedly historical terms—as a crucial location for studying the dynamics of discursive and, ultimately, cultural—change.[14] In other words, while acknowledging the ideological usefulness of a structure like observant education, I also want to examine how it undergoes or initiates change in several important contexts: in the rest of this chapter, I focus mainly on the generic terms in which observant education shapes narrative practice in both pedagogical writing and the novel; in chapter 3, I will turn to the equally formative sociological, political, and popular cultural circumstances in which supervisory instruction becomes manifest. Given those parameters, the term *functional indeterminacy* serves best to describe how the Lockean arrangement of supervisory education can both perform important conceptual and finally cultural work, as well as shift in its contours or uses given new pressures on its unstable framework.

In the context of *Some Thoughts concerning Education*, the narrative kernel contained by the structure of observant pedagogy proves functionally indeterminate by accommodating the demands loosely formed by Locke's epistemological and political agenda, and by deviating in that process from the protocols of rigorously rational discourse. In Locke's own terms, the *Education*'s storylike pattern is "literary," but that supposedly less pristine discursive mode, as Eve Sedgwick observes, is precisely what enables an ideological program to do its "chiasmic" work of grappling with mutually resistant elements in the process of making those "subjects cross each other in a rhetorical figure that conceals their discontinuity."[15] In Locke's case, it is a constellation of rhetorical figures that serves to compose the socially useful fiction of the unified, gentlemanly self.

Narrative Openings and Novelistic Innovations

The *Education*'s narrative inventiveness was by no means identified by contemporary readers as the hallmark of a new kind of educational writing, though it is clear that the renowned author of the *Essay* and the *Two Treatises* helped give new prestige and importance to a subject that soon was discussed at virtually every level of English society—by journalists, pamphleteers, theologians, female activists, philanthropists, and novelists. The reasons for this interest spanned a wide spectrum of concerns, which included moral, religious, social, economic, and political emphases. The late seventeenth and eighteenth centuries produced, in effect, a virtual explosion of new educational institutions and texts, perhaps the largest in England's history. The Society for Promoting Christian Knowledge, the charity school movement, and the Sunday school crusade at midcentury, among other educational drives, drastically changed the pedagogical landscape. And as Samuel Pickering has persuasively argued, Locke's extremely specific advice about how children should learn through reading—coupled with a new technology enabling cheap, mass publishing—spurred an extensive new industry of producing children's books.[16]

We turn then to consider the new generic experimentalism that generally accompanied the advent of supervisory educational narrative, including the ways that both natural and theatrical tropes could embody both the early Enlightenment's confidence and its anxieties about how such educational or literary innovations could improve England's social circumstances. Although the *Education*'s narrative tendencies may have gone unnoticed, their disturbance of the conventional generic waters fits the general movement Margaret Doody describes in Restoration and early eighteenth-century poetry from "closed" to "open" forms. In her view, this is an era of volatile experiment, a portrait that complements Michael Mc-Keon's discussion of "generic destabilization" in prose genres during the same period.[17] The *Education* proves both a cause and a symptom of that phenomenon: already given its markedly hybrid composition, educational writing in the eighteenth century becomes a virtual discursive laboratory, in which writers invoked still other philosophical, theological, or scientific conventions, explored the implements of dialogues, inset stories, or political rhetoric. Shaftesbury, who often inveighs against "forced instruction and solemn counsel," and the "dogmaticalness of the schools," confirms this point. In recommending the more gentle instructiveness of conversational writing in the form of the miscellany, he attributes a new vitality in English letters to the recent adoption of that multiply constituted form:

> This the miscellaneous manner of writing, it must be owned, has happily effected. It has rendered almost every soil productive. It has disclosed those various seeds of wit which lay suppressed in many a bosom, and has reared numberless conceits and curious fancies which the natural rudeness and asperity of their native soil would have withheld. . . . From every field, from every hedge or hillock, we now gather as delicious fruits and fragrant flowers as of old from the richest and best cultivated gardens. Miserable were those ancient planters who . . . made it so difficult a task to serve the world with intellectual entertainments, and furnish out the repasts of literature and science.[18]

Though an admirer of Locke's work, Shaftesbury here invokes a Lockean garden that promotes, rather than curtails, the more disruptive elements of natural excess. He makes a virtue out of what would apparently (for Locke) be a vice: now wit's "conceits and curious fancies" offer benefits reminiscent of a Lockean drama— the instructive but playful "intellectual entertainments" and other learned "repasts."

Shaftesbury's endorsement of natural excess, however, does not entail formulating a more egalitarian or expansive social vision than Locke's. As the grandson of Locke's seventeenth-century protégé, the first earl of Shaftesbury, and as someone who had once been one of Locke's pupils, Shaftesbury was thoroughly familiar with

Locke's epistemological, political, and pedagogical theories. But he also viewed Locke's empiricist description of acquired knowledge as part and parcel of a moral relativism that, as in Hobbes's work, had the pernicious aim to deny the existence of either universal ethical principles or an innate human disposition toward sociability.[19] While that characterization of Locke's views distorted his assertion in the *Essay* that God's moral laws were the primary foundation for human conduct, Shaftesbury's disagreement with him illustrates how naturalized imagery suggestive of supervisory education—as articulated by Locke or his other contemporaries—could be refurbished to house very different perspectives on human sociability and sociopolitical order. In Shaftesbury's case, the vocabulary of natural exuberance was anything but "carnivalesque" in the sense Mikhail Bakhtin describes it.[20] While it registered Shaftesbury's confidence that Nature had designed human beings to be innately inclined to social interaction, it was also framed by his aristocratic insistence that however unruly discursive raillery or spontaneous social intercourse might appear, it should be securely constrained within a social hierarchy whose gentlemanly code of "the club" should remain unchallenged.[21] Hence recommending a gentler education or miscellaneous discursivity did not necessarily imply promoting middle-class ascendancy or greater enfranchisement of women.

Still, given his claim that dialogue was the premier genre in which to foster a greater degree of intellectual open-mindedness and social tolerance in England, Shaftesbury offers one example of the way that a commitment to natural protocols could be tied to a "dramatic" sense of performing cultural improvisation. As one of the two terms in that natural-artificial formulation, the metaphor of gardening was not only ubiquitous in the pages of the educational works by Locke, Mary Astell, François Fénelon, Thomas Sheridan, Damaris Masham, William King, and many others, but it also became the most frequently invoked figure in even the most casual remarks on education or personality during the eighteenth century. Compare that trope to the one made prominent by John Amos Comenius, who had a substantial impact on British educational thinking before the advent of supervisory perspectives. The difference is striking: Comenius's natural metaphor, part of the title of one of his books, is "the labyrinth of the world," a phrase suggesting a bewildering educational pilgrimage, rather than the composure of supervisory tutelage linked to the language of husbandry.[22]

The garden plot would indeed undergo various adaptations and modifications, each with different agendas or consequences. In 1748, for instance, the same year that he became a justice of the peace, Henry Fielding writes that in order to preserve social order, a system of education was needed that subordinated "learning" to the improvement of moral virtue. This Lockean proposal turns out to be even more so: "such a System of Education as may serve for all good Purposes, and which may so cultivate the Human Mind, that every Seed of Good in Human Nature may be reared up to full Perfection and Maturity; while all which is of evil Tendency is weeded, and, as it were, pluck'd by the Roots from the youthful Disposition, before it spreads, and is strengthened by Time." Metaphorical naturalness could harbor an even greater threat, since Fielding then proceeds to decry teachers in English schools who espouse Jacobite ideals, which he claims will result in "spreading the Contagion" and "dangerous Disease" of civil unrest. To guard against that affliction, he recommends a supervisory relationship between the English government and teachers reminiscent of a supervisory pedagogical arrangement: preventing a Jacobite epidemic "can be only done by a thorough Inspection and Scrutiny into the Characters of all those who are intrusted with the Tuition and Instruction of Youth, from their earliest Season of Erudition, till they become their own Masters."[23] Cultivating the "Seed of Good" in English citizens therefore includes the ideological task of fending off politically undesirable loyalties.

The association between teaching and gardening seems to have been so common that merely *visiting* a garden could conjure the contemplation of education. That is at least the claim of Steele in a letter in *The Spectator*, which is chock full of horticultural paraphernalia of all kinds. He begins: "As I walked t'other Day in a fine Garden, and observ'd the great Variety of Improvements in Plants and Flowers beyond what they otherwise would have been, I was naturally led into a Reflection upon the Advantages of Education, or moral culture. . . . " This remark—evoking the language of observation and stressing the naturalness of his train of thought—is the prologue to a virtual gardening catalogue, including the "choking" of virtue by noxious "Weeds," the value of supportive moral "Soil," the role of "proper Manuring, necessary Pruning, and an artful Management of our tender Inclinations," and "Botanists" and "Flowers" from a multitude of nations and locales.[24] It is a miscellaneous description sprung from Shaftesburyean flourish, affirming once again the possibility of making nature and human artifice mutually productive.

This kind of horticultural exploration seems appropriate in a publication such as *The Spectator*, whose self-defined mission since its inception in 1711 was to educate its public readership, composed particularly of a burgeoning middle class, concerning new philosophical, intellectual, or cultural developments. In his introductory remarks to the journal's first issue, Addison anonymously claims: "I live in the World, rather as a Spectator of Mankind, than as one of the Species. . . . I have acted in all the Parts of my Life as a Looker-on, which is the Character I intend to preserve in this Paper."[25] But as in the case of dramatized education, Addison of course would complement his discerning observations with active interventions—the very act of publishing his views for the edification and improvement of his readers. *The Spectator* would in the course of its publication also frequently expound Locke's ideas for a popular audience, on several occasions discussing "his celebrated Treatise *of Education*" and its pedagogical proposals.[26]

In 1711, Addison's instructive role also incorporated his own kind of notable horticultural elaboration in his extended consideration of the imagination, a discussion that suggests the literary or fictional potential of the gardening trope. Addison too constructs an elaborate metaphorical description, though perhaps more precisely than Steele:

> [I]t is the part of a Poet to humour the Imagination in its own Notions, by mending and perfecting Nature where he describes a Reality, and by adding greater Beauties than are put together in Nature, where he describes a Fiction.

He is not obliged to attend her in the slow Advances which she makes from one Season to another, or to observe her Conduct, in the successive Production of Plants and Flowers. He may draw into his Description all the Beauties of the Spring and Autumn. . . . His Rose-trees, Wood-bines and Jessamines, may flower together, and his Beds be covered at the same time with Lillies, Violets, and Amaranths. . . . If all this will not furnish out an agreeable Scene, he can make several new Species of Flowers. . . . In a word, he has the modelling of Nature in his own Hands, and may give her what Charms he pleases, provided he does not reform her too much, and run into Absurdities, by endeavouring to excell.[27]

The impossible natural world created by the poetic imagination, however, is answerable to more than the goal of pleasure, for like representations of human misfortune, pleasant fictions also "teach us to set a just Value upon our own Condition." As in the supervisory pedagogical program, the key to staging "an agreeable scene" lies in satisfying competing aims, including poetic license and natural limitation, fanciful reverie and rational constraint. It was a goal that Defoe certainly strove for in his publication of *The Family Instructor* (1715, pt. 1; 1718, pt. 2), a popular piece on Puritan education presented in the form of an episodic series of dialogues among a family's parents and children; and it was an ideal that Bernard Mandeville would parody in his slippery discussions and dialogues concerning education in *The Fable of the Bees* (1714; 1728). But the "just Value" of one's "Condition" would not necessarily be assessed by a narrowly bourgeois agenda. As Terry Eagleton has argued, *The Spectator* and the *Tatler* were the "catalysts in the creation of a ruling bloc in English society, cultivating the mercantile class and uplifting the profligate aristocracy."[28] Hence in some contexts a naturalized educational program could form a provisional alliance between otherwise disparate social ranks or classes.

Both Addison and Steele's horticultural flourishes are embedded within the framework of *The Spectator*'s strongly spatial sense of experience and understanding, which is a manifestation of Richard Kroll's point that after the Restoration, knowledge was imagined "as inhabiting a *scene*, . . . a space, an architectonic fabric composed of discrete, atomic components"—such as "the library, the labora-

tory, the landscape garden."[29] To this list should be added the theater, certainly the most problematic way to model acquiring
knowledge or educating the public. When it came to drama as a literal medium or metaphorical emblem of education, late seven-
teenth- and early eighteenth-century commentators were often divided, or at least troubled, concerning its power to form desirable
English citizens. Jeremy Collier, the most well-known and prolific
critic of drama's deleterious effects on the populace, acknowledges
that plays could be morally edifying, although he stresses in *A Short
View of the Immorality and the Profaneness of the English Stage* (1698)
that since the Restoration, "nothing has gone farther in Debauch-
ing the Age than the *Stage Poets*, and *Play-House*."[30] Collier's position sparked a heated debate that lasted at least until the 1720s, but
rather than attempt to survey the antitheatrical debate during this
period,[31] I want to focus instead on the writers specifically concerned with education, because many of them took an approach to
drama or theatricality that is particularly instructive for considering
how educational writing was to contribute to novelistic storytelling.

Regarding plays themselves, educationalists could take strongly
opposing positions. The Frenchman Charles Rollin, whose *New
Thoughts concerning Education* was translated into English in 1738, re-
iterated Collier's concerns by concluding, "Comedies and Tragedies, even of those which seem to be wholly free from such Sentiments as are repugnant to Modesty and sound Morals, may be of
very dangerous Consequences to young Persons."[32] But Rollin's assertion clearly troubles his unnamed translator, who inserts a long
footnote indicating just how divisive the relation between education and the theater has been, while also reclaiming the theater for
instructive purposes. The translator writes:

> The Stage has . . . from time immemorial, opened a large field for
> controversy. On one side, the Partizans of the Theatre have fre-
> quently applauded it as a perfect School of Morality and Virtue;
> whilst, on the other, its Enemies have censor'd it as the Nursery of
> Vices. However, 'tis certain, that the Stage is good in itself, and
> might be productive of the most happy Effects, were it not abused. If
> the Actors would but lead a regular Life, and exhibit such pieces only

as are of a Virtuous cast, there is no doubt but drammatick Poems would work a great Reformation in the Morals of Mankind.[33]

Echoing a similar sentiment, Judith Drake remarks, "In short, were it not for the too great frequency of loose Expressions, and wanton Images, I should take our Theaters for the best Schools in the World of Wit, Humanity, and Manners; which they might easily become by retrenching that too great Liberty."[34]

Just why the theater should be such a problem becomes clearer when we remember that drama or dramaticality was often characterized as specifically attached to women as creatures who could be easily captured by a play's alluring surface, its fashionable milieu, or its powerful emotional stimulus. As an early example of that mentality, Richard Brathwaite, in *The English Gentlewoman* (1631), exhorts his female readers to be mindful of life's brevity this way: "Thinke how this *World* is your *Stage*, your *Life* an *Act*. The *Tiringhouse*, where you bestow'd such care, cost and curiosity, must be shut up, when your *Night* approacheth." In referring to the dressing room or "tiring-house" used by stage actors, Brathwaite has used the theater as an emblem of women's excessive concern with their appearance. But he has also identified another common theme regarding "curiosity," linked to women's inclination to be fascinated with the baubles of "novelty." Hence Brathwaite urges his women readers not to attend plays, "wherein you expect some new Scene of mirth," because the result is to "runne in a maze, while you lay the *Scene* of your *Mirth* on *Earth*."[35] By contrast with writers like Brathwaite, later female educationalists make it a point to insist that women have become emotionally or intellectually facile by virtue of years-long cultural conditioning, rather than inherent deficiency. But many are equally suspicious of a play's ability to perpetuate women's cultural bondage to trivialities. In the late seventeenth century, for example, Bathsua Makin lumps together "Cards, Dice, Playes, and frothy Romances," and two decades later, in 1694, Mary Astell deplores women's tendency to think about the world in terms of "Plays and Romances," since these "very Instructors are Froth and emptiness."[36] In the early 1700s, Mary Chudleigh announces her aim to "perswade 'em [women], instead of spending so much of their Time in reading Plays and Romances, to bestow a part of it in studying Moral Philosophy," although she also acknowledges considering both tragedies and comedies "very innocent, and very agreeable Diversions."[37]

Thus the content of plays—their themes or examples of behavior—could be potentially damaging to maturing young men or women, but so could the implications of their form—the way plays model either the "nature" of individual identity or the dynamics of a functioning community. At its most extreme, a play's artifice, like the fictionalized quality of the supervisory scenario, could produce the sense that nothing is natural, that everything about a person's subjectivity is first, the result of deliberate social staging, and second, only an impersonation of supposedly "natural" ideals.[38] At the very least, that possibility could undermine a reliable differentiation between the sexes—a potential problem not unique to English culture after the Restoration, although the new appearance of women on the stage seemed to aggravate concern about that prospect all the more. These kinds of anxieties are in any case also attributable to a larger phenomenon: the fact that plays not only represent examples of society on the stage but they also form, in the production process and their engagement with an audience, a miniature version of community that could have indirect, though disturbing, influence on English society at large. This was the reason for the perennial complaint that playhouses provided a place for the indiscriminate mixing together of people of all ranks and kinds—men, women, the "middling" classes, paupers, nobility, libertines, prostitutes, and the like. The concern amounted to worrying that the smaller model of community within the theater could have effects on increasingly larger circles of communities outside it, including the family, parliament, even the nation.

The complex intersection of fears regarding naturalness, gender, and community is exemplified particularly in the case of the educationalist James Burgh, who, in *Britain's Remembrancer: Or, The Danger Not Over* (1746), views theatricality as a threat to the entire national character. In near hysterical tones, Burgh argues that the Jacobite uprising in 1745 is evidence that British society is on the brink of collapse because it has been guilty of the twin sins of "Luxury and Irreligion," which had been promulgated in part by lax education of British citizenry.[39] As part of his catalogue of Britain's social infirmities, Burgh lists "epidemic Unbelief and Immorality" (23), insobriety, and sexual promiscuity—as well as theater. In his diatribe against the deleterious effects of drama on its audiences, women play the key role of literally embodying its contaminating power:

> [T]he Theatre is at present on such a Footing in *England*, that it is impossible to enter it and not come out the worse for having been in it; for now-a-Days, a good Play is no other than *a Trap* to draw in the modest and innocent, to a Love of Theatrical Entertainments; and the Minds of the Spectators are not the safer from being polluted and debauched, tho' the Play itself be in the main decent and modest; since the ingenious Contrivance of the Managers entirely prevents the good Effect of any worthy Sentiment expressed in the Play, by introducing *a painted Strumpet at the End of every Act, to cut Capers on the Stage in such an impudent and unwomanly Manner, as must make the most shocking Impressions on every Mind*; and lest the Audience should chance in spite of all this to carry away somewhat that might make their Hearts the better, a ludicrous and shameless Farce concludes the whole, and with one Stroke erases all the little Traces of virtuous Sentiments that were formed by the Play itself. (25–26; last two emphases mine)

Like the farces that conclude the night's entertainment, women on stage punctuate each of the play's acts with an exhibition that irresistibly unhinges any of their moral sentiments. What is more, they symbolically represent Britain's national emasculation, since Burgh repeatedly associates female weakness or affectation with the effects of indulging in luxury. Like the Assyrians and Persians before them, he claims, "the People of *Great Britain*, formerly a Nation of Heroes, are now so enervated and effeminate, that if they happen to be destitute of an Army trained to War and Hardship, they are before an Enemy as a Flock of Sheep before Wolves" (18). And these dislocations in gender are attributable to the theater's creation of a community as "a Trap," a collocation of players and audience members in which the latter will be deviously tricked out of their real (or potential) virtue.

Burgh's view is certainly extreme, but it suggests what was often beneath the anxiety—particularly expressed by male educational writers—about the connections between theatricality and "irrational" forces such as wayward individuality, insubordinate femininity, and even the insurgence of historical change. Aside from Burgh's rhetoric of crisis, however, literal or figural theater in the work of educationalists such as Locke, Astell, or Drake is crucial, because in addition to marking the artificial component of an instructional process that should also be natural, the theater emphasized the communal dynamics of education—the entire scenario of tutor, student, parents, servants, onlookers, and so on—whose mutual relationships were far broader in scope than the one-on-one interaction (between teacher and student) usually stressed in medical or gardening metaphors. Hence the combination of dramatic and natural tropes could grasp both the public and the private dimensions of the pedagogical process (an issue considered in detail in chapter 3). At its best, moreover, such a combination could serve to naturalize the dramatic element, as Addison and Steele do in their horticultural elaboration of dramatic "scenes," or as Locke does when he rejects the artificiality of "Affectation" in favor of the acquired naturalness of "Breeding." In Bourdieu's terms, the result would be to move acculturated values—temporarily, at least—from the sphere of debatable orthodoxy to that of *doxa*, the realm of things that could be taken for granted.

There are two additional ways by which educational authors could make theatricality more amenable for supervisory instruction; both suggest how early modern pedagogical theorists were unique in making innovations that had an impact on novelistic storytelling. The first strategy is linked to reconfiguring communal relations, the second to literary method. The authors I call *educationalists* were first of all more willing than other writers who attacked the theater to reimagine what kind of community might be implied by a dramatized pedagogical arrangement. While this does not mean that authors such as Locke or Astell formulated a full-scale model of education based on dramatic community, it does indicate that their theatrical descriptions—such as of tutors who were cagey "directors," or of adults who were generous audience members always willing to applaud pupils' progress—constituted a potentially new way to form the bonds of social life in the process of teaching children. The anonymous author of *The Advice of a Father: Or, Counsel to a Child* (1688), for instance, exhorts his son, "thou art entering upon the Stage, I am going off; so act thy part, that at thy *Exit*, the Spectators may clap their hands."[40] He advises his son in the role of both gentle director and as older, fellow-traveling actor, suggesting a congenial atmosphere completed by the approval of a receptive and virtuous audience. Locke envisions a similar situation: he endorses a flexible and companionate pedagogical approach, balancing it against a clearly stratified communal arrangement of the appropriate roles for student, tutor, parents, and servants—a stark contrast to the reputed social disarray of playhouses. Despite Mary Astell's rejection of plays per se, she also uses drama as a way to redefine women's desire for self-improvement within acceptable limits: "'Tis true we profess that we desire Riches and Honour, a great Reputation and Theater in the World, on no other account but to do GOD Service. But if we are real in this, why don't we perform so much as we might in our present Station?"[41] Here too, Astell portrays herself as directorial actor, a usefully ambivalent position whose uncertainty is further reflected in an appeal to being "real" in one's chosen performative role.[42] It was also the means by which to promote the sisterly comradery she wanted in her "academical retreat."

The second innovation in educational writers' texts can be traced by a circuit traveling from the theater to one of its chief tools or effects, "novelty," to the novel itself as a new genre. Authors such as Astell, Behn, and Essex would often note the dangers of novelty for students, including its attending features of extravagance, inconstancy, and cheap fashionableness. As Astell remarks, the "insatiable desire of Novelty" must ultimately be driven by "Fancy or Passion, . . . rather than Right Reason."[43] But given the terms of improvisational subjectivity, Astell also realizes the new is in fact essential to supervisory education's methodology: unless as students we are "Affected with the Newness of an Object, or some other remarkable Circumstance, so as to be attentively engag'd in the Contemplation of it, we shou'd not be any wise mov'd, but it wou'd pass by unregarded" (251). As a genre whose name designated it as the age's chief innovator, the eighteenth-century novel is particularly invested with the problems of theatricality—the reasons include its frequent identification as a form of women's scribbling, its intrigue with documenting criminal or quasi-criminal elements, and its vexed association with the heritage of romance, often cited as drama's literary counterpart. As David Marshall has indicated, since the production of plays underwent severe bureaucratic control and curtailment after the Licensing Act in 1737, the figure of theater would mutate and reappear in a variety of written forms including "fiction writing, moral philosophy, aesthetics, and epistemology."[44] In emerging during the same period, the novel could also be said to be the dubious beneficiary of this discursive displacement.

Ultimately, novelists would negotiate a persistent, though pragmatic, ambivalence about the trope of theatricality by employing a strategy similar to that of many educational writers: appropriating the very conventions of dramaticality in the project of educating others. In late seventeenth- and early eighteenth-century writing on education, there emerged a number of "literary" variations on the conventions of expository prose which were at times more modest and at others more radical than the ones in Locke's *Education*. In reflecting the kind of improvisational eclecticism that characterized supervisory instruction, educational texts of all kinds—conduct and courtesy books, language textbooks, or more abstract treatises—increasingly adopted the format of the miscellany, combining prose with verse, invented stories, historical accounts, and dialogues. Dialogues were particularly popular, especially as the dramatization of a pedagogical exchange. In *The Gentlewomans Companion* (1675), Hannah Woolley inserted a concluding section entitled "Pleasant Discourses and witty Dialogues between Males and Females, as well gentiliz'd by Birth as accomplisht by generous Education," and François Fénelon briefly staged conversations among pupils and teachers in *The Education of Young Gentlewomen* (1699). In the aim to educate eighteenth-century women about philosophical or scientific topics, entire volumes were published such as *The Philosophy of Sir Isaac Newton explained, in Six Dialogues on Light and Colors between a Lady and the Author* (1742).[45] Taking a different tack, Lewis Maidwell, in *An Essay Upon the Necessity and Excellency of Education* (1705), aimed to illustrate his more abstract discussion of learning by inserting in his text two exemplary historical narratives, one entitled "The Life of Plato" and the other "The Life of Cicero."[46] With a bolder gesture of combinatory flair, Stephen Penton published in 1688 *The Guardian's Instruction, Or, The Gentleman's Romance*, in which he told the extended story of a young man's turbulent experience during his first years at Oxford University. Penton explained that he had resorted to fiction, or a "*Romantick* manner of Writing," since he intended his work to be read by those average young men for whom "Fiction and Intercourse was [*sic*] somewhat more diverting than uniform *Narrations* or dogmatical *Propositions*."[47]

Perhaps the most striking discursive improvisation that anticipates the novel was Bernard Mandeville's *Fable of the Bees*, a work to which he continued to add material for a decade after its first appearance in 1714, until it was virtually a mongrel text devoting most of its pages to discussing philosophical, psychological, and sociopolitical aspects of education. In addition to his infamous essay that attacked charity schools as monuments to upper-class self-aggrandizement, Mandeville's two-volume work incorporated a panoply of genres: besides allegory, history, and dialogue, Mandeville used aphorisms, paradoxes, and comedic skits; he combined the conventions of epistemology, satire, and theology; and he drew on political tracts, utopian discourse (in the well-known opening poem "The Grumbling Hive: or, Knaves Turned Honest"), and literary criticism (which parodically analyzed "The Grumbling Hive"), to name only a few. Even when the surface of his prose appears smooth and untrammeled, Mandeville frequently shifts tone to mimic the sobriety of a sermon, the perspicacity of natural philosophy, or the piety of a moralistic pamphlet. As a work whose tone and heterogeneity qualifies it as an early modern form of Menippean satire, *The Fable of the Bees* suggests the trajectory Mikhail Bakhtin finds in the relation between much earlier examples of Menippean satire and the novel's eventual discursive consolidation.[48]

What distinguishes Mandeville's text from novelistic form,

among other things, is its lack of a single, identifiable perspective from which the melange of generic elements he juxtaposes can be imagined a coherent whole. For Mandeville, part of the point seems to be to thwart readers' attempts to attribute to him a consistent—or at least simple—position regarding human sociability or venality. But despite Mandeville's particular brand of elusiveness, there is an important way in which the format of supervisory education finds an analogue in—and, given the novel's educational mission, partially shapes—the function of point of view. Tutorial "seeing" and narrative point of view are eminently compatible in terms of the eighteenth-century novel's self-definition as being morally uplifting and instructive to its readers, and this is particularly true of those works provisionally identifiable as novels of education. The act of seeing, or of surveying in narrative, is more than a question of data collecting or information dispersal—it is more, in other words, than a matter of pure epistemology. It is further—and more pressingly, in Enlightenment terms—an issue of the moral, social, and finally political implications of perceiving clearly and acting appropriately. In those terms, any act of narration—and especially one presumably educational—must confront the difficulties similarly staged in the Lockean pedagogical theater: how to "excite" or entertain without sacrificing edification, and how to instruct without impounding the audience's/reader's autonomy or intelligence.

The strategy of observation, intervention, and resolution proves useful both as an instructional device and a means of deploying point of view, for the operations of observant pedagogy and novelistic narration prove to be analogous. The aim now, of course, is to educate the reader through the experience of the protagonist; the author and narrator must perform a kind of pedagogical triangulation, in which even when a character misses the import of his behavior or environment, the message will nonetheless be instructive to readers, the surrogate pupils. Here the dynamic tension between pedagogical spontaneity and imposition finds its counterpart in the choice in storytelling between relating the unadorned "facts" as they happened, or imposing conventionalized artifice. In the first arrangement, the narrative assumes the veracity of "true history," one of the most frequent claims of the eighteenth-century novel to validate its moral qualifications to teach readers via the natural sequence of real events untarnished by human meddling or manipulation. It frequently occurs in the novel as a moment when the distance between the author/narrator and reader is deliberately collapsed, supposedly making them both witnesses to the same unfolding story and subject to the same expectations or surprises. That tactic is particularly evident in Robinson Crusoe's presentation of his journal, whose putative spontaneity and fragmentary quality further authenticate the veracity of his story. Such moments advocate the lack of narrators' mediation, in the service of unalloyed edification.

The counterpart to such naturalized plotting is narrative intervention, in which the narrator steps in to adjust initial impressions made on the reader, often to the extent of offering the correct interpretation of a particular scenario. That gesture can be double pronged: in addition to addressing readers directly in order to instruct them in the appropriate response, such intervention can often take the form of actually toying with the events as they were originally described, adding new details or mitigating circumstances. In the example of Crusoe's journal, both aspects prove true in Crusoe's often subtle additions to the original entries, for those additions offer new information about particular moments of his conversion, as well as providing a correct Puritan perspective on his behavior. For Defoe, Charlotte Lennox, and other novelists, narrative intervention can also appear in the guise of invoking particular generic conventions of closure or credibility. As in *The Fable of the Bees*, where Mandeville's ironic persona frequently brings his readers abruptly behind the scenes of his storytelling, which has allegedly followed the rules of narrative probability, novelists can similarly demonstrate with bravado the contrivance of their own discursive maneuvering.

The ambidextrous employment of narrative "observation" and "intervention" in some ways recalls the description of the late eighteenth-century novel offered by Eric Rothstein. For Rothstein, the novel is constituted by a dual matrix of "systems of inquiry" and "systems of order," the first formed by inductive discernment (by fictional characters or readers of fiction) and the second by deductive imposition. Novelistic plot, he contends, as well as the reader's process of assimilating it, is created by the cycle of formulating interpretive rules from experience, rules repeatedly challenged and modulated by the intricacies of more experience—of the world, or of the reading process itself.[49] The pattern of supervisory education or narration bears resemblance to this description particularly because novels of education also create a series of episodes in which characters (and readers) must encounter unfamiliar experience, form a response to it, and learn its effectiveness, while guided by the watchful eye of the tutor/narrator. In addition, the repetition of similar experiences or problems—recall Crusoe's compulsion to travel—suggests a narrative equivalent to Locke's proposal for the formation of good habits by the insistent rehearsal of the same behavior until it takes full root. The difference, however, is that unlike Rothstein's description, which he claims applies as an educational paradigm to virtually all eighteenth-century novels except for *Tristram Shandy*,[50] supervisory educational narrative functions more specifically at a cultural level, rather than only a generalized epistemological one. Calling Rothstein's pattern "educational" can be heuristically useful, and since the eighteenth-century novel in general staked a major claim on its edifying capacity, it is not surprising that the novel of education shares with it some significant aspects. But settling on a virtual equation between the two would fail to account for the distinguishing features of contemporary pedagogical discourse and their manifestation in the novel of education, including supervisory narrative point of view and especially the aim of describing a development of profound acculturation, rather than mere knowledge-gathering. A similar point applies to Lennard Davis's perceptive claim that eighteenth-century novels compose "factual fictions," a double status constituted by a generic heritage in both journalistic "news" and the aesthetics of inventive storytelling.[51] That description also resembles the "supervisory" narrative pattern, although I will be focusing primarily on the ideological stakes behind such a distinction, because beyond the philosophical puzzle of the novel's truth status lies an array of social, gender-specific, and political issues that the program of observant education is intended to address.

The Novel of Education and the Syndrome of Virginity

The mixing, matching, and melding of genres in early modern pedagogical writing, a process in which fictionalizing education was only one discursive development among many, provided a crucial impetus for two historical developments: first, the novel's eventual literary pedigree as a genre genuinely capable of edifying readers; and second, the novel's emerging, though not exclusive, focus on the process of improvisational education for its protagonists. One suggestive way to begin telling that story is to trace first a discursive trajectory that travels, roughly, from Locke's *Education* to Rousseau's *Emile, or On Education* (1762), which has been called "the first *Bildungsroman*."[52] In his persistent attempts to answer Locke's proposals in the *Education*, Rousseau in fact adopts the Lockean strategy of staging a "natural" education, but in pedagogical orchestrations far more elaborate—even baroque—than his predecessor's. The greater challenge of such complicated educational sequences, accompanied by Rousseau's imperative that he test the applicability of his abstract hypotheses, compels him to write his book as a kind of philosophical novel: he claims that he must tell "fictions"—from *roman*, meaning "romance," "fiction," or "novel"—in order to find the truth of educating children.[53] Accordingly, Rousseau intersperses lengthy stories about his pedagogical protagonists, Emile and Sophie, among his more generalized arguments, attempting in the meantime to make them mutually informative. And in the process, he employs Defoe's *Robinson Crusoe* as a key instructive device for teaching Emile self-reliance.

Rousseau's *Emile* indicates that by midcentury educational prose has proceeded from the inadvertent or occasional appearance of mediating narratives to the self-conscious implementation of novelistic techniques. But that is, at best, only half of the story, particularly given the rather insipid characterization Rousseau provides Sophie as the blushing prize at the end of Emile's educational accomplishments. A very different sense of female development emerges from tracking women writers beginning with Aphra Behn, the reputed author of a posthumous, quasi-fictional volume entitled *A Companion for the Ladies-Closets: or, the Life and Death of the Most Excellent the Lady*———— (ca. 1712). In this book, the focus is more on edifying readers via this lady's purportedly factual exemplary life, rather than documenting carefully her own educational experience. Among the episodic sections devoted to her various virtues, which are arranged in nonchronological order (based on topics such as charity, modesty, etc.), the reader gains glimpses of the protagonist's self-instruction, as in the process of having "so improv'd her self by discoursing and reading, that she would talk very pertinently to any thing, even the *Law*, or *Astronomy*" (5). In Delarivière Manley's *New Atalantis* (1709), by contrast, one finds a more recognizably novelistic treatment of female education, with the additional difference that it is based on a pattern of virtually wholesale loss, scandal, or seduction in the series of young women's lives readers witness. As the narrative frame for this account of Queen Anne's England in disguise, Astrea, goddess of justice, has come to Atalantis to learn about human life, and does so in the company of Virtue, her mother, and the gossiping Intelligence, with both of whom she conducts a dialogue throughout. Readers encounter two distinct models of female education: one for the characters, whose moral or social knowledge usually comes by way of mishap or misfortune, often induced at the hands of men; the other pattern—as part of Astrea's acknowledgment that " 'tis necessary I should be th[o]roughly instructed"[54]—follows a gradual accumulation of sobering understanding about human foibles. This dual pattern indicates a tension in women novelists' portrayal of female development I will come back to in a moment. From here a historical line can be traced to works such as Mary Davys's *The Reform'd Coquet* (1724), which offers a more sanguine view of feminine reform in the story of Amoranda's eventual reclamation for virtue given the intervention of her lover-turned-mentor, Alanthus. In chapter 5, I explore how Davys follows a version of female instruction both acknowledged and rejected by Charlotte Lennox in *The Female Quixote* and by Eliza Haywood in *The History of Miss Betsy Thoughtless* at midcentury.

Particularly in the work of Eliza Haywood, we can outline relevant parts of a lengthy career in fiction that begins in the era of scandalous histories like Manley's and ends in the 1750s under the auspices of a much more sober perspective on women's social identities. While in novels such as the popular *Love in Excess* (1719–20), Haywood portrays female passionateness and experience in ways comparable to Manley's work, her publishing history takes her eventually to the issuing of conduct books such as *The Husband* (1756) and *The Wife* (1756), after writing novels such as *Life's Progress Through the Passions* (1748) and *Betsy Thoughtless* (1751), which depict human development for both men and women as a less catastrophic process.[55] In *Life's Progress*, for example, the narrator sets out to document how "the passions operate in every stage of life," a process for Natura, the allegorically named protagonist, recorded in exhaustive detail.[56] While much has sometimes been made of what seems Haywood's capitulation to straitlaced propriety in the last part of her life, I do not aim to characterize Haywood's career as a falling away from some kind of more authentically "feminist" agenda to a regrettable moral quietism. Instead, I want to treat her publishing history as a series of improvisations spanning nearly forty years, during which, even in the end, she retained a crucial sense of irony about women's need to "perform" proper feminine behavior, as is particularly evident in *Betsy Thoughtless*.[57] Even in *The Wife*, which seems a numbingly conventional treatment of femininity, Haywood insists that when confronted with abusive husbands, wives have the full right to leave and divorce them, a claim that would be controversial for many decades to come. In the latter part of her career, the persona Haywood adopts for her narrators, as well as for her chastened heroines such as Betsy, is similar to the one taken by the Female Spectator, who, at the beginning of Haywood's venture in journalism from 1744 to 1746, describes herself as someone whose "too great vivacity of my nature became tempered with reflection," enabling her to "judge of the various passions of the human mind, and distinguish those imperceptible degrees by which they become masters of the heart, and attain dominion over reason."[58] But this placid self-description could also harbor a notably sharp awareness of the social inequities that affected women on a daily basis.

In the last two chapters of this book, my aim will be to trace the contribution of both male and female authors to the novel of education during the first half of the eighteenth century by examining in detail Defoe's *Robinson Crusoe*, Lennox's *The Female Quixote*, and Haywood's *Miss Betsy Thoughtless*. These three works—and related fictionalized educational discourses—gather a number of supervisory themes, forms, and structures, chief among them the general assumption that the individual is profoundly malleable, gradually formable, and intellectually and morally *re*formable. Human development, moreover, is recurrently portrayed both as a series of "falls" from innocence to moral guilt requiring restitution and as a more secular accumulation of the necessary experience to make one's way in the world. These texts tell the story of the novel of education's development along several trajectories: these include a shift from Defoe's ambivalently Puritan representation of Crusoe's spiritual reformation to Lennox and Haywood's more secularized, often theatrical, treatment of women's desire for improved prerogatives via self-education; and a move from Defoe's nearly unqualified endorsement of Crusoe's Edenic colonialism to Lennox and Haywood's critique of women's "empire"-building in domestic or romantic relations. I will highlight a stark contrast between *The Female Quixote*'s strikingly aggressive portrayal of women's desire for self-improvement and Haywood's more subtle approach in *Betsy Thoughtless*, with an eye toward assessing how, by midcentury, female authors of the novel of education negotiated the task of improvising the strictures of acceptable femininity. By the 1750s, Lennox's and Haywood's work suggests the novel of education's basic outlines, although there is no clear-cut sense of its generic definition, just as the novel in general remains in tentative generic configurations. Without set traditional conventions to describe, one can nonetheless sketch the general outlines of novelistic works focusing on the issue of education, for there are several common, though mutable, contours to be traced.

If Defoe's, Lennox's, and Haywood's fiction provides an exemplary history of the novel of education's early development, then its exemplarity also requires a brief accounting of the literary context out of which it emerged, including those works antithetical to its improvisational agenda. The novel of education and its generic counterparts can generally be distinguished from those works depicting individual human nature as adamantine and virtually unchanging. Protagonists such as Richardson's Pamela or Clarissa, for instance, are who they are precisely because they *resist* change— particularly the threat posed by any kind of onslaught against their virtue. In the pattern R. F. Brissenden describes as "virtue in distress,"[59] heroines and heroes in the sentimental vein are traumatized by the prospect of moral degradation, and it is only by their steadfast perseverance in the face of adversity that their true, original worth is proven. This scenario often draws on the conventions of tragedy, which poses change as the ineluctable—and irreversible— ravages of time, misfortune, or error. There is little room here for gradual rehabilitation or piecemeal recovery. Even should a heroine like Pamela escape the drastic fate of a Clarissa, her innate virtue continues to exert itself even after the salubrious event of marriage, when she remains singularly reluctant to consummate her vows. However much the designation of "sentimental" may seem generically impressionistic, there seems good reason to agree with George Starr that the sentimental novel is in fact antieducational in its assumptions about human nature and the development of plot.[60]

To some extent, the same can be said for *Sir Charles Grandison*, since even though Richardson explicitly conceived of his last novel as offering a moral vision congruent with conduct book imperatives, neither of his two main characters—Grandison and Harriet Byron, his eventual bride—undergo the kind of serious reformation characteristic of supervisory narrative. Thematically, Richardson's novel concentrates heavily on the benefits or pressures resulting from characters' education, and stylistically, as Jocelyn Harris notes, "the pattern in *Grandison* of maxim, illustrative scene, and commentary is traceable to the conduct books."[61] In addition to frequent conversations about education, readers can witness how Grandison's largess and care succeed in guiding his charge, Emily Jervois, toward genuine virtue, or how his patience helps reform individuals such as Charlotte Grandison, his sister, or William Wilson. But despite Grandison's own personal foibles such as pride, or Harriet's being "Defective . . . in the way of Vivacity," as Richardson puts it, both characters demonstrate an innate goodness and

"Purity of Manners" that qualify them for being more virtuous exemplars than candidates for improvisational self-transformation.[62]

Even in a work such as Fielding's *Joseph Andrews*, where Joseph and Fanny seem at least to learn about the dangerousness of the outside world, Fielding persists in demonstrating that, like the "young Horse . . . vicious in his Nature," human beings may trick themselves out to be other than they are, but in the end, the truth will win out. As Joseph himself explains, drawing on his experience with equine malice in the stables: "I take it to be equally the same among Men: if a Boy be of a mischievous wicked Inclination, no School, tho' ever so private, will ever make him good; on the contrary, if he be of a righteous Temper, you may trust him to *London*, or wherever else you please, he will be in no danger of being corrupted."[63] To be sure, like his contemporaries, Fielding still holds out the possibility of character change through sincere repentance and Christian conversion, but that view of altering human nature also differs from one based on supervisory pedagogy. In the case of Defoe's *Moll Flanders*, his protagonist's spiritual redemption while in prison is nothing other than a deus ex machina enabling Moll's dramatic change from a hopelessly degraded condition to a newborn state of virtue and industriousness. Unlike a supervisory approach of gentle and discreet tutorial adjustments, Moll's apparent conversion is a massive upheaval of personal identity and motivation, after a prolonged and repetitive series of errors. If Moll's transformation of character should be taken seriously, then the colossal and instantaneous regeneration typical of this "redemptive" pattern has little resemblance, for instance, to Locke's pedagogical gradualism and ambivalent secularism.

In making this distinction, however, I should briefly reconsider the educational status of Henry Fielding's fiction, because the trajectory from *Joseph Andrews* (1742) to *Tom Jones* (1749) to *Amelia* (1751) indicates that Fielding maintained an extremely ambiguous—or at least variable—line between defining human character as essentially fixed and characterizing it as thoroughly malleable. In effect, Fielding seriously renegotiated the delineation of human malleability in each of those novels, although it could be said that doing so confronted him with an increasingly less satisfying or se-

cure sense of being able to calculate individuals' moral virtue or sociability. In *Joseph Andrews*, Fielding distinguishes strongly between
characters' inherent virtue and their grasp of practical knowledge, a
fact illustrated particularly by Parson Adams, whose stalwart moral
goodness is jarringly contrasted by his naive bearing as "an Infant
just entered" into the world (19)—a condition, furthermore, that
hardly changes in the course of the story. Both Joseph and Fanny,
however, who are equally virtuous and untutored in the ways of
the world, follow a more identifiable path of accumulating what
could be called the *technē* of virtue: the body of pragmatic knowledge and useful tools by which to recognize and fend off genuine
threats to their moral selves. In the character of Tom Jones, by contrast, the demarcation between innate virtue and practical experience is partly elided. While characters such as Squire Allworthy
may be "replete with Benevolence" (with names to match it), and
while others, such as Mr. Square or Reverend Thwackum, have
virtually no redeeming moral features, Tom himself endures the
liminal condition of having to acquire at least part of his ethical
selfhood.[64] This is an ambiguous process defined, in a kind of ret-
rospective glance to *Joseph Andrews*, by Tom's having a full store of
one of the two main features Fielding stresses in Christian virtue—
charity—while also being deplorably lacking in the second—
chastity.[65] Like Joseph and Fanny, he too must learn about the vice
residing in both the country and the city. But the larger purpose of
the novel's episodic structure is to reshape gradually his libidinous
spontaneity to the point that it no longer undercuts his otherwise
palpable goodness. With its project of reconciling a strict definition
of charity with a looser notion of masculine chastity, the story of
Tom Jones seems to be as long as it is in order to chart an incremental negotiation between Tom's "natural Gentility" (692) as a literal
member of the gentry and his need for substantial, but not total,
ethical reformation in order to merit that standing. To put it another way, having partially detached the intimate connection that
originally held between sexual abstinence and genuine virtue,
Fielding must now go to near-epic lengths (while also mocking
them) in order to demonstrate how gentrified virtue in men could
be both partially secure and partially reformable.

When he writes *Amelia*, Fielding has reached an even more acute sense of virtue's malleability. In this novel the problem is not that English society at large is any more venal or pernicious than it was in *Joseph Andrews* or *Tom Jones*, but that even the most admirable individuals who must make their way in it are dangerously susceptible to the same flux of passions or motives animating the least commendable persons. This seems precisely why, given his own disillusionment with the prospect of fixed virtue, Fielding is so unnerved by the specter of Mandeville—in the narrator's words, that "charming fellow *Mandevil*"—whose trenchant view of ineluctable and irrational human self-interest is advocated by both Booth and Miss Matthews.[66] While Booth ultimately rejects his Mandevillean outlook, the novel registers an underlying worry that human affairs may at least verge on the scenario Fielding's moral arch-nemesis described.

It is a relatively simple task to note the various ways in which most of the characters—including Booth, Miss Matthews, Sergeant and Mrs. Atkinson, and Colonel James—are moved by compulsive self-investment. But more important are the ways in which even Amelia is momentarily stirred by the same impulses. Identified by Mrs. Atkinson as "one of the worthiest and best of Creatures," Amelia is reported by the narrator to have "Virtue [that] could support itself with its own intrinsic Worth" (345, 160). But this does not apparently guarantee that Amelia has not inadvertently "injured the Captain" (her husband, Booth) as Mrs. Atkinson puts it, because of Colonel James's refusal to bail Booth out of prison in order to pursue his sexual designs on Amelia (345). The more important dilemma arises, however, when, despite her devoted loyalty to Booth, Amelia finds herself unexpectedly intrigued by Mr. Atkinson's addresses:

> To say the Truth, without any Injury to her Chastity, that Heart which had stood firm as a Rock to all the Attacks of Title and Equipage, of Finery and Flattery, and which all the Treasures of the Universe could not have purchased, was yet a little softened by the plain, honest, modest, involuntary, delicate, heroic Passion of this poor and humble Swain; for whom, in spite of herself, she felt a momentary Tenderness and Complacence. (482–83)

This is an admittedly minor tremor in the context of the other characters' sins; Amelia's chastity has been grazed, but remains intact. But this moment is extremely striking because of what it suggests about a woman who belongs to Fielding's group of angelic female characters such as Fanny and Sophia Western. Unlike them, Amelia has revealed herself to be emotionally vulnerable to a convulsively passionate, implicitly sexual, appeal. This is significant in light of Fielding's insistence in *Joseph Andrews* that men should observe the same rule of chastity as women, because by choosing to form a moral circuit running from women to men (rather than vice versa), Fielding is signaling where he considers the more profound source of virtuous standards to reside.[67] Thus while there may be Allworthys in the world, Tom Jones would never be able to reclaim his moral and social heritage without the unrelenting standard of virtue offered by Sophia. By the same token, even given the crucial role of Dr. Harrison in extricating Booth from his legal difficulties, Booth would never reach his enlightened state by the story's end without Amelia's immovable goodness. But in *Amelia*, his last novel, Fielding indicates that he doubts even her redoubtable morality is completely impregnable to the assaults—apparently well meaning or otherwise—by those around her.

In Fielding's fiction virtually none of his female characters, unlike Tom Jones, have the chance of successfully reforming their initially wayward identity. The corollary of that gendered formula is that his truly virtuous women characters remain essentially unchanged. In *Amelia*, Mrs. Bennet reflects this idea when she remarks, "the Woman who gives up the least Out-work of her Virtue, doth, in that very Moment, betray the Citadel."[68] This construction of femininity could be called the "virginity syndrome": by modeling morality strictly in terms of sexual innocence or experience, it makes the prospect of women's gradual reformation problematic, if not infeasible. Among male educationalists, Charles Rollin supports this concept when he writes about young girls, "in the Dawn of Life, the most inconsiderable Thing will sully a Virgin Purity and Innocence. 'tis a Flower of so tender and delicate a Nature, that the least puff . . . may blast and quite destroy it."[69]

This is a view of virtue that several women educationalists attack, as Damaris Masham does in *Occasional Thoughts in Reference to a Vertuous or Christian Life*, when she argues:

> [Virtue is] a *Term* which when apply'd to Women, is rarely design'd, by some People, to signifie any thing but the single Vertue of Chastity; the having whereof does with no more Reason intitle a Lady to the being thought such as she should be in respect of Vertue, than a handsome Face, unaccompany'd by other Graces, can render her Person truly Amiable. Or rather, *Chastity* is so essential to, yet singly, so small a part of the Merit of a Beautiful Mind, that it is better compar'd to Health, or Youth, in the Body, which alone have small Attractions, but without which all other Beauties are of no Value.[70]

Masham enacts here several realignments in the delineation of femininity; two of the most striking are reassigning the code of bodily beauty to interior consciousness, and then in turn allocating virginity to a condition of the body's health. These moves are important to Masham's redefinition of virtue itself, which she says is "not (tho often so misrepresented) included in Innocency; or does consist in a partial Practice of Actions praise-worthy; for its extent is equal to our liberty of Action; and its Principle the most Active one of the Mind" (11). In effect, rather than being based on relative inaction—or the periodic need for *re*action to outside threats—Masham's description of female virtue, like Bourdieu's characterization of the habitus, is based on an active implementation of inner principles.

While the syndrome Masham rejects might seem predictable in early modern views of education held by men, as Mrs. Bennet's remark suggests, it could be compelling for women as well. This problem is particularly evident in Manley's *New Atalantis*, where Astrea's judgment of female characters' sexual or emotional indiscretions is strikingly ambivalent. In musing over the case of Charlot, who is seduced and then abandoned by an aristocrat, Astrea resolves that "Modesty is the *Principle*, the *Foundation* upon which they [women] ought to build for *Esteem* and *Admiration*, and that once violated, they totter, and fall, dash'd in pieces upon the obdurate Land of Contempt, from whence no kind Hand can ever be put forth, either to rescue or to compassionate 'em."[71] Later, regarding the similar fate of Delia, Astrea comes to the same conclusion, with the additional sense that even an education in modesty will not be a sufficient guard: "we see the tender Sex, with all their *Native-Timorousness, Modesty* and *Shame-fac'd* Education, when stung by Love, can trample under Foot the consideration of *Virtue* and *Glory*, tho' by the loss, they are reduc'd to be the despicablest part of the Creation."[72] Taking this position did not mean leaving men unscathed, because Astrea offers these opinions in the context of condemning both rapacious men and society's willingness to scapegoat the women harmed by them. In Manley's text, however, women's virtually inevitable education by catastrophe is juxtaposed with Virtue's endorsement earlier of the benefits of "a generous Education" for both sexes (1:5); and as mentioned earlier, the logic of instructive loss is set against Astrea's more gradual assimilation of wisdom about human affairs. In the meantime she does not waver from steadfast ethics as the goddess of justice.

Not all women's novels during the early eighteenth century would be structured by such a drastically polarized conception of female education, though it creates a significant tension in works such as Davys's *The Reform'd Coquet*. In that work, Davys puts a benevolent face on the phenomenon of lover-turned-mentor, which in Manley's texts would be a sure formula for eventual disaster. Amoranda, Davys's protagonist, is tutored by Alanthus disguised as Formator, who is periodically torn between his desires as lover and his sense of responsibility as teacher. Formator represents one logical literary embodiment of supervisory education's interest in staging a covert form of instruction. That connection is particularly evident in an earlier application of the same idea, in François Fénelon's *Les Aventures de Télélmaque, fils d'Ulysse* (1699)—translated the same year into English as *The Adventures of Telemachus*—where he draws on his previous work on indirect instruction to portray Telemachus's education on his journeys. Fénelon's *Telemachus* had an important impact on English readers, being reissued in several editions during the early eighteenth century and eventually translated anew by Tobias Smollett in 1776.[73] In his novel, however, the gender relations in Davys's text are reversed, because Minerva, goddess of wisdom, disguises herself as the masculine Mentor, who accompanies Telemachus as guide and tutor until he reveals his real identity at the end of the novel. This difference is important because as the transgendered Mentor, Minerva is untouched by any kind of erotic interest in her protege. But in Davys's work, as in other eighteenth-century novels by women, the male lover-as-mentor always poses at least the suggestion of the dual possibilities of either the young woman's gradual edification, or her sudden fall from grace.

In the ensuing chapters, my aim will be to trace the ways that Charlotte Lennox and Eliza Haywood reformulate the problem of lovers-as-tutors, since they both reject the conventional pattern offered by Davys. In that process, I will also revise Michael McKeon's description of the function of the "aristocratic," "progressive," and "conservative" ideologies which characterized novelists' work until the mid-eighteenth century, in order to outline the historical connections among novelists such as Defoe, Lennox, Fielding, and Haywood. By McKeon's account, aristocratic ideology asserted the inherent link between rank of birth and innate virtue and formed the basis for progressive ideology, which by contrast defined a sense of personal industriousness empowering individuals to acquire genuine virtue and in the process merit higher social standing. In these terms, Defoe's portrayal of Robinson Crusoe fits the progressive ideal by affiliating it with the dynamics of a supervised and improvised education. When it comes to conservative ideology, however, which McKeon finds in Fielding's novels, the work of Lennox and Haywood suggests an alternative construction of female virtue. For its part, conservative ideology offers a skeptical perspective on both the aristocratic and progressive ideals: it finds the claims for virtue attached to birth or individual accomplishment inconsistent and misleading, and often guilty of suborning either rampant self-indulgence in the nobility, or materialistic self-promotion in the middle classes—though in the meantime, "conservativism" will not offer any clear alternative for defining virtue of its own.[74] What becomes clear in McKeon's discussion of the role of gender in these ideological relations, however, is that they share a version of the "virginity syndrome" found in both Manley and Fielding. If in the aristocratic perspective female chastity ensures the purity of noble heritage, then in the progressive outlook, it is the moral anchor that stabilizes women's ascension up the ladder of social rank or economic class, as in Richardson's *Pamela*.[75] But if, as an exemplar of conservative ideology, Fielding is skeptical of his contemporaries' assumptions about the lexicons of birth or economic self-improvement, he does not reject the shared idea that women, unlike men, could not be thoroughly reeducated after a significant lapse in virtue. In fact, given its exacerbated sense of human frailty, especially in *Amelia*, Fielding's conservative outlook seizes on stalwart feminine virtue as one of the few available places where other individuals' resocialization could be founded.

Like Fielding, both Lennox and Haywood illustrate in their novels why either an investment in the social authority of birth, or an intrigue with the possibility of economic self-advancement, offers an unsatisfactory basis for their protagonists' development. But they also redefine conservative ideology by rehabilitating the progressive perspective with a feminist twist. This did not mean making female chastity unimportant, but it did mean, as in *The Female Quixote*, representing Arabella's near paranoia that she is about to be ravished as a parodic comedy of virginal manners. Rather than concentrating, moreover, on the possibility of women's economic self-improvement, Lennox and Haywood apply a "progressive" spin to the issues regarding gender by treating it as a *separate* social category, with the aim of improving women's lives in the realm of domestic relations. In Lennox's novel, this takes the form of appropriating the vocabularies of romance, legal justice, and political government in order to form a basis for Arabella's increased sense of power in the home; in *Betsy Thoughtless*, it appears in Betsy's cumulative understanding of how the world of plays can apply to her self-image as a woman performing a public role. Since they relate to the question of personal "empire," these literary improvisations form part of the historical interconnections among Defoe's, Lennox's, and Haywood's fiction. But before examining the relations among their work, I will discuss the larger social context of the novel of education's emergence by examining a range of educational practices—including those in new pedagogical institutions, physiognomy, and popular culture—that sprang up during the late seventeenth and early eighteenth centuries.

CHAPTER THREE

Pedagogical Politics and the Idea of Public Privacy

The art of forming men is in all countries so strictly connected with the form of the government, that, perhaps, it is impossible to make any considerable change in public education, without making the same in the constitution of states.

—Helvétius, *De l'esprit*

In 1697, John Locke wrote to the London Board of Trade that England and particularly London were in crisis. Requested by the board to offer his ideas for solving the alarming increase of pauperism in English cities, Locke submitted a report that attributed the new poverty neither to economic hard times nor to lack of available employment, but to "the relaxation of discipline and corruption of manners," which had caused "the streets everywhere [to] swarm with beggars, to the increase of idleness, poverty, and villainy."[1] In response to this emergency, part of his proposal recommended the institution of state-supervised working schools for children from the age of three to fourteen. Invoking a rhetoric of national calamity, Locke pronounced harsh treatment for such "begging drones" and "idle vagabonds" who threatened civic peacefulness and English productivity. In addition to prescribing severe penalties for those who resisted working or who begged for alms without legal sanction, he proposed making children learn the skills of spinning or knitting to earn their food, until the age of fourteen when they could be dispatched as apprentices.

Here the pastoral gentility of *Some Thoughts concerning Education* is stripped away, revealing a grim urban program that seems to bear no relation to Locke's earlier concerns with inculcating morality or wisdom. Nevertheless, there are several aspects of his privately monitored educational plan—as well as parts of his contemporary educationalists' supervisory proposals—that provide for its transformation into a form of mass education, if only in menial skills. In the context of the Lockean pedagogical corpus, this twist suggests that the *Education* and its specific sociopolitical applications do anything but fulfill the theoretical agenda of Locke's political philosophy, for they skew his emphasis there on private property—including individual life, liberty, and estate—to propound a view of the individual as a strikingly public entity. In the *Second Treatise*, Locke described in general terms the ways by which individual liberty or property could be accommodated within a larger system of political rights, as in the cultivation of children's innate rationality which, when fully mature, would qualify them for complete status as citizens. However, in the *Education* a very different picture emerges, since there Locke portrays children's individual identity as something always and already a public entity: rather than rationality providing the autonomous basis by which children become free, when adults, to choose their social options, it is instead a capacity that from the beginning is profoundly shaped by the standards of public interest that children should embrace upon reaching adulthood. What is more, that public shaping takes place initially by rousing in children irrational responses such as pride or satisfaction, produced in order to compensate for their still-fledgling rational powers. In investigating this swerve from his original formulation of private selfhood, we can then evaluate how the sociopolitical implications of Locke's pedagogical concepts fit within the larger context of the competing political model of republicanism, the new educational institutions that drew on both, and the important inflections produced by both class and gender.

Establishing the intriguing turn in Locke's educational ideas away from his ostensible political precepts will be the aim of the first part of my argument before I turn to the further point of considering its implications for novelistic plot. The results should be measurable, because critical assumptions about Locke's psychological and political portrayal of the individual have produced particular ways of interpreting the eighteenth-century novel as a form influenced by Lockean premises. Past treatments have portrayed Locke as the ultimate individualist, who insisted on individual civil rights protected by the state and subject to restraint only when impinging on others' similar rights, and who found, furthermore, that individual consciousness is the epistemological touchstone for acquiring knowledge. That portrait has elicited a description of the eighteenth-century novel as taking as its first priority—if not its cause for celebration—the protagonist's discovery of unique identity and a profound psychological interiority. The intense introspection of fictionalized Puritan autobiography, as in *Robinson Crusoe*, or the compulsion for privacy, as in Richardson's *Pamela*, for instance, then offers proof of the novel's focus turned predominantly inward. The result is often to conclude, as does Ian Watt, that the eighteenth-century novel poses a worldview that "presents us, essentially, with a developing but unplanned aggregate of particular individuals, having particular experiences at particular times and at particular places."[2]

Watt's explanation, however, leaves out the fact that Lockean pedagogy and its novelistic counterparts remain emphatically "public" in their concern with monitoring personal behavior, conforming it to social norms, and thereby coordinating civic community. More recently, Nancy Armstrong has argued that early modern conduct books constructed the idea of internalized personality—first for middle-class women, later for men—by assembling a new set of protocols concerning self-inspection and feminine domesticity that also found their way to the novel.[3] This chapter examines the kind of interiority Armstrong describes as part of a pedagogical system intent not only on generating that interiority but also on instilling in individuals a psychological circuit that could reliably communicate between their inner and outer (more public) selves and could also be monitored in the interest of social organization.

Locke's own description of education will chart a version of that project, which was part of a much larger sociological approach to pedagogy in eighteenth-century England.

The aim of this chapter will be to situate the novel of education in the broadest social context considered thus far, by examining supervisory instruction and its manifestation in improvisational fiction as part of a large, loosely knit network of diverse genres, institutions, and practices—including the "high" cultural forms of scientific discourse such as physiognomy, the "low" forms of popular engravings, and the innovations of the charity school movement bolstered in part by Locke's proposals to the board of trade—all of which converged under the rubric of education to shape a similar view of English subjectivity based on the concept of what I call *public privacy*. This is not to say, of course, that these various forms or practices were entirely congruent, particularly given their divergent ideological positions regarding the malleability of human identity or the centrality of "scientific" or Christian explanations for human motivation or action. But the notion of public privacy would nonetheless emerge from these sometimes competing discourses or institutions as an overdetermined social space or category that could provisionally accommodate such differences in the interest of managing the potentially disruptive energies of private desire or impulse.

Understanding the novel of education's role in this development prepares the way for considering in future chapters the specific treatment of improvisational subjectivity in fiction by Defoe, Haywood, and Lennox. Tracing the parallels and divergences among various educational discourses and practices will make for a necessarily brief consideration of the several ways in which the concept of the publicly private gradually materialized. I will begin by considering the crucial polemic during the Enlightenment between republican and liberal constructions of private and public identity, before examining Locke's narrative treatment of public privacy in the *Education* and then discussing how publicly private identity also emerged from the Christian ethos in both physiognomical representations of human character and William Hogarth's portrayal of the apprenticeship process. Turning then to the institutionalization and literary portrayals of charity-based schooling, I will link these various phenomena to the novel's specific role in depicting the intersection of the public and private spheres.

Dueling Ideologies: *Lockean Liberalism and Republican Humanism*

There is good reason to view Locke as the intellectual champion of liberal individualism, because even in the context of the seventeenth and eighteenth centuries, his views on individual liberty, rights, and virtue sharply contrast with the political ideology of republicanism, which was already strongly in place before Locke entered the scene. Given the pervasiveness of the republican perspective that individual citizens were by definition public entities whose private lives were either politically irrelevant or antithetical to ideal civic community, it is useful to consider its doctrines before exploring Locke's position in more detail.

The historian J. G. A. Pocock has offered the most rigorous account to date of the enormous impact of classical and Italian republicanism on English political writers during the years immediately following the Civil War of 1642 and into the next century. He pinpoints the beginning of that influence with James Harrington's *Oceana* (1656), which appeared when the republican ideals of a mixed government and balanced constitution were attractive strategies for solving England's problems of civic order and the extent of monarchical authority. Republicanism's absorption into English political thinking was not an easy one, since it had to contend with the previous model of English government, whose structure was hierarchical and largely regulated by the accumulation of customary laws. The process was one of combative adaptation, and by the end of the seventeenth century, a modified republicanism had established itself firmly on English soil, contributing to the Restoration and finally becoming a key vocabulary in English politics during the eighteenth century.

The main source of this transformation was Renaissance republicanism, whose doctrine was diligently laid out in Florence and which drew on Aristotle's argument that the best government combines the rule of the One, the Few, and the Many. These three powers, represented by the prince, the aristocracy, and the general populace, should be separate branches, operating independently but coordinated by a balanced constitution. This arrangement, according to Aristotle, can draw on the benefits of each version of government—monarchy, oligarchy, and democracy—while also diminishing their respective disadvantages. Such a broadly based political system requires the active participation of all its members, leading to the Renaissance doctrine called *civic humanism*, which claimed that the realization of the individual's human potential is based on those activities contributing to the republic's sustenance. Since, as Pocock puts it, "the Aristotelian tradition was emphatic that the highest form of human association was political,"[4] the citizen is by definition a *zōon politikon*, a political creature who must take part in activities such as serving in the military, holding public office, and voting. Only this *vita activa* can nourish the most important value in republican life—virtue.

Virtue proves essential because it provides the main bulwark against the republic's worst enemy: *fortuna*, the implacable force of mutability, unpredictability, and chaos. Since from its inception the republic is an ideal arrangement, its stability is inevitably threatened by historical change. As a result every citizen must cultivate virtue diligently in order to prevent the republic's corruption and eventual demise. Pocock explains that the term *virtue*, derived from the Greek *aretē* and the Latin *virtus*, had two main meanings: "first, the power by which an individual or group acted effectively in a civic context," and second, "the moral goodness which made a man, in a city or cosmos, what he ought to be" (37). The citizen's essential nature *as* citizen is determined by the intersection of these two aspects of virtue: virtuous citizenship depends on mustering one's power, will, and reason against the threat of fortune and subordinating that effort to the public standards of ethical behavior.[5] For my present purposes, I will designate the first aspect by the common Italian (*volgare*) term *virtù*, which in Machiavelli's sense means "the skill and courage by which men are enabled to dominate events and fortune" (92). The term *virtue* will indicate its more conventional sense of moral goodness.

According to Pocock, the double nature of virtue meant that "the operations of fortune were no longer external to one's virtue, but intrinsically part of it; if, that is to say, one's virtue depended on cooperation with others and could be lost by others' failure to cooperate with one, it depended on the maintenance of the roles in a perfection which was perpetually prey to human failures and circumstantial variations" (76). Moral society depends on the citizen's power to act ethically, but since individual capacity does not necessarily rely on ethical standards, it could pose the ever-present threat of corruption, or "the replacement by private relationships of those public relationships among citizens by which the republic should be governed" (93). The impulse for such self-interested behavior was frequently portrayed during the Italian Renaissance as the feminine figure of *Fantasia*—"a nonrational creative force immanent in men, by which each is driven to fulfill his own individuality, sharply distinguished from the universal values fulfilled by and in each individual according to the thought of Aristotelian Christianity: a self-created uniqueness of bent, in pursuing of which each man acts out his fantasies and determines his individual personality" (96). Human fantasy, in other words, is an internal, individualized version of fortune's threat to civic virtue. Its disruptive force is unleashed when *virtù*, gone awry, becomes contumacious and self-seeking—and this is the moment, moreover, when virtue becomes divided against itself, when power and morality clash.

Faced with this dilemma, republican education must serve at least two functions: it should provide fledgling citizens with the necessary skills and knowledge to establish their *virtù*; and it should supply moral direction for those abilities once acquired. This task falls not only to tutors or teachers in their private studies but also to the public function of the military, the example of the prince, and the formative powers of good laws.[6] Keeping *virtù* thus fastened to public morality is a hallmark of republican pedagogy's design.

This brief overview suggests a handful of meeting points between republican humanism and Lockean liberalism, but the differences in fact remain more striking. Like civic humanism, Locke endorses the system of a balanced constitution while stressing as well the importance of moral virtue. But the similar terminology can be misleading, especially in the case of "virtue." In the *Essay*, for instance, Locke seems to make virtue a *non*political element of either private or civil life. When describing the standards by which people measure the "Rectitude, or Obliquity" of their actions, Locke sets out three kinds: divine law, civil law, and "the Law of *Opinion* or *Reputation.*"[7] It is only when Locke turns to the third criterion, what he also derogatively calls the "Law of Fashion" (2.28.12), that he uses the terms *vice* and *virtue*; his argument is that the value of virtue is too often arbitrarily set by the passing standards of the day, rather than by a genuine gauge of "what is in its own nature right and good" (1.3.18). The result of this claim is not to eliminate using the terminology of virtue altogether, for Locke turns to it again, for instance, in the *Education*. But it seems clear that rather than being a communally sustained quality of political existence, sometimes contaminated by self-interest, virtue in Lockean terms is a question either of absolute immanence or of noncivil relativism. Individual virtue could always impinge on the quality of social or political life, but it is not by definition formed by observing public offices such as voting or serving in the militia.

Given his formulation of virtue, Locke's concept of citizenship is based on a collection of individual rights rather than a concerted participation in the political arena. In the *Essay*, he defines a citizen as "one who has a Right to certain Privileges in this or that place" (2.28.3), a definition he uses in the *Second Treatise* to elaborate how civil government protects and maintains private rights, including the prerogative of accumulating property. In a sense, the difference in emphasis between this arrangement and that of republicanism is the difference between striving, on the one hand, to protect individual citizens from encroachment by each other and by the state itself (especially the monarch), and laboring, on the other hand, to protect the integrity of the republic from the degenerative pressures of its citizens' self-interest. Put another way, it is the difference between stressing individual entitlement to civil sanctuary and accentuating individual obligation to communal unanimity.

This is the general contrast drawn by Pocock and other similar-minded historians between the assumptions of republican and Lockean citizenship. Pocock not only finds them fundamentally incompatible but also concludes on this basis that given the pervasive political rhetoric of eighteenth-century England, the republican ideology ruled the day, leaving Locke "among the tradition's adversaries."[8] But for many authors during the seventeenth and eighteenth centuries, the strict lines between republican and liberal formulations of public or private life were apparently less adamantine than Pocock indicates. More recently, several historians have explored the ways in which writers about political, economic, and literary issues could draw on both traditions in forming their arguments. Steven Pincus, for instance, has examined how as early as the years from 1642 to the 1680s, English essayists such as Matthew Wren and John Fell were adopting a form of republican rhetoric that (sometimes tentatively) incorporated the "liberal" requirements of burgeoning commercial trade.[9] In the context of political argument, Shelley Burtt describes how by the 1740s, the debates about liberal rights and civic virtue in early eighteenth-century England produced a new, hybrid concept of "privately oriented civic virtue," which indicated that good citizens could "serve their country and preserve its liberty for reasons rooted in personal interests and commitments, private concerns that also dispose [one] to virtuous public action."[10] This kind of terminological redefinition, I would maintain, both partly produced and was partly made possible by the invention of a new idea of public privacy, whose conceptual fluidity could support a mixed sense of English citizenship. Equally important is James Kloppenberg's claim that in late eighteenth-century America, there was a "moment of alliance between the virtues of republicanism and the virtues of liberalism"— an alliance which was also linked to Christian representations of virtue and which ultimately enabled the colonies to formulate a broadly based concept of national destiny.[11] In the following discussion, I will adapt Kloppenberg's thesis to Enlightenment Britain in arguing that a similar, tripartite linkage among republican, liberal, and Christian perspectives was provisionally formed in the interest of educating ideal British citizens, and that in lasting for more than the "moment" of a few years, this pedagogical alliance proceeded in piecemeal, provisional fashion throughout the 1700s to produce the concept of public privacy.[12]

One of the key places where that linkage was negotiated was in early modern educational discourse, which deployed a notable conceptual plasticity and philosophical eclecticism in the interest of promoting a practical approach to instruction. Turning to educational writing is also telling, because past efforts to characterize the republican and Lockean traditions as incompatible have relied almost entirely on an analysis of the *Two Treatises*, without taking into account the distinct political agenda suggested by *Some Thoughts concerning Education*. By the apparent terms of the *Treatises*, Locke's educational program might be expected to devote itself exclusively to teaching youths how to exercise their individual rights, particularly regarding the maintenance and extension of private property, with communal restraints relegated to an afterthought. But as we have already seen in chapter 1, the *Education*'s foremost priority is to instill the reflex of self-denial, the "great Principle and Foundation of all Vertue and Worth."[13] This agenda suggests that, regarding the pragmatic institution of political deportment, rather than the theoretical construction of an abstract civil model, Locke's pedagogical project supplements, and thereby partially displaces, his political hypothesis, introducing in effect a foreign itinerary in the formation of public life.

That difference is historically decisive, since by most accounts Locke's pedagogical treatise proved to have a larger readership than either the *Essay* or the *Two Treatises* (see my introduction). In the *Education*, the public constitution of individual subjectivity does not take the same shape as that in civic humanism, but its design amounts to much more than merely training children to cooperate with communally defined norms. Instead, its tactic turns out to be to provide the individual with an intact sense of intellectual or emotional privacy while simultaneously making it possible to penetrate the far reaches of that alleged interiority for the purposes of social management. This articulation of publicly private selfhood would supply the springboard for adapting Locke's genteel educational program to the demands of urban public supervision. Furthermore, it makes a negotiation between republican ideals and Lockean educational politics a feasible cultural project.

The 'Education': Natural Signs, Public Privacy, and the Pedagogical Marketplace

Locke is the first pedagogical theorist of his time to place such persistent emphasis on attending to a child's individual "*Temper, . . . Predominant Passions,* and *prevailing Inclinations*" (sec. 102), an imperative that requires in turn avoiding the heavy strictures of prohibition and rule memorization. Locke reminds his readers in the *Education* that however strenuous or rigorous the educational program, a child's "Byass will always hang on that side, that Nature first placed it" (sec. 102). In fact, the attempt to overhaul completely his "Natural Genius . . . will be but Labour in vain: And what is so Plaister'd on, will at best sit but untowardly, and have always hanging to it the Ungracefulness of Constraint and Affectation" (sec. 66).

The first priority of this individualistic emphasis, however, is anything but fostering self-actualization; instead, observing a boy's particular propensities serves later for encouraging or redirecting them toward the chief aim of normalizing his moral and civic persona. Locke consistently discusses individual character in the context of figuring out how to adapt it most efficiently and painlessly to public mores, leaving the sense that if, in the meantime, a student's unique personality traits emerge, that is fine—so long as they do not interfere with establishing virtuous conduct. If on the contrary a child's individuality threatens to disrupt such pedagogical goals, then the response is swift, if not implacably harsh. Locke bluntly admonishes, for example, that a young man's natural talent for versifying be "stifled, and suppressed, as much as may be," because should he become a "successful Rhymer," debauchery, "gaming," and financial ruin would inevitably follow, shattering his ability to maintain an inherited estate. And if, as another instance, he should persist in following his own inclination and resist the prodding of instruction, then he is guilty of "Obstinacy," which is then justifiably punishable—and repeatedly—by the last resort of corporal punishment "carried to the utmost Severity": "the Whipping (mingled with Admonitions between) [should be] so continued, till the Impressions of it on the Mind were found legible in the Face, Voice, and Submission of the Child, not so sensible of the Smart, as of the Fault he has been guilty of" (sec. 87).

Locke's language of "reading" children's internal state via the external signs of bodily expression or behavior is not incidental, because the design of supervisory education can function successfully only if such external appearances are reliably interpretable—or, put another way, if the tutorial gaze can readily pierce the outer surface to perceive its relation to what goes on underneath. There prove to be two ways to ensure such pedagogical accuracy, and the first recalls Locke's invocation, in a passage considered earlier, of both science and the theater:

> [T]he peculiar *Physiognomy of the Mind* is most discernable in Children, before Art and Cunning have taught them to hide their Deformities, and conceal their ill Inclinations under a dissembled out-side. Begin therefore betimes nicely to observe your Son's *Temper*; and that, when he is under least restraint, in his Play, and as he thinks out of your sight. . . . And if you carefully observe the Characters of his Mind, now in the first Scenes of his Life, you will ever after be able to judge which way his Thoughts lean, and what he aims at, even hereafter, when, as he grows up, the Plot thickens, and he puts on several Shapes to act it. (secs. 101–2)

Drawing on the techniques of physiognomy allows the tutor to work effectively during two stages of a pupil's development: the first when internal conditions are unambiguously written on the childish face (the emblem, to be sure, of unique personal identity); and the second when the older student may decide to camouflage true feelings, without realizing that in the meantime a newly formulated, substitute physiognomical system allows the instructor full understanding. It is a scenario in which the powers of "science" are prodigious (as we will see in a moment) and where the theatrical illusion of truly private performance persists only for the child.

A second and no doubt more powerful measure for guarding against the "dissembled out-side" is the preventive process of "breeding," which Locke places third in his hierarchy of pedagogical goals, after virtue and wisdom and significantly before learning. Breeding turns out to be more than the veneer of social class or conventions, since in that case, it would remain simply artificial, the "Plaister'd on" facade Locke refers to regarding affectation. Instead, breeding provides what could be considered the armature of virtue—the practical means by which genuine internal qualities such as generosity or benevolence can be smoothly channeled to the exterior sphere of expression, gesture, or demeanor. With no breeding (or a poor version of it), virtues become ineffectual: "Courage in an ill-bred Man, has the Air, and scapes not the Opinion of Brutality: Learning becomes Pedantry; Wit Buffoonry; Plainness Rusticity; Good Nature Fawning. And there cannot be a good quality in him which want of Breeding will not warp, and disfigure to his Disadvantage" (sec. 93). By contrast, good breeding, like the habits forming it, becomes "woven into the very Principles of his Nature"—by becoming *second* nature, immediate and graceful reflex (sec. 42). As Locke puts it, "The Actions, which naturally flow from . . . a well-formed Mind, please us . . . as the genuine Marks of it; and being as it were natural Emanations from the Spirit and Disposition within, cannot but be easy and unconstrain'd."[14] Hence breeding can occupy a usefully ambiguous position between being an acquired naturalness of manners and being a manifest actualization of innate gentility.[15]

The naturalization of the artificial is already a familiar gesture of Locke's observant education, and it has the effect of molding a child's selfhood such that each and every internal ethical, cognitive, or emotional fluctuation is immediately communicated in bodily expression. In effect, Locke's aim is to make the child a natural sign—that is, to make the connection between body and mind causally determined and therefore reliably interpretable, without the prospect of slippage or uncertainty characteristic of artificial code systems.[16] Given the importance that seventeenth- and eighteenth-century philosophy placed on natural sign systems, this is no small strategy for ensuring the operation of supervisory education. The result is to "exteriorize" the self, bringing to the outside whatever is rumbling on the inside, or, what is almost the same thing, making the difference between them pedagogically negligible.

In addition to making the student eminently scrutable, Locke's education also alters what we might expect should be taught to children concerning the value of property. Given the key role property has in the *Second Treatise* for defining the privileges and limits to private rights, we would expect that in the *Education* Locke would propose teaching children the importance of appropriating from nature property that could be properly and justifiably their own. He does indeed claim that "Children cannot well comprehend what *Injustice* is, till they understand Property, and how particular Persons come by it," but his strategy for teaching them this principle virtually deprives children of having claim to property that is actually their own. Locke continues, "the safest way to secure *Honesty*, is to lay the Foundation of it early in Liberality, and an Easiness to part with to others whatever [children] have or like themselves."[17] As Frances Ferguson has astutely noted, this has the effect of making a boy "treat his property as if it were nature (what is freely and equally available to all)," while at the same time Locke stipulates that he should never attempt to appropriate others' possessions. Ferguson comments further, Locke's "two contradictory lessons about property teach the child first that property rights are highly contingent when they are his but (because he has to yield his property as soon as someone else wants it) absolute when they are others'. Locke's plan for educating a gentleman's son thus encourages the child not to define himself by his possessions and participates in the traditional view of the gentleman as cultivating himself rather than his assets, putting himself beyond the category of need."[18]

Ferguson goes on to observe that Locke's recommendations for how to make learning enjoyable hinge on the child's "taking that learning as a possession belonging to someone else" (74). Her examples include one considered earlier in this study, when Locke describes getting a boy to want to learn to read by characterizing it as "the Privilege and Advantage of Heirs and Elder Brothers."[19] A second case is Locke's comment when describing a game of dice with letters: "To keep up his eagerness to it, let him think it a Game belonging to those above him" (sec. 151). Ferguson's bracing conclusion is that "property is conceived throughout *Some Thoughts* as something available only to other people, and this is as true of the self as of any objects to which it might try to lay claim. For the adeptness with which a gentleman is 'able to deny himself his own Desire' is possible because desire itself is always rendered as someone else's . . . the self in Locke's account is the formal product of the desires of others."[20] In other words, the "possessions" of a young gentleman—including his property, knowledge, even inclination—are supplied by the surrounding pedagogical environment and ideological lesson designed by the tutor. Paradoxically, nonpossessive education or self-cultivation is possible precisely because the gentleman already has (or will inherit) substantial property: the imperatives of private property Locke outlined in the *Second Treatise* remain peculiarly tied to a child's instruction in the public properties of moral obligation.[21]

Ferguson's argument, though striking, does not sound inordinate in the context of the "exteriorized" self I have already described or in terms of Locke's frequent evocation of the public domain when describing education. In addition to his horticultural, medical, and theatrical tropes, Locke also draws frequently on the language of the marketplace and economic class. It is a usage that seems less metaphorical than metonymic by virtue of foresight because his project, after all, is preparing a gentleman's son to be a sound "Man of Business,"[22] though by that phrase he means not so much a financial entrepreneur or capitalist investor, as the person primarily responsible for the maintenance and operation of the affairs at a country estate. To begin with, Locke characterizes the selection of a good tutor as the parents' prudent investment in their children's future:

> In all the whole Business of Education, there is nothing like to be less hearkn'd to, or harder to be well observed, than . . . that Children should from their first beginning to talk, have some *Discreet, Sober,* nay *Wise* Person about, whose Care it should be to Fashion them aright. . . . I think this Province requires great *Sobriety, Temperance, Tenderness, Diligence,* and *Discretion;* Qualities hardly to be found united in Persons, that are to be had for ordinary Salaries. . . . As to the Charge of it, I think it will be the Money best laid out, that can be, about our Children. . . . He that . . . procures his Child a good

> Mind, well Principled, temper'd to Vertue and Usefulness, and
> adorned with Civility and good Breeding, makes a better purchase
> for him, than if he laid out the Money for an Addition of more Earth
> to his former Acres.[23]

And in the case of the tutor himself, he must be in full possession of
the "Knowledge of the World" and breeding, since Locke remarks
that otherwise it "is no where to be borrowed, for the use of his
Pupil" (sec. 94).

   As for children themselves, they should not perceive their
learning experiences as "Business," since that would burden them
with a tiresome agenda of required tasks (secs. 76, 129, 150, 151).
But they are nonetheless implicitly incorporated in a general
"economy" of education in which they acquire assets such as rationality or virtue at first only *on loan*, until reaching adult maturity.
This system is administered chiefly by the mechanism of "Reputation," or praise and blame, which motivates children to pursue desirable conduct. But as Locke tells us, this impetus is not drawn
from their own intact roster of values, since "the Esteem they have
for one thing above another, they borrow from others: So that
what those about them make to be a Reward to them, will really
be so" (sec. 129). Furthermore, the esteem that adults demonstrate
for their children, what Locke casually calls "Credit," is often given
to them without their having fully earned it. When an inquisitive
child's "Reasons are any way tolerable," Locke comments, "let him
find the Credit and Commendation of it."[24] And since children
"love to be treated as Rational Creatures sooner than is imagined"—and also, he later adds, sooner than is fully justified—he
recommends treating them so from the very beginning (sec. 81).

   The point is that besides teaching children to value public reputation, this system constitutes their individual reasoning skills and
moral values by a communal network of publicly defined merit.
The student circulates in this pedagogical economy without the
requisite collateral for the complete credit he receives, though he
remains unaware of that fact. For him, generosity to others is "always repaid, and with Interest" (sec. 110) because Locke tells parents to reward the child for it; but that terminology is curious given
Locke's earlier portrayal of the child's emphatic lack of secure prop-

erty. The student may finally accumulate the intellectual properties of reason and morality, but the initial investment in private *account-ability* is provided by the public, whose recompense (or dividend) is the future maturity of individual conformity.

One last aspect of this publicly oriented education is that in addition to the child's desire being determined by others, Locke's program instills in him a perception of the world in terms of hierarchical rank or economic class. As I have noted, Locke's pedagogy uses children's relationships with their "betters" to motivate their learning. Their conduct can be readily altered, he tells us, "especially if they see the Examples of others, whom they esteem and think above themselves. And if the Things which they observe others to do be ordered so, that they insinuate themselves into them, as the Privilege of an Age or Condition above theirs, then Ambition, and the Desire still to get forward, and higher, and to be like those above them, will set them on work and make them go on with Vigour and Pleasure" (sec. 76). The effect of this process is to associate, at least implicitly, the mature capabilities of intellection with a social position raised above what Locke calls "the low Rank" of childhood (sec. 95).

That low rank proves to be rationally and morally measurable, as well as determined by economic class, because Lockean education characterizes improvement in the first instance as an ascension from the slough of the laboring populace. Locke sternly warns against leaving children vulnerable to the "Folly and Perverseness of Servants" who, as members of "the meaner sort of People," always pose the danger of "infecting" children with the "contagion" of ego-boosting flattery (secs. 59, 68, 70). Some of the same kind of language also appears in Locke's vivid discussion of why childish lies should be immediately quashed, because his terminology for moral quality becomes infiltrated by social and economic inflection: should a gentleman become known as a liar, it is a "mark that is judg'd the utmost disgrace, which debases a Man to the lowest degree of a shameful *meanness*, and *ranks* him with the most contemptible part of Mankind, and the abhorred Rascality; and it is not to be endured in any one, who would converse with People of Condition, or have any Esteem or Reputation in the World" (sec.

131; my emphasis). In these terms, the false representations of flattery are comparable to outright lying, and the "untowardly Tricks and Vices" of servants are the infectious agents of lower moral and economic status.[25] By being placed somewhere in the middle of this socioethical scale—below his "betters" but above common servants—the child's development of presumably private rational and moral understanding is caught up in a larger scheme of social rank and economic class. Individual rationality—perhaps at first unconsciously for the student, but always consciously for the tutor—becomes constituted by the public categories of caste and privilege.

In summary, physiognomical exteriorization, the de-privatization of property, and the constitution of individual subjectivity in the public network of marketplace credit and economic class—these three factors of Lockean education suggest a sociopolitical agenda that is powerfully communal rather than stalwartly private. In these terms, rather than the philosophical cornerstone of civil life, private subjectivity or personal identity is in fact the end product of public organization—perhaps even the side effect of the social edifice. This claim may be deliberately provoking, but given the long-standing emphasis accorded Locke's individualism, it is a necessary tactic in the attempt to revaluate the importance of his work in the Enlightenment. There is no doubt that Lockean epistemology stimulated new concern about what was sometimes called "this Individuality,"[26] but that should not obscure the ways that his pedagogy offered profound measures for making individual privacy routinely scrutable—not only during education but also in the general run of social and political life.

Although Locke never framed it as such, the public "economy" in his articulation of supervisory education served historically as an indirect response to republicanism's protocols of communal citizenship, and as such, it came to function as a conceptual space in which educationalist authors with liberal or republican predilections could choose to explore ways to improve both personal and national virtue. Given the widespread perception that Locke's *Education* had described a genuinely natural form of instruction which was therefore free from the taint of political partisanship, by the early 1700s his program had become a generalized model that was readily adopted by authors with divergent ideological or political commitments. Hence supervisory education played a key role in conceiving the idea of public privacy because it provided a supple model of instruction that could be adapted to other, sometimes competing, political or economic agendas. But before considering that phenomenon in detail (in the last part of this chapter), we will turn now to the third element that made a crucial contribution to the articulation of public privacy—those discourses and institutional practices that drew on a powerful sense of Christian faith or virtue. In the next three sections, I sketch a broad picture of how a Christian perspective helped form the concept of public privacy during the period from the late seventeenth to the late eighteenth century, focusing on three exemplary instances: the "science" of physiognomy, the moral vision of William Hogarth's art, and the implementation of schooling for the poor and for upper-class women.

Faces, Apprentices, and the Christian Story of Exteriorized Selfhood

During the seventeenth and eighteenth centuries, it was of course commonplace that divine authors such as Isaac Watts or William King published works extolling the values of Christian instruction,[27] and in similar fashion, the general run of other educationalists readily acknowledged the importance of instilling Christian piety in children. With Locke, however, the period's overall commitment to promoting Christian faith was quickly complicated by an attempt to negotiate between strict orthodoxy and more secular aims or assumptions regarding everything from human nature to national purpose. It is particularly in this context that the category of public privacy gradually took shape, because very often, it was articulated as a more secular version of the biblical tenet that the soul was always open to God's irresistible scrutiny. In other words, while reiterating an emphasis on Christian virtue, public privacy also emerged from an attempt to expropriate the powers of spiritual inspection and judgment with the aim of consolidating a

pedagogical technology that could serve the secular interests of
monitoring British civil society and forming ideal British citizens.

That ambivalent project often took a literal, visual form, since
the idea of making the private public often suggested the process of
embodying hidden qualities in a palpable image for every eye to
see, and during the eighteenth century, the most systematic approach to representing that process was the so-called science of
physiognomy, which relied heavily on visual tools such as engraving and painting to conduct—and prove—its analyses. As Barbara
Stafford points out, the study of physiognomy often constituted a
form of "scientific theology," a spiritual-secular hybrid that, among
other things, was "necessary to the spiritual health of those in the
commerce of the world."[28] It was also important to the project of
education, as Locke himself indicated when advising that a tutor
should approach a student's public persona by decoding his "peculiar *Physiognomy of the Mind*."[29] In fact, the development of physiognomical research and publication during the seventeenth and eighteenth centuries indicates that Locke's passing remark has important
resonance with other discourses also intent on locating the connections between inner self and outer appearance. Hence rather
than considering the host of authors whose general Christian convictions moved them to advocate a renewed dedication to education, I have chosen here to focus on two men—Johann Lavater as
methodical scientist and William Hogarth as popular artist—who
both offer instructive examples of how Christian devotion was
given a modern slant by a physiognomical perspective that manifested the notion of public privacy in its use of impressively detailed
illustrations. A brief examination of these influential practitioners'
work shows how a concern with the human face (which had its
counterpart in chiromancy's with the hand) could endorse Christian virtue while also abetting a more secular and educational need
to penetrate the body's surface in calculating children's amendment.

LAVATER AND THE EYE OF PHYSIOGNOMY

At the time Locke published the *Education* in 1693, physiognomical discourses of the seventeenth century, which had been
strongly tied to the system of astrology, were becoming increasingly

imagined as a project that could be a genuine part of the natural and human sciences. In the most well-known physiognomical texts to appear in English during the 1650s to the 1670s—including Richard Saunders's *Physiognomie and Chiromancie* (1653; 2d ed. 1671), Marin Cureau de La Chambre's *The Art How to Know Men* (1665), and John ab Indagine's *The Book of Palmestry and Physiognomy* (1651)—reading the body was only minimally a matter of locating individuals' inner nature. There was a far greater interest in being able to use astrological signs associated with the hands—as in figure 3—or with the face—as in figure 4—in order to predict future events. In Saunders's *Physiognomie*, for instance, he displays a number of faces for his readers' inspection, interpreting the lines of the face for clues to the future. In a few instances, this includes identifying the individual's basic personality: of a man's forehead in figure 5 (upper left), he writes, "Lines bowing in this manner, denote a base nature, and the worst of manners." But otherwise, he concerns himself with the fact that one woman's countenance "denotes ill conditions," another's "a favourable, good, and gentle fortune."[30] In Saunders's physiognomical mapping of the body, on the one hand, the microscopic surface appearances of moles on a woman's face were reticulated within a distinctly astrological framework, as shown in figure 6; on the other hand, even in entering visually the depths of the body to the point of reaching its skeleton, Saunders's focus is on associating parts of the skeletal structure with the astrological symbolism of the moon or the planets, as he does in figure 7.

In La Chambre's *The Art How to Know Men*, by contrast, the emphasis is significantly greater on determining the inner mind. He tells us, for instance, that Nature

hath not only bestow'd on Man voice and tongue, to be the interpreters of his thoughts; But out of a certain distrust she conceiv'd, that he might abuse them, she hath contriv'd a language in his forehead and eyes, to give the others the Lye, in case they should not prove faithful. In a word, she hath expos'd his soul, to be observ'd on the out-side, so that there is no necessity of any window, to see his Motions, Inclinations, and Habits, since they are apparent in his face, and are there written in such visible and manifest characters.[31]

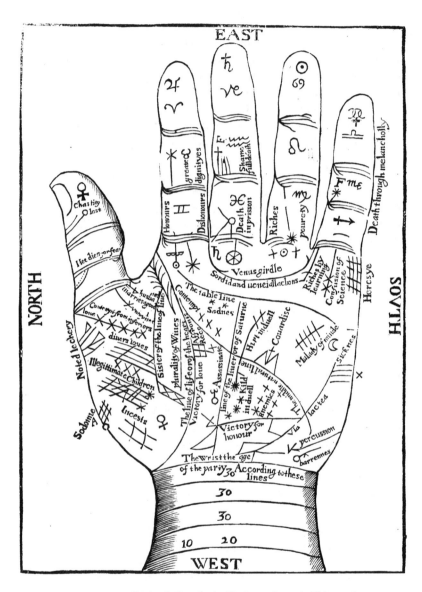

FIGURE 3. Richard Saunders, *Physiognomie, and Chiromancie, Metoposcopie*, 2d ed., 1671. This plate illustrates the astrological signs associated with chiromancy, a form of palm reading. Courtesy The Huntington Library, San Marino, California.

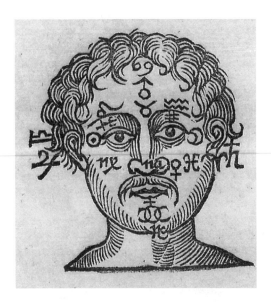

FIGURE 4. Richard Saunders, *Physiognomie, and Chiromancie, Metoposcopie*, 2d ed., 1671. This plate indicates the astrological signs of the face for predicting the future. Courtesy The Huntington Library, San Marino, California.

La Chambre also explicitly identifies physiognomical reading as a useful part of the pedagogical arsenal, since "there are few actions whereby it [the art of reading people] is not necessary; as for instance, the Education of children, the choice of Servants, Friends, Company, and most others, which cannot be well done without it" (sig. B6ᵛ).

Still, even with La Chambre's apparent confidence in his methods, a certain "Jam[es] Howell," who wrote a brief preface for the book, cautiously remarks that physiognomy "is an Art as full of incertitude as any. The lineaments of the Face, and lines of the Hands, are not streight enough to lead us unto it, . . . though the Eyes be as the Casements of the Soul, yet, many times they prove false Glasses; though . . . every Man's Fate and Fancy be written in his Forehead, yet the letters are so obscure, that we cannot read

Lines bowing in this manner, denote a
bafe nature, and the worft of manners.

A Line thus oblique in the forehead,
denotes ill conditions.

Thefe Lines denote a Murtherer, and
one that fhall fuffer a violent death.

A Line bowing thus, fhews a fordid bafe
condition.

Such Lines denote a favourable, good,
and gentle fortune.

A Line thus branch't, fignifies a mutable,
wavering, unconftant minded perfon.

Thefe

FIGURE 5. Richard Saunders, *Physiognomie, and Chiromancie, Metoposcopie*, 2d ed., 1671. These diagrams are examples of metoposcopy, the art of reading foreheads, which was a subsidiary discipline of physiognomy and its more holistic attention to the entire face. Courtesy The Huntington Library, San Marino, California.

FIGURE 6. Richard Saunders, *Physiognomie, and Chiromancie, Metoposcopie*, 2d ed., 1671. This plate charts how to interpret the position of moles on the face and neck, with astrological signs marking the column in the center of the forehead. Courtesy The Huntington Library, San Marino, California.

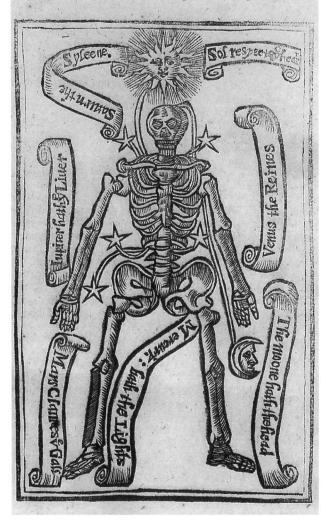

FIGURE 7. Richard Saunders, *Physiognomie, and Chiromancie, Metoposcopie*, 2d ed., 1671. This chart associates astrological signs of "The Seven Planets" (including the sun and moon) with parts of the skeleton and body organs. Courtesy The Huntington Library, San Marino, California.

them" (sig. A8ʳ). John ab Indagine echoes this sentiment in his book when he comments on the application of physiognomical analysis to children. In his words, adults should "use moderation, and do nothing rashly, neither unadvisedly to give judgement of any man in his nativity," because this "science" is difficult to use accurately.[32] In physiognomy's indeterminate status between "Art" and "science" lies the problem of its reliability. What is more, the frontispiece to La Chambre's text—showing a physiognomical analyst working at measurements on a bust inside, while in the background there is visible a small group of people conversing outside the doorway (fig. 8)—suggests another version of this problem. It is possible that, in the relation between the scholar's activity inside, assisted with various instruments of measurement, and the group's activity outside, the point is to contrast the precision of careful study to the more spontaneous exchange of social conversation. But it could be equally possible to suggest, in the context of Indagine's warning, that this student of physiognomy is isolated— and thereby perhaps also alienated—from the "real" world of social commerce or commonsense communication.

Whatever the case, by the mid- to late eighteenth century, physiognomy had appropriated the mantle of scientific authority, which can be found particularly in the work by the most famous author on the subject during the period, Johann Caspar Lavater, who was also the most popular author on the subject for English readers.[33] During the years spanning the period from the Revolution of 1688 to the American Revolution in 1776, physiognomy expanded its disciplinary provenance and strengthened its analytic purview, in part by assimilating itself, among other things, to the system of phrenology, which purported to be the scientific study of the size, shape, and topology of the human skull. Within that rough sketch of physiognomy's history, a quick look at Lavater's work suggests the trajectory of early modern physiognomical thought, especially with regard to its interest—shared with Locke—of calculating an educational narrative based on visual scrutiny. In the hands of Lavater, that project also served the larger goal of reproducing a definitively Christian hermeneutic.

In the older form of physiognomy, a story was of course often

FIGURE 8. Frontispiece to Marin Cureau de La Chambre, *The Art How to Know Men*, 1659; London, 1665, showing the physiognomist at work in a setting detached from public converse. Courtesy The Huntington Library, San Marino, California.

produced of the individual's life. As La Chambre explains, studying the face "promises to shew, what were, or will be, the inclinations and passions, past and to come, the strength and weakness of mens minds, the dispositions they have to certain Arts and Sciences."[34] But in Lavater's influential *Essays on Physiognomy, Designed to Promote the Knowledge and the Love of Mankind*, he intends to articulate a more exacting sense of both momentarily static character and its temporal unfolding. Lavater's *Physiognomische Fragmente,* published in German from 1775 to 1778, was rapidly translated after its first appearance, reaching English audiences in portions from 1775 to the 1790s (the first full volumes appearing in 1789). His description of his project suggests the kind of analytic accuracy Locke anticipates in his description of tutorial insight while also illustrating an even greater faith in the physical sciences. Lavater explains that physiognomy is a "Science" in the more modern sense while also being intent on "discovering the relation between the exterior and the interior—between the visible surface and invisible spirit which it covers—between the animated, perceptible matter, and the imperceptible principle which impresses this character of life upon it—between the apparent effect, and the concealed cause which produces it."[35] Given Lavater's commitment to the body as natural origin, he rejects the idea that "Every thing in Man depends on education, culture, example—and not on original organisation and formation; these are universally the same" (1789–98 1:143). But he is nonetheless sure of the impact physiognomical understanding can have on educational technique. At one point, he asserts, "Let a man transport himself in idea to the sphere of a Politician, of a Pastor, of an Instructor of youth, of a Physician, of a Merchant, of a Friend, of a Father, of a Husband—and he will presently feel what advantage each of these may derive from Physiognomical knowledge. It is possible to compose a particular Physiognomy for every one of these situations" (1789–98 1:76). While his seventeenth-century predecessors had also sometimes contemplated the political applications of physiognomical skills,[36] Lavater imagines here an analytical system that can serve this purpose while also saturating an entire range of social fields including familial, economic, pedagogical, medical, and religious activity.

Turning to consider the exhaustive documentation Lavater offers to support his claim to scientific comprehensiveness—various English editions, for example, included from three to eight hundred engravings of faces and profiles—reveals how his interest in children could apply to several venues that would be pertinent to both parenting and educating the young. At the most elemental level, Lavater documents how to read the face's registry of momentary emotions, and when considering the example of "fear and terror," he offers a visual template recording its features in a range of ages from infancy to adulthood (fig. 9). From here one can observe the way Lavater's explications of the contours or lines of the face become animated by an emerging moral or psychological evaluation. The alternation between description and appraisal can be both subtle and sudden, as in Lavater's account (in its entirety) of a young boy's image (seen in fig. 10):

> STRONGLY impressed with the character of truth: all is exact all harmonious; a plenitude of activity, of numerous talents.—Between the eyebrows, only, is there something foreign, empty, insipid. The eyebrows, likewise, are too weak, too indefinite, in this, otherwise, strong countenance, the power and fortitude of which might easily degenerate into vanity and obstinacy. (1789 2:103)

In other instances, Lavater works comparatively, offering contrasting images of two youths for study, or equally commonly, presenting an array of profiles with slight variations in order to ferret out what Lavater considers "immensely" different constitutions of character: one child is "Phlegmatic-melancholic, perfectly good-natured" (fig. 11, no. 1), while another is "completely stupid" (fig. 11, no. 8), and still another's mouth "is too intelligent for his age" (fig. 11, no. 5; 1797 3:133–34). In an educational context, these features form the topos of pedagogical calculation—with warning signs of eventual trouble, or evidence of promise. With the correct evaluation, the prospective instructor of the boy in figure 12, for example, knows to be patiently tolerant, because this fellow's nose denotes "little superiority of mind," and regarding his countenance in general, "if it does not attract, [it] does not raise expectation" (1789 3:289–90).

Lavater's facial semiotics also generates a reliable system of nat-

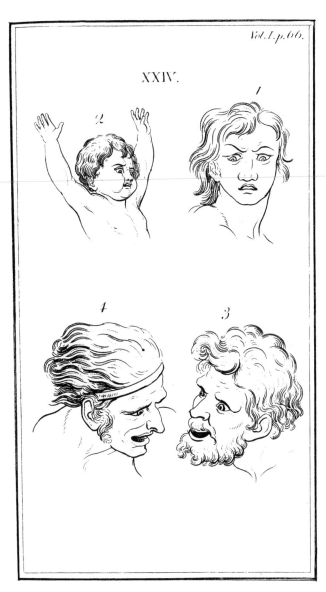

FIGURE 9. John Caspar Lavater, *Essays on Physiognomy*, vol. 1, pl. 24, trans. Thomas Holcroft, 1789. In these comparative examples from infancy to old age, nos. 1 and 2 illustrate "fear and terror," while nos. 3 and 4 show "terror, heightened by native indocility of character." By permission of The British Library (shelfmark cup.407.kk.44).

FIGURE 10. John Caspar Lavater, *Essays on Physiognomy*, vol. 2, pl. 4, trans. Thomas Holcroft, 1789. Portrait of a young boy with "numerous talents," whose eyebrows nonetheless indicate potential "vanity and obstinacy." By permission of The British Library (shelfmark cup.407.kk.44).

ural organization for the sexes. In comparing two images of the same boy, for instance, he concludes that while registering different degrees of "energy," both "denote a manly, and generous character" (fig. 13, E; 1797 3:135). Profiles of women appear less frequently, yet they too produce gendered evaluations—as well as sug-

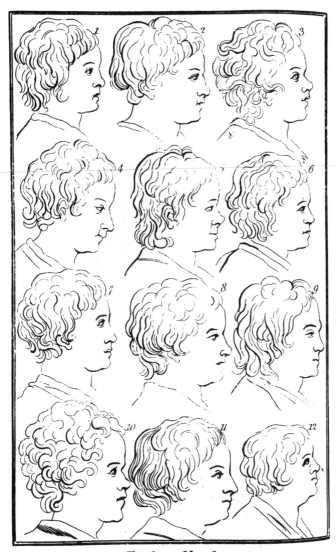

Twelve Heads

FIGURE 11. John Caspar Lavater, *Essays on Physiognomy*, vol. 3, trans. C. Moore, 1797. The often slight differences among these twelve boys' profiles prove surprisingly decisive: no. 1 is "good-natured," no. 7 has "gentleness and dignity," and no. 11 is a "man designed for the cabinet." Courtesy The Newberry Library, Chicago, Illinois.

FIGURE 12. John Caspar Lavater, *Essays on Physiognomy*, vol. 3, pl. 98, trans. Thomas Holcroft, 1789. In this boy's profile, "Not a single feature, separately considered, is excellent." By permission of The British Library (shelfmark cup.407.kk.44).

gestions of innate aristocratic virtue—as in the case of one young woman (fig. 14) who is "NOBLE, full of vivacity, youthful frolic, sanguine, capable of friendship, innocent, mild, faithful, modest, and in the outline of the nose, especially, charming effeminacy" (1789 3:311). When a female image does not evoke a catalogue of the sex's ideal traits, at times it can register instead an enthusiastic endorsement of women's supposedly natural domesticity. Of the profile in figure 15, Lavater's brief comment is, "COULD I see nothing of this countenance but the nose, I could not be so certain of the mild goodness and tranquillity of the character, and of its various housewifely virtues; yet the nose would be pledge to me of its superior discretion" (1789 3:242). In this gendered morphology, even the qualitative degree of women's relative domesticity can apparently be calibrated.

Finally there is the issue of the narrative of development or education that Lavater's physiognomical analyses embody. The stories Lavater implicitly or explicitly suggests are for him initiated by the natural origin of the body, and the task of physiognomical measurement is to assess those origins in order to imagine a sequence of pertinent events. In the interest of a more exacting inquiry, furthermore, Lavater makes a distinction between physiognomy proper, "which considers the character when in a state of rest," and "pathognomy," which "examines it in action"—that is, when the passions have created "moving power" in the self (1789–98 1:23). Hence pathognomy could apply in deciphering the two images of the boy already considered in figure 13. But the twin analytical tools of physiognomy and pathognomy are also mutually constituted, since personality's foundation in the body implies a plotline based on natural origins. Even in cases such as the representation of the state of fear (in fig. 9), there is an implicit story line in the sequence of figures (from left to right, top down) suggesting a prognosis for the infant's future experience of the same passion as a much older man. Perhaps the most example of imagining a future narrative based on a static image is figure 16, which depicts one of the youngest of Lavater's subjects, apparently a female infant no more than three years old. Lavater launches his commentary with "EXTREMELY delicate—May be said to be formed for religion, a contempt of the world, and to calm, attentive, domestic industry. Never intended for great actions, but to patient contemplation on God" (1789 3:270). Here is the entire trajectory of this girl's future life, complete with an itinerary of her simultaneous detachment from the quotidian world and her secure place in the home. Any pedagogue would know how to proceed from here.

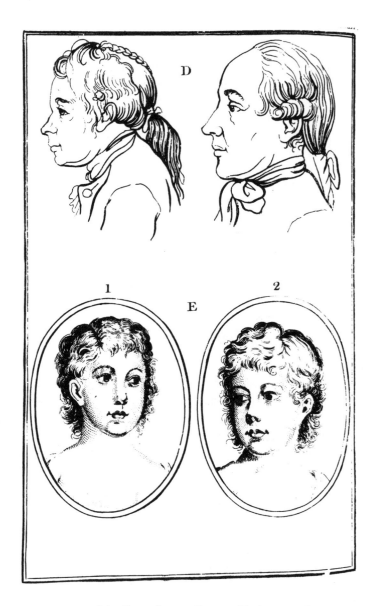

FIGURE 13. John Caspar Lavater, *Essays on Physiognomy*, vol. 3, trans. C. Moore, 1797. In these two portraits (E, nos. 1 and 2) of the same boy, the first indicates "gentleness, cordiality, and delicacy," the second "energy and vigour." Courtesy The Newberry Library, Chicago, Illinois.

FIGURE 14. John Caspar Lavater, *Essays on Physiognomy*, vol. 3, pl. 143, trans. Thomas Holcroft, 1789. This young woman is "NOBLE, . . . innocent, mild, [and] faithful." By permission of The British Library (shelfmark cup.407.kk.44).

Ultimately, a second kind of educative narrative proves to be the organizing framework for Lavater's specific analyses, and that is the process of his readers' absorption of the cultural criteria by which Lavater evaluates his subjects, leading to readers' eventual arrival at a spiritual appreciation of God's handiwork. Lavater's career

FIGURE 15. John Caspar Lavater, *Essays on Physiognomy*, vol. 3, pl. 3, trans. Thomas Holcroft, 1789. This woman's nose produces the conclusion that she has "mild goodness" and "housewifely virtues." By permission of The British Library (shelfmark cup.407.kk.44).

FIGURE 16. John Caspar Lavater, *Essays on Physiognomy*, vol. 3, pl. 63, trans. Thomas Holcroft, 1789. Lavater knew the father of this infant girl, whom he declares is destined for "domestic industry" and "patient contemplation on God." By permission of The British Library (shelfmark cup.407.kk.44).

as a Protestant pastor becomes especially evident when he explains the larger religious implications of his subject of study:

> Physiognomy is a source of delicate and sublime sensations; it is a new eye which perceives in the creation a thousand traces of the Divine Wisdom and Goodness, and which contemplates in a new point of view, the adorable Author of Human Nature, who possessed the skill to introduce so much truth and harmony into this work of his hands.
>
> Where the weak and unpractised eye of the inattentive spectator suspects nothing, the experienced eye of the connoisseur discerns an inexhaustible source of moral and intellectual pleasure. (1789–98 1:77)

As Lavater's fellow-travelers in this physiognomical theodicy, his readers may also gain the experience necessary for arriving at the expertise of being "connoisseurs" of both humanity and divinity. And in the process, their individual "I"s can converge on the singular "eye" of acquired Christian piety. Lavater's brand of theological science, therefore, produces a version of public privacy both physiologically and morally calculable.

HOGARTH AND THE EMPLOTMENT OF VIRTUE

My discussion of Lavater's physiognomy suggests both the similarities and the differences between his approach to individual interiority and Locke's in his pedagogical program. Probably the two most important distinctions arise from Lavater's decidedly antiempiricist outlook and an enthusiastic religiosity that would have made Locke at least a little anxious. Still, in the context of supervisory education's own ambiguous relation to the putatively natural origin of human passion or impulse, Lavater's analyses indicate one way that that uncertainty might have been resolved several decades later. Most importantly, however, Lavater's physiognomy illustrates that from the early seventeenth to the late eighteenth century, the aim to articulate a juncture between inner and outer selves had several similar goals, among them the founding of an overseeing perspective that could monitor that juncture, and responding to the narrative pattern that emerged in the process of those selves' complex interaction. Hence the issues of observation, narrativization, and individual exfoliation—the concerns of a variety of early modern educationalists—also compelled people in a broad range of other intellectual, scientific, or even artistic disciplines.

With that in mind, I want to discuss one other context for the public emphasis characteristic of supervisory education in order to consider how it manifested itself in eighteenth-century popular culture—specifically, Hogarth's series of twelve engravings entitled *Industry and Idleness*, which first appeared in 1747. Taking this tack has several historical nuances, including the fact that Hogarth was well known in England for his engraved studies of striking faces and that Lavater selected some of them in his *Essays* for the purpose of performing his own kind of physiognomical procedure (one of those images came from a plate in *Industry and Idleness* itself). In *Industry and Idleness*, the lack of an accompanying explanatory text for its plates may make its Christian themes more subtle than in Lavater's work, but they emerge nonetheless in developing a palpable story line about the rewards of Christian piety, especially since Hogarth provides readers with one or more scriptural quotations at the bottom of each plate. Furthermore, his depiction of the progress of two apprentices, one diligent and the other lax, is particularly relevant to the novel because it portrays these youths' instruction and subsequent fortunes as a narrative sequence that offers a suggestive example for how other narrative treatments of education—including fiction—might proceed. Hogarth's engravings also provide several visual parallels to supervisory pedagogy, although the differences must be noted as well, especially Hogarth's treatment of the story as an allegory of Christian virtue, whereby innate moral character remains steadfastly the same in determining Francis Goodchild's glowing successes and final appointment as Lord Mayor of London, and Tom Idle's degenerative slide to the gallows. As John Bender points out, there is no moral reeducation here, although he also remarks that the series "veers toward the supervised workshop as a social model."[37] In Bender's analysis, Hogarth's series is a transitional text poised between the older system of social organization—based on liminality and what he calls "the closed city"—and the emerging regime of discipline, which relies on the narrative process of penitential reform. Hence for Bender, Hogarth diagnoses the shortcomings of the old system, without really entering the new one; he concludes, "Hogarth has novelized, and thereby exposed sequentially to view, the covalance between authority and its abdication in the liminal arena—the definition of each by an alien or 'other'" (128).

While that analysis concisely explains how *Industry and Idleness* is still party to an ethos largely foreign to supervisory education, I want to suggest further that Hogarth's series nonetheless partially articulates an approach to character resembling the supervisory aim of exteriorizing individuals' identity in the process of scrutinizing their personal development. In this sense Hogarth employs a physiognomical technique that represents both Idle's and Goodchild's

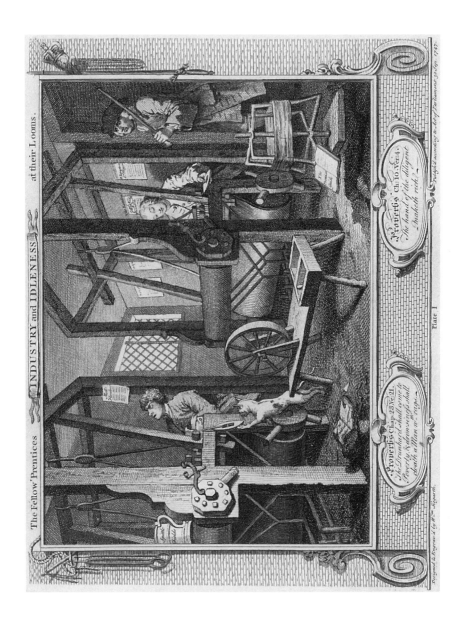

The Fellow 'Prentices at their Looms.

INDUSTRY and IDLENESS

Proverbs Chap. 23 Ver. 21.
The Drunkard shall come to
Poverty, & drowsiness shall
cloath a Man w.th raggs.

Proverbs Ch: 10 Ver 4.
The hand of the diligent
maketh rich.

Plate 1

Designed & Engrav'd by W.m Hogarth.

Publish'd according to Act of Parliament 30 Sep. 1747.

164

progress in life as an exfoliation of character, and in the meantime, he also produces an ambivalent instructive moral for his several audiences that brings to light how otherwise implicit differences in social status can generate drastically opposing responses to the same story. In reading Hogarth's series this way, I will put a slightly different spin on Bender's comment that it "promulgates a discourse situated in the public sphere, a discourse in which the multiple voices of the present can take concrete form" (135).

The first plate, entitled "The Fellow 'Prentices Industry and Idleness at their Looms" (fig. 17), depicts a paradigmatic moment of supervisory education: both youths sit at their machinery, one intently working and the other napping, unaware that in the meantime they are being watched by a figure in the upper-right-hand corner, whose authority is represented both by his slight elevation above the scene and by a staff he holds whose extension off the border of the picture is topped by the mace of the Lord Mayor of London (this emblem is similarly placed on the border of all twelve plates).[38] The subtlety of this unobserved observation is accentuated further by the engraving's compositional arrangement: the viewer's eye rests first on the central area of the shop, initially unaware, like the apprentices, of the man's presence. Although it is not entirely clear whether this man is part of the manufacturing establishment or the representative of some kind of civil authority, he is likely the former, the apprentices' master.[39] In any case, that slight ambiguity underscores two important themes in the series: authority's interventions may not always be perceptible or at least foreseeable; and apparently small or private matters have, in the end, large-scale public consequences. Several other surrogates for this figure, similarly dressed and wielding some form of authority, appear in the ensuing plates.

FIGURE 17 (facing page). William Hogarth, *Industry and Idleness*, pl. 1 (Second State), 1747. While Thomas Idle sleeps at his loom and Frances Goodchild labors diligently, both are unaware of the man of authority behind them checking their progress. On the floor, Goodchild's copy of "The Prentices Guide" is in perfect shape, while Idle's is in tatters. By permission of the Trustees of The British Museum.

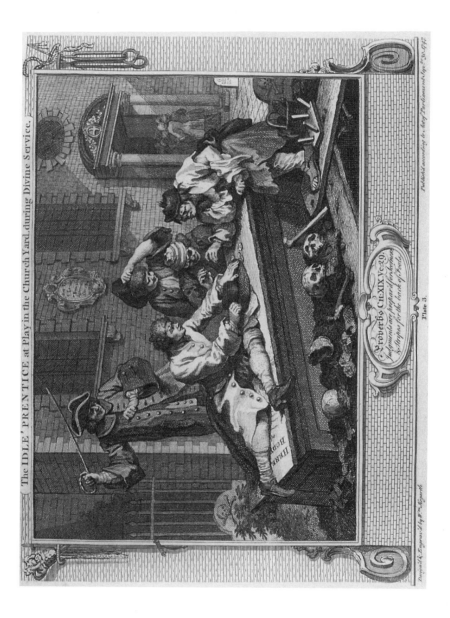

The IDLE 'PRENTICE at Play in the Church Yard, during Divine Service.

Proverbs Ch.XIX.v.29.
The companions of fools shall be destroyed.
& stripes for the back of Fools.

Plate 3.

Those figures appear again in plates 3 and 4, when Hogarth presents two different forms of adult intervention in the course of the apprentices' conduct. Tom Idle, engaged in gaming in the churchyard cemetery while his counterpart attends the service inside, is symbolically sprawled on the top of an unburied coffin, his horizontal slouch a further gesture of moral negligence and a spiritual mortality soon to be made physically literal (fig. 18). Behind him stands a man, apparently a beadle, poised to apply "Stripes for the back of Fools" (reads the inscription), administering what Locke would consider just punishment for such blatant obstinacy. The first figure's staff of authority has now become the rod of correction. Meanwhile, Goodchild enjoys the fruits of his labor, when his master rewards him with new responsibilities and benefits, including a "Day Book" for keeping records and a set of keys (fig. 19). His erect and well-groomed posture contrasts sharply with his counterpart's previous slumping demeanor, and it is complemented by his master's less domineering pose, which includes putting his arm amiably on the apprentice's shoulder. Industriousness has earned the pupil a tutorial response of supervisory friendliness, represented here also by the gloves clasped in a handshake on the desk. And this is more than an instance of reward, for by taking this

FIGURE 18 (facing page). William Hogarth, *Industry and Idleness*, pl. 3, 1747. While Goodchild attends church service inside, Idle is outside gambling and about to receive a corrective blow from a beadle. By permission of the Trustees of The British Museum.

FIGURE 19 (page 168). William Hogarth, *Industry and Idleness*, pl. 4, 1747. Goodchild is rewarded for his labor and made a supervisor by Mr. West; his new post is elevated above the loom stations, which are in the background, in order to facilitate their easy inspection. By permission of the Trustees of The British Museum.

FIGURE 20 (page 169). William Hogarth, *Industry and Idleness*, pl. 9 (Second State), 1747. Idle is about to be seized by the authorities in a "night cellar," which is a combination of murderous activity and claustrophobic close quarters. By permission of the Trustees of The British Museum.

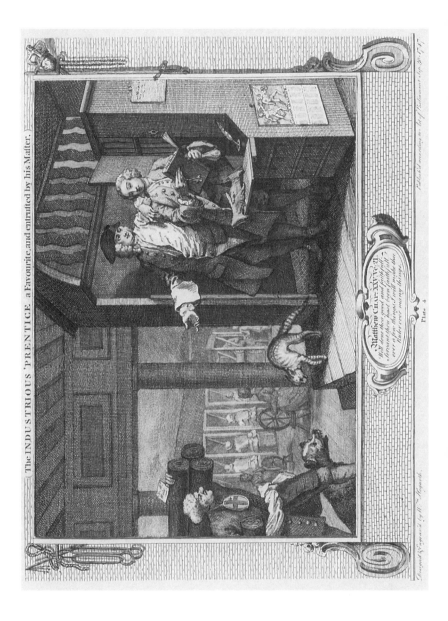

The INDUSTRIOUS 'PRENTICE, a Favourite, and entrusted by his Master.

Matthew Chap: XXV. Ve: 21.
Well done thou good and faithfull
Servant thou hast been faithfull
over a few things, I will make thee
Ruler over many things.

Plate 4.

168

The IDLE 'PRENTICE betray'd by his Whore, & taken in a Night Cellar with his Accomplice.

Proverbs CHAP: VI. Ver.26
The Adulteress will hunt for
the precious life.

Plate 9

action the master will be teaching his understudy a new set of tasks and procedures.

In the following plates emerge the final consequences of the distinct trajectories already initiated by these apprentices. The most striking contrast is that they are portrayed in physical settings that reflect their respective expanding or contracting horizons. The indolent youth, for instance, is presented in increasingly "narrow" straits that are literally confining, including a small rowboat when he is sent to sea for rebelliousness, a cramped prostitute's garret with the door jammed shut with boards, and a subterranean night cellar claustrophobic by virtue of its inmates' riotous activity (fig. 20). Goodchild, by contrast, enjoys the increasingly open spaces of the celebration of his marriage to his master's daughter, and the spacious Guildhall where he commemorates his appointment as London's sheriff.

For the moment, Idle's status—unlike that of his moral better—has become obsessively private, as he seeks to hide the degeneracy of his whoring or thievery. But in figure 20, that secrecy is abruptly torn away, exposing him later to the public humiliation of being brought before Goodchild who has now become Alderman of London. And the beadle, the familiar figure of civil power who appears once again, bears the authorizing staff with the Alderman's crest. In the final two engravings of the series, this pattern is brought to completion by the juxtaposition of two drastically different, but equally public, scenes (figs. 21 and 22): the first is the preparation for Idle's execution, against a backdrop with the most heavily populated audience so far; the second depicts an equally crowded street scene in the parade celebration of Goodchild's ascension to Lord Mayor.

In both cases, however, as different as they may be, there is the clear sense that an integral part of bringing moral conduct to its just end is making the persons involved, as well as the appropriate social rituals, prominently—and perhaps painfully—public.[40] For the hapless idler, that boils down (punningly) to the scriptural warning: "Be sure your sins will find you *out*" (Numbers 32:23)—out in the excruciating arena of personal tragedy made public. For the upstanding citizen, a similar lesson applies regarding virtue, and in jubilant terms. In both final plates, moreover, the individual protagonists are virtually lost in the hubbub of the attending crowd—Idle in the cart approaching the gallows, Goodchild inside his coach. In addition, there is in the entire series the further sense that "mere" private activity or enterprise is always in some way already public. This notion is first suggested by the quiet appearance of civil authority in the first engraving, whose presence will prove virtually ubiquitous in the series. And viewers of Hogarth's allegorical series are themselves conclusive evidence that this process is singularly and consistently communal.

To be sure, *Industry and Idleness* is not without its invidious ironies—such as Goodchild's being surrounded at the Guildhall banquet by gluttonous, but respectable citizens. Furthermore, as Ronald Paulson has persuasively argued, Hogarth designed these engravings with the purpose of delivering a double message: he intended those in polite society he called "readers of greater penetration" to perceive the subtleties qualifying or undermining Goodchild's apparent triumph; and he appealed to the class resentments of another viewing public, the apprentices, by clandestinely making Idle an underdog's hero.[41] Even given these ambivalences, however, Hogarth's series nonetheless illustrates how a young protagonist's life becomes grist for narrative adaptation by those social powers intending to use it for the instruction of others. In the case of Tom Idle, for instance, his story becomes in the end the basis for two putatively edifying texts: in plate 11, being hawked in the fore-

FIGURE 21 (page 172). William Hogarth, *Industry and Idleness*, pl. 11, 1747. Idle on his way to execution at Tyburn, while a distraught woman holding a child (center, bottom) carries a copy of his "Last Dying Speech & Confession." By permission of the Trustees of The British Museum.

FIGURE 22 (page 173). William Hogarth, *Industry and Idleness*, pl. 12 (Second State), 1747. The procession for Goodchild's becoming Lord-Mayor of London. A figure at bottom right reads a copy of the account of the "Ghost of Tho. Idle." By permission of the Trustees of The British Museum.

The IDLE 'PRENTICE Executed at Tyburn.

Proverbs Chap. I. Ver. 27.28.
When your fear cometh as desolation, and your
destruction cometh as a whirlwind; when
distress & anguish cometh upon them, then they shall
call upon me, but I will not answer.

Plate XI

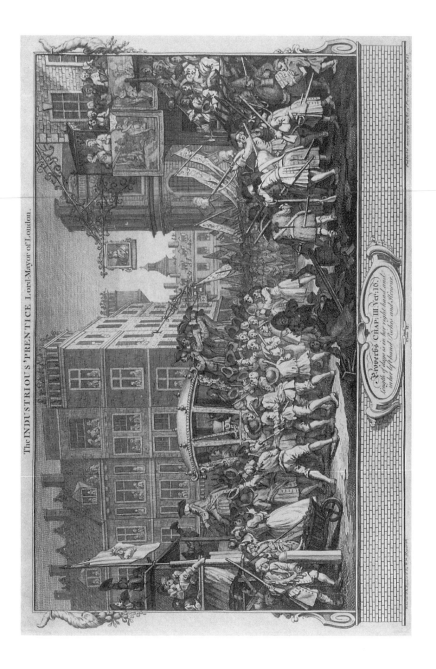

The INDUSTRIOUS 'PRENTICE Lord-Mayor of London.

Proverbs CHAP: III Ver: 16.
Length of days is in her right hand and
in her left hand Riches and Honour.

ground is "The Last Dying Speech & Confession of Tho. Idle"; and in plate 12, a figure on the right reads "A Full and True Account of ye Ghost of Tho. Idle." Whether morality or profit is the chief motive here, Idle's story has been put to the task of social tutelage.[42]

More importantly, in Hogarth's series, ensuring the proper administration of reward and punishment is facilitated by the general application of supervisory education—both within the workshop walls and without. The idea that pedagogical technique is eminently adaptable for general civic or political application was not original with Hogarth.[43] As part of its history, that notion had followed the semantic transformation of the word *government*—to include both political rule and pedagogical guidance—that began in the late seventeenth century and persisted into the eighteenth century. Supervisory education, moreover, offered the additional benefit of regulating students or the general populace by a less imposing use of sociopolitical power—ruling by what was sometimes called the "hidden hand" of government. Such an arrangement proved strongly attractive to eighteenth-century writers and politicians, just as it was for Fielding: regarding the state regulation of schooling, he recommended "a thorough Inspection and Scrutiny into the Characters of all those who are intrusted with the Tuition and Instruction of Youth, from their earliest Season of Erudition, till they become their own Masters."[44] As we shall see, the application of supervisory methods was not only a hypothetical possibility but finally an institutional reality.

Regulating the Poor: Working Schools and Supervisory Pedagogy

Hogarth's partial articulation of disciplinary surveillance in the workplace brings us back to Locke's memorandum to the London Board of Trade concerning the new influx of the poor in English cities and parishes, with an eye toward considering how activist Christian resolve would make a version of his working schools part of the history of what Foucault calls "panopticism," thereby institutionalizing the notion of public privacy at a full-blown national scale. Locke's proposed working schools correspond to Foucault's remark that rather than "bending all its subjects into a single uniform mass," disciplinary organization "separates, analyses, differentiates, carries its procedures of decomposition to the point of necessary and sufficient single units. It 'trains' the moving, confused, useless multitudes of bodies and forces [them] into a multiplicity of individual elements—small, separate cells, organic autonomies, . . . combinatory segments."[45] In this sense, Locke's proposals form part of the general response Foucault describes in Europe during the early modern period when the British and continental nations, confronted with massive demographic changes and upheavals—including a surge of poor populations, the crowding of urban areas, and the attending problems of health and crime—gradually adopted and institutionalized disciplinary methods because they offered the most efficient way to maximize social regulation and economic productivity.[46]

There are several striking resemblances between Foucault's description of the emerging disciplines and Locke's account of pedagogy in the *Education*, for not only does the operation of disciplinary power have distinct parallels to Lockean protocols, but also Foucault's discussion of its social precedents and applications is often couched in similar language. Foucault's description of the Panopticon and related disciplinary formations is particularly intriguing in this context because he relates them to medical, natural, and even theatrical phenomena, which are, of course, the hallmark of supervisory programs advanced by both Locke and his contemporaries. Since the administration of public health control, for instance, was one of the earliest manifestations of social discipline, Foucault argues that subsequently, in disciplinary thinking, "the image of the plague stands for all forms of confusion and disorder"[47]—the very kind of social malady intended to be remedied by disciplinary projects of all kinds. He points out further that the design of the Panopticon prison system was based in part on the research approach of the natural sciences in observing, classifying, and categorizing species under study (203); it was a precedent not strictly horticultural in origin, but certainly pertaining to the interests of husbandry. In commenting in another context on discipline's "natural" status, Foucault remarks that "the order that the disciplinary punishments must enforce is of a mixed nature: it is an 'artificial' order, explicitly laid down by a law. . . . But it is also an order defined by natural and observable processes: the duration of an apprenticeship, the time taken to perform an exercise" (179). Adding still another suggestive parallel to supervisory pedagogy, Foucault writes in a moment of rhetorical flourish that the Panopticon's prison cells are "so many small theatres, in which each actor is alone, perfectly individualized and constantly visible" (200).

Foucault's analysis indicates that the supervisory educational program—articulated variously by the metaphorical models of medicine, horticulture, theater, and economy—plays a substantial part itself, both theoretically and practically, in forming the outlines of eighteenth-century disciplinary organization. In practical terms, Locke's plan for working schools demonstrated a rigor characteristic of disciplinary administration. Locke recommended a variety of measures for contending with the problem of the poor, vagrant, and homeless on city streets. In addition to stressing that already existing laws should be rigorously enforced, his proposals included: reducing the number of vagabond beggars by putting those who were able-bodied and without legal passes to hard labor at sea (for three years); sending those unable to work to "houses of correction"; putting children ages three to fourteen in working schools so that they and their mothers could be kept from mischief and simultaneously brought to contribute to the nation's productivity; and setting up a state governing system of "guardians of the poor" who would set tax levies, distribute funds, and generally coordinate the efforts of individual parishes. The penalties for administrators and the poor were harsh, ranging from financial forfeiture (for embezzlement) to imprisonment and transportation to the colonies. The point of all this was not merely moral indignation but improving England's gross national product: Locke quickly calculated that his labor-intensive program could in eight years "make England above a million of pounds richer."[48]

Locke, however, devotes the most time in his proposal to laying out his plan for working schools, whose main purpose is an ed-

ucation in labor, since he mentions no other subjects of study. It is
an education both in specific working-class skills as well as in the
general lessons of shouldering the burden of hard work. And it answers Locke's concern that poor children's "labour . . . is generally
lost to the public till they are twelve or fourteen years old"; he
claims further that they are best off when "from infancy [they are]
inured to work" (2:383–84), no doubt because that certainly should
be their lot in life as adults. The only other instruction he does
mention concerns giving children "some sense of religion," since
their schoolwork will take place in the local parish, where they can
also be compelled to attend services (2:385). Children will be
obliged to come to the schools and apply themselves to work,
Locke predicts, because with their mothers also at work elsewhere,
"otherwise they will have no victuals" (2:384). For the most benefit to the kingdom, Locke recommends that the schools "be generally for spinning or knitting, or some other part of the woollen
manufacture" (2:385), and he proceeds then to describe the details
of the schools' administrative organization, the procedure for ap-
prenticing students, and the management of the flow of incoming
raw materials and outgoing finished product.

Locke's working-school system may be able to prevent children
from being "utter strangers both to religion and morality as they
are to industry" (2:385), but otherwise it seems to bear little resemblance to the *Education*'s stress on virtue and wisdom, let alone the
finer points of genteel bourgeois breeding. This is why in revising
Foucault's thesis that discipline constitutes a wholesale installation
of what he calls "complete" institutions, one must identify the specific historical ways by which class, gender, or other forms of social
status delineated distinct kinds of supervisory programs that could
vary in panoptic penetration, administrative severity, or discursive
rhetoric. But it is also imperative to locate the similarities. What
does carry over from Locke's treatise to his working-school model
is the underlying structure of supervisory education, including on
occasion its attending metaphorical language. There is striking resonance, for instance, in Locke's repeated use of the phrase "over-
seers of the poor," which recalls his description of the observant tutor (see, e.g., 2:378–79, 380, 383). And after he has graphically de-

scribed the streets "swarming" everywhere with beggarly and homeless "drones"—who are as much the refuse of the English social hive as a threatening "disorder" of its national health—it is hard not to hear the words of a stern pedagogical physician in Locke's subsequently proposed "effectual remedy" that takes the form of working schools.[49]

These resemblances point to the structural adaptability of supervisory education to the requirements of a new kind of mass pedagogy, because if the *Education*'s student from the gentry or perhaps the middle class is circulated in an implicit economy of communal "credit" and class position, then that system could be effectively modified to administer a program more directly linked to large-scale economic productivity. Although Locke's poor law proposal was not adopted into law by Parliament despite several tries, its working-school component served as a model both for later state legislation, especially the General Act of 1723, as well as for the even more broadly based efforts of the charity school movement.[50] The supervisory arrangement of observation, intervention, and resolution was particularly useful for all three endeavors— Locke's proposal, state working schools, and charity schools—because they confronted the same, complex problem: how to cope with an often overwhelming number of students in an educational system that purportedly was financially self-supporting by virtue of manufacturing goods, but whose obviously limited funds could afford only a minimum number of teachers. Educational supervision, then, became not so much a way to facilitate the "natural experience" of children's learning, as the means to achieve greater institutional efficiency. Now a single instructor would have the task of surveying the progress of a large number of students, interposing correction where necessary, and allowing the rest to take its course until the need again for further comment. It was a design that walked a tightrope between efficient organization and the disorder of children's en masse unruliness—needless to say, the schools often exercised a stringency that belied any kind of supervisory liberality or hidden authority. Here, it became necessary that students be constantly aware they were being observed (or might be), in order to prompt their good conduct.

The Society for Promoting Christian Knowledge (SPCK)—the organization responsible for spearheading the highly successful charity school movement that persisted well into the late eighteenth century—as well as its counterpart in various other philanthropic societies, provides a good case in point about the general institutionalization of supervisory education in Britain during the 1700s. As a hybrid of Lockean pedagogy and Christian mores, in fact, the charity school movement produced by far the eighteenth century's most important innovations in pedagogical institutionalization—for both boys and girls—for a number of reasons. Almost from the beginning, the movement was enormously successful because it introduced a new economic method for supporting philanthropic work: it borrowed from Fleet Street the joint-stock system, consolidating for each school smaller "subscriptions" from many charitable donors, rather than relying, as in the past, on an endowment from a single wealthy patron. This financial innovation seems appropriate given the economic emphasis of both the *Education* and Locke's board of trade memorandum; the Society also drew heavily on Locke's working-school model for its own establishments, including the ages when children would be admitted or apprenticed, the kind of labor they would be set to, and the ultimate goal of making each working school as financially independent as possible. The SPCK coordinated from London a broad campaign that included not only England but also Scotland, Ireland, and Wales. Though the Society records were often feebly maintained and are unreliable for the last half of the eighteenth century, they show that by 1723 there were in the country parishes of the British Isles at least 1,329 schools, a number that slowly increased until the end of the century. As the best historian of the movement, Mary Jones, reports, the pace of instituting charity schools, especially in Scotland and Wales, was often explosive: in Scotland, for example, between 1709 and 1730, more than five hundred schools were added to those already in place.[51]

At any given time during the eighteenth century, the number of working schools generally amounted to no more than one-fourth of the charity school establishments, although at various points along the way—motivated by uneasiness concerning the poor acquiring a "literary" education, by enthusiasm to increase national productivity, or by the commitment to ensuring the working classes' availability for labor—working schools became the main priority for Society administrators, parish clergy, and subscribing donors alike, causing their numbers to surge periodically. The interest in working schools was particularly high pitched in England during the early 1700s and again in the last decades of the century, and in Ireland from 1720 to 1750; in Scotland and Wales, working schools received less, though concerted, attention.[52] Charity schools of all kinds ended up drawing on a supervisory organization for their education, because instructing large numbers of pupils with few teachers required it, regardless of whether the content was reading, writing, religious dogma, spinning, or husbandry. For the purpose of considering briefly how supervisory structure informed actual pedagogical practice, I will concentrate on examples of working schools.

In England, by 1704, the Grey Coat Hospital in Westminster was one of the first schools to introduce spinning wheels and spinning mistresses to train children, particularly young girls, in manual labor, which was supplemented by religious instruction. Along with the schools at Findon and Artleborough, both in Northamptonshire, it provided impetus for other similar workhouse-schools that soon appeared across the country, a development heavily endorsed in the SPCK's circulating letters which used language reminiscent of Locke's: they urged "introducing all proper measures to inure children to labour and industry," lest "the advantages they received from a pious education should incline them to put too great a value upon themselves."[53] Perhaps the best example of supervisory education in action is the Artleborough institution, which at its peak housed more than one hundred students and was operated— by all accounts, single-handedly—by Mrs. Harris, whose indefatigable energy and resourcefulness became legendary in charity school annals. She instructed the children in church catechism, trained them in knitting and spinning, gathered stubble with them in harvest time, taught them to sing, as well as orchestrated the administrative duties of bookkeeping and purchases. All this was best accomplished by the ability to observe and assist her students' progress as efficiently as possible, an arrangement made effective as much by an architectural design that anticipated Jeremy Bentham's Panopticon, as by diligence: as Jones reports, "during the fifteen hours' day the mistress was on constant duty in a school-house constructed so that she might see two floors at the same time, and direct and order all the children at pleasure."[54] In other schools the same effect was achieved by housing instruction in factorylike buildings, or, where it was possible, by reducing the student-to-teacher ratio, but in all events the prerogative was the easy surveillance of student activity.

In Ireland, a similar approach of compartmentalizing pupils' tasks into individualized spaces, while simultaneously coordinating them within a broadly superintended program, was applied to the endeavors of both agriculture and weaving. In the highly praised project by Sir Richard Cox at Donmanway, for instance, large fields were divided into smaller, individualized enclosures for raising flax, and students were given prizes for the best crop, as well as for spinning and weaving the flax. This allowed for motivating individual effort and learning while keeping them incorporated within the accomplishments of the student body as a whole; and in this context, Jones's remark that the "morals of old and young [were] carefully inspected" (237) suggests the supervisory character of the school. That prospect is confirmed by a report written in 1721 about another institution, the Green Coat Hospital in Cork, which endorsed supervisory gentleness in the interest of Protestant and nationalist ascendancy: "forasmuch as mild and gentle Methods are in their own nature most effectual for the Propagation of Religion, this may be justly reckon'd a farther Reason for *Erecting* Charity Schools in this Kingdom, wherein *Children* of *Popish Natives* being Instructed, Cloathed, and taken Care of along with our own, may be won by our affectionate Endeavours; that the *whole Nation* may become *Protestant* and *English*."[55]

Ireland proved to be an intense laboratory for educational reform and experiment, in part because for the English authorities, the populace's attachments to Popish doctrine and seditious political sentiment were vices frequently linked to the degeneracy of pandemic sloth. In 1733, in response to a petition to the king requesting aid "to Instruct these great Numbers of People in the Principles of True Religion and Loyalty," in order to avoid the "Prospect . . . that Superstition, Idolatry, and Disaffection will, from Generation to Generation, be propagated among them," the Incorporated Society in Dublin for Promoting English Protestant Schools in Ireland was granted a patent and funding by the crown.[56] The Dublin Society's rapid success with working schools similar to Richard Cox's led in 1747 to the first parliamentary grant to elementary education in the history of the United Kingdom; those funds continued to flow until the turn of the nineteenth century. The celebrated achievements of the Society also spurred on the activities of other organizations, including the Royal Dublin Society, which also instituted agricultural working schools that Jones aptly terms "their little labour colonies" (241). As the seal of one society read, the byword was "Religione et Labore." The promise of a neatly tilled Ireland, well spun with patriotic Protestantism, fueled one of the first British attempts at a nationalized education supervised and guided by the agenda of watchful English policy.

Despite the often-recounted triumphs of the Mrs. Harrises or Richard Coxes, the working charity school did not prove to be an unmitigated success. Trustees found the requirements daunting, if not frequently defeating, because it was difficult to ensure regular labor from the children, locate skilled workers who could also teach effectively, juggle financial obligations, and find a market for produced goods that were often substandard or defective. Many working schools closed or discontinued a program teaching skilled labor, including the Grey Coat Hospital, having become convinced that the concept was overly ambitious and impracticable. Still, that did not prevent the periodic revival of working-school proposals during the rest of the century.[57] (They became particularly popular once again in the 1780s and 1790s under the rubric of "schools of industry," and were championed by the pious ideals of people such as Sarah Trimmer, Hannah More, and Robert Raikes.)

What may be the institutional apotheosis of supervisory education for teaching the poor would come in the early nineteenth century, when Andrew Bell and Joseph Lancaster independently devised what came to be called the "Mutual or Monitorial System" of instruction. Bell worked from his experience with a charity school in Madras, India, where the main issue was establishing a firm hand over numerous students; Lancaster's method grew from his concern to reduce drastically the cost of financing schooling for the poor. Both their proposals shared the plan of using elder pupils to serve as monitors, tutors, or assistant teachers, thereby increasing the scope of instruction possible while reducing the task of the teacher in charge, as well as the lessons' expense. Here supervision became delegated across a hierarchical scale of authority, and it was facilitated by the essential arrangement (according to Jones) of "a large room, with desks around the walls for the writing lessons, and a floor space chalked out into squares, in which the children stood in classes for their lessons."[58]

Unlike supervisory pedagogy, this approach relied heavily on memorization, although it similarly stressed the importance of moral instruction. The most striking aspect of this monitorial concept, however, was how it revised and broadened a supervisory program's effectiveness. As Lancaster puts it in *The British System of Education*:

> The Master should be a silent by-stander and inspector. What a master says should be done; but if he teaches on this system, . . . *the system*, not the master's vague, discretionary, uncertain judgment, will be in practice. . . . In a common school the authority of the master is personal, and the rod is his sceptre. His absence is the immediate signal for confusion and riot; and in his absence his assistants will rarely be minded. But in a school properly regulated and conducted on my plan, when the master leaves school, the business will go on as well as in his absence as in his presence, because the authority is not *personal*. This mode of ensuring obedience is a novelty in the history of education.[59]

One of the key aspects of this newly efficient system is that its ambition to evacuate personal "tutorial" authority in order to replace it with pedagogical systemization comes the closest of any preceding instructional projects to realizing Bentham's panoptic vision. Moreover, in putting behind the ambivalence characteristic of previous charity school curricula split between the paradigms of industry and "learning," this approach readily meshed them at the

FIGURE 23. John Lancaster, *The British System of Education*, pl. 4, 1810. This engraving illustrates the Monitorial System's efficiency and cost-effectiveness: eight groups of seven boys each are being taught by tutors who are only slightly older than their pupils. Courtesy The Huntington Library, San Marino, California.

level of organizational administration. Figure 23, one of Lancaster's illustrations of the monitorial system, shows that consolidation of purpose was made possible by the system's neat efficiency, as well as by its ability to reproduce the same instructional unit ad infinitum into the projected horizon of further pedagogical necessity (here, proceeding visually off to the upper-left side of the engraving).[60] Not surprisingly then, the similarity between the mechanical composition of monitorial schools and that of the new factories was not lost on contemporaries. As one educational commentator wrote, "The principle in schools and manufactories is the same. The grand principle of Dr Bell's System is the division of labour applied to intellectual purposes."[61] But as I will suggest in a moment, examining the case of previous early modern versions of disciplinary organization, particularly among women, presents a very different sort of institution.

Mary Astell's Female Academy and the Supervision of Friendship

It is no accident that Joseph Lancaster's Monitorial System has such a powerful resonance with Foucault's description of discipline in action, because Lancaster, like Andrew Bell, was a contemporary of Bentham, Foucault's discipliner par excellence. However, the austerity of educational programs such as both Lancaster's and Bell's—including their magisterial orchestration of authority and their factorylike production of conformity—should be correlated to the particular conditions of class or rank in which they functioned. In the case of Bell, the ideological dynamics of colonialism are also relevant, since his school system was transplanted from India in order to reach the poor in Britain. The way gender is imbricated in pedagogical institutionalization is equally significant, moreover, though up to this point the lot of poor boys and girls in the charity school system has seemed equally grim. There were several ways in which gender served to organize and differentiate working-school operations, including the assignment of labor based on assumptions about masculine or feminine abilities—such as

spinning and weaving for young girls, versus husbandry or carpen-
try for young boys—and the focus in related tracts or treatises (or
Locke's board proposal) on how to reclaim supposedly derelict
mothers for better motherhood by inducing them to work in poor-
house settings much like the ones faced by their children.

For the moment, however, I want to consider briefly the ways
that the differences of both gender and upper-class standards could
also generate very different circumstances for a pious education, by
way of illustrating that especially in the hands of women, the apparent monolith of early modern disciplinary practice could in fact
be seriously improvised. Mary Astell is a good case in point: she
was intimately involved in the charity school movement while also
having proposed her own "academical retreat" for women in part
I of *A Serious Proposal to the Ladies* (1694) and reiterating its prospective value in part II (1697). As Ruth Perry points out, Astell
had a high profile in early eighteenth-century England as a pa-
troness of philanthropic projects, and as a sponsor of charity
schools, her name was often associated with those of other SPCK
reformers such as Robert Nelson and Dr. John Sharp.[62] Astell
therefore clearly supported the work the charity school movement
was doing in English culture, although as we have already seen in
chapter 1, her proposed academy for women who were from the
upper-middle-class, gentry, or nobility took on a very different social complexion.

In arguing that the clamors of everyday English life had had
the deleterious effect on women of at least distracting them from
more important intellectual and spiritual concerns, Astell proposed
that her female readers should join together in sponsoring a form
of "*Religious Retirement*": it would serve a dual purpose as "a Retreat from the World for those who desire that advantage; but
likewise, an institution and previous discipline, to fit us to do the greatest good in it."[63] In effect, Astell's school would be only a temporary oasis for women's study and self-examination, before they
reentered the world to take up their lives as daughters, wives, or
mothers.[64] Her institute would further promote a utopian community of women who could escape from what Astell characterized as
men's "Tyranny" in perpetuating women's "Ignorance and Folly,

since it is in your Power," she exhorts her female readers, "to regain your Freedom, if you please but t'endeavour it."[65] It would also shift women's preoccupation with the baubles of novelty to a new sense of idealized feminine solidarity:

> Happy Retreat! which will be the introducing you into such a *Paradise* as your Mother *Eve* forfeited, where you shall feast on Pleasures, that do not, like those of the World, disappoint your expectations, pall your Appetites, and by the disgust they give you, put you on the fruitless search after new Delights . . . ; but such as will make you truly happy *now*, and prepare you to be *perfectly* so hereafter. Here are no Serpents to deceive you, whilst you entertain your selves in these delicious Gardens. (pt. I:67–68)

In the reconstituted, exclusively female paradise of Astell's academy, then, there would not be even the suggestion of men's dangerous influence represented by the emblem of the phallic serpent. Hence the husbandry of Astell's pedagogy would aspire to Edenic proportions.[66]

Still, the gentle and genteel community Astell describes would also mean hard work, since as her earlier mention of "discipline" indicates, she insists that her female pupils should apply themselves constantly to reading mainly pious and religious texts, examining their inner lives, and finding charitable ways put their new enlightenment into practice. Astell strives in her description of these pupils' education, moreover, to formulate an ideal balance between rigorous training and tolerant easiness. In part I of *The Serious Proposal*, for example, Astell denominated her retreat a definitively Protestant "*Monast[e]ry*" which, rather than apply the strict dogmatism of that usually Roman Catholic institution, would sponsor a more open encouragement of inquiry and self-motivation (pt. I:60). (Later, in part II, given her critics' complaint about Popish taint, Astell emended her description of her academy to "Seminary" [21].) Therefore she explains that in her academy,

> Piety shall not be roughly impos'd, but wisely insinuated by a perpetual Display of the Beauties of Religion in an exemplary Conversation, the continual and most powerful Sermon of an holy Life. And since Inclination can't be forc'd, (and nothing makes people more uneasy than the fettering themselves with unnecessary Bonds) there

shall be no Vows or irrevocable Obligations, not so much as the fear of Reproach to keep our Ladies here any longer than they desire. (pt. I:104–5)

As further evidence that Astell aims to moderate discipline with gentleness, she describes the relationship between her students and tutors in markedly supervisory terms, which include the vocabulary of inspection, natural indoctrination, and medicinal remedy. This tensile combination merits quoting her account at length: the tutors, she explains, will be

> Watching over their [the women inmates'] souls with tenderness and prudence; applying Medicines with sweetness & affability. Sagacious in discovering the very approaches of a fault, wise in preventing, and charitable in bearing with all pityable Infirmities. The sweetness of whose Nature is commensurate to all the rest of their good Qualities. . . . Yet know how to assert their Authority when there is just occasion for it, and will not prejudice their Charge, by an indiscreet remissness and loosning the Reins of discipline. Yet what occasion will there be for rigour, when the design is to represent Vertue in all her Charms and native Loveliness, which must needs attract the eyes, and enamour the hearts of all who behold her? To joyn the sweetness of Humanity to the strictness of Philosophy, that both together being improv'd and heighten'd by grace, may make up an accomplish'd *Christian*. (pt. I:103–4)

As one last component in judiciously relaxing the "Reins of discipline," Astell also puts special emphasis on the function of friendship not only between her teachers and students but also among the students themselves. The idea of friendship's pedagogical value was not a new one. In Locke's account, a tutor should employ a companionate friendliness after a more stern assertion of authority during a pupil's younger years. Much like the master's amicable embrace of Goodchild in *Industry and Idleness*, this strategy served as a form of pedagogical reward. But generally, strong friendship among boys is not much discussed in early modern pedagogical texts. In the education of girls, by contrast, some male educationalists, such as François Fénelon and John Essex, were emphatic about the usefulness of promoting friendship between a student and her peers. As Fénelon put it, the point was to create in a girl "an affection for those Persons who may be profitable to her. Friendship will well near lead to all those things which you can expect from her: You have by this a certain Bond to draw her to Goodness."[67]

In Astell's hands, by contrast, the idea of female friendship serves less as a useful device to induce pupils' affectionate emulation of moral examples, than it does as a means by which to model women's relationships long after they have left her institution. As she notes, friendship is "without doubt, the best Instructor to teach us our duty to our Neighbour, and a most excellent Monitor to excite us to make payment as far as our power will reach."[68] In effect, the "Monitor" Astell invokes functions as a feminized, displaced version of either the tutors' superintending gaze or a possibly centripetal point of social surveillance akin to Foucault's description. This improvised concept of pedagogical inspection, furthermore, functions at its best as a *de*centralized, disseminating version of educational inspection forming female solidarity. In Astell's words, nothing "shou'd hinder them [the female students] from entring into an holy combination to watch over each other for Good, to advise, encourage and direct, and to observe the minutest fault in order to its amendment. The truest effect of love being to endeavour the bettering the beloved Person" (pt. I:140).

A particularly vivid example of how Astell's proposal for supervision and female friendship could take concrete fictional form emerges in Sarah Scott's *Millenium Hall* (1762), a novel that seems in many ways to have adopted and enlarged Astell's challenge to imagine a new social order for English women. In Scott's utopian story, the middle- and upper-class women who have established Millenium Hall have succeeded in achieving a more permanent version of Astell's Edenic academy, since as the narrator tells us, their pastoral community has become an "earthly paradise" whose "enchanted ground" provides a refuge for women who wish to live genuinely educated, pious, and productive lives for the rest of their years.[69] For the more privileged members, a rigorous attention to virtuous behavior and its corresponding manifestation in physiognomical expression is combined with a sense of community based on egalitarian friendship, since Millenium Hall's society is founded on the principles of "mutual confidence, reciprocal services, and correspondent affections."[70] There is no better example of mutual, friendly instruction than the story of the cofounders of Millenium Hall, Miss Louisa Mancel and Miss Melvyn, who in their childhood became friends at a girls' boarding school whose superficial curriculum prompted them to initiate their own, more substantial, education. As the elder of the two (at about fourteen years old to Louisa's ten), Miss Melvyn improves Louisa's mind with reading books on geography, philosophy, and Christian devotion (91), but her younger charge proves to enhance Miss Melvyn's sensibility as well when Louisa proposes to pay for Miss Melvyn's extra lessons in other subjects. Despite her conviction that the boundaries of property were "broke down by true friendship; and all property laid in one undistinguished common," Miss Melvyn refuses her companion's repeated offers until she realizes she has found "a superior degree of delicacy, and a generosity much more exalted, in one so young, than she had felt in herself" (93). In much the same way Astell describes the benefits of mutual inspection, Miss Melvyn revises her estimate of her own and Louisa's virtue, forming a bond the two will use later as a model for establishing Millenium Hall's ideal community. Inspired by Miss Melvyn's example, Louisa learns to evaluate her own imperfections "with very scrutinizing and rigid eyes," gaining a sense of autonomy and accountability that will serve as the basis for her later life in Scott's exemplary society.[71]

Ultimately, however, in both Astell's proposed academy and Scott's fictional feminine retreat, the agency of friendship would not completely disperse or dislocate the effects of supervisory education's cultural and ideological effects on upper-class women. But Astell's example suggests that in the attempt to improvise on the more restrictive, masculinist versions of instruction available in early modern England, promoting the love of friendship among women could have a significant role not only in resisting the "Tyranny" of men's cultural privilege that Astell mentions but also in formulating an alternative, more egalitarian locus for conducting education and social relations generally.[72] In a sense, the phrase "supervision of friendship" itself suggests the double valence that educational sorority would have in Astell's formulation, because on the one hand, it indicates the way that women's localized companionships could potentially atomize or at least deflect disciplinary structures, while on the other, it marks the way that friendship could remain still one more property "of" supervision—and thereby assimilated within that larger edifice.

In the case of *Millenium Hall*, Scott's ambivalent relation to supervision is more pronounced, since in addition to maintaining egalitarian relations among themselves as peers, the upper-class members of her utopian society administer separate communities within the whole that are charitable institutions for the poor, destitute, and even the physically disabled. In providing housing for both elderly and young women—the latter who are eventually given in marriage to men of the appropriate virtue and station— the elite women of Millenium Hall offer genuine help to their social inferiors while constantly maintaining the original standards of division between the working and upper classes. In ways reminiscent of the age's charity schools, the administrators of Millenium Hall vigorously educate their charges in Christian values, use daily and "particular inspection over the performance of these girls," and train them "either for the care of a house or children" (160). As the narrator reports, they "watch with so careful an eye over the conduct of these young people, as proves of much greater service to them than the money they bestow" (167). In effect, the society of Millenium Hall forms two societies, combining a form of feminist, decentered education among peers comparable to Astell's academy with the institutional techniques of charity schools, which sustain the very economic inequities affecting women in the first place.

Despite that ambiguity in both Scott's and Astell's genial academies, however, their description of a paradisal institution for women had one further important function, because rather than being a form of Christian nostalgia, it was in fact a way to suggest a dramatically different model for the formation of knowledge than the one that was historically part of the Western tradition. A clue to this improvisation on Paradise appears when Astell describes the inevitable ways that women's improved education would disturb the status quo arrangement men had usually enjoyed: "Men will resent it," she tells her female readers, "to have their enclosure broke down, and Women invited to tast[e] of that Tree of Knowledge they have so long unjustly *monopoliz'd.*"[73] This brief reformulation of the original Fall story captures precisely the nature of Astell's general educational argument, because rather than imagine the province of knowledge as forbidden by virtue of divine decree, it underscores that, especially in the case for women, knowledge had been prohibited to them on the basis of *cultural* narrowness—on the privileges men had arbitrarily usurped for themselves, observable in most of the male characters who populate Scott's novel, including Sir Charles Melvyn, Mr. Hintman, and Mr. Morgan. Thus in contrast to the usual cast given in the West to the acquisition of knowledge, Astell's approach indicates that ignorance and innocence are not in any way genuinely congruent—that, in other words, women's acquisition of "learning" would be no fall from grace (defined socially or otherwise), and that for them, *tasting*, rather than avoiding, the Tree of Knowledge was not only their prerogative but also their spiritual obligation. In the meantime, Astell would also limit to some extent the range of knowledge proper for her students; hence in claiming that they should concentrate on reading only those "useful Authors" whose work had immediate applications to religious piety, Astell erects a secondary, though less formidable, "enclosure" that would demarcate the distinction between men's and women's domains of knowledge (pt. I:77). But even at that, Astell's revised Eden suggests an enormously different approach to female education, because it implicitly invokes the claim made previously by Bathsua Makin, for instance, that historically, women in early modern England had lost a legacy of female learning that had its origins in antiquity. In 1673, the title of Makin's treatise provided her main thesis—*An Essay To Revive the Antient Education of Gentlewomen, in Religion, Manners, Arts & Tongues*—which argued that since biblical and classical times there had been a substantial tradition of learned women who had been linguists, orators, logicians, philosophers, mathematicians, and poets. Reclaiming this tradition, Makin explained, could also have the kind of spiritual benefits Astell imagined, since "Many Women have improved their humane Knowledge, [which] . . . by Gods Blessing hath been a means of their obtaining Spiritual Knowledg[e]."[74] In Astell's case, she endorsed a smaller corpus of works for women's reading, while Scott remained relatively vague about what selection of texts would be appropriate. But both women's academies nonetheless pointed to a comparable way back to both the Eden of women's spiritual enlightenment and the lost historical origins of female erudition.

Ultimately, even given its roots in the historiography of female learning, Astell's proposal for an Edenic female community may retain an aura of otherworldliness. But for the purpose of considering the genuine cultural work Astell's ideas could do in early eighteenth-century England, there is really no liability in remembering, for instance, that Astell's academy was never finally built. Like Bentham's Panopticon, which was also never constructed, Astell's school is an idealized model that found its way through other channels into English discourse and culture, as exhibited in the case of *Millenium Hall.* The point in future discussions will be to trace the earlier connections that run from Astell's pastoral representation of female friendship and self-enlargement via education to the literary practice of authors such as Charlotte Lennox and Eliza Haywood, whose work appeared in the decades before Scott's novel.

Whatever may be the very broad points of comparison between Astell's and Bentham's "idealization" of their sociopedagogical institutions, however, the similarities end there. For Bentham, his prison promised the ecstatic result of "Morals reformed—health preserved—industry invigorated—instruction diffused—public burthens lightened—Economy seated, as it were, upon a rock—the gordian knot of the Poor-Laws not cut, but untied—all by a simple idea in Architecture!"[75] In Astell's case, however, the social "knot" of gendered hegemony could not be so easily resolved—she proposed instead the more localized, pragmatic approach of forming powerful intellectual and emotional ties among better educated, and thereby more independent, upper-class women. While that aim may seem modest, Astell realized that it could create an important rift in the cultural privileges men were accustomed to enjoying, and Scott later confirmed her conviction that women could challenge the gendered inequities of English life. In chapter 5, I will explore how women's fiction often captured the same sense of disruption when female characters asserted their desire for their own kind of knowledge. What is more, in Lennox's *Female Quixote* and Haywood's *Betsy Thoughtless*, feminized pedagogical friendship also plays a significant part in these authors' revaluation of women's socialization: at the very least, it offers a temporary alternative to traditional, masculinist intervention (as for Arabella), and at its best, it provides a crucial rational guide in the face of moral confusion and even the emotional violence exerted by men (in the case of Betsy).

Political Peregrinations: Education's Novel Experiment

In the picture of eighteenth-century England traced thus far, the idea of public privacy could be both a capacious and a strikingly diverse category, since it was constituted by a variety of social, cultural, and discursive phenomena—including Lockean pedagogy, physiognomical semiotics, popular media, charity and working schools, and feminist formulations of ideal community. These elements formed a composite, but by no means complete, definition of the new concept, and while Locke's particular depiction of exteriorized identity was influential, it was also located within a much larger sociopolitical network of revisionist or competing discourses and institutions. This important point brings us back to the issue of eighteenth-century republicanism and its perspective of civic humanism, because while often drawing on the tenets of Christian faith, the protocols of supervisory education provided partial grounds for negotiating a practical working relation among Lockean, republican, or potentially other political agendas. From that final point, we can survey the novel's general relation to the newly defined intersection of private and public life.

As elaborated earlier, Pocock considers the Lockean formula of universal natural rights adjudicated by civil government fundamentally incompatible with civic humanism's concept of communal maintenance of civil virtue. But this ideological divide can be breached even further than has been suggested so far if we consider Foucault's comment on the relation between a political system based on rights and the function of disciplines:

Historically, the process by which the bourgeoisie became in the course of the eighteenth century the politically dominant class was masked by the establishment of an explicit, coded, and formally egalitarian juridical framework, made possible by the organization of a parliamentary, representative régime. But the development and generalization of disciplinary mechanisms constituted the other, dark side of these processes. The general juridical form that guaranteed a system of rights that were egalitarian in principle was supported by these tiny, everyday, physical mechanisms, by all those systems of micro-power that are essentially non-egalitarian and asymmetrical that we call the disciplines. . . . The real, corporal disciplines constituted the foundation of the formal, juridical liberties.[76]

Without assuming so readily that the disciplines are more "real" than their juridical or discursive counterparts, we can detect here a suggestive way to revaluate the import of Locke's work to eighteenth-century political thinking and practice. Certainly his *Essay* had described with philosophical rigor and rhetorical persuasiveness the worst enemy of republican civic virtue—unpredictable individuality. In the face of that daunting explanation of individual intransigency, coupled with the perception of alarmingly rampant self-promotion and avarice, republicanism needed all the help it could get to align citizens' *virtù* with public virtue. Thus one of the instruments that could offer such help was the operation of supervisory management—sometimes articulated in specifically Lockean terms and sometimes in others—not because it could always ensure that alignment, but because it offered the polity a way to perceive immediately the threat of incorrigible self-interest and to respond in turn with appropriate corrective or protective measures.

Assessing in full the extent to which advocates of republicanism invoked a supervisory educational vocabulary would no doubt pose an intricate and daunting task for any historical account of early modern English culture. But I will at least suggest that there is a strong chance that for eighteenth-century writers or politicians, who had probably drawn a less adamantine boundary between republican and Lockean concepts than has Pocock, the prospect of a pragmatic and even piecemeal accommodation between civic humanism and supervisory education was not unthinkable for the purposes of dealing with specific and concrete social problems. It is here that observant education's functional indeterminacy is crucial: that pliancy could make the articulation of public privacy a tractable model for adoption or emendation by diverse ideological elements, whether republican, Christian, or otherwise reformist. If, for instance, the individual self could be exteriorized, the citizen made private and (nominally) equal yet public and unequal, then that characterization offered a provisional purchase for republican application. The differences, to be sure, would always offer resistance to such efforts: the main friction would be the difference in emphasis between public *participation* (in republican terms) and public *management* (in the disciplinary, supervisory sense). As one example of the attempt to negotiate that connection, in *The Fable of the Bees* Bernard Mandeville's peculiar formula of "private vice, public benefits" provided precisely the grounds for drawing on both an empiricist vocabulary for individual motivation and a republican emphasis on the public domain, with an eye toward exploring both private and public approaches to moral standards.[77]

There would also be other ways that eighteenth-century authors would tie republican rhetoric about the commonweal to a concern about education that sometimes also invoked supervisory ideas. One particularly urgent issue was the prospect of preserving the blessings of the Revolution of 1688: in *Cato's Letters* (1723), John Trenchard and Thomas Gordon claimed that there had been a drastic social degeneration in England after the revolution's promising turn of events, because the country's leaders became interested in fostering their own welfare, rather than building on the people's new freedoms. Hence, they explain:

> Nothing was ever done to rectify or regulate the Education of Youth, the Source of all our other Evils; but Schools of Literature were suffered to continue under the Direction of the Enemies to all sound Literature and publick Virtue: Liberty, being deserted by her old Friends, fell of Course into the Hands of her Enemies, and so Liberty was turned upon Liberty.[78]

Here Trenchard and Gordon agree with the supervisory principle that in education, liberty must be deftly guided with wise constraint. And they combine this conclusion with the common republican theme that the nation must maintain constant vigil against the deteriorating effects of historical change induced by individual self-interest, confirming Pocock's observation that education in England had a "long career as a perceived mode of counteracting the course of social development."[79]

After the Jacobite uprising of 1745, in addition to Fielding's stern advocacy of "inspecting" the political credentials of school teachers, others such as James Burgh, in his aptly titled *Britain's Remembrancer: Or, the Danger Not Over* (1746), perceived the rebellion as divine punishment for the English people's sins, particularly their failure in an age of wealth and prosperity—two of the greatest threats to the republic's civic integrity—to maintain the traditional standards regarding everything from the times of getting up in the morning to the more vital need to teach children properly. In fact, according to Burgh, these two things are symptoms of the same general national decline from England's idealized past. He laments the present conditions this way:

> Where are the sober and regular Manners of our Fathers, when it was the constant Custom for the Citizens to rise betimes according to the Order of Nature. . . . When the Exchange was shut at Twelve, and Dinner over every where by One; when they spent their Evenings at home in instructing their Children, Apprentices and Servants, in the Principles of Virtue and Religion, and concluded every Day with the laudable Exercise of Family-devotion?[80]

Having invoked a kind of republican nostalgia, Burgh finds present-day England alarmingly changed; among the signs of social decay in his contemporaneous English citizens is the fact that "the joking Club, the wanton Play-house in Winter, and the luxurious Musick-Garden in Summer, call them from the peaceful Enjoyment of their Families at home, [and] from the Instruction of their Children and Domesticks."[81] But rather than devote his time to promoting the potential benefits of supervisory education, Burgh remains preoccupied with their deplorable lack.

The case of Thomas Sheridan, however, deserves more extensive exploration, because his work is a telling example of the tripartite alliance of republican, liberal, and Christian themes invoked earlier in this chapter. On the face of it, Sheridan makes an argument similar to Burgh's in a treatise whose protracted title delivers his claim: *British Education; or the Source of the Disorder of Great Britain, Being an Essay toward proving that the immorality, ignorance and false tasks which so generally prevail are the natural and necessary consequences of the present defective system of education* (1756). From that point, Sheridan proceeds to describe a program of active reform far more explicit than Burgh suggests: drawing on a Christian resolve against "irreligion," he affiliates the concerns of civic humanism with the aim of deploying the techniques of supervisory instruction.[82] Sheridan's discussion is thoroughly republican in emphasizing the need to restore an original sense of civic responsibility based on classical models, which means in part improving the education of gentlemen, since they are "born to be legislators, . . . the bulwarks of our constitution" (25). But in also drawing heavily on Locke's *Education*, Sheridan proposes a hybrid project that becomes unmistakably clear when he praises both Locke and Milton as the "two eminent physicians" who had helpfully diagnosed the English "disease," as he frequently puts it, of faulty education.[83] In effect, Sheridan has made Milton, a classical republican to the last, an educational compatriot of Locke, whose political views were drastically incompatible with Milton's. And yet at the level of pedagogical procedure, Sheridan is confident that his two educational heroes can together provide a useful prototype of social reform.

This composite approach would of course have serious complications. In terms comparable to the republican notion of rule by the One, the Few, and the Many, Sheridan describes the English state as a political composite of three principles of government: the first is the law, which rules by fear; the second is the monarch's employment of honorific reward; and the third is the "legislative or republican part," which operates on the basis of virtue (41). But Sheridan also counters the implacable rule of the law by applying Locke's premise of gentle, noncoercive education to the way that Christian religion should unify the nation: Christianity's role, he says, should be to "direct, [rather] than govern; [to] restrain, [rather] than impel," giving "no umbrage to a free people" (44). The strain of this combination is further exacerbated when Sheridan admits that the *Education* may not offer a complete solution for the republic because "Locke . . . seems to despair of any effectual reformation in the publick established system; he has therefore turned his whole thoughts towards private education." That will not be a genuine remedy, Sheridan contends, because Locke's "method is the best calculated for despotick states, and if it became general, wou'd be the surest means to establish arbitrary power" (25–26). Hence an emphasis on the polity's public liberties becomes the grounds for rejecting private instruction.

Despite those difficulties in allying a republican and Lockean approach to the public sphere, Sheridan offers another way to accommodate that combination when he describes his own version of public privacy by proposing to "revive the long lost art of oratory" (vi). Oratorical skills should be inculcated in gentlemen, says Sheridan, because they will provide the traditional benefits of making young men effective leaders while also bolstering the persuasive abilities of the clergy. But in addition, oratory provides a way to measure the population's successful internalization of sound English values. When "eloquence was despised, all men were at liberty to speak their thoughts publickly in their own manner" (111), thereby inflicting their lack of morality or wisdom on everyone. But a systematic promotion of eloquent speech, asserts Sheridan, would produce an eminently tangible mark of personal virtue that could assure the public of one's public reliability. In the face of degenerating adherence to republican conduct, as well as his own more liberal perception of individual prerogative, Sheridan has in effect formed an overdetermined national project made possible by the equally overdetermined realm of citizens' public privacy. The result deviates from the usual contours of liberal individualism, since now the realm of personal privacy—even mental space—can be readily infiltrated in the interests of both education and political management. At the same time, the model of republicanism has become modified, so that the overall ability to supervise private desires or impulses has been partially substituted for the traditional requirement that individual citizens be full participants in government. In the end, Sheridan's advocacy of oratory was one way in which the emerging separation of the private from the public sphere could be compensated for by inventing a liminal zone between social and personal life. And the result was a provisional domain in which liberal and republican perspectives could form at least an uneasy association in order to save the nation from moral and political deterioration.

Despite Sheridan's ambivalence about Lockean pedagogy, an underlying similarity remains in that, as with Locke's memorandum to the Board of Trade, education is conceived as both the manifestation of and solution to crisis. Therefore Locke's working-school proposals as well as the *Education*'s more genteel features would be periodically reformulated by authors such as Sheridan in the vigilant need to reinscribe the principles of human management. In addition, on a broader pedagogical canvas, the work of educationalists such as Richard Peers, Mary Chudleigh, Judith Drake, or William Hirst would play a part in offering alternative ways for England to aright itself from what seemed a chronically wholesale lapse in national virtue. The pedagogical task of social remedy, moreover, fell also under the auspices of morally edifying writing, which was the status aspired to by the novel and its generic counterparts. Narrative discourse offered a useful malleability for the purposes of describing educational supervision, but it was also perceived in other contexts as the best means to discern the quality of human motive or character. In 1744, James Harris expressed this view in his discussion of the comparative value of painting versus what he generally termed "poetry":

> As to that System of Qualities *peculiar* to *Aeneas* only, and which alone *properly constitutes his true and real Character*, this would still remain a Secret, and be no way discoverable. For how deduce it from the mere *Lineaments* of a Countenance? Or, if it were deducible, how few Spectators would there be found so sagacious? 'Tis here therefore, that Recourse must be had, not to *Painting*, but to *Poetry*. So *accurate* a Conception of Character can be gathered only from a *Succession of various, and yet consistent Actions*; a Succession, *enabling us to conjecture*, what the Person of the Drama will do in the *future*, from what already he has done in the *past*.[84]

In this case, Harris is skeptical of the kind of physiognomical optimism exhibited by Lavater; relying on the familiar trope of the theater, he places his confidence instead in witnessing a narrative sequence that can surpass the agency of static images. Still, although he is concerned mainly with philosophical questions of genre, Harris's comments have serious social implications, particularly since the ability to predict human behavior also has crucial import for the execution of good "government"—whether pedagogical or political. For those at the other end of the political spectrum (the governed), the narrative abilities of poetry or drama, not to mention the novel, could even be palpably onerous, since they were potentially accessible and instructive to the less educated classes, who bore the burden of being less "sagacious." The popular readership's consumption of morally and politically correct narratives, then, could compel this audience to apply similar lessons to itself.

In these terms, the eighteenth-century novel of education was a concrete form of political practice, not so much because it always explicitly engaged the competing agendas of liberalism or republicanism—frequently, it did not—but because in the process of enunciating or testing particular educational hypotheses (themselves often inflected by such agendas), it could foster a more general inclination in readers to have their private values shaped by the ministrations of public policy. This is to say that the efforts of authors such as Sheridan, who ventured to affiliate liberal and republican versions of education at the level of political argument, served as a discursive backdrop for the novel's more broadly based contribution to the formation of publicly private identity. Conceiving the novel's political function this way presents for cultural analysis an area left unexplored by Foucault's discussion of the disciplines. Although he briefly mentions the general historical "passage from the epic to the novel" as a corollary to the emergence of disciplinary culture,[85] Foucault nowhere considers those discursive formations that functioned in part to support the panoptic institutions he describes, or whose persuasiveness was in turn measurably buttressed by those institutions. In her account of early modern conduct books' construction of interiorized feminine identity, Nancy Armstrong has made an important connection between such discursive formations and the novel's representation of fictional character.[86] Taken together, this chapter and the previous ones add another dimension to that cultural picture by aiming to articulate the dual, semiautonomous phenomena of both supervisory educational narrative

and its corresponding social or institutional practices. One link between them is an analogous pattern of displacement or sedimenta-
tion: if, in Foucault's terms, the operation of the social system rests
on a universally coded, egalitarian scheme of juridical rights, which
is supplemented and put into effect by the constraining machinery
of the "corporal disciplines," then the generic or discursive analogue is the initial installment of philosophical description using rationally sanctioned language, which is then submitted to the
metaphorical elision and narrative sinuosity of pedagogical emplotment. The key words here are *elision* and *sinuosity*: on the one hand,
emplotment can often produce, as John Bender argues, disciplinary
uniformity or calculable order;[87] on the other hand, it can also introduce improvisational elements—intentional or otherwise—that
produce significant reorientations of the cultural system, such as
imagining the productive space of Mary Astell's or Sarah Scott's female academy.

In addition to employing agricultural, medicinal, and theatrical tropes depicting a secularized version of the Fall, the pedagogical plot of the novel of education pursues a trajectory along the
asymmetrical fault line dividing the private from the public
sphere—a division whose precise contours or dynamics would be
widely debated during the eighteenth century, for the most part
without arriving at a general consensus. That feature of the novel
of education is not surprising given the *Education*'s procedures for
externalizing the pupil's internal psychology in the context of a
public economy of morals and social status. But it is also relevant to
the *Education*'s generic status as a written work, for it too is ambivalently constituted as a (revised) public record of what originally
was personal correspondence between Locke and Edward Clarke.
As such, it registers the double marks of familiarity and formality,
of a specific and later a broadly conceived audience, of an apparently genuine reluctance on its author's part to have his private
"thoughts" *public*ized. That aspect of Locke's treatise was often
characteristic of his other texts: as Richetti comments concerning
the *Essay*, "Locke certainly began his work in a private context,
but that privacy became in due course part of his public manner as
a writer."[88] Such ambivalence finds its institutional counterpart in

the charity school movement, which Jones remarks took the "intermediary position between private-venture education on the one hand, and state-controlled education on the other."[89]

In this context, the novel of education's cultural function is to rehearse the competing dynamics of individual privacy and public management, demonstrating in the meantime that they can be tacitly—or sometimes not so tacitly—directed by narrative emplotment and, by implication, the correlative sociopolitical agency of attentive observation and prompt response. The indeterminacy of public privacy, however, is more than a symptom of general (or simple) cultural indecision, for the point is to make the apparent intransigence of that gordian knot (recalling Bentham) ideologically functional by incorporating it within the domain of authorial control, the protagonist's ultimate social conformity, and the novel's obligation to educate the public in moral responsibility. In that sense, rather than heralding what Richard Sennett calls the eighteenth century's "fall of public man,"[90] the novel of education contends with that danger by reinscribing and ultimately subduing it within the formation of the protagonist's publicly scrutable self. Defoe's Robinson Crusoe, like Hogarth's Goodchild, may, on the one hand, provide occasion for celebrating the singular value of individual industriousness or perseverance, but on the other, that individuality is shaped by being eminently legible—both to the eyes of Providence and those of the viewer/reader.

The imperative of social "observation"—as a form of scrutiny as well as conformity to norms—therefore could lessen and perhaps even obviate the scandal often associated with the eighteenth-century novel's appropriation of initially "private" genres, including letters, memoirs, journals, and to some extent autobiographies. Although that tactic was a feature of all sorts of novels, the point for the novel of education was not merely to turn "private" genres inside out, exposing their contents to a generalized readership, but to situate them in such a way that they could elucidate a gradual convergence between malleable individual identity and public criteria for conduct. One way of doing this could be to juxtapose putatively "private" forms against traditionally or recognizably "public" ones, such as dialogues, miscellanies, sermons, tracts, or political pamphlets, thereby providing a context by which the issues and obsessions of individual development could be judged or measured. *The Fable of the Bees* offers a protonovelistic example of that strategy, where Mandeville presents a patchwork of various discourses—including the fabliau, moral diatribe, religious meditation, dialogue, and speculative "history"—to argue his view of education as a precarious process mediating between "private vice" and "public benefits."

In the first novel we will consider in detail, *Robinson Crusoe*, Defoe constructs several layers of "private" discourse around the moral improvement, religious conversion, and economic enlargement of his protagonist. At the center of that work readers are privy to the confidentiality of Crusoe's journal, notably altered by additions intended to clarify the junctures of his progress for a public audience. This portion is framed in turn by a text characteristic of Puritan autobiography, a form created itself by the publication of believers' introspection usually meant at the outset only for private use; and that text is further emended by frequent economic analyses and the language of government and colonization—making Crusoe's individual successes the exemplar of calculable moral and financial values. All of these elements are further compounded by Defoe's goal of combining Puritan doctrine with the more secularized ethos of Lockean supervision.

In Lennox's *Female Quixote*, the permeable line between private and public life comes under pressure in at least two distinct ways. Having imbibed the heady stuff of French romances, Arabella has constructed an imaginary world of heroic virtue she attempts to impose on everyone in her household—and that encounter proves incendiary. As part of her ambitious self-education, Arabella also appropriates the language of "empire" and judicial powers in order to govern entirely her domestic sphere, although ultimately, this conflation of the public and private will end in her capitulation to marital conformity. Juxtaposed against Arabella's overweening ambition, Betsy Thoughtless in Eliza Haywood's novel demonstrates that in midcentury English society, a more promising approach is to acquire an ironic sense of public feminine identity as dramatic performance. For Haywood, the trick is to create for women the ability to distinguish for themselves between their private desires or even resentments of masculine mistreatment and their obligation to fulfill certain public roles—without, in the meantime, creating the specter of feminine duplicity. In Haywood's novel, the metaphor of drama provides the means for staging a "true" fiction encompassing both feminine desire and public obligation.

~~~

CHAPTER FOUR

'Robinson Crusoe,' Education, and Schizophrenic Narrative

Experience, the Instructor of those who can learn of no other Master. . . .

—Henry Fielding,
A Proposal for Making an Effectual Provision for the Poor

Daniel Defoe's concern with education was no less than a life-long preoccupation that manifested itself in a broad array of generic forms and articulated the importance of instruction for all levels of English society. His best-known instructional works include: *The Family Instructor* (1715, vol. 1; 1718, vol. 2), in which he considered a wide range of concerns for middle-class parents, children, and their hired help or apprentices; *The Complete English Tradesman* (1726), in which, while aiming to instruct aspiring businessmen in the protocols of conducting trade, Defoe also discussed how to train servants or employees; *The Compleat English Gentleman* (composed 1728–29; pub. 1890), where he turned his attention to what he characterized as the gross ignorance and lack of moral virtue indulged in by the landed gentry and nobility; and *Of Royall Educa-*

cion (composed 1731; pub. 1895), a manuscript left unfinished at his death. In these works Defoe drew liberally on the forms of the polemical tract, the conduct book, the pedagogical treatise, the moral or religious essay, and also the conventions of dialogue and drama. In some instances, he confined himself to the boundaries of a given generic mode, while in others, as with *The Family Instructor*, he experimented with new possibilities both in representing the process of education and in promoting the direct edification of readers.

For the purposes of considering a discursive link between Defoe's educational writing and his novels, *The Family Instructor* proves to be an ideal site for study, not only because it anticipates several important themes and narrative patterns Defoe uses a few years later in *Robinson Crusoe* (1719), but also because it undoubtedly offers one of Defoe's most innovative approaches to writing about education. As we shall see, Defoe's generic experiments in the *Instructor* prove instrumental to the dynamics of novel writing, particularly in the first volume, where they incorporate several principles of a supervisory educational program while retaining crucial aspects of the Puritan perspective on the patriarchal family.

Pedagogical Writing and the Theatrics of Liberty

As Defoe—or his narrator/commentator—claims early in *The Family Instructor*, one of the chief aims of the work is to illustrate the importance of a familiar Lockean principle: "beginning early the great Work of instructing and managing . . . Children."[1] In fact, in all three stories related in the text, Defoe's concern is the pedagogical situation that stands *after* the most opportune season of educating children has already passed—when parents are confronted by the results of their negligence in providing their children with rigorous religious instruction, or when a tradesman must reform the spiritual backwardness of his adolescent apprentice, or when a husband must contend with his spouse's hardened irreligion, which results from her inadequate schooling at home. This scenario, to be sure, has ready application to what happens in *Robinson Crusoe*, and Defoe's treatment of the problem here has significant bearing on how he portrays Crusoe's development in the novel. The challenge in both works is to confront and transform what Bourdieu and Passeron identify as an established disposition's "durability"—its tendency to perpetuate indefinitely an individual's ideological orientation or social behavior. At the same time, however, the aim will be to install a second, more desirable disposition that will presumably sustain at least the same degree of durability as had the earlier, displaced habitus. In the end, not only is that educational process socially and ideologically complex, but it also requires substantial literary improvisation on Defoe's part in order to represent successfully its tangled intricacy.

In his introductory remarks to the main text, Defoe calls immediate attention to the generic overdeterminacy of *The Family Instructor*, signaling both its multipurpose function and its future malleability for novelistic adaptation. In describing his use of eighteen dialogues in the work, each framed by the narrator's introductory remarks and subsequent commentary, Defoe writes in the preface:

> The whole Work being design'd both to divert and instruct, the Author has endeavoured to adapt it as much as possible to both those Uses, from whence some have call'd it a Religious Play.
>
> It would more have answer'd that Title, had the Author's first Design been pursued, which was to have made it a Drammatick Poem: But the Subject was too solemn, and the Text too copious, to suffer the Restraint on one Hand, or the Excursions on the other, which the Decoration of a Poem would have made necessary.
>
> As to its being called a Play, be it called so if they please; *it must be confest, some Parts of it are too much acted in many Families among us: The Author wishes that either all* our Plays *were as useful for the Improvement and Entertainment of the World, or that* they were *less encouraged.* (preface, n.p.)

Defoe depicts here his difficulty in matching content to form, since the conventions of dramatic poetry appear inappropriate, while the frivolity of plays is unsuitable for the moral seriousness of his message. This dilemma recalls Locke's ambivalence concerning his theatrical metaphor both for educating children as well as composing his treatise: like Locke, Defoe must struggle with the promising boldness of his innovation in the tradition of conduct books while running the risk of undermining his aim to edify readers by employing the techniques of drama—his book too might devolve into mere spectacle. This point has further resonance with Defoe's later claim that at least two of the children he portrays have been profoundly corrupted by play-reading and play-going. His text, oddly enough, must both dramatize and denounce the dangers of the theater.

In this passage, Defoe seems to shrug off this difficulty by literalizing the metaphor of the theater—by quickly shifting his attention to the "real" families his text represents that "act" the roles *The Family Instructor* describes. But this explanation apparently proves insufficient, for he returns to the problem of his chosen method in the following introduction to part 1. At this point, however, the problematic term is not *drama* but *novel*, and this shift in terminology suggests the kind of rationale any early eighteenth-century "novelist" might need to invoke:[2]

> The way I have taken . . . is *entirely New*, and at first *perhaps* it may appear something *Odd*, and the Method may be contemned; But let such blame their own more irregular Tempers, that must have every thing turned into new Models; [and that] must be touch'd with *Novelty*, and have their Fancies humour'd *with the Dress* of a thing; so that if it be what has been said over and over a thousand times, yet if it has but a different colour'd Coat, or a new Feather in its Cap, it pleases and wins upon them, whereas the same Truths written in the divinest Stile in the World, would be flat, stale, and unpleasant without it.
>
> If then, after all the pains which have been taken by ministerial Labour and Instruction, and by the pressing Exhortations and moving Arguments of eminent Divines, even of all Opinions, in their Writings on this Subject, this mean and familiar Method should by its Novelty prevail, this will be a happy Undertaking, but no Reproach at all to the Labours of others. (2–3)

At first it seems that Defoe is proposing a distinction between salutary "newness" and degenerative "novelty." It turns out, however, that he is offering a peculiar defense of novelty by condemning novelty itself, or at least by attacking its most superficial obsession with surface appearance. Furthermore, the question of drama reenters the stage, since Defoe characterizes the fetish of novelty as a fascination with mere costuming or accessorizing. That leaves a paradoxical function for his own work, which must use a "mean and familiar Method" while simultaneously succeeding in its "Novelty."

This double gesture is further underscored in the Newcastle edition of the text, in which Defoe adds the following:

> If you Object against the Novelty or Humour of the Work, blame your own vitiated Appetites which would not relish it in its old and better Dress, not because it was improper or improbable, but because it was old.
>
> *Be it so then* that this is the humour of the Times, and let the Crime of it be never so much to be blam'd, yet *at the same time* that I blame the Cause, I endeavour to comply with the Evil, and first gratify it, in order to reform it.
>
> Since you then will have a Toy, a Novelty, *here it is for you*, read it YE PARENTS who neglect instructing . . . your Children. (3)

While conveying the tone of moral diatribe, this passage suggests a kind of novel vertigo, where solid mooring to traditional precedent becomes impossible, and novelty becomes the standard of both social evils and their reparation. Defoe's best tack must be to trust in his novel method because it is a *moral* novelty, a *sober* drama—but the ambiguities of this strategy remain unresolved, as I will explore later in Defoe's prefatory remarks to *Robinson Crusoe*.

One last feature of this double gesture of novelty is Defoe's curious contention that his work is clearly neither fact nor fiction, an ambiguity that is reminiscent of the characterization of supervisory education by Fénelon, Locke, and others. Defoe reports: "Tho' much of the Story is Historical, and might be made [to] appear to be true in Fact, yet the Author resolving not to give the least hint that should lead to Persons, has been obliged to leave it Uncertain to the Reader, whether it be a History or a Parable" (5). This deliberate uncertainty pertains first of all to Defoe's goal that his work function as "a general Reproach to those that are guilty, [rather] than a pa[r]ticular Satyr upon Persons or Families,"[3] but it also tellingly rehearses the uncertainty Locke describes in the ideal ped-

agogical situation, in which the pupil's learning process is conducted most successfully by his inability to tell the difference between "real" events in his experience and the artificial interventions orchestrated by the tutor. Hence Defoe performs his role as
author in characteristically supervisory fashion, instructing his readers by blurring the distinction between fact and fiction; he even extends that uncertainty to the difference between his identity as the
"genuine" author of the text and the persona of his speaker/
narrator. As his introductory remarks indicate then, Defoe's work is
a textual hybrid, part history and part fiction, part satire and part
religious meditation, part play and part "novel"—attempting to deploy each of these generic modes successfully via the organizing intention of educating adult readers.

In turning to the dialogues, Defoe considers several pedagogical, religious, and family issues, stressing all along that his goal is
genuinely ecumenical, at least in avoiding any partiality concerning
particular Protestant group interests, whether Anglican High
Church or Dissenter (3). His dialogues aim instead to promote a
more inclusive premise regarding the many "Advantages of Religious Conversation" both in the home and the workplace (209).
The *Instructor's* three sections concentrate on the areas Defoe believes need the most attention: first, parents' responsibility to inculcate religious piety in their children at a young age, and failing that,
instituting proper spiritual protocols as soon as they recognize the
error of their previous negligence; second, employers' responsibility not only to ensure their children's religious instruction but also,
as surrogate "parents," to administer the same for their employees
or apprentices; and third, the need for patience, determination, and
generosity of spirit when a spouse needs to be corrected concerning his or her religious duties in the home.

Defoe's dialogues compose a series of conversational vignettes,
relating three distinct narratives. Part 1 tells the story of an urban
middle-class family whose mother and father have neglected the
early religious instruction of their children; after being jolted into
realizing this mistake by the spiritual distress of their youngest son,
Tommy, they begin to stipulate rules of prayer, Scripture reading,
and the like for the entire family. Mary and her older brother (who

remains unnamed), however—the two eldest children apparently in their late teens or early twenties—are outraged at the imposed family dictates, and rebel furiously against the new order.[4] Leaving this situation unresolved until part 3, Defoe's narrator then turns to part 2, which tells the story of two families and their respective employees. The father of the first family is a middle-class clothier, a devout and virtuous man who employs the spiritually untutored apprentice Will; the father of the second family, an Alderman who runs a more lucrative business, has a reputation for an honest but irreligious life, and employs a cherubic apprentice named Tom. The ensuing dialogues happily recount both Will's conversion to Christian piety through Tom's influence, and Tom's master's similar realization that he must take charge of his employees' religious edification. Next, reaching part 3, Defoe's narrator takes up the narrative thread from part 1, presenting the story of Mary's eventual reconciliation with genuine spirituality through the persistence of her long-suffering husband, as well as the dispiriting consequences of her brother's intransigence, which concludes in irreparable alienation from his father and a painful death.

Each of these narratives shares the common situation I mentioned earlier—the problem of children and also adults being past the point of seasonable, ready education; hence parents, their offspring, and those in their employ must all labor under the burden of *re*educating themselves or others. It is a task to which Defoe takes two very different, if not incompatible approaches—the first founded on the principles of gradual, supervisory pedagogy, the second entrusted to the more austere authority of Puritan patriarchy. Defoe's work attempts to negotiate a difficult path between these two perspectives, providing a useful precedent for considering the dynamics of *Robinson Crusoe*.

Although Defoe does not cite the pedagogical work by Locke, Fénelon, or Astell in *The Family Instructor*—in fact, he rarely refers to any earlier authors on education in his pedagogical texts[5]—his discussions of child psychology and pedagogical technique demonstrate a clear understanding of the fundamental precepts attached to indirect instruction while also reflecting a similar approach to creating in individuals a social disposition poised delicately between the imperatives of freedom and conformity. In addition to his emphasis on the importance of early instruction, there are several other telling contact points, including the familiar ideas regarding the dangerous potential of bad habits (63, 68), Defoe's claim that with virtually no prompting, children can learn fundamental spiritual truths by "the mere Power of Natural Reasoning" (58), and his general assumption that moral character is finally more important than knowledge of skills or books.

Before considering the supervisory elements in Defoe's text in detail, we should note here that they draw on and augment the pedagogical principles implicit in casuistry, that long-established discourse concerning matters of conscience based on the notion that inherited moral rules frequently needed to be revaluated in their application to specific circumstances. On that assumption, casuistical analysts wrote to enlighten their readers without dogmatic prescriptions, proceeding instead on the basis of instructive examples that could suggest, rather than dictate, solutions, and they consistently maintained that individual readers always had the prerogative—and burden—of making their own ethical decisions, which should nonetheless be translatable into the terms of recognized morality. As George Starr points out, in *The Family Instructor* Defoe drew heavily on the themes and conventions of casuistry, retaining its penchant for dialogue and episodic narration while also pushing those features one step further into an extended, quasi-fictional exploration of his characters' ethical quandaries.[6] Hence although it was a distinct methodology, casuistical procedure proved amenable to the more dramatic innovations of supervisory education. If casuistry relied on the importance of examples, observant education stressed further the invention of a nearly complete instructional environment, and where casuistry espoused a versatile examination of ideas, supervisory education advocated creating a fluid process in which individuals could apparently learn with natural facility.

Thus while drawing on casuistic principles, *The Family Instructor* approaches supervisory ideals most strikingly in its frequent stress on relaxing the impositions of authority. In cautioning against neglecting children's religious education until "their green and tender Years are past," for instance, Defoe stresses the noncoercive powers of adult authority, employing Locke's corresponding metaphor of pliable wax: in their tender years, he claims, children can be "moulded *like Wax to a Seal*, to receive such first Impressions as the Perswasion and Example of Parents are apt to make."[7] Throughout *The Family Instructor*, Defoe repeatedly points to the enormous impact of adult "example" to bring children gently to proper religious and moral behavior (see, e.g., 41–42, 69, 276) while echoing supervisory education's scaling down of adult power. In part 1 of the text, moreover, the children themselves realize the value of the steady, step-by-step pedagogy of the sort Locke and other educationalists like him espoused. As the eldest brother remarks concerning his parents' sudden imposition of religious instruction, "had they done this *gradually*, and begun it *sooner*, we might by degrees have been brought to ha' *liked it*" (152). Similarly, when describing by what methods a recalcitrant spouse should be educated in proper spiritual conduct, Defoe urges that the goal is to "exhort and perswade, intreat, instruct, and *by all gentle means* if possible, prevail upon and engage one another to a Religious Holy Life" (297); later, echoing this sentiment, one of the characters remarks that Mary, the spouse in question, "may be wrought upon by Degrees to be sensible of her Mistake" (300).

But given the tardy circumstances of these children's education, the supervisory metaphor of gently molding individual character comes under stress, giving way to a more harsh and unpleasant scenario. As Defoe's narrator observes:

> The Heart of the tender Youth, by forbearance of Instruction, grows opinionated, and obstinately embraces the Follies he has been indulg'd in, . . . and this renders late Instruction fruitless: THEN *as to Correction*, the Heart being hardned, as before, by Opinion and Practice, and especially in a Belief that he *ought not to be corrected*, the Rod of Correction has a different Effect; for as *the Blow* of a Stripe makes an Impression on the Heart of a Child, as stamping a Seal does upon the soft Wax, the Reproof even of Words on the same Heart when grown up, and made hard, is like striking upon Steel, which instead of making an Impression *on the Metal*, darts back sparks of Fire in your Face. (68–69)

Here Defoe reveals a readiness for corporal punishment that would probably unnerve a supervisory educator's resolve to save it as a last resort, but in addition to that, Defoe's suggestion is that despite the partial usefulness of dealing gently with children such as Mary, who in part 3 is already a full-grown (and married) woman, something more dire is needed, which Defoe generally presents as the staunch and resolute reassertion of parental prerogative, particularly in the person of the father, who, in Puritan terms, embodies the proper head of familial and spiritual order.

In fact, Defoe seems to be of two minds regarding the imposition of stern authority when gentler methods prove ineffectual. On the one hand, at times his narrator presents that step as simply the only (if regrettable) alternative at hand given the imminent danger that children's religious edification may go entirely unaccomplished—much like Locke's reluctant acknowledgment that severe punishment may finally be necessary for intractable pupils. On the other hand, Defoe's commentator sometimes suggests that such last-ditch efforts are excruciating precisely because of earlier "forbearance" or leniency—because the commanding authority of the family patriarch was not soundly established from the beginning. And that patriarchal authority differs markedly from the one described by Locke or Fénelon, because rather than merely setting, as unobtrusively as possible, the acceptable boundaries of a child's behavior, it exercises a more imposing jurisdiction over family life, readily proscribing behavior and meting out punishment. It is a government of command and submission, doubly enforced by divine mandate, as the father in part 1 indicates when he says to his family, "I think it my Duty to let all of you know, *that* as I have no reason to doubt but the Command of *God* is clear, *and that* I ought to see it obey'd; I join to my own Command, *viz., That* in my Family, I will have *no more* prophaning the *Lord's Day*; *no more* going to Plays; *no more* Swearing Drunkenness, or Immorality whatsoever . . . ; and I expect to be put to as *little Trouble* as possible in having this order submitted to" (139–40).

But even in resounding assertions of patriarchal authority such as this one, there frequently appears the language of a more gentle approach, indicating the double bind in familial conduct. As the father puts it: "I am willing to indulge you in every thing that is reasonable and just; but as I am convinced that what I desire is not only *your Duty*, but *your Interest* to comply with, . . . if you will oblige me to use violent Methods to restore you, and to restore my Family, altho' I shall *be sorry for it*, yet as it is my Duty *I must do it*" (138). That ambivalence is further underscored by the contrasting metaphors of horticulture and disease or sickness, which, as in Locke's *Education* or Astell's *Serious Proposal*, suggest alternate perspectives on the pedagogical process. For the most part, Defoe and his fictional characters invoke the language of planting and of curing illness to suggest distinct measures of urgency or danger in children's waywardness. In fact, the trope of cultivation often indicates an unforeseen benevolence in the pedagogical situation, as when the narrator comments in part 1 that should religiously untutored children show their parents "common Respect, *as above*, it must be all owing to that very Grace, which in spight of the Obstructions of a Godless Education, has been planted in the heart by the powerful Influence, and invincible Operation of the Spirit of God" (56). Such parents must bear the shame of realizing that "the Knowledge, the Piety, the Fear of God, which is found in their Children, is no Product of their planting, no Fruit of what they had sown" (55). Later, this is exactly the experience of the father when contemplating his second eldest son's unexpected piety: he exclaims, "*how I am ashamed!* when I look into my own House, and see what a Soil I have had to plant in, and have neglected to cultivate it; *what Children* would these have been, if I had begun betimes to instruct them!"[8]

Even when the horticultural trope does indicate the hazards of poor instruction, it nonetheless pales by comparison with the graphic and visceral details of physical disability. As the narrator comments in striking, consecutive paragraphs:

> The Child *may* be wrought upon; Nature like some Vegetables, is malleable when taken *green* and *early*; but hard and brittle when condens'd by Time and Age; *at first* it bows and bends to Instruction and Reproof, but afterwards obstinately refuses both.
>
> The Temper of a Child misled by Vice or Mistake, *like a dislocated Bone*, is easie to be reduc'd into its Place, *if taken in time*; but if suffer'd to remain in its dislocated Position, a callous Substance fills

up *the empty Space*, and by neglect grows equally hard with the Bone, and resisting the Power of the Surgeon's Skill, renders *the Reduction* of the Joynt impossible. (68)

In this passage, as in the other moments when the metaphors of illness or disease come into play, there appears a more alarmed and drastic response to children's spiritual condition—whether their religious ignorance is compared to when they "are taken sick" and need "Applications for the Recovery of their Health" (56–57), or whether they are in danger of being *"infected* with the Disease" of "Songs, Plays, Novels, Romances, *and such like Stuff*."[9] In this sense, Defoe's religious (and dramatic) treatise must perform a kind of homeopathic operation for readers' eventual edification, drawing on the very cultural forms that in larger, less controlled doses could induce spiritual malaise rather than moral diligence. Moreover, Mary's near fatal illness in part 3, like Crusoe's similar fever recorded in his journal, is further evidence of the profound correspondence between physical ailment and spiritual malady.[10] In these cases, the most expedient remedy is reconciling oneself with and submitting to the patriarchal father—or, at a second remove, the heavenly Father Himself—whose familial and spiritual authority is powerfully restorative.

The Family Instructor, then, is deeply divided in its presentation of the pedagogical process, either because Defoe is offering a Puritan corrective to perceived deficiencies inherent in the supervisory program, or because in studying the test case of education already gone bad, he is implicitly comparing the relative merits of the two approaches. At this juncture, it is necessary to pause briefly to reflect on the history of Puritanism and supervisory education, because in important ways, they are less opposed as traditions than this discussion may have suggested thus far. Put bluntly, the issue comes down to how "patriarchal" Puritan pedagogy may really be. Soon after the Reformation, Puritanism had advocated—and partly effected—a substantial weakening of the power wielded by the state, the king, and the clergy, thereby reducing their ability to dictate matters such as individual faith, and in this arrangement, the family took on a much more important role in maintaining the standards of both religion and civil society. In general terms, then, it could be said that on the one hand, Puritanism—and Protestantism in general—was a less patriarchal culture than its precedents, but on the other hand, its more explicit dispensation of authority in the family also made the head of the household—the father—a more powerful social figure. In the public sphere, therefore, Puritanism supported a more liberalized approach to male authority figures, while in the domestic sphere, the rule of the patriarch became at least potentially more emphatic (and could be especially daunting for the family's female members). This profoundly ambivalent strain in the Puritan tradition indicates why it can be perceived as both amenable and antithetical to the emergence of supervisory instruction. Certainly Puritan soteriology—with its emphasis on the individual's particularized journey to salvation—is an important historical source for Locke's empiricist experimentation, antiauthoritarian introspection, and individualism—all of which are key components in supervisory procedure. And yet the Puritan emphasis on prohibition, especially in Defoe's hands, ends up reinstating the license of the father, since it is ultimately on his authority that prohibition depends for its force. It is noteworthy that, in many ways, the father's predicament in part 1 of *The Family Instructor* is based on a crisis of prohibition, because he has failed to establish constraints early enough for his family. Hence he is caught between the dictates of his responsibility as patriarch and his genuine desire to be benevolently lenient.[11]

Puritanism's complicated relation to supervisory instruction means that despite their differences, Defoe would not have been able to engage them in a productive dialogue in *The Family Instructor* (or later, in *Robinson Crusoe*) except for the fact that they also share some common ground—including the project of endorsing individual experience while also reconciling it to established standards of virtue. With its greater capacity for systemic pliancy, supervisory education could provide a way to accomplish that goal while accommodating Puritan pedagogy at the same time. Thus in key situations in each of the three narratives in *The Family Instructor*, Defoe employs the trademark strategy of precognitive education—

the process of observation, intervention, and resolution—as a way of balancing the imposition of tutorial power with the student's need for freedom.

At the outset of part 1, that scenario initiates the entire process of the family's reformation. As the narrator reports, "the Father walking in a Field behind his Garden, finds one of his Children [Tommy] wandred out, all alone, under a Row or Walk of Trees, sitting upon a little rising Ground, by it self, looking about, and mighty busie, pointing this way, and that way; sometimes *up*, and sometimes *down*, and sometimes *to its self*; so that the Father coming unperceived pretty near, . . . after much Observation, and some Surprise, discovering himself, asks the Child *What he was doing*, and so sits down by him, which Question begins the FIRST DIA-LOGUE" (5–6). Readers learn soon after that the Father has inter-vened at the precise moment when Tommy needs reassurance and direct instruction regarding his own discoveries about the existence of God and His will for humanity. This intervention is fortuitous, more a sign of Defoe's wisdom than the father's, because the con-versation proves mutually instructive: for his part, the father soon learns of his dreadful error in not educating Tommy and his siblings earlier in basic scriptural truths. It is Defoe's way of accommodating the supervisory paradigm, as he also does in part 2, to the necessary reversal—at least momentarily—of the roles of teacher and pupil. The adults, as much as the children, must acknowledge and repent their mistakes; as the father remarks later, his youngest son has been an indispensable "Instructor" (61).

In part 2, a similar process is enacted when the prosperous Al-derman, stung by the realization that he must take charge of his employees' spiritual well-being, goes to tell them his intentions. Upon hearing them already in conversation about the matter, he hides "*undiscovered*" in a nearby closet (283), where he listens to them discuss at length their resolve to appreciate prayer and godli-ness. When one of the apprentices concludes with the wish that their master would "begin with us and try" to instruct them, the Alderman emerges from his hiding place both to reveal his own further understanding from their discourse and to seize the oppor-tunity to bring their resolve to fruition (291). This is one more in-

stance when the teaching process is bilateral and when the authoritative imposition of order is rendered unnecessary by the more
natural process of conversation and opportune intercession.

By contrast readers also witness the educational wisdom of the
more exemplary adults in Defoe's work, such as the pious master
and mistress in part 2, who proceed in the most discreet and gentle ways possible to reform the unruly apprentice Will, making it
"their Business to observe him more narrowly" for opportunities to
instruct him. Such a moment comes, when, "seeing him one
Evening take a Candle, and go up into a Room over their Work-
house, by himself, the Mistress silently followed him, and plac'd her
self so, as she might see him, and he perceived nothing of it" (212).
After watching Will's restive reading of the Bible, during which he
becomes overwrought to tears concerning his sure damnation as a
sinner, the mistress intercedes, showing Will there is indeed hope
for repentance and redemption. Following Will's rapturous response, the narrator tells readers, "she wisely withdrew; believing it
was a happy Juncture, in which the Child ought to be left alone,
that he might give himself full Vent, with Fervency and Earnestness
to call upon God" (227). This is supervisory education performed
to perfection, with all the benefits of its naturalized procedure.

In part 3 of the *Instructor*, Mary's husband employs subtle instructive measures at every opportunity in order to reclaim her
from her life of irreligion and dissolute fashionableness. This proves
a tricky business, for despite Defoe's indication that the proper role
of the husband is to instruct his wife (and not vice versa: see 273,
275), Mary remains a full-grown adult, entitled to the respect and
tenderness appropriate in marriage's "Dominion of Love" (342).
By his "obliging Carriage," her husband "prevented many little Ex-
cursions which her Inclination would otherways have led her too
[*sic*]" (345). And by means of his ingenious, indirect stratagems, the
"Worship of God was quietly introduced into the Family" (346),
but these measures nonetheless provoke Mary's resentment that her
behavior is being manipulated.

In Mary's arguments with her husband and her conversations
with her older brother, Defoe reveals what is finally at stake here—
the prospect of adult autonomy in the face of the Puritan mandate

that patriarchal authority remain fully intact. For rather than objecting to the religious pieties both her husband and father have attempted to inculcate in her, Mary rejects the manner and timing of their imposition. Indeed throughout Defoe's work his sympathies lie with affirming the jurisdiction of the patriarch over his family members even when his children are full-grown, as witnessed in the exile and death of Mary's older brother. But as Mary's speeches make equally clear, Defoe gives considerable credibility to the Lockean premise that when children come of age, they owe their parents appropriate respect for their station, but not obedience to their commands. In one of the most moving moments of the *Instructor*'s dialogues, Mary tells her aunt:

> My Father and Mother had bred up me and my Brother as you know, till we were come to be what we call Men and Women: We had been used to Company, to good Manners, to Converse in the World with People of Quality and good Breeding; and were come to an Age, in which we might be thought fit to be trusted with so much of the Government of our selves, as to be past Schooling and Tutelage: We made no other use of those Liberties than became a modest Behaviour; they can charge us with nothing Criminal or Scandalous: No Vice, nothing injurious to our Reputation; when all of a sudden without any Notice, we were fallen upon, abridged of all lawful Liberties, were to have new Lectures of Family Discipline read to us, which we were absolutely to submit to, and *to commence Children again*.[12]

Both Mary's father and her husband, as well intentioned or gentle as they may be, threaten to do exactly that—to render her (or her brother) a child again, depriving her of the right to autonomy she has already gained.

The problem is how to negotiate both the imperative of spiritual well-being and the prerogative of adult self-determination. Although the plot apparently comes down on the side of the former, Defoe's text nonetheless presents a compelling case for the claims against patriarchal authority, despite Mary's eventual reconciliation with her father and her acknowledgment of the justice in her brother's final isolation. With the exception of her father, none of Mary's family members contest her claim to adult individuality, and furthermore, her husband's steadfast commitment to gentle methods of persuasion implicitly confirms the justice of her declaration. Later, even her father acknowledges the wisdom of Mary's husband's chosen strategy, going so far as to exclaim, "*Dear Son*, you are fitter to be a Father than I am" (368, 371). Even after the sobering tragedy of her brother's death, we can still hear resonating Mary's earlier protest, which gains further power from her brother's exclamation that his father's behavior has made him childishly vulnerable—"*as it were upon a Stage*, to be a Spectacle to all People" (399). This is indeed a moment of full visibility, when the rebellious self becomes thoroughly scrutable both to the fictional characters as well as to readers, but unlike the dramatic scenario Locke imagined, it is a moment of tortuous exposure, when the stripping away of the illusion of self-contained privacy is simultaneously accompanied by dire loneliness. Therefore without completely undermining the auspices of patriarchal authority, the brother's words are an indictment of his father's insistence on enforcing a form of familial alienation that strongly resembles the kind of spectacular punishment described by Foucault in *Discipline and Punish* as key to the older system of judicial judgment.

Rather than resolve the double bind between liberty and patriarchal authority, Defoe's work must finally enact its narrative vacillations, and the form he chooses provides a capacious arena for negotiating a textual relation between contending perspectives. Just as Locke does briefly in the *Education*, Defoe uses the dynamics of dialogue to include opposing voices and claims. *The Family Instructor* is remarkably "dialogic" in Bakhtin's sense by virtue of its fluid, protonovelistic presentation of several voices, none entirely dominant by the work's end.[13] What is more, Defoe's dialogic vignettes themselves trace the outlines of a supervisory discursive practice, since the reader's edification by what the narrator terms the "natural" flow of conversation is complemented in each case by his own emending interventions, which are meant to ensure the text's persuasiveness. The narrator is quick to remark, for instance, "how naturally the Connexion of Gospel-Truths, one with another, appears" in part 1 (39)—its naturalness apparently in need of supplementary explanation. His interventions appear not only in the framing discussion for each dialogue, as in this example, but also in the middle, as when the narrator inserts this comment within one dialogue: "*the Father blusht, or at least ought to have done so*" (9). This and many other asides during the course of the characters' conversations serve as periodic guideposts for the gradual process of our enlightenment, for Defoe's novel experiment with the "natural" features of dramatic dialogue must inevitably justify itself by alternating such naturalness with clarifying explanations. The "new" therefore authorizes itself by a natural process that itself may not yet be naturalized in the sense of being readily assimilable.

The supervisory dynamics of *The Family Instructor*, then, offer a way into the peculiar narrative flow of *Robinson Crusoe*, since they provide an instructive prototype for examining the persistent repetitions and sometimes boggling circumlocutions in Defoe's novel. In *Crusoe*, as in the conduct book, there is the challenge of education coming too late, the collision of Puritan, patriarchal structure with an empiricist experimentalism and gradualism, and the problematics of novelty—all of them managed by a narrative dexterity alternating "natural" presentation with pointed commentary. And that narrative management will emphasize all the more what the *Instructor*'s narrator calls the role of "providential Accidents" in "surprising" the protagonists into their duty (267). In Defoe's Puritan adaptation of supervisory pedagogy, Providence, as much as tutorial or authorial control, plays a crucial role in cultivating the soil of instructive experience.

'Robinson Crusoe' and the Pedagogical "Chequer-Work of Providence"

The discussion in the previous section confirms Paula Backscheider's general observation that *The Family Instructor* was a "transitional work" in Defoe's "increasing interest in 'life writing,' character creation, and point of view."[14] In addition, it also casts light on the thematic and structural affinities between his conduct book and *Robinson Crusoe*, which appeared only a few years later in 1719. The fact, moreover, that the *Instructor* was second only to that novel in popularity among Defoe's works—reaching its eighth edition within five years of its first publication—suggests there might be an underlying link between these two texts, both in their author's mind and in their readers'. The author of *Lives of the Poets* (1753), in fact, evaluated *Robinson Crusoe*'s merits in the context of Defoe's oeuvre using terms that recall Defoe's own sense that his method in the *Instructor* was "*entirely New*":

> The natural abilities of the author (for he was no scholar) seem to have been very high. He had a great knowledge of men and things, particularly what related to the government, and trade of these kingdoms. He wrote many pamphlets on both, which were generally well received, though his name was never prefixed. His imagination was fertile, strong, and lively, as may be collected from his many works of fancy, particularly Robinson Crusoe, which was written in so natural a manner, and with so many probable incidents, that, for some time after its publication, it was judged by most people to be a true story. It was indeed written upon a model entirely new, and the success and esteem it met with, may be ascertained by the many editions it has sold.[15]

Although *Crusoe*'s "model entirely new" is by no means identical to the *Instructor*'s framework, Defoe's prefatory remarks to the novel indicate a telling correlation to his conduct book, particularly in the attempt to promote the notion (as the author of *Lives of the Poets* also notes above) that the text is "a true story." But as in his pedagogical work, Defoe complicates that idea by blurring the distinction between its factual or fictional status, especially with regard to either discursive mode's moral effectiveness: "*The Editor believes the thing to be a just History of Fact; neither is there any Appearance of Fiction in it: And however thinks, because all such things are dispatch'd, that the Improvement of it, as well to the Diversion, as to the Instruction of the Reader, will be the same*."[16] As Defoe puts it in the *Instructor*, the work should prove compelling, "whether it be a History or a Parable," since "it may be either way adapted to the sincere Design" of edifying as well as entertaining readers (5). In this case, however, there appears to be little anxiety about potential melodramatic distractions in using bold new form.

In *Crusoe*, Defoe expands the narrative experiment he began in the *Instructor* by attempting to infuse Puritan autobiography with supervisory pedagogy. It was quite a different story, however, to create a sustained, coherent narrative in *Crusoe*, whose episodic quality Defoe attempts to consolidate by tracing the thread of Crusoe's spiritual pilgrimage. His efforts are further complicated by the fact that the two main narrative patterns he employs—one characteristic of Puritan autobiography, the other emerging from indirect instruction—contain extremely contrary, if not incommensurate, designs. And that double narrative thread is drawn out in a tension reminiscent of the *Instructor's* contention with the dual strands of traditional patriarchal authority and the newer emphasis on individual liberty.

One of the most striking features of Defoe's novel is its turbulent narrative flow—the sudden occurrence of storms, shipwrecks, or other threatening dangers, Crusoe's abrupt seizures by guilt or euphoria, the unexpected discoveries and truncated exposition. Over and over again, often in a matter of a few paragraphs, Crusoe's mental state swings from what he calls his "Discomposures"— which occur when he imagines himself "so absolutely miserable, so without Help abandon'd"[17]—to his exuberant faith both in his own abilities and in those of Providence. These extremes, of course, are the symptoms of having abandoned the secure "middle State" of life recommended by his father, and Crusoe's unflagging capacity for being "perfectly confounded and amaz'd" (164) is an effect created at least in part by the exotic quality of the island. But the very violence of such narrative seesawing and, furthermore, its persistence even after Crusoe's spiritual conversion indicate that the reason goes beyond unfamiliar circumstances or even Crusoe's headstrong rebellion against parental authority.

A particularly instructive example of this narrative oscillation occurs midway through *Robinson Crusoe*, in a passage that binds adverse thematic, formal, and ideological elements so tightly that it is worth examining in detail. It is an episode forming a virtual allegory of Crusoe's repeated attempts to reconcile inherent inquisitiveness with Christian faith, material appearance with spiritual substance. In perhaps the most exalted terms he ever uses, Crusoe claims that during a period of five years, "I liv'd mighty comfortably, my Mind being entirely composed by resigning to the Will of

God, and throwing my self wholly upon the Disposal of his Providence. This made my Life better than sociable, for when I began to regret the want of Conversation, I would ask my self whether thus conversing mutually with my own Thoughts, and . . . with even God himself . . . was not better than the utmost Enjoyment of humane Society in the World" (135–36). But only shortly after, having finished his new boat, Crusoe sets out "to make a Tour round the Island" (136), an endeavor seemingly innocent enough, but, as it turns out, fraught with moral and spiritual dangers. When he comes upon a treacherous ledge of rocks traversed by two opposing currents—one moving powerfully out to sea, and the other, an eddy, circling back to the coastline—Crusoe spends two days on shore, attempting to calculate from his vantage point on a hill when the conditions will be favorable for safe passage. On the third day, despite his precautions, Crusoe fails to negotiate a course from the first current to the second and is swept uncontrollably out to sea, becoming "a warning Piece," he says, "to all rash and ignorant Pilots":

> [A]ll I could do with my Paddlers signify'd nothing, and now I began to give my self over for lost; for as the Current was on both Sides of the Island, I knew in a few Leagues Distance they must joyn again, and then I was irrecoverably gone. . . .
>
> And now I saw how easy it was for the Providence of God to make the most miserable Condition Mankind could be in *worse*. Now I look'd back upon my desolate solitary Island, as the most pleasant Place in the World. . . . Thus we never see the true State of our Condition, till it is illustrated to us by its Contraries; nor know how to value what we enjoy, but by the want of it. (138–39)

It may seem puzzling at first that Crusoe attaches such enormous importance to a simple miscalculation by harshly condemning his attempt to explore by boat much of the same terrain he has already surveyed on foot. But he provides a clue to that judgment when he finally regains the shore: Crusoe reports that he "gave God Thanks for my Deliverance, resolving to lay aside all Thoughts of my Deliverance by my Boat" (141). That comment suddenly illuminates the spiritual subtext of Crusoe's venture, since it recalls a crucial turning point earlier in the story, when Crusoe, at the point of conversion, realizes that "Deliverance from Sin [is] a much greater Blessing, than Deliverance from Affliction" (97). In other words, despite his claims of Christian resignation, Crusoe's exploratory venture manifests his lingering desire to place earthly condition over spiritual welfare. It is, moreover, a reenactment of what he later calls his "ORIGINAL SIN" (194), since it was in traveling by sea that Crusoe first rebelled against the constraints of his life in England. In the simplest terms, this scenario indicates that travel on land corresponds to accepting one's station, while ventures by sea, in contrast, demonstrate dangerous personal willfulness.[18] Just after he has left home, Crusoe himself corroborates the logic of this scheme by remarking that the "Current of [his] . . . Desires" erodes his good sense and moral stability (9).

This episode has further significance because it encapsulates two narrative structures composed of intransigent elements that are the raw material for making Crusoe's story what he calls "a Chequer-Work of Providence" (156). On the one hand, as in the case of the eldest son in the *Instructor*, there is Puritan restraint: under that dispensation, divinely sanctioned law prescribes that its dictates be obeyed, and that punishment be the consequence for the failure to do so. This is a familiar theme in Crusoe's oppressive guilt and in his conviction that almost any misfortune is a punitive measure taken by Providence. In terms of narrative order, this pattern follows the archetype set by the Fall story: rebellion is met with punishment, resulting in repentance, and finally, redemption. In the case of Crusoe's marine junket, he is ultimately "delivered"—both physically and spiritually—from his own attempt to muster deliverance.

This pattern, on the other hand, is opposed by Crusoe's robust adventurousness, a restless curiosity not only essential for his survival on the island but also instrumental in his spiritual growth. In fact, it is nothing less than the catalyst for acquiring knowledge in classic Lockean fashion, in which direct sensory experience is the first step. In *An Essay concerning Human Understanding*, Locke calls such motivation "*Desire*; which is an *uneasiness* of the Mind for want of some absent good."[19] He considers it an essential impulse preceding abstract reasoning and compelling human will. This key feature of Crusoe's psychological profile complements other critics' arguments that Locke's *Essay* provides a crucial conceptual framework for Defoe's novel, particularly in terms of its exploration of individual identity, its meticulous recording of sensory detail, and its plain style.[20] Eve Tavor, for instance, applies this connection to Defoe's fictional narrators: "In reproducing [the] world of perceptions, reflections and reasonings, Defoe follows Locke in showing how his narrators proceed by degrees from their immediate perception of concrete particulars to more and more general ideas."[21]

This general scheme applies equally well to Crusoe as protagonist, whose career on the island serves to illustrate Locke's claim in the *Essay* that in giving human beings experiential understanding, God has provided them both "Whatever is necessary for the Conveniences of Life" as well as "Light enough to lead them to a Knowledge of their Maker."[22] For Crusoe, in short, the difficulties endemic to the process he calls "Experiment" are not only inevitable but also necessary. His mishap with the boat provides an exemplary instance of that fact, since the calculations and projections he performs on the hill prove no substitute for taking the plunge. Crusoe's conclusion that "we never see the true State of our Condition, till it is illustrated to us by its Contraries" makes Locke's epistemological premise all the more emphatic by apparently devaluing abstract contemplation or speculative imagination. This possibility also has consequences for Crusoe's own self-knowledge, since he does not even seem cognizant of his compulsion to escape the island until his ordeal is over.

Defoe's combination of the Puritan and empiricist paradigms results in such a violent narrative ebb and flow that Crusoe—as both protagonist and narrator—often comes close to being overwhelmed. These contrary currents, in fact, threaten Crusoe's story with a kind of narrative schizophrenia—at least to the degree that Crusoe's autobiography is composed of two antithetical, yet inextricable, elements. One of the symptoms of schizophrenia is the inability to tell a coherent story, and Crusoe's abortive tour of the island suggests exactly that possibility: Crusoe's attempt at self-description, like his efforts in the boat, could "signify nothing."

Whether or not we put the case in such dire terms, Defoe's

work nonetheless presents a signal moment in the discursive and cultural development of the novel of education, for its competing narrative patterns register one of the most compelling issues in England after the Restoration—namely, how to reconcile the contending values of individual liberty and political stability, personal faith and orthodox theology, and last, but not least, the rational autonomy of children and the requirements of moral or social responsibility. In short, although the proposal by Locke, Masham, and other educationalists to approach these problems in a tolerant, liberal fashion was, in general, extremely influential, in *The Family Instructor*, that idea is met with considerable resistance, particularly from those with affinities for Puritan stringency and patriarchal hierarchy. Even a sympathetic attempt to assimilate a supervisory perspective to a Puritan ethos, such as the one Defoe makes in *Robinson Crusoe*, must confront the incompatibilities of their respective generic forms. In that sense, Defoe's work poses an ideal instance in which the seams and sutures of that combination are clearly visible. Of crucial assistance in that uneasy alliance, I argue, are the narrative strategies implicit in the supervisory educational theory. But first I must consider the specific pedagogical themes in Defoe's work.

Crusoe's story, to be sure, portrays his religious conversion in terms of spiritual and moral reeducation. Crusoe begins, in fact, by recounting his educational background, explaining, "My Father . . . had given me a competent Share of Learning, as far as Home-Education, and a Country Free-School generally goes, and design'd me for the Law."[23] What Crusoe lacks, however, and what he must gain under the duress of his "afflictions," is a profound religious faith. He observes that despite his parents' "good Instruction" in spiritual matters, he leaves his home with only a "little Sense of Religion," which is soon dissipated by keeping company with godless seafarers.[24] Having abandoned his familial tutors, Crusoe must learn the value of salvation, he says, "without any Teacher or Instructor; I mean, humane" (221)—his qualification of an initially absolute claim acknowledging Providence's tutorial role while also indicating his impulsive self-dependence.[25] During his arduous spiritual education, furthermore, Crusoe considers his isolated helplessness to be childlike (113). That role will later be reversed, however, when it is incumbent upon Crusoe to teach Christian faith to Friday, whose uncivilized affections are "like those of a Child to a Father" (209).

The term Crusoe uses most in this context is "instruction," a word carrying significant overtones of the prescriptive emphasis in the Puritan "guide" tradition, which has already been considered with regard to *The Family Instructor*. J. Paul Hunter confirms that link by arguing that *Robinson Crusoe* has "important thematic affinities" with the *Instructor* and the guide tradition, including the topics of rebelliousness, divine guidance, and obedience.[26] But the connection is structural as well, since Defoe's narrative experiment in the *Instructor* strongly resembles the pattern of Crusoe's gradually emerging disposition in the novel. Several of the *Instructor*'s miniature stories, like Crusoe's episodic ventures, exhibit the same cycle of selfish willfulness, discontent, contrition, and reconciliation—the pedagogical equivalent, on a lesser scale, of spiritual rebellion, affliction, repentance, and redemption. Later in this section I will explore how the commentator's function in the *Instructor* also has strong parallels with Crusoe's role as narrator and interpreter of his past actions.

Crusoe's pedagogical progress, however, traces a clear supervisory trajectory. His piecemeal acquisition of domestic skills, as well as his cumulative spiritual understanding, follows Locke's claims, for instance, that a pupil should not "be *taught by Rules*," that "*Curiosity* should be . . . carefully *cherished*," and that education should proceed "by safe and insensible degrees."[27] Those elements add further support to the argument by Jay Fliegelman, one of the few critics to have observed a connection between Locke's pedagogy and *Robinson Crusoe*: he persuasively claims that for Defoe, Crusoe's leave-taking of his parents is finally justified, because he is acting on Locke's premise that children should be subject to parental authority only as long as they are under age.[28] Crusoe's apparent rebellion, then, is in fact his appeal to a higher authority—Providence—for his spiritual well-being, and his ensuing "afflictions" are not punishment for disobedience, but an unavoidable part of searching, through individual experience, for his relationship to God. In

Fliegelman's cogent formulation, Crusoe turns out to be a persistent pilgrim, rather than what he often calls himself: a prodigal son.

In these terms, Crusoe's repeated wrestling with virtually the same problems—say, the desire to escape the island—is the narrative exemplar of supervisory educationalists' proposal that habit formation offers the chief method by which to teach a student without relying on confusingly abstract principles, prohibition, or severe punishment. In his case, Locke strongly opposes "the trouble of repeated Injunctions, and multiplied Rules of Doing and Forbearing,"[29] since they easily confound the rational capacity of children, and even dispose them toward doing the very thing they have been prohibited. (Consider this point, for example, with regard to Crusoe's father's strong "advice" not to travel.) That approach, Locke claims, must be accompanied by stringent enforcement of the rules, usually corporal punishment, which he calls "the worst, and therefore the last Means to be used in the Correction of Children" (sec. 84). Locke proposes instead that tutors teach their pupils moral habits, accomplished by "a repeated Practice, and the same Action done over and over again, under the Eye and Direction of the Tutor" (sec. 66). This process applies to Crusoe, despite the fact that he has competent powers of reasoning, because as we have already seen, he consistently proceeds, in near childlike fashion, as though firsthand experience were the only means to understand himself or the will of Providence. Crusoe himself invokes habit as a key element for his spiritual sensibility: "I had been well instructed by Father and Mother; neither had they been wanting to me, in their early Endeavours, to infuse a religious Awe of God into my Mind, [and] a Sense of my Duty. . . . But alas! falling early into the Seafaring Life, . . . that little Sense of Religion which I had entertain'd, was laughed out of me by my Mess-Mates, by a harden'd despising of Dangers; and the Views of Death, *which grew habitual to me.*"[30]

If Crusoe's "divine Knowledge" (88), as he calls it, is gradually eroded by recurrent, degenerate behavior, then it follows that, on the island, his attempt to regain it must also follow the arduous path of repeated trial and error. The first process Crusoe summarizes rapidly, in the matter of a few sentences; the second, however, he

takes care to lay out in exhaustive detail. Readers are thus witness
to the perplexing fact that although shortly after arriving on the island, Crusoe can articulate—and to some extent even analyze—
the principle of resignation to the will of Providence, he still reen-
acts, over and over again, the process of reaching that conclusion.
Despite the usefulness of rational contemplation—as in the island
"tour"—Crusoe can fully gain that dispositional perspective only
by colliding with it head on, until he absorbs its meaning almost
corporeally—until it becomes, like habit, second nature. As he endures this recurring pattern, Crusoe's frequent seesawing from exuberance to frustration might be accounted for by Locke's description (by now familiar) of a tutor's dual purpose: "he that has found
a way to keep up a Child's Spirit, easy, active, and free; and yet, at
the same time, to restrain him from many things he has a Mind to,
and to draw him to things that are uneasy to him; he, I say, that
knows how to reconcile these seeming Contradictions, has . . . got
the true Secret of Education."[31] This proposal proves to be the test
of Providence's tutorial expertise, since Crusoe needs to maintain
his experimental curiosity, at the same time that he becomes
morally and spiritually responsible.

In summary, then, Crusoe's educational career is mutually constituted by the distinct pedagogical paradigms offered by the Puritan guide tradition and supervisory instruction. But there is still
one more textual layer to consider. The narrative tension generated
by Defoe's discursive combinations is intensified further by the fact
that *Robinson Crusoe* also draws on Puritan spiritual autobiography,
which has strong affinities with the guide genre while introducing
an even greater emphasis on the theological theme and the process
of personal salvation.[32] A major difference between the guide tradition and spiritual autobiography can perhaps best be summarized as
the difference between spiritual *education* and spiritual *conversion*.
Puritan guides, to be sure, set out to teach the principles of Christian faith, but for the most part, they do not focus on the moment
of salvation. Spiritual education, in the guide tradition, provides the
general, preparatory concepts for redemption, while that event, in
spiritual autobiography, is made specific, articulated at the level of
personal self-description. In *The Family Instructor*, Defoe had begun

to narrow the gap between those two generic approaches, but even there he had not focused as intensely on a single individual, or documented the exhaustive amount of daily minutiae characteristic of spiritual autobiography.

These differences make the contrast with "precognitive" pedagogy all the more pronounced, particularly given the secular, pragmatic orientation provided by Locke's version of it. In the supervisory educational process, the pupil undergoes a four-part process: after experimenting with new data, he commits errors, receives correction, and assimilates new understanding. Puritan autobiography, by contrast, enacts a sequence of rebellion, punishment, repentance, and redemption. Even the smallest details become invested with the aura of spiritual consequence. This contrast is useful for summarizing several of the differences I have already alluded to: (1) Rather than characterize student errors as "faults," which are readily remedied, spiritual autobiography portrays human errancy as "sin," the manifestation of being spiritually unregenerate. (2) Rather than employ periodic, reasoned correction for such errors, spiritual autobiography emphasizes punishment, usually accompanied by the overtones of righteous anger. (3) Rather than rely on the accumulation "by gentle Degrees" of instructive lessons, spiritual autobiography—even in its attention to the details of daily experience—hinges on the single moment of sudden transformation that assures one of salvation. Supervisory pedagogy, in short, is a process of degrees, while spiritual autobiography turns on the distinction of kinds—articulated by the adverse categories of the divine and the satanic, spirit and flesh, salvation and damnation.

Despite such sharp contrasts between indirect instruction and the Puritan genres of guide and autobiography, these forms have important similarities that allow Defoe to link them, however uneasily. Puritan autobiography, for example, is a genre that—by the very act of writing it—affirms salvation as profoundly experiential: it attests to the conviction that the text of God's will is found not only in Scripture but also in the pattern of daily incidents which, if dutifully recorded and carefully scrutinized, will yield their spiritual meaning. During the eighteenth century, in fact, Locke's work provided epistemological and pedagogical confirmation for that earlier theological premise. The Puritan guide, for its part, shares the supervisory commitment to organizing the development of children in order to assure their social and spiritual happiness. These similarities present an initial basis for generic accommodation, although in the process the supervisory and Puritan paradigms prove mutually exacerbating. On the one hand, despite the attraction of its more fluid, responsive approach, indirect education poses the threat of moral laxity, if not social—or even spiritual—chaos. The Puritan genres, on the other hand, while having a strong sense of scrupulous pedagogical management, share an authoritarian stringency that Astell, Fénelon, and Essex, among others, found insupportable.

As part of this discursive triad, supervisory pedagogy functions as a kind of *generic intermediary*, supplying provisional, though often strained, linkages between autobiographical and didactic orientations. Because of its strong individualist emphasis, for instance, it can mediate between the intensely personal quality of Defoe's story—the "I" of autobiography—and the larger concerns of social or moral responsibility by employing an incremental, repetitive process operating under the auspices of providential wisdom. In a moment, I will examine the specific narrative form by which this mediation takes place. But in general terms, Defoe's novel is overdetermined—in the broadest sense of that term—by the conjunction of these generic strains. At times, Crusoe's development seems nearly bifurcated, swinging as it does between the "Contraries" of compulsive action and oppressive guilt. In other instances, however, the incidents in Crusoe's life and the way he interprets them are curiously composite, as though the components of supervisory and Puritan orientation have become hybridized, the ascendancy of one or the other apparently indeterminate. There are moments, for example, when the process of gaining knowledge by firsthand experience takes on perceptible overtones of Puritan didacticism. At one point, when confronted with grapes of uncertain quality, Crusoe reports he "was warn'd by my Experience to eat sparingly of them, remembring, that when I was ashore in *Barbary*, the eating of Grapes kill'd several of our *English* Men who were Slaves there."[33] Being warned by experience in the face of potential bodily harm may in fact be appropriate, but the word *warn* is also one of the key words in the guide tradition of exhortation, which often prescribes behavior using the language of severe precaution. That sense is reinforced on several occasions, among them in Crusoe's comments on proper industry (which are reminiscent of Locke's principle concerning the moral use of property).[34] After remarking on the island's abundance of food, Crusoe concludes: "In a Word, The Nature and Experience of Things dictated to me upon just Reflection, That all the good Things of this World, are no farther good to us, than they are for our Use" (129). In this instance, when even the inference of his reason "dictates" to Crusoe correct ethics, the elements of natural process and emphatic command become inextricably intertwined.

The motif of the garden is a particularly instructive instance of such narrative ambivalence, since it is both a reigning emblem of Puritan symbology, as well as a central metaphor in supervisory educationalists' portrayal of the learning process. By placing Crusoe on the island as a consequence of his "Original Sin," Defoe is of course replaying the Fall story with a new twist, since Crusoe has been both banished from the "Eden" of his homestead, as well as situated in a paradisal setting where, in the end, he can savor the fruits of his redemption. It is no coincidence that in the preface, Defoe echoes the opening lines of *Paradise Lost*, claiming that the novel's purpose is "*to justify and honour the Wisdom of Providence in all the Variety of Circumstances, let them happen how they will*" (1). Within this symbolic framework, Crusoe's life on the island repeatedly follows the typology of the Fall, rehearsing the pattern of willfulness, punishment, and reconciliation. In these terms, the Edenic island serves as the setting for Crusoe as an active agent, whose decisions or actions will periodically prove misguided and require contrition.

In contrast, when Crusoe at one point comments that the island seems "like a *planted* Garden" (99; my emphasis), his remark suggests the possibility that Defoe is drawing on indirect instruction's pervasive metaphor of education as horticulture. Defoe himself employs that imagery in *The Compleat English Gentleman*, urging that "the principles of virtue, religion, and subjection to government are to be planted in the minds of children from the very first moments that they can be made capable of receiving them, that they . . . may have some time to take root, before the taste of pleasure and a loose levity and folly can have access to supplant them."[35] Although Defoe's urgent tone reflects Puritan foreboding, and although it is also possible that Defoe might disagree with Locke or like-minded educationalists as to exactly when "the very first moments" of rational capability in children should arrive, his comment reflects a similar view of "cultivated nature" that applies to Crusoe's gradual spiritual education on the island. This pedagogical perspective views nature—however errant—as eminently malleable; its approach is more relaxed and patient, and therefore amenable to the process of incremental habituation.[36] Crusoe himself often remarks on what he perceives as Providence's infinite long-suffering, inclined toward gentle proddings and slight adjustments, rather than submitting his behavior to severe punishment.

Not surprisingly, Defoe's "Garden-Plot"—both in the sense of image and narrative sequence—sharply contrasts with Puritan typology. It seems likely that while writing the *Education* in 1693, Locke had Milton's *Paradise Lost* in mind as the example of the Fall story he intended to revise. Rather than follow the lead of Puritan pedagogy, however, which rehearses a lapsarian paradigm, Locke poses the garden scene as one without prohibition, in which human subjects are less active agents than the objects of tutorial management. This apparently simple alteration is of enormous consequence, because Locke in effect eliminates the event of the fall. It does not, of course, completely remove what Locke calls "Fault," or error, but it does dispose of the colossal failure that brings calamity, and even permanent loss.

This nonlapsarian quality of Crusoe's development should be underscored, particularly given the theological concept of the "Fortunate Fall," which also attempts to moderate the consequences of original sin and, in many respects, applies to Crusoe himself. Under the dispensation of the Fortunate Fall, man's loss of Eden precipitates both his sustained quest to recapture its benefits and his achievement, in the end, of a "heaven" of even greater proportions. In *The Family Instructor*, for instance, Mary's aunt suggests this pattern when she reassures Mary's worried parents that "sometimes our Falls are made the first Steps to our Recovery, and the very particular Sins that we commit, are the Introduction to our Deliverance from the Dominion of Sin in general."[37] As Jay Fliegelman has convincingly argued, moreover, that paradigm applies equally well to Crusoe, who grieves for his lost "middle Station of Life" at home, but finally gains an economic and social position of greater scale, in addition to spiritual happiness.[38] This modified version of the Fall clearly approaches Locke's pedagogical model, since it at least poses the possibility of a paradise regained (if not exceeded). Nevertheless, it does not go so far as to be readily assimilated to a narrative design that practically eradicates a fall and its dramatic consequences.[39] A Lockean model, in fact, adds a secular twist to what Fliegelman calls "the paradox of the Fortunate Fall":

> [F]rom one perspective Adam and Eve are sinful prodigals who are deserving of their punishment and, yet, from another, they are victims more sinned against than sinning, who, by courageously accepting their fate, are transformed ultimately into hero and heroine. From one perspective, Jehovah is the most gracious of parents; for he has allowed Adam and Eve to fall only so that he might sacrifice his son to permit their progeny the opportunity to choose to return to his embrace. From another perspective, however, Jehovah may be seen as a parental tyrant enforcing a covenant of works that, as it demands perfect obedience, extorts an excessive payment from those who are guilty of nothing but natural inability. (83–84)

The points of contact between Locke's pedagogy and Adam and Eve's fortunate salvation through divine grace are certainly only approximate, but the comparison suggests that a nonlapsarian approach to education makes an already existing tension in Puritan discourse all the more pronounced.

The garden motif, then, provides a thematic and structural overlay of two distinct pedagogical approaches. In the Puritan scenario, it presents Crusoe as an Adam who dares taste the fruit of personal adventure, while in supervisory terms, it implies that his actions are analogous to the unconscious impulses of vegetable vitality. Noting that contrast can help explain, among other things, the fitful quality of Crusoe's psychology, what Leopold Damrosch calls "the peculiar opacity and passivity of character in Defoe's fiction."[40] More importantly, the garden motif functions as a metaphoric intersection of diverse generic strains, particularly the three I have focused on in this discussion: spiritual autobiography, Puritan guide, and supervisory pedagogy. As their nexus, the garden registers virtually all of the narrative tensions discussed so far—including spontaneity versus deliberation, Puritan prescription versus indirect inference, and lapsarian allegory versus secular drama.

Until now I have focused on the individual generic components of Defoe's work and their uneasy cohabitation in the narrative. But despite such contrary currents, the burden for Defoe, of course, is to negotiate those narrative streams successfully, to present his readers a plausible—even if at times perplexing—story about his protagonist's spiritual education and conversion. His primary method of accomplishing that task is to assign Crusoe, as narrator, the pedagogical function of consolidating all discordant narrative elements, with the aim of educating the reader. To be sure, that goal was new to neither fictional nor nonfictional writing of the Enlightenment, but in facing new generic obstacles to that purpose, Crusoe's narration draws on a supervisory model for the pedagogue's relation to his pupil's development. The supervisory tutor scrupulously observes the progress of his student/protagonist, periodically intervenes to correct errors, and then withdraws to witness the resolution of that particular educational episode: it is a matter of balancing covert and overt instruction. As we have already seen, Defoe partially adopted this pedagogical model in *The Family Instructor* by forming self-contained educational stories framed by prefatory remarks and interpretive commentary. In introducing this innovation to the guide tradition, Defoe could assume the role of the reader in "observing" the characters' actions and dialogue while also being able to address the reader with direct religious exhortations.

In *Robinson Crusoe*, Defoe employs the supervisory narrative pattern less schematically, adapting it to the conventions of autobiography, in which Crusoe plays the part of protagonist, who provides the "raw material" of lived experience, particularly in the journal, as well as the narrator, who couches his instructive commentary in the form of personal observations on his past. Crusoe's narrative commentary, in fact, is saturated by the vocabulary of "observation," which has at least three semantic registers: it occasionally refers to Crusoe's perceptions in a strict epistemological sense; it articulates Crusoe's increasing skill in perceiving patterns or logical relationships; and, most importantly, it records his ability to appreciate the moral or spiritual import of even the smallest story element. Significantly, Crusoe invokes the terminology of observation in the context of learning both practical and spiritual lessons. He reports, for example, "not observing the proper Time" for sowing his corn, thereby having to learn the hard way good methods of farming.[41] In a more serious passage, when Crusoe remarks that he has not learned the principles of salvation from "any Teacher or Instructor" except Providence, the themes of experiential education, observation, and redemption combine: "I cannot refrain from observing here also from Experience . . . How infinite, and inexpressible a Blessing it is, that the Knowledge of God, and of the Doctrine of Salvation by *Christ Jesus*, is so plainly laid down in the Word of God" (221).

Crusoe's observant commentary varies from the strict protocols of the supervisory pedagogical paradigm, since Crusoe offers such remarks as a gesture of direct intervention in the reader's interpretation of the story. Despite that difference, however, Crusoe nonetheless proceeds in a recognizably supervisory manner to modulate between direct, sometimes didactic, "telling," and implicit, naturalistic "showing." That modulation (as I argued in chapter 1) is the narrative analogue of the precognitive pedagogical pattern, in which on the one hand, the tutor lets the student experience his education "naturally," without an awareness of the tutor's orchestrations, while on the other, the tutor must also periodically intercept his pupil's waywardness with pointed instruction.

In *Robinson Crusoe* that alternating approach is articulated as the difference between fact and fiction, between natural truth and aesthetically shaped discourse. As the putative "Editor" of Crusoe's manuscript, Defoe claims that it is *"a just History of Fact; neither is there any Appearance of Fiction in it"* (1), although it seemed clear even to Defoe's contemporaries that the story followed familiar allegorical patterns.[42] There is no better example of this dual strategy than Crusoe's journal, which has the strongest claim for representing his experiences in an unmediated, mimetic fashion. Even here, however, Crusoe does not refrain from interpolating explanatory comments—in fact, they often seem more urgent in tone, given that the journal documents Crusoe's eventual repentance and reconciliation to God. Particularly in this context one can observe Crusoe repeatedly rehearsing the supervisory pedagogical pattern: he presents the journal's entries, which record his recurring distress and afflictions; he explains the reasons for and significance of his condition while also relating how Providence was instrumental in assisting him; and then he reports the beneficial results of that providential assistance. Crusoe's interjected explanations are most diligent and lengthy at precisely the same points that Providence intervenes in the story, a feature of the narrative suggesting Crusoe somehow mistrusts the reader's ability to perceive the meaning of those crucial turning points.

Such implicit distrust is further evident in the generic sleight of hand operating in the journal, because at times it becomes difficult to distinguish the original entries from Crusoe's commentary. Toward the beginning, Crusoe signals his remarks by using "N.B.," even indenting such explanations to make the difference palpable (see, e.g., 76). Later, however, Crusoe increasingly elides the distinction, so much so that one can read several paragraphs before realizing they are not in fact part of the original journal. At times it is almost a shock to come across Crusoe's transitions such as "I return to my Journal" (97), while turning back to discover exactly where Crusoe begins his interpolated comments often proves impossible. Even after becoming aware of Crusoe's subtle insertion of his interpretations, the reader may not recognize their appearance.[43]

This narrative indirection has important connections to supervisory tutorial modulation, which could achieve what Locke called "the true Secret of Education" by making the student feel "easy" and "free" while also bringing him "to things that are uneasy to him"—namely, the principles of moral restraint, social cooperation, and political conformity. Crusoe as narrator performs an analogous pedagogical function on two levels. First, he makes as coherent as possible his experience of desiring complete self-dependence and pursuing a grand sense of personal liberty while, at the same time, becoming increasingly constrained by the dictates of providential and social order. This theme finds its most potent articulation in the island as prison, an image persistently haunting Crusoe's imagination. In telling that story, Crusoe attempts also to produce a similar effect in his readers, presenting them with the "natural" and true events of his life while simultaneously guiding them to the proper interpretation of their import.

Finally, Defoe's adaptation of Crusoe's role to a supervisory narrative pattern significantly alters the conventional function of the spiritual autobiographer. For in addition to telling his story and providing the proper spiritual perspective on its significance, Crusoe must also negotiate a satisfactory relation among the competing generic elements associated with Puritan and supervisory pedagogy—which include the blurring of fact and fiction, the didactic emphasis on orderly, if not hierarchical, values, the claims of individual liberty, and the secularization of human development.[44] Confronting that task places a new emphasis on the narrator's role as the instrument of narrative coherence, an emphasis that will become characteristic of novelistic discourse, particularly in suggesting an analogue for a flexible, yet reliable approach to social organization and control.

Crusoe's task as narrator, then, can best be described as a form of narrative *government*, since that term has several personal and public nuances pertinent to its double register of political administration and pedagogical supervision. This double sense was the basis for frequent claims that the English political system—by the example of its officials, if not also by the very structure of its organization—should play a key role in teaching the public correct civic values and behavior. The goal of education, furthermore, whether public or private, is *self*-government, the power and obligation to submit one's passions or inclinations to rational adjudication authorized by social mores. In that context, Crusoe's apparently whimsical self-designation as "Governour" of the island has both political and pedagogical significance, particularly with regard to his treatment of Friday.

Social Identity and the Extraordinarily Ordinary Self

In *Robinson Crusoe*, Defoe resolves—or at least eases—the tug-of-war between patriarchal authority and supervisory liberality much differently than he does in *The Family Instructor*: unlike his counterparts Mary or her brother, Crusoe does not finally have to submit himself to the dominion of his earthly father. His parents' deaths conveniently dissolve Crusoe's responsibility to reconcile with them. But more importantly, this narrative twist signals Defoe's apparent message that Crusoe has no need for such self-abasement, since he has consolidated his more important relationship with his Heavenly Father.[45] In a way, Crusoe fulfills what Mary's father tells her when he acknowledges her repentance of past rebellion: "your Offence against me is nothing, but *as it was* a Sin against [God]," he concludes, "my Joy and Comfort is, That God has given you a due and deep Sense of your Offences, *against him*, and I hope has pardoned you also."[46] Crusoe's case differs, however, in that he need not mend his relationship with Providence via a mediating earthly father.

One consequence of this difference is that the last part of *Robinson Crusoe* shifts its focus to a new, complicated issue: Crusoe's emerging role as a public, even political figure on the island—a development that surprisingly reintroduces the problem of patriarchal authority and its function. After Friday arrives on the scene, Crusoe not only becomes a surrogate "Father" to Friday and his childlike affections (209) but also a ruling "Lord," "Governour," and "King" over the entire island and its accumulated populace by the end of the story. Much earlier, Crusoe has enjoyed substantial pleasure in thinking "this was all my own, that I was King and Lord of all this Country indefeasibly, and had a Right of Possession; and if I could convey it, I might have it in Inheritance, as compleatly as any Lord of a Mannor in *England*" (100). Later, this whimsy gains apparent substance in a much quoted passage where Crusoe muses on the kingdom he has established with the new inhabitants:

> My Island was now peopled, and I thought my self very rich in Subjects; and it was a merry Reflection which I frequently made, How

like a King I look'd. First of all, the whole Country was my own meer Property; so that I had an undoubted Right of Dominion. 2*dly*, My People were perfectly subjected: I was absolute Lord and Law-giver; they all owed their Lives to me, and were ready to lay down their Lives, *if there had been Occasion of it*, for me. It was remarkable too, we had but three Subjects, and they were of three different Religions. My Man *Friday* was a Protestant, his Father was a *Pagan* and a *Cannibal*, and the *Spaniard* was a Papist: However, I allow'd Liberty of Conscience throughout my Dominions. (241)

Although Crusoe's self-designation as king is the result of "merry Reflection"—and perhaps we should smile along with him at its bemused levity—he should nonetheless be taken seriously, because Defoe devotes considerable time to the importance of Crusoe's governing role on the island.[47] Crusoe's capacity as fatherly monarch or governor is key to understanding the final stage of his religious, moral, and social reeducation. As the above passage suggests, however, the political significance of Crusoe's kingdom-in-microcosm is unclear, particularly with regard to its credentials as a patriarchy. On the one hand, his assertion of being "absolute Lord and Law-giver" indicates the classical function of the patriarch in the *pre*political state that Locke describes exhaustively in the *Second Treatise of Government*. On the other hand, there is Crusoe's staunch commitment to religious toleration, which would have its foundation in a Lockean separation of church and state. This ambivalence provokes a troubling question: What, finally, is the significance of Crusoe's apparent break from the dictates of familial patriarchy, if the end result takes the form of Crusoe's so-called kingship?

Not surprisingly, critics' answers to this question have been sharply divided. Richard Braverman, for instance, argues that Crusoe's relationship with Friday follows the Lockean, nonlapsarian guidelines of companionate parenting and rational liberality. "Friday's appearance," he claims, "legitimates Crusoe both in his separation from his past and his fathering of the new world of the island."[48] Manuel Schonhorn, by contrast, collects persuasive evidence from Defoe's other political works such as *Jure Divino* to show that Crusoe ultimately fulfills the benighted role of what Schonhorn calls the "gentleman-warrior-prince"—the man who, modeled after Defoe's heroic King William, commands the day by virtue of his martial courage and patriarchal leadership.[49]

Without attempting to resolve all the issues at stake here—and without, furthermore, indulging in mere fence straddling—we can usefully extend the logic of *Robinson Crusoe*'s dual narrative in order to suggest that Crusoe's political stature is composed by an uneasy coalition of *both* supervisory and patriarchal elements. The best place to consider that combination and its implications is in Crusoe's tutoring Friday, because there rests the origins of the sociopolitical community Crusoe forms by the end of the novel.

Crusoe is nothing less than enthusiastic about his new companion and pupil in Friday, whom Crusoe calls "the aptest Schollar that ever was."[50] As he teaches Friday new religious, moral, and cultural values, it becomes clear that Crusoe's pedagogy follows several aspects of supervisory education's premises, particularly as set out in Locke's *Education*. Crusoe speaks, first of all, of his aim to "imprint right Notions in his Mind" (217), invoking the Lockean metaphor of the wax tabula rasa present in the *Instructor*. Crusoe also acknowledges in Friday "the same Powers, the same Reason, [and] the same Affections" as are enjoyed by all human beings under God's universal dispensation (209), thereby treating his student in good supervisory fashion by appealing gently and confidently to Friday's inherent rational powers. And last, but not least, Crusoe further approaches Friday's education with all the affection and patience Locke advocates in ultimately making a child one's fellow companion by the end of the process. As Braverman points out, it seems hard to imagine a more companionable—and Lockean— tutorial relationship than the one Crusoe has with his charge.

Crusoe triumphantly claims that during these years he and Friday live together "perfectly and compleatly happy, *if any such Thing as compleat Happiness can be form'd in a sublunary State*" (220). That kind of assertion leads Braverman to argue that Friday's learning experience is a "utopian education," based on Locke having envisioned "innocent children in a state of nature."[51] Such a sweeping assimilation of Crusoe's pedagogical approach to Lockean, or more generally supervisory, principles, however, is not fully persuasive, first because supervisory educationalists' view of Nature is not untroubled, and second because there are significant aspects of Crusoe's educational procedure that do not match the supervisory program. Although Locke, for instance, substantially detoxified the traditional view of sinful childhood by secularizing the Fall paradigm in his pedagogy, his approach nonetheless retained a profound cautiousness, even distrust, of childhood's natural state and its impulses. Similarly, despite its disarmingly quaint earnestness, Friday's learning process is not simply an object lesson in Elysian pedagogy.

A key difference between Crusoe's tutorial practice and that of a supervisory instructor is that Crusoe does not generally conduct Friday's education by temporarily effacing his authority as teacher in order to observe his pupil's behavior before intervening. Instead, Crusoe's pedagogy draws on the model of Puritan didacticism: he approaches Friday by direct instruction, using "long Discourse"[52] to teach him theological and intellectual ideas. One reason for this may be that since Friday is a young man of "about twenty six Years of Age" (205) with a fully formed and distinct cultural background, Crusoe assumes he must launch his education head-on, in order to produce his spiritual (and, in a way, culinary) conversion as quickly as possible. It is worth recalling that when he embarked on his marine adventures, Crusoe himself was not much younger and also thoroughly versed in English cultural values and life. The difference, however, is that unlike his master, Friday does not have the individual prerogative—or luxury—of employing trial and error in the process of reforming his beliefs or practices. The reason for that difference is analogous to the difference between the education Locke proposes for the sons of the landed gentry and the one he advises for the children of the poorer underclasses: after his arrival, Friday's role as the island's chief source of manual labor is, after all, decisive. In this case it is more a matter of race or cultural heritage than economic class that determines Crusoe's education by a cruder, scaled-down version of supervisory pedagogy.

Although Crusoe describes Friday's appearance as having "all the Sweetness and Softness of an *European*," indicating he is a "tawny" Indian rather than a black (205), racial or ethnic background is finally a key determinant of the quality of Crusoe's so-

ciopedagogical relationship to his pupil. To be sure, Crusoe has af-
fectionately adopted Friday as his spiritually newborn son while
conducting his education in gentle supervisory fashion. Despite
that fact, however, Crusoe's teaching Friday never culminates in the
individual liberty Locke or Astell envisions, because Crusoe's relationship to Friday is severely overdetermined. For in addition to
being father/son and teacher/pupil, their relationship is also
lord/servant and master/slave. In the case of the first two affilia-
tions, there is the prospect for Friday's eventual self-determination
as an "adult" Christian; but in the case of the second two, both
of which are based on a matrix of ethnic or cultural inferiority,
Friday is destined—really, doomed—to remain Crusoe's devoted
subordinate.

Even when Crusoe proclaims Providence's universal distribution of rational capacity, with an eye toward Friday's future instruction, his qualifications and further addenda are telling: Crusoe is
struck that

> it had pleas'd God, in his Providence, and in the Government of the
> Works of his Hands, to take from so great a Part of the World of his
> Creatures, the best Uses to which their Faculties, and the Powers of
> their Souls are adapted; yet that he has bestow'd upon them the same
> Powers, the same Reason, the same Affections, the same Sentiments
> of Kindness and Obligation, the same Passions and Resentments of
> Wrongs, the same Sense of Gratitude, Sincerity, Fidelity, and all the
> Capacities of doing Good . . . that he has given to us. (209)

While providing this long list of characteristics shared by all human
beings, Crusoe suggests that some people are nevertheless designed
for "the best Uses to which their Faculties, and the Powers of their
Souls are adapted" (209). Though vague, this proviso seems to indicate the limitations of Friday's role as native Indian and helpmate
to Crusoe. Also pertinent to Crusoe's perception of Friday's usefulness as native servant are the other qualities he includes with universal reason—the sentiments of "Kindness and Obligation" and
the "same Sense of Gratitude, Sincerity, Fidelity." These features
readily explain Friday's demonstrative gratefulness to Crusoe for
saving his life, as well as his consistent loyalty. In the guise of uni-

versal human characteristics, they provide the basis for cultural and economic subordination.

The dichotomy between Crusoe's relaxed, genial tutoring of Friday and his more stern, even anxious approach based on patriarchal authority is particularly evident in the several dialogues Crusoe has with Friday while educating him. As in *The Family Instructor*, these dialogues provide a space for the exchange of contending points of view, even the collision of potentially unresolvable differences. Here Crusoe negotiates a fragile relation between subtle supervision and patriarchal austerity, ultimately consolidating the basis for managing Friday and his future colony in miniature. In the first dialogue, Crusoe questions Friday to see whether "he had any hankering Inclination to his own Country again" (214). Their brief conversation is more for informing Crusoe than instructing Friday, because Crusoe worries that a lingering desire to return to his homeland may motivate Friday to murder his new master. More than anything else, it is a test of Friday's potential dangerousness administered by a suspicious Crusoe.

In the second dialogue, however, when Crusoe attempts to teach Friday about the Devil, there emerges a new openness in pedagogical exchange. This time, Friday initiates the discussion by interrupting Crusoe's instruction to ask, "*[W]hy God no kill Devil, so make him no more do wicked?*" (218). After Crusoe finally composes himself enough to answer that God has reserved Satan's destruction for last, the two men engage in a discussion as perplexing for Crusoe as it is humorous. When Friday concludes, "*you, I, Devil, all wicked, all preserve, repent, God pardon all*" (219), Crusoe gives up the lesson in frustration. He interprets Friday's misunderstanding of Scripture as "a Testimony . . . how the meer Notions of Nature, though they will guide reasonable Creatures to the Knowledge of a God, and of a Worship or Homage due to the supreme Being," inevitably fall short of genuine spiritual insight. "Nothing but divine Revelation," he concludes, "can form the Knowledge of *Jesus Christ*, and of a Redemption purchas'd for us; . . . the Word of God, and the Spirit of God . . . are the absolutely necessary Instructors of the Souls of Men, in the saving Knowledge of God"

(219). As it turns out, Crusoe never relates the moment of Friday's divine revelation that would be necessary for his qualifying later as a full-fledged "Protestant." But whatever one believes about Crusoe's interpretation of this conversation, there is clearly a modicum of tolerant open-endedness in its conclusion.

In a third series of dialogues between himself and Friday, Crusoe confirms his sense of Friday's reliability and solidifies the basis for their ensuing relationship. In these discussions of Friday's desire to see his native country, Friday comes to understand Crusoe's intent that they be lifelong companions. But more importantly, Crusoe himself learns a key lesson emphasized in Locke's pedagogy: how to interpret correctly the physiognomical signs of a student's countenance and body language. He learns, in effect, to trust his first observations of Friday's appearance: "He had a very good Countenance, not a fierce and surly Aspect; but seem'd to have something very manly in his Face, and yet he had all the Sweetness and Softness of an *European* in his Countenance too, especially when he smil'd" (205). Early in their third set of conversations, at the mention of Friday's homeland, Crusoe "observ'd [that] an extraordinary Sense of Pleasure appear'd in his Face, and his Eyes sparkled, and his Countenance discover'd a strange Eagerness" (223–24). But Crusoe's suspicious interpretation of this "observation" proves mistaken. Although he "was every Day pumping him to see if he would discover any of the new Thoughts, which I suspected were in him," Crusoe finds "every thing he said was so Honest, and so Innocent, that I could find nothing to nourish my Suspicion" (224). Their conversations culminate in Crusoe's full trust in Friday's loyalty, and in Friday's declaration that he would rather die than leave his master. Crusoe has finally learned to capitalize on his ability to perceive the Christian and Western potential in his native pupil.

At this point, Friday's further exhortation that Crusoe extend his instruction to Friday's entire people—"*you teachee them Good*" (226)—suggests not only Crusoe's missionary capacities but also the expansive powers of Crusoe's emerging role as chief pedagogue and governor of his own island. As Crusoe himself reports, teaching Friday turns out to be a process of *self*-instruction, for in "laying

Things open to him, I really inform'd and instructed my self in many Things, that either I did not know, or had not fully consider'd before" (220). But in addition to grasping more firmly the tenets of his own Christian faith, Crusoe acquires the skills of pedagogical management that also apply to establishing the bonds of loyalty and cooperation in sociopolitical government. Crusoe has gained the ability to read his subjects' motives and character, to maintain social hierarchy and stability with benevolent paternalism—to act, in short, as a kind of supervisory patriarch who is both tolerant and strong. Negotiating this dual role is no easy task; it is a piecemeal process full of fits and starts, as are Crusoe's dialogues with Friday. Notwithstanding those difficulties, here one witnesses Defoe's version of the instantiation of the colonial system: the incorporation and adaptation of supervisory pedagogical techniques to establish the social, intellectual, and even emotional dynamics of a rational and gentle colonialism. In fact, having learned the lessons of training Friday, Crusoe becomes an even more effective observer-governor when he uses techniques of spying and clever orchestration on the fractious mutineers in order to produce their submission to his authority on the island. The first stage of that process is captured in an illustration from the sixth edition of the novel (fig. 24), where in the upper-left-hand corner of the picture, Crusoe perches himself on a hill with a telescope in hand, surveying the sailors' activity. He will then proceed to assist the captain of the ship, even going so far as to represent himself as only the assistant to a more powerful "governor" ruling the island.[53] And when he finally secures the mutineers' willing cooperation, he has established a full-blown colonial system that will operate after he leaves. Thus if the first stage of Crusoe's education results in spiritual conversion, the second stage produces a new, hybrid form of socioeconomic enterprise.

In demonstrating how ultimately Crusoe's island enterprise becomes a financial and sociopolitical success, Defoe's *Farther Adventures of Robinson Crusoe*, the sequel published in the same year as the first volume, confirms that the indirect techniques of supervisory education continue to be effective tools in colonial management. When Crusoe returns to his island, he finds it generally thriving,

An Engliſh Ship comes to R. Cruſoes Iſland. *V.I.p. 296.*

but given the roguish behavior of several of the Englishmen, particularly the ringleader William Atkins, it has become chaotic and woefully lacking in Christian virtue. The Spanish inhabitants on the island, it turns out, have been unsuccessful in trying to convert the natives living in the region, and the miscreant Englishmen have lived in near ignorance of Christian faith, to the point of living with native women they have never married. For both Crusoe and the French Catholic priest accompanying him, religious education becomes the first order of business, and they therefore teach Atkins and his cohorts an ecumenically defined set of Christian values, in order that they in turn should convert their soon-to-be wives. The priest's adage that "attempting to teach others is sometimes the best way of teaching our selves"[54] recalls Crusoe's remark about his experience with Friday and proves equally true for Atkins's English mates, who readily convert their female companions into both wives and Christians.

Atkins's case, however, requires more delicate supervisory managing: when Crusoe and the priest go out to find him for another conversation, Crusoe ends up improvising a restrained form of observation in order to monitor Atkins's progress. Crusoe describes reaching a point in the landscape

> where the Trees were so thick set, as that it was not easy to see thro' the Thicket of Leaves, and far harder to *see in*, than to *see out*; when, coming to the Edge of the Wood, I saw *Atkins* and his tawny Savage Wife sitting under the Shade of a Bush, very eager in Discourse; I stopp'd short 'till my Clergy-man came up to me; and then having show'd him where they were, we stood and look'd very steadily at them a good while. (166–67)

Although Crusoe and the priest are too far away to hear his words, Atkins turns out to be converting his wife to Christianity—and, in the process, himself—in a scene that recalls Defoe's aim in *The*

FIGURE 24 (facing page). Daniel Defoe, *Robinson Crusoe*, 1719; 6th ed., London, 1722. While the mutineers cause havoc on the island, Crusoe observes their activity using a telescope at a safe distance (upper-left-hand corner). Courtesy The Huntington Library, San Marino, California.

Family Instructor to fashion a successful religious play. Both Crusoe
and the priest become so overwhelmed with emotion at the silent
drama of the couple's conversion that the priest begins to expostu-
late until Crusoe "entreated him to with-hold himself a while, that
we might see an End of the Scene, which to me, I must confess,
was the most affecting, and yet the most agreeable that ever I saw in
my Life."[55] Only when Atkins and his wife have finished talking do
Crusoe and the priest intervene by questioning Atkins about his
newfound faith, after which Crusoe offers his readers a full tran-
scription of the conversation. So moved is he by the intensity of
Atkins's conversion, Crusoe declares "*the Man was made a Teacher
and Instructor to me, in a most surprizing and unexpected manner*" (174).
This encounter produces the turning point for Crusoe's ability to
consolidate the island's realm into "a kind of Common-Wealth" in
which both the native and European inhabitants can live peacefully
and prosperously (192). In this dramatic affirmation of Crusoe's
original social fantasy, supervisory colonialism proves able, once
again, to reverse spiritual deterioration, induce the ready cooperation of the native population, and generate the bonds of a secure,
yet tolerant, community.

Ultimately, the outcome of Crusoe's pedagogical adventures—
including the narrative seesawing between Puritan and supervisory
guidelines, Crusoe's erasure of the distinction between spontaneous
"facts" and their contemplated interpretation, and his cultivation of
pedagogical skills for sociopedagogical management—the crucial
outcome of Crusoe's story is not the formation of a unique individual whose private self is the hallmark of his identity. As peculiar
as Crusoe's temperament may seem and as unusual as his personal
success may appear, his story is more about the eventual *effacement*
of strictly private selfhood in favor of lucidly public and political
identity. In that sense, Defoe's novel follows the Lockean pedagogical protocol of "exteriorizing" the student's inner dynamics in the
process of conforming his behavior to public social standards. The
general movement of *Robinson Crusoe* is therefore from opaque personal motive to transparent religious commitment, from individual
singularity to sociopolitical readability. If Crusoe's youthful urge to
adventure baffles even himself—as when he exclaims "I know not

what to call this"[56]—then the mystery of his personal reasons finally gives way to the ability to expose and name their significance, when, for instance, he calls his indulgence in wanderlust his "Original Sin."

Furthermore, Crusoe's emergence from excruciating privacy and self-concealment marks his final development of social maturity. When he is terrified of discovery by the cannibals, Crusoe seeks out "the most retir'd Parts of the Island," finding places "as private indeed as my Heart could wish for" (162). But as he reports, such measures are ultimately ineffectual, because "Fear banish'd all my religious Hope" (156). Only when he decides to intervene in the cannibals' activity and then acts on that decision, does Crusoe regain his spiritual confidence and step into his role as preeminent ruler of the island. Just as what is painfully private must be *public*ized, apparently personal promptings also turn out to be part of a larger providential order. Crusoe remarks that he never fails to heed "those secret Hints, or pressings of my Mind, to doing, or not doing any Thing"; but he later learns that those intuitions are in fact the "secret Intimations of Providence" (175–76). In acknowledging this larger order and his inextricable public role in it, Crusoe succeeds in completing his reeducation.

Although it may finally prove impossible to disentangle entirely Crusoe's private self from his public one, that indeterminate result is no drawback, since the goal of supervisory education is precisely to affiliate individual privacy and public conformity so intimately that they facilitate exemplary consociation. In the end, Crusoe becomes a version of Foucault's "calculable man": he has come full circle only to be circumscribed by the very values of "the middle Station" in life his father so urgently recommended. Crusoe ends up the apotheosis of middle-class values—including industry, frugality, persistence, and self-discipline—although the very success of those principles nearly exceeds the parameters of middle-class livelihood. More importantly, while Crusoe's acquired disposition seems to be thoroughly determined by a bourgeois calculus, he also presents a telling example of social and pedagogical improvisation by which he has allied the agendas of Puritan patriarchy and supervisory liberality in the guise of both colonial administrator and fictional narrator. The socially useful paradox of Robinson Crusoe is that he has endured and appropriated the experience of rare adventure, while that process proves to be only the extraordinary means for finding a remarkably ordinary self. But as we shall see in the next chapter concerning Charlotte Lennox's heroine Arabella, the definition of "ordinary" disposition harbors a powerful distinction regarding gender, because the very prospect of successfully engaging "adventure" has troubling complications for an English woman who, in significant ways, aspires to the same boldness championed by Crusoe.

CHAPTER FIVE

Romancing the Home:
'The Female Quixote,' 'Betsy Thoughtless,' and the Dream of Feminine Empire

> Do not amuse yourself with reading romances; they warm the imagination, without enriching the mind; and altho' they represent virtue in the highest degree it can ascend to, yet they conceal abundance of poison beneath beautiful flowers, and especially to young people.
>
> —Philippe Dufour, *Moral Instructions of a Father to his Son*

> [Women should not expect] any one Man of Wit should arise so generous as to engage in our Quarrel, and be the Champion of our Sex against the Injuries and Oppressions of his own. Those Romantick days are over, and there is not so much as a *Don Quixot* of the Quill left to succour the distressed Damsels.
>
> —Judith Drake, *An Essay in Defence of the Female Sex*

She wanted, this woman, to have a heroic life. But for Arabella, Charlotte Lennox's heroine in *The Female Quixote* (1752), her quest for self-empowerment through romance proved to be strangely caught between insight and delusion, bold innovation and implicit nostalgia. For educational writers such as Philippe Dufour, the problem was much simpler, since he perceived in romance only the appearance of genuine morality, beneath which lurked the real core of dangerous frivolity; and if that threat should prove a strong caution for young men, then it would apply all the more to young women, whose presumably frailer constitutions would make them all the more susceptible to romance's poisonous charms. For men, and especially for women, reading romances produced unwieldy imaginations: in that sense, Dufour identifies the traditional sense in which Lennox's protagonist has been interpreted as a feminine variation on Don Quixote's whimsicality in Cervantes's famous novel.

But Arabella also captures another sense of quixotic behavior that is key for understanding how women authors from the late seventeenth to the mid-eighteenth century chose to represent the process of making their way in English society. Arabella embodies a distinct—though often self-contradictory—sense of female assertiveness advocated by women educationalists such as Mary Astell, Damaris Masham, and Judith Drake since the turn of the century. Both Masham and Drake, in fact, explicitly identified women who insisted on their right to a better education as female Quixotes: women who would be perceived as at least amusingly distracted and at most mentally imbalanced. In *Occasional Thoughts in Reference to a Vertuous or Christian Life* (1705), Masham argues that there are obvious advantages for both men and women, as well as children, if women were to gain substantial instruction in their Christian faith. Still, she pessimistically remarks, women who took that reasonable initiative would face daunting opposition:

> The Law of Fashion or Custom, is still to be obey'd, let Reason contradict it ever so much: And those bold Adventurers are look'd upon but as a sort of *Don Quixots*; whose Zeal for any Reformation puts them upon Combating generally receiv'd Opinions, or Practices; even tho' the Honour of their Maker be concern'd therein: Or (what is nearer to most) their own Private and Temporal Interests.[1]

In *An Essay in Defence of the Female Sex* (1696), Drake is equally critical of the social conventions regarding gender when she explains that women are at a great disadvantage in defending themselves against men's attacks on their intelligence or abilities "because through the Usurpation of Men, and the Tyranny of Custom (here in *England* especially) there are at most but few [women], who are by Education, and acquir'd Wit, or Letters sufficiently quallified for such an Undertaking."[2] But that acquired deficiency should not lead women (as she explains in the epigraph) to hope for rescue by a gallant man. The bonds of masculine homosociality, she insists, are so strong—since "Men are Parties against us"—

that women should not look for a "Champion of our Sex against the Injuries and Oppressions of his own," because those "Romantick days are over" (23, 3–4). As dry-eyed realists who recognize that modern English culture will not produce a "*Don Quixot* of the Quill," women must instead become Doña Quixotes of their own making in the struggle to overcome "the advantages Men have over us by their Education, Freedom of Converse, and variety of Business and Company" (3–4, 6).

For both Masham and Drake, then, their feminism entails a kind of romantic antiromanticism: it is not so much the complete banishment of heroic idealism, as it is a displacement of its location from an investment in masculine protection or authority to a stake in female enterprise against the cultural odds. But in Drake's text, there is also a rehabilitation of men's potential heroism suggesting a near nostalgia for the supposedly lost gallantry of a bygone age. Drake reports that in endorsing better education and social opportunities for women, she intends to improve the mutual society of men and women, and thereby ultimately preserve the long-standing preeminence of England as a nation. In the context of that project, the more traditional values of romance are crucial, because Drake recalls "an Opinion of a very Ingenious Person, who ascribes the Ruine of the *Spanish Grandeur* in great measure, to the ridiculing in the Person of *Don Quixot*, the *Gallantry* of that *Nation* toward their *Ladies*."[3] Hence Drake describes gallantry as one of the key things men learn best in the company of women, although now, rather than an exhibition of masculine strength or superiority, it is a "mixture of Freedom, Observance, and a desire of pleasing" in civil society (142). This is a gallantry with a new, gentler twist while also fully recognized and sanctioned by social tradition. Ultimately, Drake's approach to quixotism defines both a newfound feminine innovation and an attempt to preserve the legacy of English stature.

While in Lennox's novel, Arabella shows little concern for England's national ascendancy, she finds herself similarly situated between endorsing a strategy for female emancipation and perpetuating a more restrictive code of social behavior that has its origins in an earlier heroic or classical age. In the end, both dimensions of Arabella's romantic revisionism come down to the problem of what, and how, to teach, since in effect, Arabella uses French heroic romances in order to instruct the men around her in submissive obedience to her, and in turn, those efforts produce two countervailing pedagogical effects. Her stubborn insistence on the factuality of romantic stories reinforces the old stereotype of women's intellectual inadequacy, which in turn provokes her father (the Marquis), her suitor (Granville), and other male acquaintances (such as Sir George) to embark on their own individual and collective attempts to educate her about the "real" world. It is a case of dueling pedagogies, not just dueling agendas. At stake is what kind of knowledge women should learn from men, and what kind men should learn from women, as well as women from each other and for themselves. But equally important is what kind of instructive technique is appropriate or necessary for the improvement of relations between the sexes. There are several competing models for education deployed by the characters, including those following a direct, even harsh, didacticism, and others drawing on the indirect or covert methods characteristic of supervisory instruction. In this mix of conflicting methodologies, it becomes evident that the ideal function of supervisory education, which is to generate an evolutionary narrative successfully mediating between individual innovation and social tradition, virtually grinds to a halt. Under the pressures of the gendered inequities in Arabella's life, a supervisory approach proves unequal to the task of promoting an expanded sense of women's social entitlement while also maintaining a secure sense of the culture's traditional continuity.

This chapter explores how, as a figure caught in the crossfire of incompatible educational modes and agendas, Arabella demonstrates the ways gender difference drastically complicates the prospect of successfully improvised identity for mid-eighteenth-century English women who were intent on enlarged social participation. In being torn between epistemological illusion and the potential for social equalization or reform, Arabella closely resembles her literary predecessor, Cervantes's Don Quixote, who was similarly a figure of both willful befuddlement and staunch idealism a century and a half earlier. But in coming after the advent of recognizably "modern" feminist critiques of English culture during the late seventeenth and early eighteenth centuries—with authors including Bathsua Makin, Mary Astell, Mary Chudleigh, and Damaris Masham—Arabella's uneasy association of misprision and reformist zeal assumes a newly ambitious, and hence more vexingly polemical, character. In her daring bid for personal power, therefore, Arabella enacts in her own way Astell's exhortation in *A Serious Proposal to the Ladies* that women should seek through self-education to establish their own form of "empire." The combative suggestions of that metaphor, however, combined with the martial affinities of quixotic heroism, also pose the possibility of radically fracturing not only the social ties between men and women but also the often tenuous link between individual autonomy and social sanction. It threatens to split Arabella into two selves: one, as Leland Warren comments, "fully congruent with society's expectations, the other revealing the character's individual desire."[4]

This potential split has produced opposing interpretations of Arabella's reliance on romance as a cultural mandate. For Ronald Paulson, for instance, Arabella's staunch commitment to romance values transforms her into "a monster of egotism or self-sufficiency," while for many critics writing more recently—including Margaret Doody, Laurie Langbauer, Deborah Ross, Patricia Meyer Spacks, and Jane Spencer—her romantic gambit is an admirable, though ill-fated, gesture toward a feminist sense of women's genuine power and capacities.[5] But even a commitment to feminist solidarity has not produced a consensus on the individual or social value of Arabella's assertiveness. Katherine Green, for instance, argues that Arabella's identification with romance heroism ultimately "enrolls her under the masculinist illogic of romance," so that her "perception of herself through the distorted mirror image of romance entangles her in an ominously fragile imaginary construct . . . reflected by the male gaze."[6] Strangely, Arabella has the capacity to seem part monstrosity and part revolutionary, part female rebel and part masculine objectification. But the double valence of her story may have less to do with competing critical perspectives than it does with the result of portraying female education as the formation of a *female* (Don) Quixote, a woman who will be a cultural Amazon, fiercely intent on both seizing masculine prerogative and championing an idealized, recognizably traditional, femininity. This chapter will consider exactly how Arabella's conception of female empire produces an enigmatic model of education for women, a model that by the mid-eighteenth century would seem excessive and also outmoded in the face of increasingly conservative definitions of women's place in England. Lennox's novel proves to be the boldest fictional exploration of earlier women educationalists' interest in bolstering female entitlement, but it will also mark the failure of "empire" as a useful cultural metaphor for that purpose, at least in prose fiction. In the last two sections of this chapter, I turn to consider how in *The History of Miss Betsy Thoughtless* (1751), published one year before Lennox's novel, Eliza Haywood offers a more viable alternative for the midcentury's fictional representation of female education and development. Haywood in effect considers and then rejects female empire as a trope for a woman's successful maturation, proposing instead a more subtle approach to female identity conceived as ironic performance rather than imperious mastery.

Romance and the Canons of Female Education

By the time Arabella meets the unnamed Countess who befriends her late in the novel, the narrator reports that "romantick Heroism, was deeply rooted in her Heart; it was her Habit of thinking."[7] Like the hypothetical—and hapless—students often described by seventeenth- and eighteenth-century treatises on education, Arabella has fallen victim to the effects of dangerous habituation, whose grip is characterized in the familiar terminology of horticultural *root*edness. Viewing her world through romantic lenses has been for Arabella "a Principle imbib'd from Education" (329), and in a way generally similar to Robinson Crusoe's experience, she will have to undergo a psychological and moral ordeal in order to be adequately reeducated in acceptable behavior.

In Arabella's case, however, her initial education as a child has the peculiar distinction of being both meticulously micromanaged and extremely neglected. After his retreat from public life and the death of his wife, Arabella's father takes the unusual step of taking personal charge of her instruction. When she is four years old, he removes her from the care of her nurses, permitting her

> to receive no Part of her Education from another, which he was capable of giving her himself. He taught her to read and write in a very few Months; and, as she grew older, finding in her an uncommon Quickness of Apprehension, and an Understanding capable of great Improvements, he resolved to cultivate so promising a Genius with the utmost Care; and, as he frequently, in the Rapture of paternal Fondness, expressed himself, render her Mind as beautiful as her Person was lovely. (6)

On the one hand, the Marquis has followed the advice of Locke, Masham, and others, who recommended that parents take an active and frequent hand in their children's education; his closing sentiment, furthermore, echoes precisely Locke's dictum that education's holistic aim should be to produce "A Sound Mind in a sound Body."[8] On the other hand, the Marquis's rapturous enthusiasm about his daughter's intellectual abilities seems to have made him a "fond" parent in the worst sense that Locke describes that condition: his fondness has created an indulgent neglect of the most serious aspects of her instruction. While he makes sure she learns French and Italian, as well as music and dancing, he does not insist on anything else, although the narrator seems intent on placing the blame on Arabella rather than anyone else: "she would have made a great Proficiency in all useful Knowlege, had not her whole time been taken up by another Study"[9]—namely, reading French heroic romances.

In effect, after teaching her to read and write, the Marquis has made his daughter into a virtual autodidact by giving her free access to his library, an arrangement not uncommon in those households of the nobility or gentry where the patriarch's largess allowed a daughter or wife to study on her own. In part, then, Arabella is a warning about the dangers of women having no other recourse than to teach themselves, even though Masham, Drake, and other female educationalists argued that women may ultimately have no other choice. But the significance of Arabella's reading of romances is complicated further by the literal location of those texts in the family estate. As the books her mother had read in order to alleviate the burden of isolation from social intercourse, these romances offer Arabella a direct link to the mother she has never known. They therefore represent, both personally and historically, a female legacy that inspires Arabella's desire for broader social horizons. But since the Marquis has later incorporated the romances into his own library, where Arabella finds them, he has conferred on them a curious—though only partial—discursive legitimacy as part of the canon of texts officially sanctioned by male authority. Because they are housed along with the philosophy, history, and tomes on rhetoric, romances seem part of the respectable canon, though the Marquis's response to Arabella's reading them indicates they are quite the opposite.

The ambiguous status of romance in Arabella's household reflects a larger debate that had gone on for at least the previous one hundred years about whether or not romances could be an acceptable or even desirable part of instructing young or adult readers. The general agreement concerning young men reading romances was that at best it polluted their rational capacities. In the mid-1700s Philippe Dufour echoed Jean Gailhard's earlier conclusion in *The Compleat Gentleman* (1678) that reading "Romantical Adventures" inflamed boy's wayward fancies; Gailhard's views were widely known, especially during the late seventeenth century, when the popularity of his treatise in England prompted publishers to reissue it repeatedly.[10]

When it came to women reading romances, however, there was no clear consensus one way or the other—among either male or female educational writers. For many men, such as François Fénelon, romances were alarmingly inflammatory to the female imagination. In *Instructions for the Education of a Daughter* (1707), in fact, Fénelon describes a condition uncannily similar to Arabella's. Young women who become entranced with "Romances, with Plays, with the Relations of Chimerical Adventures," he laments,

> fill their Minds with empty Notions, by using themselves to the magnificent Language of the Heroes or Heroines, in Romances; they spoil themselves hereby for the World: For all these fine Airy Sentiments, all these Generous Passions, all these strange Adventures . . . bear no sort of proportion to the true Motives which are the Springs

of our Actions in the World, and upon which our Affairs do turn. . . . A poor Girl fill'd with the moving and surprizing strains which have charm'd her in her Reading, is astonished not to find in the World real Persons, who resemble these Heroes: She would live like those imaginary Princesses who are in the Romances, always Charming, always Adored, always above all kind of Want: What a disgust must it be for her to descend from this Heroical State to the meanest parts of Housewifery.[11]

Fénelon's argument is surprisingly blunt in preferring for women one form of distaste over another, since he indicates that women should be trained to endure admittedly repelling menial labor. By contrast, women educationalists who shared Fénelon's revulsion to romance drew on a notably different rationale. Bathsua Makin, Mary Astell, and Aphra Behn, among others, opposed "frothy Romances" in the interest of spurring women to more serious ways to educate themselves. As Astell put it, "There is a sort of Learning indeed which is worse than the greatest Ignorance: A woman may study Plays and Romances all her days, & be a great deal more knowing, but never a jot the wiser. Such a Knowledge as this serves only to instruct and put her forward in the practice of the greatest Follies."[12] For these writers, women could not afford the luxury of distracting themselves from the educational material with far greater cultural stakes.

There would be other educational writers, both men and women, who would voice cautious support for reading romances. In *Second Part of Youths Behavior, or Decency in Conversation Amongst Women* (1664), for instance, Robert Codington, in addition to insisting that women should have a full "Knowledge of Letters" and "learning," suggested a discriminating approach by endorsing for women readers romances that were "serious, generous, and of a noble Subject," without citing any particular examples.[13] Nearly a century later, while sharing Fénelon's concerns, Wetenhall Wilkes wrote to his favorite niece:

Novels, Plays, Romances and Poems must be read sparingly, and with Caution, lest such Parts of them as are not strictly tied down to Sedateness, should inculcate such light, over-gay Notions, as might by unperceiv'd Degrees soften and mislead the Understanding.[14]

Others, such as Mary Chudleigh, deemed romances "*very innocent, and very agreeable Diversions,*" so long as they did not dominate a woman's reading list.[15]

But there were also other women educationalists who perceived romances less as harmless entertainment, than as a serious way to educate women in virtue and sociability. It comes as something of a surprise, for instance, that in the rather straitlaced *Gentlewomans Companion; or, A Guide to the Female Sex* (1675), Hannah Woolley recommends that young women read both "choice pieces of Piety" and romances for their instruction. After emphasizing the study of Christian virtues, she writes:

> Some may imagine, that to read Romances after such practical Books of Divinity, will not only be a vain thing, but will absolutely overthrow that fabrick I endeavoured to erect: I am of a contrary opinion, and do believe such Romances which treat of Generosity, Gallantry, and Virtue, as *Cassandra, Clelia, Grand Cyrus, Cleopatra, Parthenissa*, not omiting Sir *Philip Sydney*'s Arcadia, are Books altogether worthy of their Observation. There are few Ladies mention'd therein, but are character'd what they ought to be, [and] the magnanimity, virtue, gallantry, patience, constancy, and courage of the men, might intitle them worthy Husbands to the most deserving of the female sex.[16]

Later, Judith Drake, similarly endorsing the value of gallantry, stresses less the moral than the practical benefits of reading romances. In *Defence of the Female Sex*, she explains that while in their formative years boys are given the liberty to run about outdoors, girls are given books of

> *Romances, Novels, Plays* and *Poems*; which though they read carelessly only for Diversion, yet unawares to them, give 'em very early a considerable Command both of Words and Sense; which are further improv'd by their making and receiving Visits with their Mothers, which give them betimes the opportunity of imitating, conversing with, and knowing the manner, and address of elder Persons.[17]

As a result, argues Drake, young women are usually more mature than their male counterparts of the same age, who have spent their time less usefully in memorizing Latin and Greek, and who, upon setting out in the world, "hoist Sail for the wide World without a

Compass to Steer by" (58). By Drake's account, then, romance is responsible for a more advantageous education for women, and it therefore undergirds her claim that men should become indoctrinated under women's more sophisticated linguistic and social tutelage. Therefore, romance is intimately tied to her project of recapturing England's former national glory.

On the face of it, Lennox's novel may seem poised among the mixed opinions about romance's value, rather than definitively choosing a particular side of the debate. Hence Arabella's attempt to enforce a romantic order within her household seems a horrible mistake, or an innocent, though disruptive, distraction, or a valid attempt to improve the level of social intercourse. By the mid-1700s, however, as critics have often noted, the novel had formed a self-description that aimed to authorize its own kind of fictional storytelling in the process of debunking "romance" conventions.[18] While praising Lennox's book in a review he wrote for *The Covent-Garden Journal* in 1752, Henry Fielding noted, for example, that "the Humour of Romance [is] . . . not at present greatly in fashion in this Kingdom."[19] One aspect of this development, as Margaret Doody points out, is that male authors were in effect declaring a female "body of lore" defunct, no longer available for borrowing or citation.[20] But another dimension was the phenomenon of appropriating one version of romance while discounting another characterized as inferior and "feminine." In a sense, this double standard is embodied in the Marquis's incorporation of the Marchioness's books in the library: it constitutes an appropriation of romance while indicating that doing so is based less on rational judgment than sentimental attachment or filial association. Therefore the Marquis both memorializes and discredits—owns and disowns—his wife's books, which represent the legacy of both women's reading and writing.

If, like the Marquis, the novel by the mid-1700s sets out to expropriate romance while also disavowing the family resemblances between them, then it was a move anticipated in educational discourse during the late 1600s, when writers were working to invent more effective ways to insinuate virtue in their readers. A case in point is Stephen Penton, who in 1688 published *The Guardian's In-*

struction, Or, The Gentleman's Romance, which deploys the "*heteroge-neous* Matter" of personal sketches, imagined scenarios, and specu-lative stories in order to inform "the *Gallant Youth* of the *English* Gentry" about the importance of "Learning and Politicks."[21] When the book first appeared, Penton wished to remain anonymous be-cause he perceived in his use of "romance" elements a generic in-novation in educational writing bound to provoke controversy. But against anticipated objections to the "*Romantick* manner of Writ-ing," he argues for its effectiveness:

> Truly, when I was of the Age of those persons in kindness to whom I write, I then thought that Fiction and Intercourse was somewhat more diverting than uniform *Narrations* or dogmatical *Propositions.* And I was about to say, that they better understand *Hobbs* his Sense and Principles by *Timothy* and *Philautus,* than from the Grand Au-thour himself: For there they see Consequences displayed, and the *Slye Connexion* between Dangerous Conclusions and Plausible Pre-misses exposed, which was palliated before under Good Style and Language, and the *Magisterial* authority of the Proponent. (sig. A3ʳ⁻ᵛ)

Drawing on "romance" is therefore more effective in appealing to the sensibilities of youth, not only because it is more entertaining but also because it implicitly challenges traditional authority by showing how acceptable "Style" camouflages shoddy thinking.

When Penton proceeds, in the guise of the "Guardian," to tell the invented story of a boy's instruction by a demanding tutor, it becomes clear that Penton's definition of romance follows the more general sense of "Fiction," rather than the conventions of heroic ro-mance. In fact, as part of his strategy to validate his employment of fictionalized narration, Penton creates an implicit hierarchy of dif-ferent kinds of "romance" based on their association with gender. When the boy in question is at first intimidated by his tutor's insis-tence on strict discipline, the father correctly refuses his requests for a different teacher, while the mother and sisters are in favor of catering to the boy's self-indulgent wishes. The women are mis-taken in their aversion to the tutor's advice to his pupil, the Guardian explains, because they "had been used to reade nothing but Speeches in *Romances*" (63). Hence romance is the culprit for an undesirable, "Womanish" demeanor, an emotional instability Penton finds in most of the women in the book, including "fond" mothers and overly delicate sisters.[22] These feminine shortcomings, undergirded by the dainty ornateness of heroic romance, stand in sharp contrast with the "Masculine Eloquence which flows upon all Occasions" in the Parliament (87), which has the Guardian's Whiggish admiration for its strong leadership as England enters a new political era.

Penton's book thus illustrates an early example of how the aim of better educating readers could lead to endorsing the "novel," in the sense of proposing an innovative, "realistic" form of storytelling set against both traditional nonfictional prose and feminized, ethereal romantic conventions. But while this tactic certainly characterizes the effect of Lennox's satire of romance and Arabella's infatuation with its niceties—in an important way, Lennox's work even seems a compressed document of the mid-eighteenth-century transition from acknowledging the validity of romance to asserting the novel's ascendancy—it does not tell the entire story about *The Female Quixote*. There is also a tendency in the book to resist the apotheosis of the novel's "masculine" ethos, a reformist impulse already indicated by Drake and Woolley's endorsement of romance in the interest of promoting women's interests. At the same time, however, the novel reveals that the very act of championing a "female" literary legacy will turn out to take on bracingly "masculine" features when Arabella reaches for the spoils of an imperious domesticity.

From Canons to Cannons: Abject Amazons and the Prospect of Empire

If a differentiated system of gendered values discriminates among more and less estimable definitions of romance, then they apply with equal weight to the idea of gaining personal and social sway in the form of "empire." This is the lesson learned from only a brief comparison of Robinson Crusoe's and Arabella's stories, which share some notable similarities. Both characters are driven by apparently irrational desires compelling them, almost uncontrol-

lably, in search of adventure. For different reasons, they are put off
by the inconsequential dullness of ordinary, "modern" English life:
Crusoe finds unacceptable the conditions of middle-class existence,
although his father advocates the benefits of the "Middle Station of
Life"; Arabella finds herself in rebellion against her father's desire
that she settle down as a submissive and loving wife, whose model
of behavior would to a great extent be similarly defined by both
middle-class and aristocratic standards. For most of the novel, she
refuses to resign herself to the ordinary role expected of women:

> What room, I pray you, does a Lady give for high and noble
> Adventures, who consumes her Days in Dressing, Dancing, listening
> to Songs, and ranging the Walks with People as thoughtless as her-
> self? How mean and contemptible a Figure must a Life spent in such
> idle Amusements make in History? Or rather, Are not such Persons
> always buried in Oblivion, and can any Pen be found who would
> condescend to record such inconsiderable Actions?[23]

Both Crusoe and Arabella take matters into their own hands
by pursuing what is initially a transgressive form of personal empire: Crusoe, by literally creating the economic and social basis for
a miniature English colony, and Arabella, by deploying what she
calls the "Laws of Honour and Romance" (116) in order to establish an "Empire of Love" (320) she can administer in her own
household.[24] Like Crusoe, who only half-playfully assigns himself
the honorific titles of "King," "Lord," and "Governour," Arabella
also appropriates political and legal terminology to validate an un-
orthodox authority over everyone who comes within arm's distance. But Crusoe's quest for empire will end triumphantly, while
Arabella's will not, for reasons that include, and also surpass, gender: Crusoe's story is of a man who learns to master the discipline
of domestic management before then applying it to the larger project of forming his personal kingdom; Arabella's story, by contrast,
is about a woman who rejects traditional domesticity by opting to
replace it with a form of feminine sovereignty. The political implications of Arabella's peculiar behavior, in fact, are observed even by
the men around her, since as Sir Charles remarks about her eloquence, "if she had been a Man, she would have made a great Figure in Parliament" (311).

Of course, even should Arabella choose to submit first to the regimen of domestic femininity, she would not then have the option to invoke some kind of quasi-political authority for expanding and transforming her traditional role. That kind of privilege applies only to Crusoe's masculine entrepreneurialism. But comparing the two protagonists nonetheless reveals how Crusoe's ultimate success depends at least in part on initially mastering the ways and means of maintaining a domestic economy—the functions usually assigned to women. As Nancy Armstrong points out, both eighteenth- and nineteenth-century theorists interested in educating young women "recommended *Crusoe* over Defoe's other works, because they thought women were likely to learn to desire what Crusoe accomplished, a totally self-enclosed and functional domain where money did not really matter. It was no doubt because Crusoe was more female, according to the nineteenth century understanding of gender, than either Roxana or Moll that educators found his story more suitable reading for girls than for boys of an impressionable age."[25] In these terms, Defoe's novel made a significant contribution to the emergence of domestic fiction, which later became fully identifiable as a genre in the hands of Richardson in *Pamela*, the book that in Armstrong's estimation consolidated a middle-class and psychologically internalized sense of feminine identity.[26]

There is at least one sense in which the representation of Arabella's experience resembles that of Pamela, since she too exhibits a genuine sense of her own psychological interiority. In addition to being pronounced by virtually everyone around her (including the narrator) as a woman of admirable intelligence—having "more *Wit*," as Glanville notes, "than her whole Sex"[27]—Arabella's restive imagination is further evidence of an inner life so self-confirming that it reproduces its fantasies in the environment around her. Her peculiar behavior—and the equally discomfiting behavior she induces in others—are external manifestations of her interior landscape. Although she is committed to living in the world of romance's grand public gestures and events, Arabella also anticipates her story being told in all the exhaustive, realistic detail with which authors such as Defoe or Richardson recorded the mental lives of their protagonists. As Arabella tells her handservant Lucy, she should

recount all my Words and Actions, even the smallest and most inconsiderable, but also all my Thoughts, however instantaneous; relate
exactly every Change of my Countenance; number all my Smiles,
Half-Smiles, Blushes, Turnings pale, Glances, Pauses, Full-stops, In-
terruptions; . . . and every Gesture which I have used for these Ten
Years past; nor omit the smallest Circumstance that relates to me.
(121–22)

Arabella seems to propose a hybrid generic approach, in which the
elements of her own romance heroism can be inscribed by the
novel's conventions of formal realism (as Ian Watt terms it[28])—join-
ing, in the process, the external and the internal.

It is also true, however, that Arabella adamantly rejects the narrative logic of domestic fiction. In the first place, her veneration for
what Michael McKeon calls "romance idealism," the conviction
that received traditions form the basis for knowledge, corresponds
to her equally strong commitment to "aristocratic ideology," which
treats moral virtues as both historically unchanging and inborn personality traits.[29] The latter interpretive code establishes a social
ethos antithetical to the middle-class valence of the new domesticity. But more importantly, for Arabella, a woman's story ends—
even literally—when she submits to marriage and the yoke of
household management. As she explains to Glanville regarding any
romance heroine, once "she at last condescends to reward him with
her Hand . . . all her Adventures are at an End for the future."[30]
Hence a woman's story can continue only so long as she maintains
a sense of independence derived from romance in medias res. That
notion, combined with Arabella's aristocratic ideals, prompts her to
reverse the narrative process exemplified by Crusoe: rather than
submitting first to the demands of domesticity, deferring until later
a claim to any kind of "public" social power—which, for a woman,
is already rendered off limits by the protocols of domestic fiction—
Arabella immediately seizes a form of romantic empire whose aggressive political implications enable her to dominate the men
around her at home. In effect, Arabella wants to "romance" the
home, transforming its typically dull and stifling furniture into the
props for a protofeminist quest for authority.

The men around Arabella—the Marquis, Glanville, and Sir

George—respond to her self-authorization by trying to teach her how history and, more importantly, how "modern" social relations between the sexes really work. Their various attempts to do so are a study in contrasting pedagogical strategies. Arabella's father, as we have already seen, has initially been very active in schooling his daughter, before apparently becoming complacent about the rest of her education. But once he realizes the extent of Arabella's commitment to romance values and of her aim to impose them on her potential suitors, the Marquis attempts to make up for lost time, though to relatively little effect. Like the father in Defoe's *Family Instructor*, the Marquis decides his last resort is to impose heavy-handed discipline, in the hopes of curbing Arabella's behavior, if not really reforming her. When he realizes, for example, that Arabella has banished Glanville from the estate, her father reacts angrily, "leading her to his Writing-Desk" and ordering her to reverse her dictum by writing him. In her letter, Arabella makes entirely clear to her suitor that her father has imposed his will on hers: "It is not by the Power I have over you, that I command you to return, for I disclaim any Empire over so unworthy a Subject; . . . it is in Obedience to my Father's absolute Commands, that you receive this Mandate" (40). Later, when he perceives that Arabella has softened in her demeanor toward Glanville, the Marquis "resolved not to interpose his Authority in an Affair upon which her own Happiness so much depended" (46). But that apparent moderation does not dispel Arabella's resentment of what she considers "a tyrannical Exertion of parental Authority" (35).

The Marquis's attempts prove to be too little too late, especially since his death prevents him from persevering in the aim of altering Arabella's disposition. That pedagogical task passes on to Glanville, who, as her future spouse, assumes the role of teaching her better behavior. Sir Charles, his father, reflects the men's general sense of how serious things are when he characterizes Glanville's prospective function in the terminology of disease and cure:

> [Y]ou may probably find the Means of curing her of those little Follies, which at present are conspicuous enough; but, being occasioned by a Country Education, and a perfect Ignorance of the World, the Instruction, which then you will not scruple to give her, and which,

from a Husband, without any Offence to her Delicacy, she may receive, may reform her Conduct. (180)

Glanville himself adopts the language of the cure, as when he later
tells Sir George, concerning Arabella's "romantic Turn," that "I
must cure her of that Singularity."[31] But where Arabella's father has
failed in that aim, Sir Charles intimates, Glanville will succeed because he will provide Arabella with consistent and gentle guidance.
And if Glanville does not always insist on correcting each of Arabella's romantic excesses, it is because his father has accurately described Glanville's intention to use the indirect methods affiliated
with supervisory instruction. He rejects outright attempting to
shock or command Arabella, as her father had sometimes done, out
of her obstinacy. As the narrator reports, "Sometimes he fansied
Company, and an Acquaintance with the World, would produce
the Alteration he wished: Yet he dreaded to see her exposed to
Ridicule by her fantastical Behaviour, and become the Jest of Persons who were not possessed of half her Understanding" (117).
Like Locke, Glanville carefully guards his pupil's sense of others'
"esteem" in order to shape her disposition as gently as possible, and
he persists in that effort even when Miss Glanville's and other people's opinion of her have become anything but complimentary. In
these and other circumstances, like Fénelon, Astell, and other educators, Glanville deploys a kind of honest deception, by which he
hopes to coax Arabella into normalcy. His chief strategy for curing
her, in fact, is only to pretend to read the romances Arabella gives
him, choosing instead to infer and mimic the behavior she expects
from him while looking for opportunities to revise, gradually, her
stubborn perceptions.

Glanville's efforts to cure Arabella homeopathetically give a supervisory twist to the way that several characters in Cervantes's
novel—including Carrasco and the Duke and Duchess—attempt to
"humor" Don Quixote into sanity. But in a more daring gambit to
rid Arabella of her illusions, Sir George goes to even greater lengths
of deceptive indirection. His duplicity surpasses Glanville's because
he seems unconcerned about Arabella's general well-being and is
intent on seducing her by pretending to an earnest belief in ro-

mance values. He therefore also goes further than Glanville in his methods, by making the claim to being a sympathetic author, as well as a reader, of romance narratives. Sir George proceeds to sway Arabella by employing his literary skills—formerly devoted, he tells Sir Charles, to tragedies, essays, and poetry (252)—in order to tell a story of his "Adventures" that *"exactly copied the Stile of Romance"* (207, 209). How much Sir George hopes this tactic will be effective can be measured by his story's lasting for almost all of book 6, until his describing a rapid transfer of devotion from one heroine to another strikes Arabella as incongruous and unworthy. But the failure of this stratagem is only a momentary setback for Sir George, who then turns to employ a version of the staged scenario that educators like Locke recommended in the interest of "cozening" pupils. When Arabella subsequently meets a woman who identifies herself as the Princess of Gaul and who relates in her "History" that Glanville has been her unfaithful suitor, Arabella nearly decides Glanville does not deserve her own affections. But as Glanville later discovers, this episode is only a "ridiculous Farce" aimed to eliminate him as a rival: in fact, Sir George "brib'd a young Actress to personate a Princess forsaken by him [Glanville]; and had taught her all that Heap of Absurdity with which she had impos'd upon *Arabella"* (382, 368).

In creating a false persona and staging a real-life fiction, Sir George partially resembles Robinson Crusoe, who creates the false story about the island's governor in order to reform the fractious mutineers and thereby to secure his personal authority. Both men attempt to recast transgressive behavior for their own purposes by drawing on the fictive plotting techniques recommended by Locke and other educators when dealing with reluctant pupils. In Sir George's case, his authority is also literally at stake, since he is intent on proving, especially to his male listeners, that his storytelling abilities mark him as a real "Author" (see 252). But it is also clear that Sir George has used "his plotting Talent" (354) in order to teach Arabella a lesson in the most cynical sense possible. He may aim to seduce her, but even that prospect failing, Sir George has worked to manipulate the circumstances until he can rudely shock Arabella out of her silly notions. On the face of it, then, particularly since

Glanville genuinely loves Arabella, his approach to her reformation may seem the best alternative offered by the men in her life. But because both Glanville's and Sir George's attempts to change Arabella's mind are based on the similar tactics of feigned behavior and hidden agendas, Glanville's apparently benevolent intentions are also tainted by masculine hubris. The fact, moreover, that neither Glanville's nor Sir George's efforts succeed suggests that Lennox finds them wanting: the novel's story line indicates that even the most gentle implementations of supervisory education are heavily stacked in favor of male manipulation and cultural hegemony.

Arabella's stalwart commitment to romance is in effect a preemptive strike against the normalizing force at least implicit in masculine attempts to reeducate her, and as such, it is direct, aggressive, and unapologetic in its aim to subdue the men around her. This is why many critics point to Arabella's employment of romance as a bid for female power, although none has considered the exact political and judicial terms in which she makes that claim. Like Mary Astell, Arabella realizes, at least instinctively, that women need to seize a version of personal "empire" in the face of England's disadvantageous social hierarchy. She repeatedly describes herself as a monarch with "absolute Empire" over her suitors, who as her "Subjects" should exhibit complete obedience to her commands (see, e.g., 40, 136, 138). To be sure, that kind of project provokes strikingly different responses not only within the story but also outside it, as in the example of the Roman Emperor Domitian. Astell, as we saw in chapter 1, uses Domitian's legendary attention to trivial—and bizarre—activities rather than the affairs of state as a way to exhort her female readers that rather than "catching Flies, . . . you should be busied in obtaining Empires."[32] This sentiment matches Arabella's determination to be satisfied with more than the usual baubles of domestic feminine activity. But Domitian could be used to prove just the opposite conclusion about Lennox's book. In the discussion framing his review of the novel, Fielding cites Domitian as an instance of "vain Curiousity and Diligence in Trifles," the result of the human tendency to apply inordinate energy to petty pursuits. "If Domitian," he remarks, "had not been of a busy as well as a cruel Temper, he would never have employed so many Hours in the ingenious Employment of Fly-spitting, which he is supposed to have brought to the highest Degree of Perfection of which the Art is capable." In Fielding's view, then, Arabella is Lennox's Domitian: for him the novel's aim is "to expose all those Vices and Follies in her Sex which are chiefly predominant in our Days, that it will afford very useful Lessons to all those young Ladies who will peruse it with proper Attention."[33]

Fielding's main concern is with women's predilection to emulate the mannered foolishness of romance, although as his comments suggest, he is equally dismissive of their attempt to gain the form of sovereignty suggested by Astell's argument. In Fielding's fiction, for example, women who have pretensions to learning, such as Jenny Jones or Mrs. Western in *Tom Jones*, inevitably become deluded or egotistical in their sense of self-empowerment. Mrs. Western's extensive reading in European history and "political Pamphlets and Journals," moreover, leads her to opine about matters of public policy in which, her brother scoldingly reminds her, "Petticoats should not meddle."[34] For both Astell and Arabella, however, using the trope of empire is not aimed to make a claim for women's full participation in the public sphere. Instead, they both maintain a strong distinction between the world of men's social and political power and the world of women's more private lives. As Arabella explains to Glanville, who has missed this point, the "Empire of Love, . . . like the Empire of Honour, is govern'd by Laws of its own, which have no Dependence upon, or Relation to any other."[35] For her, the point is romancing the *home*—appropriating the language of politics for the purpose of authorizing women's enlarged self-determination in the personal arena of family, friends, and love relationships. It is a less extensive, but no less crucial, domain.

As monarch or administrator of her empire at home, Arabella employs the language of legal regulation as the chief means to teach men how to behave properly toward her. Under the general rubric of the "Laws of Romance," the more specific "Laws of Knighthood" and "Laws of Decency and Decorum" determine when men's misbehavior—perceived or real—has become a "Crime" against her sovereignty (see, e.g., 172, 155, 161, 115). As, for in-

stance, either a metaphorical municipal judge or a monarch sitting
in judgment, Arabella stages a miniature trial of Glanville for his
possible participation in her supposedly near abduction. In alluding
to Cleopatra's test of Coriolanus's loyalty, she exhorts him to "endeavour your own Justification" until "it might be lawful for *Arabella* to readmit you, with Honour, into her former Esteem and
Friendship" (115–16). Later, in submitting to his own trial of love
by fire, Bellmour will echo Arabella's judicial terminology by declaring himself a "Criminal" deserving of his "Sentence of . . .
Death" (174). In effect, Arabella uses romance as a form of legal
precedent whose statutes reform her subjects by way of direct prescription, prohibition, and punishment. As seventeenth-century legal theorists frequently commented, the law's enforcement served
not only to maintain order but also to teach the populace acceptable conduct. By the early eighteenth century, this method of education had been discredited as archaic and coercive by educationalists such as Locke, Masham, and Astell. Hence Arabella is imposing on her suitors an alien code of civil behavior in a method
considered both outdated and harsh. And yet she deploys this double anachronism in the aim of establishing a more "modern" female
role in the household. Forceful pedagogy seems the only means she
has for improving the sexual odds.

Arabella's transformed "political" power will also have a decidedly theatrical dimension, in which she stages both her own romantic heroism and the conduct of men. While she is constantly
an object of masculine observation or eroticized admiration because of her beauty, Arabella's countenance and dress consistently
induce a kind of quiescent astonishment in her spectators, including women. Even in London, her antiquated apparel produces a reluctant respect for her act of sheer self-invention, which in turn di-
rects others' behavior, often despite themselves, by romantic standards. When, for instance, the unsuspecting Mr. Hervey becomes
caught up in the intrigue of Arabella's accusing him of being "an
impious Ravisher," he perceives himself as both audience and actor
in her fantastic drama: he "stood some Moments considering the
strange Scene he had been Witness to; and in which he had, much
against his Will, appeared the principal Character" (20, 21). Ara-

bella's theatricality also gains a mystifying, even magical, quality given Lennox's apparent borrowing, especially at the beginning of the story, from *The Tempest*. As Deborah Ross has suggested, the Marquis's self-imposed retreat from the world at court, the death of his wife, and his subsequently raising his daughter on his own resemble the situation of Prospero, whose exploits in wizardry on his island create a romantic backdrop for Lennox's more satirical intentions.[36] But the most important parallel between Shakespeare's play and the novel is no doubt that between Prospero and Arabella, since she is the one who asserts a form of magical and even theatrical power in order to establish her own self-defined domain. Arabella's self-appointed prowess in fact includes the mystical ability to "command" men to live or die. Like Prospero, she uses her romantic powers to test and reeducate the eighteenth-century equivalent of an Alonso, Ferdinand, or Miranda (perhaps even a Caliban) in the interest of forming a more ideal community. Thus she supplants her father and emulates—with a satirical twist—Prospero's masterful use of illusion and orchestration of human affairs, a role that serves as Shakespeare's model for the dramatist. And like Prospero, she too must realize in the end the value of returning to the world at large, though for her it is one determined by diminished female terms.

In performing the role, at least temporarily, of a female Prospero, Arabella underscores what is implicit in her use of political or judicial metaphors—that she is not merely a female *version* of a masculine figure but instead a woman who actively appropriates and transforms for her own purposes the role models usually designated as male. This is another form of Drake and Masham's sense of a female quixote: a woman daring enough to tilt at the landmarks of masculine authority or educational privilege and, in the process, to become a person neither entirely masculine nor traditionally feminine. The most potent figure in the novel of this improvised female identity is the Amazon, who introduces an explicitly colonial context for the notion of feminine "empire" and who represents for Arabella an emblem of idealized womanhood. As Laura Brown has pointed out, male authors' characterization of a woman as an Amazon during the eighteenth century usually served to create a scapegoat for the brutality of British empire-building, since typically an Amazonian woman represents a "domestic violence [that] displaces male imperialist violence."[37] In the hands of women authors, however, that construction of female identity would often be seriously challenged. Judith Drake, for instance, chose to treat the stories of Amazon societies as genuine historical fact, claiming there was a different origin for their initial formation than that traditionally offered—inherent female combativeness. In *Defence of the Female Sex*, noting that there had long been accounts of nations composed solely of male citizens, Drake concludes that "the Conditions of their Society were not so easie, as to engage their Women to stay amongst 'em; but as liberty presented it self, they withdrew and retired to the *Amazons*."[38] Whether or not she believes in the Amazons' actual existence, Drake apparently ignores the imperialist bias inherent in imagining a female warrior who stands in for the colonial Other that the British encountered across the globe. But she nonetheless indicates that Amazonian fierceness—even in "modern" British women—is a response to a prior hostility in men's treatment of them.

In Arabella's case, however, she treats the Amazon as more than an example of female self-defensiveness. She takes things further by commandeering its traditionally masculinist symbolism and seizing on Thalestris, the Queen of the Amazons, as a model of female identity. That move is clearly a way of doing violence to the domestic ideal—given Arabella's resistance to marriage, it is, in effect, a way to substitute martial for marital status in defining women's lives. Arabella's reluctant pupils in romance history, including Sir Charles, Sir George, and Miss Glanville, are appalled by precisely the suggestion that women could be warlike. Miss Glanville wonders, for instance, "Whether in former times Women went to the Wars, and fought like Men? For my Cousin . . . talks of one *Thaltris* [sic], a Woman, that was as courageous as any Soldier whatever."[39] For Sir Charles, it is troubling to imagine such skills giving women institutional authority over men, as Arabella reports it having occurred in the romance *Cassandra*, where Thalestris is offered the command of male forces attempting to rescue Statira and Parisatis from Babylonian captivity. He exclaims, "O shameful! . . . offer a

Woman the Command of an Army! Brave Fellows indeed, that would be commanded by a Woman!" (205).

The most innovative and unsettling aspect of Arabella's construction of Amazonian identity, however, is her claim that it in no way dispenses with genuine femininity. Her description of Thalestris's commanding femininity in fact provokes the most vociferous response of any to her assertions about Amazons:

> *Thalestris*, [Arabella said,] tho' the most stout and courageous of her Sex, was, nevertheless, a perfect Beauty; and had as much Harmony and Softness in her Looks and Person, as she had Courage in her Heart, and Strength in her Blows.
>
> Indeed, Madam, resumed Miss *Glanville*, you can never persuade me, that a Woman who can fight, and cut People to Pieces with her Blows, can have any Softness in her Person: She must needs have very masculine Hands, that could give such terrible Blows: And I can have no Notion of the harmony of a Person's Looks, who, by what you say, must have the heart of a Tyger. But, indeed, I don't think there ever could be such a Woman. (125–26)

Miss Glanville is invoking the familiar idea that an Amazon must have been a woman who had become unsexed by her commitment to martial valor. The most common emblem of that fact was that an Amazon's dedication to being an unsurpassed archer entailed cutting off one of her breasts in order to allow clear passage for her arrows. The remaining mammary served as reminder of the Amazon's natural femininity, whose harmony had become disfigured by the deliberate attempt to act "like a man."

As Laurie Langbauer points out, Arabella's Amazons certainly are "the symbol for women's usurpation of men's power,"[40] but they are also much more, because for Arabella, they represent the possibility of having masculine power without any loss of feminine virtue. In Miss Glanville's view, an Amazon offers the spectacle of a woman who has lost her natural female identity in the act of perversely seizing men's aggressivity. But Arabella's Amazon is all the more disturbing because she is viscerally abject, a being both powerfully masculine and fully feminine, indeterminately occupying both categories in a volatile combination. That possibility seems to Miss Glanville a monstrosity, an animalistic being with a "the heart of a Tyger." What she finds repulsive about Arabella's Amazon, as Julia Kristeva observes about abjection in general, is not the prospect of her physical deformity—Arabella claims she has none—but instead the fact that she "disturbs identity, system, order."[41] Ultimately, Arabella's Amazon is intent on forming a *feminine*, rather than merely female, empire. She expropriates men's political and judicial discourse for the purpose of ruling at home, and despite her aggressive displacement of male domestic authority, she retains the virtues traditionally associated with her sex, including softness and dazzling beauty.

Inevitably, there are several problems with Arabella's attempt to establish this figure of womanhood as the successful culmination her own self-education, or to use it as an effective device for schooling those around her in romance gallantry. The first difficulty is her resulting estrangement from her household community, an alienation that does not completely ostracize her, but at the very least, severely undermines her aim to be an integral and motivating figure in her family and friends' lives. She has not, like Fielding's "Amazonian Heroines" in *Tom Jones*—including Mrs. Partridge, Molly Seagrim, and Goody Brown—become so masculinized that she engages in literal fisticuffs or physical intimidation.[42] But she has some similarities with another female character Fielding associates with unseemly Amazonian behavior, Mrs. Western, whose "masculine Person, which was near six Foot high, added to her Manner and Learning, [and] possibly prevented the other Sex from regarding her, notwithstanding her Petticoats, in the Light of a Woman" (273–74). For Fielding, Mrs. Western's domineering physique matches her dour demeanor and her impingement on areas of knowledge traditionally reserved for men, but in addition to trespassing on masculine literary territory, Mrs. Western has indulged in the worst kind of "feminine" reading—"all the modern Plays, Operas, Oratorios, Poems and Romances"—becoming in the process one of the worst of Fieldingesque creatures: "a Critic" (272–73). As Jill Campbell points out, during the 1740s and 50s women such as Mrs. Western also invoked, at least implicitly, the common Whiggish characterization of the Jacobite rebellion as being motivated in part by aggressive, Amazonian women, who, in pursuing their own form of "petticoat government," bullied men into political insurrection against the throne.[43] While by contrast, Arabella has no genuine political aspirations and can muster every feminine charm imaginable, she also uses her physical appearance as a weapon on the men she encounters, her impressive beauty often subduing them at least temporarily to her desires. In the end, Lennox does not consider her heroine's aspirations anywhere near as problematic as Fielding does Mrs. Western's. But the price of the domestic prowess both women wield is a kind of partial exile: they are always marginal figures in the very circles where they live.

It should be remembered, however, that even female educationalists who strongly endorsed a better education for women acknowledged that they should prepare themselves for the probability of relative social isolation. In proposing her plan for an academic retreat, Mary Astell sought to transform that likelihood into the genuine benefit of temporary female retirement in a community of sympathetic women. But for others, such as Damaris Masham, who did not imagine retreat advisable, a liberally educated woman faced a daunting prospect. Even after she has exhorted her readers to religious understanding for nearly two hundred pages in *Occasional Thoughts in Reference to a Vertuous or Christian Life*, Masham creates a troubling list of the potential repercussions: women "conversant in Books," for instance, "might be in danger of not finding Husbands," and their "Conduct, which carry'd with it so much Reproach to Woman's Idleness, and disappointment to Men's Vanity, would quickly be judg'd fit to be ridicul'd out of the World before others were infected by the example." A knowledgeable woman, moreover, would inevitably be "in Town the Jest of the *Would-be-Witts* [*sic*]." But in the country, her fate would be worse: her being so well informed about religious issues would make her suspected of heresy, her lack of sectarianism also liable to make her accused of being "a *Socinian*, or a *Deist*"; her knowledge of philosophy would lead to suspicion of atheism; the country parson would be diffident, being nervous about her ability to challenge his authority; and finally, "the Country Gentlemen that wish'd her well, could not yet chuse but be afraid for her, lest too much Learning might in Time make her Mad."[44]

At first glance, Arabella seems to fit the role Masham describes for her female Quixote, particularly regarding the suspicion of her sanity. But ultimately, the kind of knowledge Arabella has chosen to gain for herself undermines her claim to the kind of heroism imagined by educational writers such as Masham, Astell, and others who came after them in the early eighteenth century. The problem is more than that she has committed herself to a less "serious," and therefore less effective, body of knowledge than that recommended by earlier women educationalists. It is instead that she has aimed to establish a progressive mode of female prerogative by deploying, via romance, an outmoded canon of literature or social values. It is also a difficulty like the one Judith Drake faces in trying to redefine women's social position while also harking back to the nostalgic code of masculine gallantry. Even the modest criteria of practical application suggest that Arabella has done both too much and too little in improvising a protofeminist identity. On the one hand, given Arabella's audience, she has introduced a new model for gender relationships too suddenly, exceeding virtually everyone's ability or willingness to assimilate it. On the other hand, however, her insistence on retaining the well-recognized feminine attributes of softness or beauty suggests to her listeners, despite her Amazonian ethos, that the conventional eighteenth-century perceptions of women's role remain ultimately intact—and that Arabella can herself be finally reconciled to them.

There is also one other way that Arabella has unintentionally limited or circumscribed her ability to mandate change, even in the guise of metaphorical monarch or judge. As she often tells her suitors as subjects, she is determined to apply consistent and implacable "Rigour" in declaring their sentences.[45] While on occasion, she relents in her rigorous judgments, it is precisely her rigor that prevents her from imagining her role as anything other than that of *implementing* the law, rather than creating or thoroughly revamping it. So while romance authorizes her largely to dictate the course of her relationships, it also serves as a precedent in the strongest legal sense of the term, constraining her from seriously deviating from its precepts. This is the result of Arabella's being "a strict Observer of romantic Forms" (13). As she remarks herself to Miss Glanville, "my Power is confined by certain unavoidable Laws" (182). Arabella's uncompromising dedication to romance as exemplum, David Marshall comments, induces her to conceive her main obligation as an exacting imitation of the past, so that she appears as only one more example in a predictable series of romantic heroines.[46] In terms of Bourdieu's definition of social behavior as "regulated improvisation," this means that Arabella has inadvertently stressed the regulated aspect of her desire for self-reinvention. She will confront that limitation most notably in the person of the Countess who offers an alternative model of female identity.

Female Tutelage and
'The History of Miss Betsy Thoughtless'

With the introduction of the Countess, Lennox offers readers someone who comes the closest to representing the exceptionally educated, poised, and also sometimes discredited woman imagined by Astell and Masham. While as a younger woman she was deeply influenced by reading romances, she has since mastered more serious forms of learning and therefore exemplifies the potential story line for Arabella's own development. The Countess, readers learn,

> among her own Sex had no Superior in Wit, Elegance, and Ease, [and] was inferior to very few of the other in Sense, Learning, and Judgment. Her Skill in Poetry, Painting, and Musick, tho' incontestably great, was number'd among the least of her Accomplishments. Her Candour, her Sweetness, her Modesty and Benevolence, while they secur'd her from the Darts of Envy, render'd her superior to Praise, and made the one as unnecessary as the other ineffectual.[47]

With these accomplishments, the Countess has become a less aggressive version of Arabella's Amazon queen, since she has acquired the elements of a liberal, traditionally male, education while also fostering the feminine qualities of delicacy and humility. She may not be quixotic in Arabella's sense, but like Masham's exemplar of self-instruction, she is judged as knowing "too much for a Lady" by some of those who circulate in polite society (in a telling remark by a "Lord *Trifle*") (333).

In undertaking Arabella's reeducation, the Countess appears an ideal instructor both in terms of content and form. In negotiating their discussion between Arabella's romantic diction and a more modern vocabulary, the Countess attempts to demonstrate to her pupil the historical changeability in concepts such as "Adventure" or virtue. In advocating a form of romantic idealism, Arabella believes social custom "cannot possibly change the Nature of Virtue or Vice: And since Virtue is the chief Characteristick of a Hero, a Hero in the last Age will be a Hero in this" (328). But the Countess counters by gently responding that "Custom . . . changes the very Nature of Things": regarding vice and virtue, "different Principles, Customs, and Education, may probably change their Names, if not their Natures" (328). While monitoring Arabella's feelings via the "Air of Perplexity" (329) that periodically marks her countenance, the Countess tries to change Arabella's mind by changing her view of change. In effect, she gains at least a little ground in illustrating—in persona and discourse—that a more sophisticated sense of improvisation than Arabella's might produce more successful, if not completely liberating, results. Perhaps more importantly, the Countess also exemplifies a version of applying supervisory education by means of female friendship, especially as Mary Astell had imagined it. For Astell, teaching women could avoid—or at least soften—the imposing instrumentality of surveillance by conceiving the relationship between student and teacher, and student and student, in terms of friendship, which could be all the more effective by promoting a feeling of mutual communion. In the very short time that the Countess spends with Arabella (a span of only five pages), she offers a clear alternative to the clandestine manipulation used by Sir George or even Glanville. Her example briefly suggests how educational indirection might also function as an act of genuine respect and improvement.

Still, despite her ideal attractions as a teacher, the Countess must also be ultimately judged a failure. Her abrupt departure from the story, never to return, suspends her efforts to reform Arabella, who is instead ultimately disabused of her romantic notions by the Doctor of divinity. It is difficult to decide exactly why the Countess's instructive efforts do not continue, and trying to do so inevitably leads to speculating about what decisions Lennox made in trying to conclude the novel. Later, I will consider the problems related to Lennox's authorship of the text, but for the moment, I want to remain at the level of the story itself. In the form we have it, the *Female Quixote* suggests one of two possibilities concerning why at midcentury, an observant education for women is not completely viable. The first possibility is that instruction by friendship may be complicit—perhaps unknowingly—with an implicitly masculine agenda that will finally coerce women into submission. To the extent that one sympathizes with Arabella's dilemma, then, the Countess is "saved" from functioning in so distasteful an office. The second, more likely, conflict is that even as a genuinely "female" strategy, supervisory education is fundamentally incompatible with women's resentment or even outrage about social inequity, and it is therefore ineffective in reshaping women's transgressive conduct based on that response. In that case, Lennox's novel documents a particular stratum of middle- to upper-class women's relationship to the English status quo—a frustration stemming in part from the optimism felt in previous decades by writers such as Astell, Masham, or Chudleigh.

This does not mean that just as they had become thoroughly codified by midcentury, the premises of supervisory education became defunct, even if only for female authors. Instead, it suggests that the *Female Quixote* registers an important dissenting view of supervisory instruction's desirability while offering no clear alternative except for intervention by authoritative men (in the person of the Divine). In order to understand better what kind of literary alternatives concerning female development or education were available at the same time as Lennox's novel, it is useful to consider briefly Eliza Haywood's *The History of Miss Betsy Thoughtless* (1751). That book, in contrast with Lennox's, successfully adapts supervisory elements in representing a young woman's reformation as a gradual, evolutionary process of self-reflection.

Although in *Betsy Thoughtless*, Haywood's protagonist is a commoner rather than nobility and spends the bulk of her time in London, she also exhibits a number of character traits comparable to Arabella's. Like Arabella, Betsy has suffered the death of her mother early in life, and with her father dead as well, she gains a relatively incomplete education. Also a remarkable beauty, Betsy has "a great deal of wit" and a good nature, although she is headstrong and "too volatile for reflection."[48] Like Arabella, Betsy similarly resists the prospect of marriage, but in rejecting even the idea of serious romantic commitment, unlike Arabella, she is a coquette whose preoccupation for most of the novel is engaging in emotional intrigue. Arabella is interested in the heroism of romance, while Betsy toys with romance in the more conventional sense. But even here there appears to be an underlying connection, since as several critics have noted about Arabella's apparent idealism, her fixation on romance allows her a way to invoke, at least subconsciously, the erotic thrills of a liaison with a man.[49]

Perhaps most importantly, both women are obsessively intent on gaining complete power over the men around them. In Betsy's case, at issue is "conquest," in which she is often a "tyrant, but a very gentle one"[50]—a contrast to Arabella's rigorous monarch. Betsy feels "no satisfaction superior to that of the consciousness of a power of giving pain to the man who loved her" (13). In her ultimate fantasy of female preeminence, men even become instrumental gadgets tuned in to women as a force of nature:

> "As the barometer," said [Betsy] to herself, "is governed by the weather, so is the man in love governed by the woman he admires: he is a mere machine—acts nothing of himself—has no will or power of his own, but is lifted up or depressed, just as the charmer of his heart is in the humour." (75)

In observing Betsy's elaborate machinations regarding her many suitors, her guardian, Mr. Goodman, makes a remark similar to that made of Arabella: "it was a pity she was not a man—she would have made a rare minister of state" (108).

Betsy's accumulated experiences about love and men—including her failed relationship with Charles Trueworth, her near victimization by several rakes' sexual designs on her, and her catastrophic first marriage to Mr. Munden—finally curb her attempts to assert complete control over her romantic relationships. In her case, rather than persist in her fantasy until a single blow produces its radical breakdown, Betsy undergoes a series of narrative cycles in which she is provoked to some sort of self-awareness, lapses temporarily into "her former self" (207), and then proceeds in a widening spiral to reach greater circumspection. The narrator of the story, in fact, consistently employs the empiricist terminology typical of educational treatises when she distinguishes between Betsy's proclivity to luxuriate in the sensations of emotional stimulus and her periodic improvement of her "power of reflection."[51] As this process works to refurbish her frequently described "fluctuating disposition,"[52] Betsy experiences a piecemeal enlargement of her native intelligence and a gradual dwindling of her will to power.

Like her counterpart, Betsy must in the meantime endure men's attempts to employ indirect ways of reeducating her, as with Trueworth, the man she eventually marries. Toward the beginning of their relationship, when Trueworth is troubled by Betsy's facile behavior, he decides "to appear satisfied with every thing that pleased her—and to contrive all the methods he could, without her perceiving he did so, of stealing, by gentle degrees, into her mind, a disrelish of such things as were unbecoming in her" (201). This approach smacks of Hezekiah Woodward's definition of clandestine, "precognitive" education (considered in chapter 1) and seems a more deliberate plan than Glanville's for Arabella.[53] In the end, however, Trueworth's endeavor will be equally unsuccessful. Betsy proves too stubbornly cunning for his maneuvers, and the couple breaks up until reuniting late in the story, when Trueworth has abandoned his previous stratagem. Both Betsy and Arabella therefore represent their authors' rejection of the familiar tradition in eighteenth-century fiction of a woman's moral education by her suitor, especially as it had appeared in Mary Davys's *The Reform'd Coquet* (1724), where the man disguises himself in order to effect his lover's ethical recovery. But Betsy is also distinct because, unlike Arabella, she benefits from the sustained efforts of a female mentor, Lady Trusty, who, while absent for occasionally long periods of time, is still able to administer a less presumptuous and more amicable form of supervision. Lady Trusty is intent on improving "the good she found in her [Betsy's] disposition, and of weaning her, by degrees, from any ill habits she might have contracted."[54] She realizes that "plain reproof was not the way to prevail on her to reclaim the errors of her conduct" (32). Thus in "being under the eye of so excellent an instructress" (40), Betsy eventually makes her way to both modesty and self-reliance. In ultimately recognizing, moreover, that Lady Trusty has tutored her in the spirit of mutual affection, without attempting to manipulate her conduct in secret, Betsy herself identifies her instruction as one based on the model of friendship: "the gentle reproofs you take the trouble to give me, are so many fresh marks of the friendship with which you vouchsafe to honour me, and which I shall always esteem as my greatest happiness" (447).

Another key to Betsy's successful development is learning to master a kind of social theatricality, in which women must constantly attend to how they are perceived and what standing they have in terms of "reputation." As Lorna Beth Ellis has observed about Betsy's cultural *Bildung*, she must learn the value of the "manipulation of appearances."[55] Despite having, the narrator notes, "an aversion to dissimulation," and also without falling into the temptation of becoming outright deceitful (as represented by Lady Mellasin and her daughter, Flora), Betsy eventually gains the ability to engage in a kind of "honest" theater, in which she assumes the role of self-reflective and virtuous woman.[56] As the underlying model for accomplishing that transformation, drama proves an instrumental part of Betsy's awakening. After seeing "that excellent comedy, called the Careless Husband," she "was very much affected with some scenes in it; she imagined she saw herself in the character of Lady Betty Modish, and Mr. Trueworth in that of Lord Morelove; and came home full of the most serious reflections on the folly of indulging in idle vanity" (258). Although during the eighteenth century the genre of drama was often associated with the fanciful frivolity of romance, in Haywood's hands, it becomes the centerpiece—along with modest masquerades and even opera—of moral edification. As the sensible Miss Harriot remarks, "I look upon a good play as one of the most improving, as well as agreeable, entertainments a thinking mind can take" (287).

Betsy learns to apply the motif of dramatic performance to her own behavior, especially when she has married Mr. Munden, whose lack of affection (leading later to domineering brutishness and infidelity) tempts her to question whether she should be a submissive wife. But as Lady Trusty exhorts her, "you are now . . . entered into a state, the happiness of which greatly depends on *the part you act in the first scenes of it*. . . . If any dispute happen to arise between you concerning superiority, . . . rather recede a little from your due than contend too far" (457–58; my emphasis). With Munden's imminent death, Betsy will not have to play the role of the beleaguered, virtuous wife for long. But that ordeal produces the final step of transforming Betsy's impulse to control others into the ability to demonstrate, both to herself and later to Trueworth, "the command she had over herself" (572). Betsy has thus fully internalized the conventional standards of female virtue, although that does not mean Haywood is complacent about the social disadvantages that apply even to upper-class English women. Instead, she indicates that given Munden's insupportable behavior, Betsy deserves the right to an independent life based on a legal separation, a process she initiates before his death renders it unnecessary. As Deborah Nestor also points out, there is a deliberately arbitrary quality in the plot's happy resolution, since Munden's sudden death conveniently frees Betsy to accept the affections of Trueworth, whose wife has also unexpectedly died.[57] Hence Haywood reveals the fictive strings by which happy endings for women must be manipulated, in contrast to what could otherwise be realistically expected. Her heroine, moreover, is no less practical about the inequities inherent in a social system based on staged female identity: as Betsy comments several times, she lives in a world "where innocence is no defence against scandal, and the shew of virtue more considered than reality."[58] But rather than responding in turn with Arabella's implacable commitment to Amazonian measures, Betsy develops a resigned pragmatism based on cumulative self-discipline.

For Haywood, then, the solution to the problem of educating women about the world is to situate their development in the context of sustained female friendship and to form a theatrical sense of proper female conduct. Hence Betsy's final understanding of dramatic role playing shifts from plotting the behavior of those around

her—as Arabella does, for example, with Hervey—to staging her
own self-mastery. A moderated sense of social theatricality proves
crucial, because rather than rely on actual pretense or subterfuge, it
teaches Betsy to enact an improvised identity based on the trope of
irony. This means in part accepting the discrepancies between actual and perceived virtue, but it can also mean acquiring a more
subtle form of empowerment. Thus even Haywood's apparent
message that women abandon the ambition of empire has its own
ironic compensations. When toward the end of the book, for instance, Trueworth describes to Betsy the condition of his heart
during his absence from her, he declares that "the empire you had
there was never totally extirpated" (571). By this point, of course,
Betsy has renounced her previous desire to dominate him and thus
refuses such control while also chastely repulsing his advances. But
as the narrator indicates, this very reluctance will ironically secure
her hold over Trueworth's feelings, ensuring his earnest solicitations
during the next year, until their eventual marriage. Haywood's
novel advocates an ironic sense of female identity, which gradually
unfolds a woman's productive deployment of both compliance and
assertiveness.

Female Authority and the
Deflection of "Progressive" Narrative

In *The Female Quixote*, by contrast, Arabella's reformation has
no chance for a gradual evolution. Instead, her transformation proceeds by the narrative logic of radical discontinuity: she first takes
her catastrophic plunge into the Thames and then rapidly submits
to the abrupt intervention by the Divine. As the last of Arabella's
teachers, and the only truly successful one, the good Doctor works
to instruct her via an older model of authoritative declaration and
exhortation. Their conversation, though respectful, is conducted
by the Divine's immediate assertion of his moral expertise and by
Arabella's announcement of her own "Docility": "I expect you will
exert the Authority of your Function," she remarks, "and I promise
you on my Part, Sincerity and Submission."[59] The degree to which

unequal power relations are invested in this scenario is underscored
again later, when, in finally acknowledging the "criminal" tendency of romances to encourage bloodshed, Arabella declares: "my
Heart yields to the Force of Truth" (381). The Divine succeeds in
inducing her to apply the "modern" standards of Christianity to
romances' idealization of violence or even murder. Hence he has
produced a sudden change in Arabella's mind: she has abandoned
an Amazonian valorization of martial prowess and abdicated her
function as self appointed empress, who earlier judged men's
"crimes" by very different standards.

The suddenness of Arabella's transformation does more than
underscore the Divine's didacticism, since it has inevitably provoked questions about the entangled nature of female authority and
female authorship. Arabella's drastic change of mind means she no
longer tells her own story the way she has intended; it also means
that the novel, as the document of her story, quickly comes to an
end. In the novel as a whole, as David Marshall suggests, a woman
telling her own—or even another woman's—story is problematic
at best, since with the exception of Mrs. Morris's "Narration" of
Miss Grove's promiscuous sexual history, no female character offers
readers an extended biographical or autobiographical narrative.[60] In
addition to Lucy's nervous inability to tell Arabella's story, or the
actress's rehearsal of Sir George's fraudulent "History" of the Princess of Gaul, we have even the Countess's terse account of an apparently uneventful life. She says to Arabella:

> [W]hen I tell you . . . that I was born and christen'd, had a useful and
> proper Education, receiv'd the Addresses of my Lord——— through
> the Recommendation of my Parents, and marry'd him with their
> Consents and my own Inclination, and that since we have liv'd in
> great Harmony together, I have told you all the material Passages of
> my Life.[61]

In these terms, a proper woman's life means having virtually no
story at all, or at least one without compelling interest.

The problem with women's storytelling also has implications
for the novel as a whole. If in Defoe's novel, Crusoe as narrator
successfully conveys Defoe's intentions by following the supervisory

guidelines for combining objective report with interpretive spin, then in *The Female Quixote*, the suddenness of the plot's resolution has induced readers to bypass the third-person narrator's otherwise routine delivery of the story in order to question Lennox's control of her text. For Lennox's biographer, Miriam Rossiter Small, Arabella's alteration "would be more convincing if this were done gradually through some of her actual experiences instead of suddenly at the end, but the emphasis is intended to be placed more upon the burlesque than upon character, and for the former it is essential that Arabella's whims be maintained throughout."[62] In Small's view, the problem is ultimately much larger, since she echoes the suspicion expressed since at least the mid-nineteenth century that the penultimate chapter of the novel was authored by Samuel Johnson.[63] There is no definitive proof that Johnson, as Lennox's friend and mentor, actually composed the chapter, entitled "*Being in the Author's Opinion, the best Chapter in this History*" (368). But given the stylistic similarities to Johnson's prose, and the Doctor's aphoristic resemblance to his persona, more recent critics have come to an equally damaging conclusion about Lennox's authorship. Patricia Spacks, for example, writes that "it hardly matters whether Johnson actually wrote the crucial chapter. . . . If not literally, at least metaphorically, Dr. Johnson articulates the view of the world that persuades Arabella to abandon her dream."[64] For Spacks, unlike Small, the point is cultural rather than aesthetic: in her view, Lennox is at least implicitly guilty of abdicating her authority as a female author who could end her heroine's quest for autonomy with a greater sense of accomplishment or satisfaction.

Especially for twentieth-century readers, it is extremely hard not to share Spacks's opinion. But rather than debate the merits of the novel's conclusion in terms of either aesthetic or more recently defined feminist standards, I want to consider this problem briefly in the context of the eighteenth century's earlier characterization of covert educational authority, because in *The Female Quixote*, that key aspect of the supervisory model becomes significantly skewed by the conception of female authorship. As it was particularly represented by educationalists following Locke or Fénelon, the supervisory scenario required effacing the tangibility of the tutor's authority even to the point of making him seem completely absent. The ideal was for the instructor to disappear from the pupil's view. In *Robinson Crusoe*, Crusoe offers the fictional counterpart to that paradigm, particularly in the journal, when he works to erase the evidence of his editorial revisions of what otherwise appears a spontaneous document of his experience. Thus readers are supposedly more readily edified by a relative unawareness of Crusoe as narrator or Defoe as self-declared "editor." In the case of Lennox, however, there occurs a very different version of authorial absence. It is interesting to note, for example, that in agreeing with Spacks's conclusion about novel's ending, Laurie Langbauer remarks: "What is important is that Lennox herself, literally or figuratively, must disappear; despite the persistent dreams in the book of romantic freedom for women, power and authority can enter the text only as a man."[65] What is a virtue in fiction by men—the fiction of the disappearing author—becomes a vice in a work by a woman.[66]

There are several reasons why this should be so, even when we imagine the response of eighteenth-century readers. In the first place, Arabella's antics create a thematic spotlight on the prospect of women's authorizing for themselves substantial social alternatives. Thus readers will likely be disappointed by an author who in the end seems to capitulate to normative values as rapidly as does her protagonist. There is also the problem of the dedication, which according to Boswell and eighteenth-century editions of Johnson's collected works, was composed by Johnson for Lennox as well. That claim has gone unchallenged despite the fact that Boswell is ten years off in reporting that Johnson composed the dedication in 1762. But whether or not he composed it, the dedication itself presents an implicit question about Lennox's ability or willingness to declare herself the writer of her text. In the signature, which ends a rhetorical question about Lennox's justification in claiming the Earl of Middlesex as a patron, readers' eyes come to rest in the last line not on Lennox's name, but instead on the equivocal "The Author?"[67] At the beginning, as at the end of the novel, readers are left to wonder how seriously they should doubt the strength of Lennox's authorial imprint.

That uncertainty is particularly ironic in the context of Richardson's advice to Lennox about how to end the book. In reconstructing the writers' correspondence about whether Lennox should add a third volume, Duncan Isles speculates that Lennox may have proposed to emulate both *Don Quixote* and Richardson's *Clarissa* by having Arabella discover her folly at the moment of her imminent death. Isles also guesses that perhaps Lennox planned a variation on that pattern, with the Countess returning in order to bring Arabella gradually to modest womanhood. Whatever was the case, Richardson rejected the plan because it would undermine Lennox's prestige as the originator of her own work. He wrote her:

> It is my humble Opinion, that you should finish your Heroine's Cure in your present Vols. The method you propose, tho' it might flatter my Vanity, yet will be thought a Contrivance between the Author of Arabella, and the Writer of Clarissa, to do Credit to the latter. . . . You are a young Lady . . . , and I am sure, will think that a good Fame will be [in] your Interest.[68]

In apparently having followed Richardson's advice, however, Lennox created a text that has produced precisely the kind of suspicions about her authority Richardson thought could be avoided. Given the novel's ultimate shape, readers are struck by such misgivings all the more when, in the penultimate chapter, the Doctor cites Richardson as an "admirable Writer of our own Time," who "has found the Way to convey the most solid Instructions, the noblest Sentiments, and the most exalted Piety, in the pleasing Dress of a Novel."[69] In these terms, Richardson proves the successful male author who can morally educate readers by disappearing into his text as the putative "editor" of his characters' correspondence. Lennox, by contrast, has difficulty dispelling the potency of romance and endorsing edifying fiction because to do so suggests losing the authorial prowess she has associated with Arabella's self-empowerment. Hence the spectacle of the disappearing female author inevitably suggests something else: that her aims have become indistinguishable from a masculine agenda.

In the case of Eliza Haywood, it has also been sometimes suggested that in shifting to more conservative mores during the 1740s and 50s—as in her conduct books, *The Husband* (1756) and *The Wife* (1756), or in novels such as *The Fortunate Foundlings* (1744) and *Life's Progress Through the Passions* (1748)—she merged her views disturbingly easily with those espousing "standard" early modern femininity. While there is no question that during the later decades of her career, Haywood abandoned her earlier interest in erotic scandal and powerful femme fatales, in *Betsy Thoughtless*, I have suggested, she demonstrated that eighteenth-century female identity could be measurably improvised by means of ironic social performance. In that sense Haywood was able to establish the strength of her own authorship in a way Lennox could not. There are, to be sure, several ironies about Lennox's novel as well: the most important is that Arabella employs an antiquated social code of conduct in order to "modernize" her status as a woman. Arabella often seems unaware of that ultimate design, but whatever the case, seizing control of her household in the name of romance proves to be a double-edged sword. Like Judith Drake's campaign for a revised version of English "gallantry," Arabella's Amazonian assertiveness reintroduces the very element of submissive feminine softness that had helped men discount women's abilities in the first place. The figure of the female Quixote, in other words, embodies many of the very attributes that had served traditionally to characterize women as the lesser sex. In Lennox's work, this kind of irony ultimately waylays a protofeminist bid for entitlement, rather than allowing, as for Haywood, the possibility for women's calculated indirection regarding the status quo.

Another way, finally, to understand the difference between Lennox and Haywood is to consider their work in the context of Michael McKeon's description of the "progressive" and "conservative" ideologies defining the novel's development during the first half of the eighteenth century. As I have discussed earlier (in chapter 2), both Lennox and Haywood represent at least partial versions of conservative ideology in their critiques of both progressive and aristocratic definitions of how personal merit can match social status. In the first place, both authors adhere to what McKeon calls "extreme skepticism," a distrust of the link between appearances and reality which serves as the epistemological mooring for a conservative outlook. When Arabella remarks to the Divine that "Human Beings cannot penetrate Intentions, nor regulate their Conduct but by exterior Appearances" (371), she states the unreliable condition of knowledge of which both she and Betsy Thoughtless must become fully aware before their stories end. In the *Female Quixote*, that perspective corresponds to Lennox's demonstration that noble title does not guarantee genuine honor, as Sir George amply illustrates. The novel momentarily suggests a typical progressive scenario, moreover, since at the beginning of the story Arabella's father insists on arranging her marriage with a man of noble extraction (Glanville), and Arabella's lack of initial attraction to him leads her to rebel against her father's "tyranny" in trying to enforce a union that has not been based on a trial of Glanville's genuine worthiness. In Haywood's novel, by contrast, Betsy does not need to stave off an imposed marriage, but Haywood similarly attacks aristocratic ideology by demonstrating that there is no reliable tie between individual virtue and titled rank. In Haywood's world, while there are the Lady Trustys and Lady Loveits, who represent the best of feminine benevolence, there are also characters such as Lady Mellasin who embodies the worst of female chicanery, or the salacious "Lord" (unnamed) who nearly rapes Betsy shortly after her marriage to Munden. In *Betsy Thoughtless*, complacency about social rank can prove personally disastrous, especially for women.

Both Lennox and Haywood also play out the second half of the conservative outlook by discrediting the ideals of progressive ideology. In Lennox's case, this point is perhaps more obvious, because she consistently satirizes Arabella's deluded resistance to her father's, and later Glanville's, aristocratic "tyranny." In this sense, *The Female Quixote* also seems to fit McKeon's comment that in some modes of "conservative experimentation," the point is to "mount a comprehensive critique of that general condition of credulity which is vulnerable first to aristocratic, but also to progressive, fictions of love."[70] For her part, Haywood is less interested in wholesale credulity of operatic proportions than she is in the more mundane—and ultimately more ominous—phenomenon of social climbing by way of marriage. In *Betsy Thoughtless*, progressive ideology is dealt its worst blow in Betsy's catastrophic near seduction by Sir Frederick Fineer, a presumably wealthy nobleman whom Betsy considers marrying because the only useful purpose for marriage she can imagine at this point is to gain higher social station. That hope proves ill-fated when Sir Frederick turns out to be only a fraudulent pauper. What is perhaps the most striking about this, another of Betsy's near misses with rape, is that beneath Sir Frederick's ridiculously high-blown addresses to Betsy—which are reminiscent of Arabella's romantic style—lie both a violent design on her virginity and a cheap interest in getting money. Thus Haywood, in contrast to Lennox, suggests that a woman's becoming enamored with ornate romantic rhetoric is less the material for comic farce, than it is the basis for becoming a near victim of physical and social brutality.

In several respects, Lennox and Haywood share the conservative outlook also advocated by Fielding in his fiction, particularly in *Joseph Andrews* and *Tom Jones*. Like Fielding, they remain extremely skeptical of the codes of social appearances, and like him, they attack both aristocratic presumption and middle-class interest in money for their ability to misrepresent an individual's genuine moral virtue. In the case of characters such as Tom Jones or Betsy, who have the chance to mend their ways and thereby merit real happiness, all three authors reflect the narrator's cautionary remark in *Betsy Thoughtless* that "Nature may be moderated, but never can be wholly changed"[71]: for such individuals, there is the possibility for only a muted version of the progressive opportunism and self-transformation enjoyed by Robinson Crusoe. Both Haywood and Lennox also share Fielding's criticism of the double standard in both aristocratic and progressive ideology regarding men and women's sexual conduct. Among male novelists, Fielding was the most vocal of his time in claiming that men should maintain their chastity until marriage in the same way expected of women. Joseph Andrews articulates this position most clearly when he remarks to his sister Pamela, "Chastity is as great a Virtue in a Man as in a Woman"—with the crucial difference that for a man, "his Chastity is always in his own power.["72] But in both *Tom Jones* and *Amelia*, Fielding will allow his male protagonists the possibility of learning the importance of that lesson over time, after indulging in sexual promiscuity. That prerogative, of course, does not apply to his sympathetic female characters, who, like Fanny in *Andrews*, Sophia Western in *Tom Jones*, or Amelia in his last work, must maintain a standard of unwavering chastity. To some extent, both Haywood and Lennox share this perspective on gendered virtue, since despite close calls, both their protagonists remain chaste, while in Haywood's novel, Trueworth is not disqualified as an appropriate mate for Betsy despite being guilty of sexual indiscretion with Flora Mellasin, Betsy's onetime childhood friend.

Unlike Fielding, however, Lennox and Haywood reject a strict equation between sexual chastity and genuine moral virtue, therefore taking a different view of how women might sustain or even acquire virtue in a more general sense. If female chastity is key in undergirding both aristocratic and progressive ideology—particularly for the purpose of ensuring the transmission of pure bloodlines, or securing for future generations family estate or property—then especially in Fielding's case, it seems equally important for the conservative need to find some kind of reliable ethical mooring for the English social fabric. Hence in his fiction, virtuous women's moral education is almost always accomplished before the story begins, as is true for Fanny, Sophia, and Amelia. None of his Amazonian characters, moreover, have the prospect of reforming themselves into admirable wives or mothers. In *Female Quixote* and *Betsy Thoughtless*, by contrast, Lennox and Haywood work to establish a credible claim for women's ability—in fact, *need*—to improve themselves not only intellectually and morally but also socially. Haywood succeeds with this goal better than Lennox, whose portrayal of Arabella is retarded by a secondary commitment to a form of aristocratic idealism. But both authors are appropriating for women the masculine prerogative of actively seizing the means for self-improvement, and in Haywood's case, this also means adopting for a female protagonist a narrative model of gradual reform usually applied only to male characters such as Crusoe or Tom Jones.

Another way to put this is that both Lennox and Haywood, in different ways, have attempted to redefine a "progressive" agenda for women by reinterpreting the boundary lines denoting social status or rank. While in its traditional form, progressive ideology champions women's sexual chastity in the interest of rationalizing upward social mobility for women or their (future) husbands, the point for Lennox and Haywood is to consider the demarcations of rank or class as *analogical markers* for measuring the improvement of women's social prerogatives *as women*, regardless of their change in social status in the strict terms of economics or inheritance. Rather than use a static definition of female virtue to justify women's crossing the usual boundaries of social status, Lennox, for instance, uses a constellation of social and political metaphors—including those from legal, political, and even colonial contexts—by which to define Arabella's desire for better education and standing as a noblewoman who has no apparent aspirations for anything else than improved conditions in the home. But drawing on the literary apparatus of romance proves both momentarily empowering and ultimately defeating, given its underlying investments in epistemological naivete and rigid social hierarchy. Under those conditions, Arabella's self-education proves quixotic in the worst sense, and her attempt to educate others equally flawed. In Haywood's novel, by contrast, Betsy's changes seem more a victory than a capitulation, as the narrator suggests in the last line of the story: "Thus were the virtues of our heroine (those follies that had defaced them being fully corrected) at length rewarded with a happiness retarded only till she had rendered herself wholly worthy of receiving it."[73] This new sense of "progressive" narrative does not produce Betsy's exalted social status, since in marrying Trueworth, Betsy becomes part of the country gentry, the social group to which she belonged at the beginning of the story with her parents. She has accumulated instead a larger sense of self-mastery and rational reflection which have been imparted by the trial and error of at least a part-time supervisory education. She has succeeded in improvising female identity, where Arabella has not, because she has formed for herself a repertoire of skills by which to perform her femininity—and the inherent ironies of that performance are no more lost on Haywood than they are on twentieth-century readers. Hence Haywood deploys a more practical version of improvised female identity that could serve female novelists after her, notably Frances Burney and Jane Austen, who in the later eighteenth century explore a similar interest in the ironies of female development.

The Novel of Education and (Re)Visions of Eden

The story I have been telling about the novel of education is
that it had its earliest perceptible beginnings in the advent of "supervisory" educational work—by authors such as John Locke, Mary
Astell, François Fénelon, Judith Drake, and many others—a development in turn followed by novels such as Delarivière Manley's
New Atalantis, Defoe's *Robinson Crusoe*, Fielding's *Tom Jones*,
Lennox's *The Female Quixote*, and Haywood's *Betsy Thoughtless*. The
historical collocation of these literary and nonliterary texts, moreover, which articulated a model of improvisational identity during
the late seventeenth and early eighteenth centuries, established a
provisional model of the English *Bildungsroman* that is both dramatically public and intensely private. In tracing the pedagogical and
literary elements culminating in the novel of education's formation

by the mid-eighteenth century, I have also considered three key narrative "moments," or intervals, in its accumulating discursive development.

First, there has been the large-scale investigation by both male and female educational writers into the possibility of articulating a way to create a form of human disposition that could be both natural and acculturated, free and constrained, publicly scrutable and personally intact. As Locke's *Some Thoughts concerning Education* has helped demonstrate about this first stage, the goal of negotiating among those competing elements—embodied in the desire to make such a disposition neither entirely rule governed nor dangerously unruly—was often accomplished discursively by adopting tropes from husbandry, medicine, and the theater in order to generate an accommodating sequence for instructing students. The result was a multifarious form of "functional indeterminacy": one of its effects was being able to describe a way by which to monitor indirectly the pedagogical process, thereby ensuring a pupil's successful circulation in a social economy of "credit" and social class. A second consequence was fomenting in the educational texts themselves a narrative impulse in educational writing that manifested itself in a generic experimentalism ranging from Hannah Woolley's inclusion of "witty Dialogues" in *The Gentlewomans Companion*, to Locke's interpolation of "true" stories about his pupils, to the Menippean sprawl of discursive modes in Bernard Mandeville's *The Fable of the Bees*. And finally, the agency of instructive supervision provided the analogue for novelistic point of view, by which narrators could coordinate the dual tasks of merely "observing" fictional events and of manipulating their symbolic meaning at the same time.

The second narrative stage is represented by Defoe's *Robinson Crusoe*, which serves as one of the earliest examples of the English novel of education, the first instance of the consolidation of its heritage in diverse generic elements. To be sure, in drawing on his experiments with dramatic dialogue and storytelling in *The Family Instructor*, Defoe's work is also crosshatched by contending narrative patterns or generic strains. Crusoe must make his way in fitful, even oscillating, fashion as a result of Defoe's combination of Puritan autobiography, with its lapsarian teleology, and empiricist incrementalism, with its more secularized profile. But the story of Crusoe's reeducation in spiritual truth is nonetheless sustained and finally coherent. That result is due in part to Defoe's adaptation of supervisory narrative technique, which contributes to the successful constitution of Crusoe's intense introspection, as well as his public role as "governor"—both politically and pedagogically—on his island.

By midcentury, Lennox's *Female Quixote* and Haywood's *Betsy Thoughtless* offer the third stage as a study in contrast concerning the degree to which female education or development could be improvised to accommodate women's desires for greater domestic latitude or social franchise. For Arabella this means combining two disparate vocabularies, one from French romance and another from "empire"—including judicial and political tropes—in order to assert for herself a sense of daunting "command" in her household. But in drawing on her self-instruction in romance, the feminine textual legacy of her deceased mother, Arabella has also formed a peculiar form of antique feminism, in which she insists on more social power as a "modern" woman while also reintroducing the specter of the vulnerable femininity she intended to dispel in the first place. Arabella has tried, Lennox seems to be saying, to do both too much and too little in redefining her social prospects. Despite the temporary friendship and intervention of the Countess, the final result is Arabella's capitulation to male tutelage—signifying her inability to sustain the cross-purposes of her initial self-definition.

In *Betsy Thoughtless*, Haywood is also interested in studying her protagonist's similarly imperious design to manipulate almost every man who comes across her path, but Haywood explores a different way by which to accomplish both Betsy's reeducation in self-restraint and her desire for an alternative to the typical constitution of the relation between the sexes. In Betsy's case, several different social and literary agencies produce a more gradual reorientation in her disposition, including the abandoned attempt to reprove her by Trueworth, the relatively sustained assistance of her surrogate mother, Lady Trusty, and finally—what is the narrative embodiment of Betsy's oscillation between shallow self-involvement and mature reflection—the story's cumulative cycles of failure and introspection. Perhaps most tellingly, Betsy ultimately adapts a form of potentially corrupting influence—London's theatrical productions—to her strategy to define acceptable female identity as a form of ironic social performance.

There are several very different reasons why Defoe and Haywood would be able to offer more successful representations of improvised selfhood than does Lennox, and those reasons are both literary and ideological. As I suggested in chapter 2, the female novel of education emerges during the early eighteenth century from women novelists' grappling (at least implicitly) with two contrary social models for the formation of female identity. The first, founded on supervisory notions of empiricist process and improvised disposition, characterized female experience as a matter of the incremental accumulation of knowledge or wisdom; the second, by contrast, operated on a near equation between sexual purity and virtue or its social cognates. Hence, as in Delarivière Manley's *New Atalantis*, that duality could produce what amounted to two distinct narratives of female education: one recording Astrea's gradual understanding about human frailty, and the second recounting the series of hapless women's catastrophic losses or seductions. There is interestingly a similar pattern in *Robinson Crusoe*, because Defoe's hero must also confront the collision of an empiricist version of education with one based on the biblical Fall. There are several crucial differences, however, because Defoe's interest in his protagonist is singularly asexual, although that often did not make a difference in stories about male development given early modern attitudes about male promiscuity. But there are more important reasons: unlike Manley, who uses dialogue as her novel's format, Defoe deploys the unifying device of supervisory point of view. What is more, in Defoe's work, Crusoe embodies in *his own personality* the dual story line that stratifies Manley's novel into at least two separate trajectories.

The differences of gender also mark Henry Fielding's contribution to the novel of education, especially because of the way that, initially in his fictional career, he applies a female standard of chastity to his male characters, such as Joseph Andrews who, like Fanny, must fend off would-be seducers. For that reason, the pattern of Joseph and Fanny's education about the world and themselves is much more similar than, say, it is for Tom Jones when compared to Sophia Western, or for Captain Booth when compared to his wife Amelia. Ultimately, in his last two novels, Fielding distinguishes male from female forms of acquired virtue in the attempt to accommodate a "gradualist" version of human development that he feels increasingly compelled to explore. At the same time, however, in the face of the increased volatility in human nature or social relations that this newer, supervisory model implied, Fielding also finds it increasingly necessary to locate a reliable anchor for sociability *some*where, and that place becomes female moral steadfastness. To use Michael McKeon's terminology, Fielding invokes a "conservative" ideology in order to demonstrate that Defoe's notion of "progressive" identity often cloaks a crass materialistic commercialism, while at the same time, Fielding remains skeptical of other ways of establishing moral virtue, such as the "aristocratic" investment in the legacy of birth. But in order to critique both of those alternative ideological descriptions, part of Fielding's strategy seems to have been to define female virtue as something that could perform two functions: help resist the allurements of an aggressive capitalist economy, while also found a standard of social behavior on a *gendered* version of natural birth.

If by the middle of the eighteenth century, the ambiguous conflation of the aristocratic and progressive ideologies enabled the novel (as in Fielding's fiction) to establish an identifiable set of generic and social conventions that were then subject to further cycles of discursive change,[1] then similarly, the (proto)feminist spin given the conservative outlook by Lennox, and especially Haywood, would install a recognizable outline for the novel of education for later novelists—especially women—in the second half of the century. That particular "spin," however, would also generate some acute complications in the representation of female character, particularly in *The Female Quixote*. In redefining the sense of the "progressive" as a form of feminist self-assertiveness for Arabella, Lennox demonstrates her belief in women's need to "earn" a better form of status *within* their domestic station or social standing, rather than by aspiring (as Fielding believed Richardson's Pamela did) to ascend the social hierarchy as a "reward" for immovable chastity. But that goal is strangely—and, at the same time, very understandably—thwarted by Arabella's choice of romance as her means of attaining it. Certainly Arabella takes a skeptical view of aristocratic forms of patriarchal authority, particularly as they appear in her father or Glanville, but it turns out that in effect, Arabella's commitment to romance paradoxically reintroduces a form of aristocratic ethos that ultimately derails the "progressive" train of events her efforts should initiate. In other words, Arabella's rigorous emulation of romance means that in reenacting its pathos about women's chronically threatened chastity, she has in her romantic will-to-power unwittingly created a formidable barrier against the prospect of gradually accumulating other equally important kinds of virtue. This helps explain why the opportunity for Arabella to undergo a form of "progressive" instruction with the Countess quickly fails, and it also demonstrates why the narrative corollary for a feminist "progressive" agenda—an incremental, educational story line— never manifests itself in Lennox's novel. The only recourse for Arabella's rehabilitation is sudden calamity—and submission, as Arabella puts it, to the "Force of Truth."

I offer this view of *The Female Quixote* as a description of the educational and therefore ideological difficulties Lennox had to contend with concerning early modern female identity, rather than as an evaluation of her work as a "failed" novel of education. But it is important to note why Lennox's novel would not have been able to offer an entirely useful model of feminine education for later novelists, especially given Haywood's approach in *Betsy Thoughtless*. As we have seen, Haywood's employment of a more gradual, cyclical pattern for her protagonist can explain the difference, particularly when combined with the concept of ironic female performance. But both of those differences, it seems to me, are related to another crucial distinction between Lennox's and Haywood's approach to the formation of female identity. Since the social status of Haywood's heroine is approximately middle class,[2] rather than nobility, that fact seems to fit Nancy Armstrong's argument that during the eighteenth century a bourgeois model of female interiority displaced the previous one based on aristocratic public display. But we can also say that a bourgeois model for femininity could achieve that task in Haywood's novel because it was undergirded by a supervisory concept of human inculcation emerging in England since at least the 1680s. In these terms, Lorna Beth Ellis's claim that *Betsy Thoughtless* represents the first female *Bildungsroman* in England is significant, although that possibility needs to be based on more than Ellis's discussion of the novel as "conservative" in the conventional sense of being willing to endorse the social status quo.[3] Instead, there is a need to aim for a more subtle form of ideological evaluation, because, given both its protocol of ironic female performance and its deliberately contrived happy ending, Haywood's novel could be considered less than strictly conservative in the usual sense. Taking that tack includes accounting for the way Haywood chose to respond, at least implicitly, to the masculinist ideology in Fielding's fiction, which had been "conservative" in the larger historical sense of fetishizing female virtue in the interest of critiquing both bourgeois and aristocratic interpretations of social value.

With this picture in mind of the complex ideological similarities and differences among novels of education by men and women by the mid-1700s, I turn now to suggest briefly the subgenre's historical trajectory for the rest of the century. There is first of all an important connection to the Continental *Bildungsroman*, particularly Rousseau's landmark work, *Emile, or On Education* (1762). Given the substantial educational framework of Defoe's novel, it should be no surprise that Rousseau seizes on *Robinson Crusoe* as the textual centerpiece for teaching his charge, Emile. In fact, Rousseau explains that Defoe's work is the only exception to his exceptionally strict rule that Emile read no books before the age of sixteen. The value of this novel lies in its ability to inculcate in Emile the lessons of self-sufficiency and moral detachment. Rousseau writes:

> Robinson Crusoe on his island, alone, deprived of the assistance of his kind and the instruments of all the arts, providing nevertheless for his subsistence, for his preservation, and even procuring for himself a

kind of well-being—this is an object interesting for every age and one which can be made agreeable to children in countless ways. . . . This state, I agree, is not that of social man; very likely it is not going to be that of Emile. But it is on the basis of this very state that he ought to appraise all the others. The surest means of raising oneself above prejudices and ordering one's judgments about the true relations of things is to put oneself in the place of an isolated man.[4]

Admittedly, at best this is only half the story, and Rousseau apparently assumes that Emile will not be struck by the other compelling aspect of Crusoe's story—his prolonged struggle to gain genuine Christian faith. But for Rousseau, *Robinson Crusoe* should be "disencumbered of all its rigmarole" (185)—or, rid of its preoccupation with Christian conformity—because he chooses to emphasize the Lockean half of Defoe's work. Given his extensive discussion of Lockean pedagogy in the early part of *Emile*, Rousseau is particularly tuned in to its secularized emphasis on a student's need for liberty and relative self-determination, and as a part of this interest, he employs clandestine tutorial orchestrations far more elaborate than Locke's.

Robinson Crusoe, then, supplies a crucial link between English pedagogical theory and discourse during the 1700s and Rousseau's work, which has itself been called "the first *Bildungsroman*" by Allan Bloom,[5] although that claim should probably be emended with "in France" or "on the Continent," given the context of the development of the genre in England by 1751. Still, Rousseau's work is particularly important because it had tremendous influence on the development of its counterpart in Germany. As Wilhelm Dilthey explains, Rousseau was largely responsible for having "inspired" the "interest in inner culture" that sprang up in Germany during the late eighteenth century. "The *Bildungsroman*," he observes, "is closely associated with the new developmental psychology established by Leibniz, with the idea of a natural education in conformity with the inner development of the psyche. This had its beginnings with Rousseau's *Emile* and swept over all of Germany."[6]

By this account, then, there is a tangible connection between Lockean (and supervisory) pedagogy, Defoe's novel, and the Continental *Bildungsroman*, although Rousseau's particular interpretation

of Lockean and Crusoean elements provides a clue to the difference
between the Germanic and English "novels of education." Besides
deflecting the Puritan moral of *Robinson Crusoe*, Rousseau also
chooses to emphasize almost exclusively the "natural" portion of
Locke's educational theory. Despite his own commitment to tutorial involvement, Rousseau attempts to erase the contrivance of
Lockean supervision by persistently announcing the naturalness of
his own procedure—particularly its intrepid promotion of everything "natural to the human heart" (167). But championing a Crusoe who is totally self-reliant and an emblem of such consummate
naturalness can only be achieved by seriously truncating both Puritan theodicy and the supervisory stress on selfhood's public
scrutability. In a sense, this approach takes the gardener out of the
garden—it thoroughly identifies itself with the pupil's perception of
spontaneous self-determination.

This stalwart, naturalized independence became Rousseau's
version of Locke's and Defoe's work, a posture adopted in turn by
the generation of German novelists and readers whom Dilthey describes in *Poetry and Experience* as alienated from their contemporary sociopolitical surroundings. For them, self-cultivation could be
the antidote to "an antiquated world in all its life forms"; and the
Bildungsroman accordingly "gave expression to the individualism of
a culture whose sphere of interest was limited to private life" (335).
This cultural scene poses a sharp contrast to the one we have witnessed in late seventeenth- and early eighteenth-century England.
Supervisory education's commitment to moral and civil acculturation, its goal of "exteriorizing" children's personal identity, which
is then circulated in an "economy" of public credit, and finally, the
institutionalization of these elements in various forms by the charity school movement—these educational values and social phenomena constitute a very different picture for the emerging English
novel of education and its cultural milieu. This is true not only for
the early eighteenth century, given Mandeville's republicanism or
his contemporaries' more earnest anxieties about political stability,
but also for the century's middle and second half, when the concerns of English novelists of education remained strongly tied to
exploring the public issues emphasized by their nonfictional coun-

terparts. Unlike German novelists such as Hölderlin, English authors, both men and women, sustained a close connection to the
sociological and institutional preoccupations of educational reformers, whose concerns included topics such as urban poverty and
crime, the irreligion of the working class, or the social status of
women.

There is, of course, a second important reason other than the
English novel's socially extroverted character for why the Germanic
model for the genre produces at best a distorted historical picture,
and that reason lies with the last item in the previous sentence—
namely, the way that women pedagogues and novelists have played
very little part, if any, in the conventional explanations of the English *Bildungsroman*'s beginnings during the late eighteenth or early
nineteenth centuries. Susan Fraiman's welcome *Unbecoming Women*
has more recently helped to begin reorienting the interpretation of
the English "novel of development," as she terms it, by focusing
exclusively on the work by authors from Frances Burney to George
Eliot. But the fact remains that her book stands against a large body
of work that has adopted as its approach the assumption that the
Romantic project of defining a form of universal, imaginative, and
natural personality—both on the Continent and in England—was
responsible for producing England's *Bildungsroman* tradition, without considering that this model was predominately based on a masculine model of identity. I would even argue that because many
critics have taken that perspective, they have had either to assume
that the English *Bildungsroman* had its native origins in the mid-
nineteenth century, or they have had to fill in an apparent literary
historical gap that seems to loom between earlier "important" novels in the genre—such as Smollett's *Roderick Random* (1748), Fielding's *Tom Jones* (1749), or perhaps Johnson's *Rasselas* (1759)—and
the familiar mid- to late nineteenth-century texts such as Dickens's
David Copperfield and *Great Expectations*, Samuel Butler's *The Way of
All Flesh*, or Hardy's *Jude the Obscure*. In the meantime, of course,
it has been impossible to overlook work such as Charlotte Brontë's
Jane Eyre or George Eliot's *Mill on the Floss*, with some occasional
discussion of Jane Austen's *Pride and Prejudice* or *Emma*. But even at
that, by the lights of the approach I am describing, there is a lacuna

that would have to be filled between the mid-eighteenth century and, say, the moment of Carlyle's translation of *Wilhelm Meister* in 1824, and the thing serving that purpose has been the role of German Romanticism, especially via Goethe, in shaping English letters. This is not to say that the German context is not relevant, only that it may indeed have played a smaller part than has often been imagined when considering that in England, the most important, integral, and socially effective work being done during the second half of the eighteenth century—both in pedagogy and its literary counterpart, the novel of education—was being done by women. During those decades, in fact, not only did women authors become increasingly activist in proposing and implementing educational programs for the upper, middle, and lower classes, but they also began to conceive their work as novelists in ways increasingly tied to pedagogical effectiveness or social practice.

In telling the story this way, we could begin with Sarah Fielding's novel for girls entitled *The Governess or, Little Female Academy*, published in 1749, the same year as her brother's *Tom Jones*. This text is the earliest known full-length novel written especially for young people, and it is part of the eighteenth-century's innovation in children's literature, which is probably attributable at least in part to Locke's specifications concerning the stages of children's reading abilities.[7] In drawing also from works such as Fénelon's *Instructions for the Education of a Daughter* (1707), Sarah Fielding's novel espouses a recognizable form of supervisory technique, but with a feminine cast reflecting the function of friendship that is familiar in Mary Astell and Haywood. She writes in the dedication: "The Design of the following Sheets is to endeavour to cultivate an early Inclination to Benevolence, and a Love of Virtue, in the Minds of young Women, by trying to shew them, that their True Interest is concerned in cherishing and improving those amiable Dispositions into Habits; and in keeping down all rough and boistrous Passions; and that from this alone they can propose to themselves to arrive at true Happiness."[8] With this general purpose, she tells the narrative of nine schoolgirls, interweaving among their life stories various fairy tales or folktales illustrative of relevant lessons.

In tracing the itinerary running from Sarah Fielding to later

eighteenth-century feminist work on education and women's fiction, we would also need to account for the significance of treatises
such as Wollstonecraft's *Thoughts on the Education of Daughters*
(1787), Elizabeth Bonhote's *The Parental Monitor* (1788), Sarah
Trimmer's *Reflections on the Education of Children in Charity Schools*
(1792), Mary Hays's *An Appeal to the Men of Great Britain* (1798), or
Hannah More's *Strictures on the Modern System of Female Education*
(1799). These and other texts developed educational theories that
were often carefully implemented and tested in the growing body
of children's literature. Moreover, their arguments for improving
the education of women also provided an intellectual and social
framework during the late 1700s that fostered the new novels by
women that were centered on the reformation or acculturation of
young heroines. In this context it would be particularly important,
for example, to consider the interrelation among Maria Edge-
worth's pedagogical manuals, including *The Parent's Assistant* (1796)
and *Practical Education* (1798); her fiction for children, such as *Moral
Tales for Young People* (1801); and her novel *Belinda* (1801), which
aims at refuting in fictionalized form Rousseau's thesis that
women's education should be designed for the greater pleasure of
their male companions (Wollstonecraft was among others also provoked to writing a response to Rousseau's views). Among the other
novels that would need to be studied are Anna Maria Bennett's *Ju-
venile Indiscretions: A Novel* (1786), Eliza Fenwick's *Secresy; or The
Ruin on the Rock* (1795), and last but not least, Frances Burney's
Evelina (1778) and *Camilla* (1796).

This array of educational texts indicates all the more strongly
why the insular rubric of "self-cultivation" usually associated with
the *Bildungsroman* cannot account for the way in which these novelists were writing in the context of—and usually with the express
purpose of—redressing social inequalities. This miniature historical
sketch also suggests that in order to assess more accurately the mid-
to late nineteenth-century novels by both men and women—
Brontë, Dickens, Butler, or Eliot—it will be necessary to understand more fully the ways that women were interanimating the
work of literary practice and actual schooling in the late eighteenth
century.

That said, we might begin tracing such connections by noting the thematic links between Lennox's and Haywood's novels and the fiction of female novelists later in the century. In *Emma*, for instance, Austen's protagonist has inherited a somewhat more genteel version of Betsy Thoughtless's desire to control others, since in Austen's portrait, Emma is clueless that her intrusive matchmaking renders her less than attractive, especially as a prospective spouse for Mr. Knightly—and like Betsy, Emma must gradually learn to abandon that tactic for marital happiness. As another instance, it would be possible to consider the parodic energy animating Arabella's frantic behavior in *The Female Quixote* to have been transported to Burney's *Evelina*, although in this case, rather than residing in the heroine, it motivates a host of characters around her who offer satiric exempla for Evelina's more sober reflection and eventual maturity. But rather than attempt to survey the many ways that mid-century novels of education by women were adapted and transformed later in the century, I want to conclude by considering briefly one thematic thread that could be useful in a more detailed study of the ties between early eighteenth-century novels of education by women and those also by women in the mid-nineteenth century.

I have realized in the course of writing this book that a pervasive issue in the work running from Locke to Haywood is not just "nature" in a broad sense, but nature as an educational garden that has inevitably recurring resonances with that iconic Garden, Eden itself. As the locus of an initially ideal state of being or community, perfectly natural and sublimely harmonious, Eden has also carried with it the West's cultural memory of knowledge gained through enormous loss. And that figure appears literally or is invoked structurally by a variety of discourses considered here: Locke's attempt to replace "sin" with "error" in his pedagogical husbandry; republicanism's fixation on the ideal polity always on the brink of or already fallen into disarray; Robinson Crusoe's self-recovery on his gardenlike island where he cultivates the fruit of colonialist mastery; Manley's depiction of young women's inevitable loss of chastity, the emblem of a moral paradise that can never be regained; Lavater's enthusiastic affirmation that in fact a spiritual sublimity *could* be reclaimed via the narrative of theodicy produced by physiognomical analysis; Lennox's portrayal of Arabella's wild world of romance as an idealized, though inherently flawed, representation of female empire; and, finally, even in the moment toward the end of Haywood's novel when Betsy Thoughtless, strolling unsuspectingly in a beatific garden, encounters her worst temptation in happening upon her onetime suitor Truelove, who resumes pursuing her.

For the moment, though, I want to recall one other telling example of Eden in Mary Astell's representation of her female academy as an institution that would reverse the social Fall in women's history by removing the prohibition against knowledge men had imposed on them. It should be no surprise that in the history of women's early modern writing, the idea of reinventing Eden was a common topos, because that project could potentially accomplish two things: first, attacking one of the master narratives for explaining and justifying the inequality of the sexes; and second, finding a way to reclaim some kind of social, cultural, or personal bliss that could generate genuine change in the world as women knew it. But it should be remembered that while Astell renounces men's "Tyranny" in erecting an arbitrary cultural "enclosure" inside which resided proper knowledge for men only, she herself reinscribes a more subtle version of that masculinist demarcation when she prescribes for her women students mainly "pious" works for their reading and contemplation, reminding them that their main purpose in life is spiritual refinement, rather than encroaching on the public sphere of men's secular and political life. Strangely, then, the snake reenters the reenvisioned Garden: in this educational scenario, women themselves retain the elements of their own undoing, even while learning to improve their lives.

A version of this pedagogical Eden, I suspect, runs through many novels of education by women from the eighteenth to the nineteenth century, with important variations indicating the ways by which these authors improvise on received social and literary traditions. If in the *Female Quixote*, for example, Arabella's recovery of romance is her hope for a female paradise, then in her case, that hope is shattered by a calamitous denouement to the story that has all the features of the Fall writ large. And in these terms, Haywood's use of repeated cycles of disillusionment and reflection in representing Betsy's attempts to manipulate men registers a way to subdue and reorganize a pattern of "falling" that can then be successfully pointed toward Betsy's eventual genuine maturity. I want therefore to consider briefly the Edenic patterns in Haywood's work in order to suggest how they might offer a future basis for exploring what happens to the female novel of education by the nineteenth century, and for that purpose, Brontë's *Jane Eyre* offers a particularly instructive point for comparison.

Toward the end of *Betsy Thoughtless*, when Betsy has left her disastrous marriage with Mr. Munden and is expecting some form of legal separation, she takes temporary sanctuary with acquaintances in the country, whose home has a garden that has the Edenic features of both "exotick plants" and trees that "seemed as old as the creation."[9] On these pleasant grounds Betsy finds herself contemplating her long-past relationship with Trueworth, whom she realizes has been lost to her because of her own vanity. Gazing on a picture of him she has carried with her, Betsy cannot help bursting out mournfully: "Though I no more must see himself, . . . I may, at least, be allowed to pay the tribute of my gratitude to this dumb representative of the man to whom I have been so much obliged" (568).

To Betsy's surprise, her looking on Trueworth's image has been mirrored by Trueworth himself, who has unexpectedly come upon her and has taken the "uninterrupted freedom" of locating an unexposed "view of every thing she did" (569), even of listening in on Betsy's outburst about her loss. Upon hearing her declaration of affection, Trueworth reveals himself and, spurred by realizing her feelings, attempts too much by brashly grabbing Betsy around the waist and embracing her so tightly that she has to admonish him to stop. In reminding him that she is still married, Betsy repulses his entreaties, and the narrator commends her behavior by commenting, "Till this dangerous instance, she had never had an opportunity of shewing the command she had over herself" (572).

In this small but crucial scene are several elements familiar in a feminized Eden, one of the main ones being the fact that it is the man, rather than the woman, who is the dangerous snake in this grassy garden. In fact, Trueworth's watching Betsy invokes Milton's portrayal of Satan's observation of the original couple's activities before he begins the task of causing their downfall. In Trueworth's case, of course, he has tempted Betsy compulsively in a gesture of both long-simmering passion and genuine compassion. But he has nonetheless come close to undoing Betsy's previous progress in becoming a virtuous and thoughtful young woman. For her part, Betsy has learned two things: she can now successfully resist such potential moments for failure, and she in fact loves Trueworth more than she knew. In her assertion of self-"command," moreover, Betsy represents at least a minimal example of the self-restriction I have indicated in Astell's version of Edenic existence, since Betsy has insisted on a standard of female purity that has been historically the imperative imposed by men, rather than women—and as Trueworth later realizes, her resistance is precisely what he would have hoped for in a prospective bride.[10] But for several reasons I will consider in a moment, Betsy's self-division is a far cry less than Jane's is in Brontë's novel.

In *Jane Eyre* Brontë presents the famous scene in which Rochester proposes marriage to Jane in the garden on his estate that Jane reports is "Eden-like," teeming with dense blooming flowers.[11] What is peculiar about this scene is the way that Jane appears both to be and not be at fault at the same time. Feeling anxious at the idea that she "might be watched," Jane flees into a more remote part of the garden, until her sense of foreboding suddenly upends itself. Upon meeting Rochester, she explains: "I became ashamed of feeling any confusion: the evil—if evil existent or prospective there was—seemed to lie with me only; his mind was unconscious and quiet" (260, 261). In seeking to reassure her, Rochester invokes Eden (perhaps unknowingly) once more, telling Jane that his feelings for her have evolved to the point that "when you are near me, as now: it is as if I had a string somewhere under my left ribs" (264). This particular remark not only reflects Jane's investment throughout the novel in the key element of "sympathy," but it also recalls the ideal relationship before the Fall—actually, it gestures to the emblem of the original couple's powerful intimacy, since Eve was formed from Adam's rib.

Still, as readers probably remember, a nagging worry persists for Jane that is linked particularly to the problem of an unequal relationship of power between herself and Rochester—and Jane's inability to locate or perceive just where the trouble resides. In response to Rochester's calling her a bird, Jane retorts: "I am no bird; and no net ensnares me: I am a free human being with an independent will; which I now exert to leave you" (266). If nothing else, this should recall Jane's earlier, justly famous speech claiming that "women feel just as men feel" and deserve the same opportunities as "their more privileged fellow-creatures" (115)—a speech she significantly delivers immediately before meeting Rochester for the first time. In the garden, however, unable to sustain her resolve to follow her own initiative to leave him, Jane resorts to physiognomy, attempting to resolve her fears by reading Rochester's face: "I want to read your countenance," she declares, "turn!" (267). But this too proves only one more turn on an ever-turning set of signs or signals that elude her clear interpretation.

When Rochester finally proposes marriage to Jane, all her anxieties seem at first dissolved when she realizes that she has been indeed "called to the paradise of union," though here too, as the narrator Jane states, "if I had loved him less I should have thought his accent and look of exultation savage" (268). Rochester's ominous visage indicates clearly—both to Jane in retrospect and to readers—*that* he poses a danger to Jane, though exactly what that danger is remains for the moment unspecified. In this gothicized marriage proposal—complete with flashes of lightning and the chestnut tree that "writhed and groaned" (268)—is a full roster of the players from the Fall story, except for one. If Jane plays a troubled Eve, and if Nature plays its role as a sublime emblem of divine power, then the question is what Rochester's role must be, since he seems strangely outfitted as a Byronic Adam. But because of his deception, he is, like Trueworth, really the serpent—and like him, Rochester has also spied on his object of desire before discovering himself to her.

Returning, then, to my original formulation of the feminized Eden as an apparently idealized locale that teaches as much by its positive environment as it does by its residual elements of hegemony, in this case Brontë has turned the traditional tables by illustrating that male, rather than female, deception is the culprit here. But since the residual constraints are, by Astell's example, installed by women themselves, then the result is that a secondary level of difficulty arises as a form of female failure or loss. In this case, Jane has failed to be a good reader: she has not only failed to interpret Rochester's face correctly but she has also been unable or unwilling to decipher what the chestnut tree is telling her in its groans—because ultimately, it functions as a sublime Tree of Knowledge, which, as in Astell's academy, Jane *should* taste in order to choose her actions more wisely. In effect, she has failed at attending to the "presentiments" she has championed earlier as part of those "signs" that can signal "the sympathies of Nature with man" (231). And she has failed at this task not because she succumbs to her love for Rochester, I would argue, but because she is willing to submit to him as her male "master," the name she continues to call him even after their betrothal.

In this revised Edenic scene, then, there are several parallels to the one in Haywood's novel: there is the female desire to escape men's surveillance, and a related reflex to survey them in turn; an implicitly doubled narrative of finding an apparently ideal relationship while also being checked by some form of implicitly masculinist self-constraint or confusion; and a feminist critique of masculine hegemony, joined with a form of feminine acquiescence. But the differences between Brontë's and Haywood's representations are also important: coming as it does at the end of the novel, Betsy's temptation is really more a final test than a painfully ambiguous example of failing to "read" the world, as it is for Jane, who undergoes her ordeal only halfway toward her eventual reunion with Rochester in marriage. But much more consequential are the larger historical changes that, over the course of the nearly one hundred years between Haywood's and Brontë's novels, have produced very different modes of representation. In *Betsy Thoughtless*, Betsy's garden encounter reads like a staged moment in a sentimental drama, complete with the heroine's emotional outburst in declaring her heartfelt love for a lost lover. In *Jane Eyre*, melodramatic strains can be heard as well, but Brontë's indebtedness to the gothic tradition introduces what is probably the most significant way by which nineteenth-century fiction had complicated the Enlightenment's portrayal of developing female identity. In Brontë's hands, the representation of women as publicly private figures (as discussed here in chapter 3) becomes a process of mediating between two disparate, but mutually constitutive modes of characterization: one is based on the language of psychological depth, as in Jane's familiar descriptions of the "rise" of her "vehemence of emotion" (265), or of her need to access the hidden desires of her heart; the second mode emerges from what Eve Sedgwick describes as the gothic method of presenting character, in which identity materializes from outside elements whose influence is embodied in the imagery of impinging surfaces, contagious contact, or contingent exchange. While the first mode therefore indicates the existence of an internal, purely personal core, the second makes the self integral to the public sphere, since as Sedgwick notes, in late eighteenth-century gothic fiction identity is "social and relational rather than original or private; it is established ex post facto, by recognition." The gothic novel's conventions of surfaces, she argues further, later became widely assimilated by Victorian novelists, including Brontë, who were regarded as more than narrowly "gothic" writers.[12]

In Jane's encounter with Rochester, the twin modes of narration are clearly at work, since besides her persistent efforts to pierce the deceptive veil of her own propriety (or Rochester's evasiveness), she finds herself equally compelled by sheer physical proximity to Rochester and therefore also to his vaguely disturbing desires. There is no better emblem of her being shaped by contingency than the ephemeral smoke from Rochester's cigar, whose "warning fragrance" initially alerts her to his presence nearby, and then induces her to try leaving the garden, before subtly drawing her back into a conversation with him.[13] This moment leads to Rochester's invoking the ephemeral "string" connecting their two hearts, and then, to Jane's description of her capitulation to his marriage proposal in strongly "exteriorized" terms: "sitting by him, roused from the nightmare of parting . . . I thought only of the bliss given me to drink in so abundant a flow" (268). Her resolve for independence—whose mirror image is also her internal "nightmare" about leaving—is thus dislodged by the external "flow" generated by the power of Rochester's insistent physical presence.

Such a scenario does not ultimately mean that Jane Eyre must learn to repel external influences in living her life. Instead, it reveals that her failure with Rochester is the result of having relied too much on the trope of penetrating surface elements—and doing so badly at that—without at the same time understanding how to interpret and cope with the surrounding world of surfaces themselves—especially those attached to the social influences of the places and people around her. Jane therefore needs to accommodate both the internal and the external in seeking to have future relationships founded on the basis of her personal watchword—"sympathy"—which can potentially link the two realms. In broader terms, her struggle also illustrates how the need for women to negotiate the elusive distinction between private and public life has become transmuted from the challenge Betsy faced, to one now writ large by gothicism's volatile themes and form. And as a final point of comparison, in the powerful clash of two narrative lines of development in Brontë's passage—a confrontation generated largely by gothic theatrics, which historically were adapted from the romance genre—Jane's experience of the garden registers a pattern of radically opposed elements reminiscent of the one Arabella creates for herself in *The Female Quixote*. There are no doubt a number of other important similarities or differences among the novels by Lennox, Haywood, and Brontë, connections and contrasts that would reveal a great deal about the novel of education's gradual transformation over the course of the century separating them. But whatever those details may be, the example of *Jane Eyre* suggests that during the nineteenth century, the female novel of education would continue to value and revalue the paradigm of Eden in the search for expanded female horizons.

Reference Matter

Notes

Introduction

1. Sterne, 300.
2. Sterne, 9. I am indebted to Fliegelman, 64–66, for pointing out the relevance of Locke's epistemology to Tristram's haphazard education, though I use it here for a different purpose.
3. See, e.g., Watt; Rothstein; Konigsberg; Tavor, *Scepticism*; and McKeon, *Origins*. An emphasis on epistemology is registered, for instance, in the titles of Rothstein's *Systems of Order and Inquiry in Later Eighteenth-Century Fiction* and Tavor's *Scepticism, Society, and the Eighteenth-Century Novel*; Konigsberg goes so far as to say, "[A]ll the major novelists from Defoe to Austen, in one way or another, are concerned with perception—technically, thematically, and aesthetically" (7). To a great extent, this is the legacy of Kenneth MacLean, whose *John Locke and English Literature of the Eighteenth Century* is based upon the claim that "the book that had the most influence in the Eighteenth Century, the Bible excepted, was Locke's *Essay concerning Human Understanding*" (v).
4. More specifically, these scholars have demonstrated how Locke's epistemology is manifest at the level of representation, where the novelist attempts to simulate sensory experience using the technique of formal realism (Watt's emphasis, esp. 15, 21, 30–31, 65, 102); how it underwrites character portrayal in terms of a psychology formed by accumulated memories and an aggregate identity-formation (one of Konigsberg's main points, 118–22, 169–70); how it informs narrative point of view, particularly with respect to the problem of certainty in human knowledge (Rothstein's analysis, 245–50); how it shapes the novel's emphatically skeptical treatment of rationality, morality, and social relations (Tavor's thesis, *Scepticism*, esp. 7–53); and how its thoroughgoing secularization of the tests for divine revelation (McKeon's argument, *Origins*, 77–83) contributed to the novel's insistence on historical accuracy and reliability.

5. For an example of this explanation, see Watt's mention of Locke's crucial shaping of "the eighteenth-century climate of opinion" (6).

6. For examples of treating early modern philosophy and fiction as analogical or "parallel" discourses, see Watt, 31; Tavor, *Scepticism*, 3.

7. See Watt, 31.

8. On the destabilization of generic categories, see McKeon, *Origins*, 25–64; on the new challenges to traditional concepts of virtue, 131–75; on the novel's conflation of the themes of truth and virtue, 265–70.

9. While McKeon's argument suggests a new fluidity in the boundaries between philosophy and literature, it also implicitly reproduces the traditional emphasis on epistemology, because most of his discussion of generic destabilization—both conceptually and in terms of the organization of *Origins of the English Novel*—falls under the heading of "questions of truth." In a move that resembles Watt's comparison of philosophy with literature, McKeon also links "questions of truth" to sociological "questions of virtue" by what he calls a "deep and fruitful analogy" ("Generic Transformation," 177). That strategy is certainly useful for organizing his analysis efficiently while also avoiding overly simplistic isomorphisms between texts and their contexts. The result, however, is that he tends to portray the generic alterations contributing to the emergence of the novel mainly in terms of competing forms falling on either side of the epistemological divide between truth and falsehood—the substitution, for instance, of the conventions of "history" for those of "romance" and vice versa. Hence the epistemological premises for such a distinction may sometimes be ambiguous, but they remain constant as an abstract simulacra for contemporaneous generic transactions—without themselves coming under scrutiny as a kind of writing.

10. De Man, "The Epistemology of Metaphor," 21. Also relevant to de Man's treatment of the relation between philosophy and literature is the work of Richard Rorty. See, e.g., Rorty's discussion of philosophy's role as "edification" rather than metaphysical truth-telling in *Philosophy and the Mirror of Nature*, 357–94, and his essays on the discursive status of philosophy and fiction in *Consequences of Pragmatism*, 90–109, 110–38.

11. Richetti, 46; my emphasis.

12. Richetti, 91, 100. For a slightly different view, see Wilson, who examines how "the excesses and unpredictabilities" in Locke's "literary invention go beyond the philosophy . . . in ways that, while not always subversive of the philosophic purpose, manage to seem somehow self-sustaining" (471).

13. De Man, "The Resistance to Theory," 4.

14. I use the term *educationalists* to designate early modern authors who

wrote about education but may or may not have worked as educators in the sense of being tutors, teachers, or administrators of institutions for schooling. John Locke, Damaris Masham, and François Fénelon, for instance, all wrote about education and worked at some point as instructors. Others, such as Daniel Defoe and Mary Astell, went so far as to propose new schools for educating men or women; however, their projects were never realized. Like many authors on education, they had the greatest impact in instructing readers.

15. Another way to describe the general difference between a deconstructionist and Foucauldian approach to subjectivity would be that while deconstructionists stress that individual identity is perpetually indeterminate given the supplementary operations of representation, Foucault considers identity *initially* indeterminate until it is shaped by the rigors of the disciplinary system, which produces both the "soul" and a "docile body." On this point, see esp. *Discipline and Punish*, 192–94 [hereafter *DP* in notes]. My aim is to consider the ways by which even disciplined subjectivity can retain undecidable elements that can be crucial to understanding, among other things, how social change is possible.

16. Foucault, *Archaeology of Knowledge*, 12.

17. Foucault, *DP*, 197.

18. In viewing Foucault's work this way, I am not going so far as to accuse him of "'personifying' power," as Judith Butler puts it in discrediting some of his critics (*Bodies That Matter*, 9). While I concur with Butler's view that Foucault's work can be read as generating a "disruption and subversion of [the] grammar and metaphysics of the subject," I am stressing here something she herself acknowledges when she remarks that at times Foucault seems to be "[i]nvesting power with a kind of vitalism" (*Bodies That Matter*, 9, 224).

19. For both Armstrong and Bender, Mikhail Bakhtin's work forms an important, though temporary, counterpoint to Foucault's disciplinary thesis. Armstrong remarks that "the panopticon . . . is incomplete in itself as a model of culture. It requires something on the order of 'carnival,' Mikhail Bakhtin's figure for the practices that, with the growth of disciplinary institutions, were entirely cast out of the domain of culture" (*Desire*, 23). Invoking a provisional sense of social resistance, she explains, can enable scholars to represent the eighteenth-century novel as a discourse that arises out of serious cultural conflicts over definitions of class and gender, rather than one that results from an overly simple rise of disciplinary power. For Bender, Bakhtin's view of the novel as a genuinely "heteroglossic" genre serves as one of two opposing poles defining the early modern novel's social function, the second of which is the novel's narrative representation of penitential reform. Hence as a distinctly urban discourse, the "novel acts

out . . . the interplay between the unbounded heterogeneity of population in cities . . . and the bounded unity of their walls, fortified compounds, governmental structures, and systems of communication" (61, see also 211–13).

In both critics' larger accounts of the novel's function in Enlightenment culture, however, Bakhtin's alternative perspectives ultimately give way to an emphasis on the dominant implementation of power. As Bender remarks, "I assimilate Bakhtin's ideas about the novel's antiauthoritarian embrace of diversity (its 'heteroglossia') into an account that runs opposite his main argument"; he stresses instead "the subordination of diversity to civic rule and . . . to narrative order" (274 n. 27; 61). Armstrong similarly concludes, "the reality that dominates in any given situation appears to be just that, the reality that dominates" (*Desire*, 23).

20. Foucault, *DP*, 222.

21. Bourdieu and Passeron, 10. For their full discussion of the concept of *pedagogic action*, see 5–11.

22. Mandeville, *Free Thoughts*, 253–54.

23. Bourdieu, *Outline*, 72.

24. Butler, *Gender Trouble*, 143. In echoing Bourdieu's argument that subjectivity is neither completely rule governed nor radically alien to social control, Butler also claims that "the reconceptualization of identity as an *effect*, that is, as *produced* or *generated*, opens up possibilities of 'agency' that are insidiously foreclosed by positions that take identity categories as foundational and fixed. For an identity to be an effect means that it is neither fatally determined nor fully artificial and arbitrary. . . . Construction is not opposed to agency; it is the necessary scene of agency, the very terms in which agency is articulated and becomes culturally intelligible" (*Gender Trouble*, 147).

25. Butler, *Gender Trouble*, 128. In *Bodies That Matter*, Butler presents a more cautious formulation of performance than she had offered previously in *Gender Trouble* by describing "performativity not as the act by which a subject brings into being what she/he names, but, rather, as that reiterative power of discourse to produce the phenomena that it regulates and constrains" (2). But this does not necessarily mean that some form of individual initiative may not be crucial for specific performances that can substantially change the systems in which they function. As an example, when describing Luce Irigaray's deliberately devious "miming" of Plato's theory of mimesis, Butler concludes that "she performs a repetition and displacement of the phallic economy" inherent in Plato's work (45).

26. Bourdieu and Passeron, 18.

27. For Bourdieu and Passeron's occasional remarks on this subject, see *Reproduction*, 13–14, 18, 28.

28. In *Desire and Domestic Fiction* (1987) and related essays, Armstrong's description of conduct books' and the novel's representations of middle-class female identity stresses its disciplinary determination, without accounting, for instance, for the possibility of authors' active agency in the process (see also Armstrong's "The Rise of the Domestic Woman"). Pat Gill, in "The Conduct of Ideology," offers a sympathetic and incisive analysis of this difficulty in Armstrong's work. Having acknowledged this problem herself, Armstrong has since introduced the idea of "intellectual labor" into her studies of early modern literature, particularly in *The Imaginary Puritan* (1992), which she coauthored with Leonard Tennenhouse.

29. Bourdieu, 78.

30. Bourdieu, 168. Bourdieu's conception of *doxa* is therefore quite different from Roland Barthes's characterization of it as "opinion," although his notion of the public clash between orthodox and heterodox perspectives resembles Barthes's description of *paradoxa* as "dispute" (18).

31. In characterizing the ideological function of education this way, I have adapted John Guillory's discussion of the relation between doxa and ideology in *Cultural Capital*, 134–41.

32. Sterne, 301.

33. Two recent book-length studies indicate a shift in the direction of the dual-gendered approach I will be taking here. In *Nobody's Story*, while focusing specifically on female novelists, Catherine Gallagher explains that her argument "does not claim that they belonged to a separate tradition. Rather, it takes them to be special in their extreme typicality" (xv). Taking a very different tack in *Models of Value*, James Thompson formulates a concept of eighteenth-century "economy" that comprises both the political and the domestic spheres, proceeding to discuss in detail the work of Defoe, H. Fielding, Burney, and Austen.

34. Ezell, *Writing*, 70–71. In *The Patriarch's Wife*, 62–100, this approach has also shaped Ezell's view that seventeenth-century women authors were a key part of a network of manuscript circulation and publication in which men also played an active role.

35. See Ezell, *Writing*, 66–103.

36. See Axtell, 98–99, 101–4.

37. Ezell, "John Locke's Images of Childhood," 141. Ezell goes so far as to call the first half of the eighteenth century the "Age of Education" (141).

38. Fliegelman, 12. See also Summerfield: "For three-quarters of a century, Locke's *Thoughts* was the most influential English book on child-rearing" (2).

39. For discussion of Carlyle's relationship to Goethe's work and also its

significance to *Sartor Resartus*, see, e.g., Howe, 82–125; and Buckley, 10–12, 40–41.

40. Fraiman, 13–31.

41. Howe, 6.

42. Swales, 14. For other discussions of these distinctions, see Howe, 6; Buckley, 13; Moretti, 16–17; Jost; and Tennyson. There is a fourth generic subdivision, the *Künstlerroman*, which deals specifically with the development of an artist; for my purposes here it is not a crucial distinction.

43. Moretti, 17.

44. Dilthey, 335–36. The Goethe quotation is from his essay "West-östliche Divan."

45. On the significance of this issue in the context of recent literary theory and the twentieth-century *Bildungsroman*, see my "Subjectivity, the Novel, and the *Bildung* Blocks of Critical Theory."

46. Wordsworth, 321.

47. Dilthey, 335.

48. Moretti, 4–5; Buckley, 27, 11. For further discussion of the problem of the genre's putative emphasis on interiority, see Swales, 17, 29, 150–51. See also Beddow, who stresses the *Bildungsroman*'s representation of an organic human nature opposed to Newton's mechanistic model (see 1–7, 10–15).

49. See McGann, *The Romantic Ideology.*

50. Fraiman, xi.

51. For Said's discussion of the distinction between "origin" and "beginning," see his *Beginnings*, esp. 29–78.

52. Sedgwick, *Between Men*, 14–15.

Chapter 1

1. Locke, *Education*, sec. 112–13; Locke's emphasis removed.

2. For a few other rare occasions when Locke refers to aspects of female education, see secs. 9, 152.

3. Locke, *Education*, sec. 9. In addition, while guarding against those faults that might render a male student "a *Beau*" or could "effeminate" his mind, Locke simultaneously proposes to transvaluate those kinds of differences into a genderless universality (secs. 9, 107); see also secs. 108, 113. Also striking is his admonishment to make children's emotional constitution comparable to physical—and apparently virile—toughness: "The softer you find your Child is, the more you are to seek Occasions, at fit times, thus to harden him" (sec. 115). Of course, this approach also has key class elements: a gentry son's masculinity should emulate the rugged

hardiness of the rural working class while also being refined by gentry sophistication.

4. See Locke, *Essay*, 2.1.2, 1.4.14. He discusses the state of babies' minds in 1.4.2–4.

5. Bourdieu, 72. He describes the *habitus* elsewhere as "*a matrix of perceptions, appreciations, and actions*" (83). See also his discussion of the term on 214 n. 1.

6. Bourdieu and Passeron, 36; original emphasis removed. For their full discussion of *pedagogic work*, see 31–54.

7. See Bourdieu, 91–95.

8. Locke, *Education*, sec. 7. For other references to this procedure, see secs. 94, 115, 137, 180.

9. Locke, *Essay*, 2.21.35.

10. In *Outline*, Bourdieu explains the habitus is not defined by a notion of habit as "a mechanical assembly or preformed programme" (218 n. 47), or by an existential concept of absolute self-determination (76), but by a composite of socialized inclinations that mediate between those two extremes. Hence the habitus embodies Locke's aim to combine, in the mature young adult, habitual reflex with rational reflection.

11. Locke, *Education*, sec. 66.

12. Locke, *Education*, sec. 149. See also Locke's advice of "concealing" from a child the fact that his tutor "has not the Power of the Rod" (sec. 88).

13. Bourdieu and Passeron, 10.

14. Locke, *Education*, sec. 29.

15. Locke to Molyneux, 20 Jan. 1693, in *Correspondence of John Locke*, 4:625–26.

16. F. Ferguson, 68–69. She also comments: "[T]here can be no renunciation of parental authority without a concomitant renunciation of the child. 'Parents who know their business [may] know that they do not know their business,' but they nonetheless tend to exert themselves, for example, to keep an infant from crawling into a fire. Moreover, education in the form of nurturing inevitably curtails the child's freedom" (68).

17. Hunter, *Before Novels*, 270.

18. This kind of characterization can have very different historical or ideological motivations, with varying degrees of plausibility. In *Prodigals and Pilgrims*, Jay Fliegelman argues persuasively that Locke's new concept of limited parental authority produced, among other things, the American colonies' disposition to justify political revolt. Nathan Tarcov, in *Locke's Education for Liberty*, is less successful in aiming to align Locke's pedagogical views with his political philosophy and the ideals of a historically triumphant liberal humanism.

19. See Webster, *The Great Instauration*, 104–15.

20. Winstanley, 43, 58.

21. Comenius, *The Great Didactic*, 252; he is quoting Cicero. In *Pioneers of Modern Education, 1600–1700,* John Adamson considers the link between Bacon and Comenius to be so strong as to assert that "the *Great Didactic* is the *Novum Organum* of pedagogy" (53).

22. For an account of Comenius's language texts, see, e.g., Monroe, 123–41.

23. Comenius, *A Reformation*, 7.

24. Woodward, 19. He goes on to remark that a child "shall seeme idle and think he is in sport, when he is indeed serious, and best employed."

25. Milton, *Complete Prose*, 2:368. For discussions of the similarities and differences in Milton's and Comenius's views on education, see Milton, *Complete Prose*, 2:364–66 nn. 9–10; Ainsworth, 20–21; and Webster, *The Great Instauration*, 113–14, and introduction, 22–42.

26. For an account of Comenius's visit, see esp. R. Young. See Sadler for an extended discussion of Comenius's concept of "universal" education.

27. In Comenius's *Pansophiae prodromus* (1639) and *A Reformation of Schooles* (1642), both of which were brought out by Hartlib, the chapter headings of the *Didactica Magna* were listed for readers' information, but the entire work was not published in English until M. W. Keatinge's translation in 1896.

28. Gailhard, pt. 1:16; Walker, preface, sig. $\pi 3^r$, 1. Gailhard would go so far as to assert the importance of learning using this anecdote: "One day, *Aristotle* being asked, *what a difference there was between learned men and unlearned; Such,* said he, *as between the living and the dead*: being of opinion, that a man without learning is a statue more than a man." He then remarks that learning is "necessary to many, and convenient to all; it doth enrich the mind, rectifie the will, regulate affections, quickens and perfects natural parts, and is an ornament to the whole man, whom it doth fit and dispose almost for every thing: But this is most certainly true, that it is neither a burthen nor a hinderance to any" (pt. 1:30–31).

29. Armstrong and Tennenhouse, 101. For them, literacy has the "modern" sense of being associated with literary skill and an internalized personal consciousness. For a very different description of literacy emerging since the Restoration—one based on the assumption that literary, scientific, and theological forms of knowledge are equivalent—see Kroll.

30. If for Armstrong and Tennenhouse, the English Revolution in the 1640s provides the primary analytical fulcrum—and critical mythology, in Barthes's sense—by which to tell the story of modern individuality (see their discussion, 47–68), then in this account, the Revolution of 1688

functions as an equally important juncture in the formation of the early modern habitus.

31. Walker, 9.

32. For many earlier authors, the fallen human inclination to sin was the dangerous origin for behavior that could become habitual. For examples where the problem of bad habits is discussed, see Gailhard, pt. 1:9, 92; pt. 2:10; Brathwaite, *English Gentlewoman*, 10; Codington, 31–41; Woolley, 6; Dufour, 89, 94. For instances where installing good habits is discussed, see Brathwaite, *English Gentlewoman*, 216; and Walker, 72.

While the term *habitude* was in use since at least the fifteenth century, the *Oxford English Dictionary* lists two distinct definitions that suggest the modern version I describe was beginning to emerge during the seventeenth century. It cites the older sense of habitude, the "Manner of being or existing; constitution; inherent or essential character," as being first employed in 1400. But the one closer to a concept of habitus—"A disposition to act in a certain way, arising either from constitution, or from frequent repetition of the same act"—is first cited in 1603, with increasing usage during the eighteenth and well into the nineteenth century.

33. Drake, 135, 139.

34. Astell, *Serious Proposal*, 82, 61. The symbolic proximity of Astell's proposed retreat to Catholicism, in fact, especially because she called it "a *Monastry* [*sic*]" (60), drew criticism from her readers. In part II of the *Serious Proposal* (1697), she answers her critics by reasserting her Protestant convictions, choosing to call her retreat a "Seminary" (21).

35. Fénelon, *Instructions*, 17, 36. For some of his other frequent discussions of habit, see also 29, 62, 103, 109, 149.

On this point, Fénelon differs from Lacanian theorists, who perceive a child's entry point into socialization as the symbolic—that is, the acquisition of language. For an impressive application of this idea to Enlightenment theories of language and fiction, see Dorothea von Mücke's *Virtue and the Veil of Illusion*. By contrast, Bourdieu concurs with Fénelon's view, explaining that the body, as much as cognitive response, can be key to forming the habitus. See *Outline*, 87–90, especially his remark that in a "symbolically structured environment, without specialized agents or specific moments," a pupil can gain "practical mastery" of cultural behavior "without attaining the level of discourse" (87).

36. See, e.g., Hough, *Sermon* (1705), 18–21; Peers, *A Serious Call to Christianity* (1715), 13–14; Clarke, *An Essay upon the Education of Youth* (1720), 105; and Wilkes, *A Letter of Genteel and Moral Advice to a Young Lady* (1744), 80.

37. Fénelon, *Instructions*, 33, 42, 38.

38. Chévremont, sig. A2ᵛ; Lowe, 9.

39. Masham, *Occasional Thoughts*, 190–91. For examples of other authors advocating a gentle, indirect pedagogical approach, see Ronksley, *The Child's Weeks-work: or, A Little Book, So nicely Suited to the Genius and Capacity of a Little Child, Both for Matter and Method, That it will infallibly Allure and Lead him on into a Way of Reading With all the Ease and Expedition that can be desired*, 4 (and esp. the title); Essex, xx, xxii; *An Humble Attempt to Assist Parents and Masters*, preface, sig. A1^r-v; and Wilkes, 8.

Two other specific cases are particularly notable. In *Serious Proposal To the Ladies*, Astell assures her readers that her religious retreat will not impose any kind of Catholic austerity:

> Piety shall not be roughly impos'd, but wisely insinuated by a perpetual Display of the Beauties of Religion in an exemplary Conversation, the continual and most powerful Sermon of an holy Life. And since Inclination can't be forc'd, (and nothing makes people more uneasy than the fettering themselves with unnecessary Bonds) there shall be no Vows or irrevocable Obligations, not so much as the fear of Reproach to keep our Ladies here any longer than they desire. (104–5)

Several years later, in *A Sure Guide to Hell . . . Containing Directions I. To Parents in the Education of their Children . . .* , Benjamin Bourn gives this theme a demonic twist by having Satan describe to young people how in order to train them in the ways of damnation, he "must use gentle Methods with thee at first, drawing thee on, step by step, in the broad Way" (31).

The advent of a more gentle pedagogy during the seventeenth and eighteenth centuries was partly due to changing views about childhood, which included the emerging sense that children were more than "small" adults, that their maturation required instructional methods keyed specifically to their condition, and that they could even undergo adolescence. For discussions of these kinds of changes, see, Ariès; Bayne-Powell; Boas; Coveney; DeMause; Marcus; Pinchbeck and Hewitt; Plumb; Somerville; Spacks, *The Adolescent Idea*; Spacks and Carnochan; and Stone.

40. Woodward, 20–21. The only other early example I have found that approaches recommending the "cozening" of children is in Gailhard, *Compleat Gentleman*, where he writes: "When a Scholar is not in a humour, or disposed to learn . . . instead of making him learn with reading, one should teach him with telling, or take some other way to cheat him, as it were, into learning" (pt. 1:21).

41. See Drake, 54; Wilkes, 9; Sheridan, 11–13; and Clarke, 9, 71–79, 121. Clarke was so enthusiastic about Locke's *Education* that he declared: "If the Method there laid down for a private Education . . . was duly fol-

lowed by those whose Circumstances very well enable them to bear the Expence, it would produce, I believe, another Kind of Reformation in the World, than any Means yet made use of, ever did" (126).

42. Astell, *Serious Proposal*, 108. In part II of *Serious Proposal*, Astell invokes another Lockean concept when she describes how judgment creates probable knowledge:

> For knowing nothing without [outside] us but by the Idea we have of it, and Judging only according to the Relation we find between two or more Ideas, when we cannot discover the Truth we search after by Intuition or the immediate comparison of two Ideas, 'tis necessary that we shou'd have a third by which to compare them. But if this middle Idea be wanting, . . . yet we are Ignorant of those Truths which wou'd arise from the Comparison, because we want a third by which to compare them. (71–72)

43. The epigraph reads: "*Ill Habits*, when once contracted, like *Errors* in their first Concoction, are the most difficult Things in Nature to be remov'd————Lock." Locke was certainly familiar with Fénelon's work; Harrison and Laslett, 134, report that his library contained both Fénelon's *Education des Filles* (1687) and *The Adventures of Telemachus* (1699–1700).

44. Fénelon's text, sometimes called *Instructions for a Governess*, appeared in the 1699, 1707, 1708, and 1750 editions (among others) of *Instructions for the Education of a Daughter*; it was also sometimes appended to other authors' treatises, often in abbreviated form, as in Essex's *The Young Ladies Conduct*, chap. 11.

45. Fénelon, *The Accomplish'd Governess*, 25–29.

46. Bourn, 13–16.

47. See *The Order of Things*, xxii, where Foucault defines an *episteme* as an "epistemological field" constituting the fundamental conditions for articulating knowledge.

48. See von Mücke, chaps. 1 and 3.

49. Here I am drawing on Raymond Williams's explanation, in *Marxism and Literature*, 121–27, that in addition to a culture's "dominant" ideology, there are nonconforming "residual" strains and, under certain conditions, equally important counterideologies.

With regard to eighteenth-century descriptions of change in the history of education, George Hickes, the translator of Fénelon's *Instructions* in 1707, draws on the very logic of gentle coercion advanced by the text itself. In his address "To the English Reader," Hickes recounts the success of Fénelon's text in France this way: it "scarce came forth at Paris, but, tho' it overturn'd all the former Methods of Education, it *gently forc'd* its own way into the Best of Families of France, against the strong Torrent of Opposition" (sig. A9ᵛ–A10ʳ; original emphasis omitted).

50. Fénelon, *Instructions*, 179, 252. For similar views by men writing about women's education, see Essex, vii; and Rollin, 38. In *Britain's Remembrancer: Or, The Danger Not Over*, James Burgh says to his "fair Countrywomen" regarding their education: "Your Characters as to Virtue and Vice greatly depend on your Fathers and Husbands; your tender Minds being naturally so pliant as to be susceptible of whatever Impressions are made on them by our Sex" (42).

51. Drake, 124–25, 57. Several years earlier, in *An Essay To Revive the Antient Education of Gentlewomen, in Religion, Manners, Arts & Tongues* (1673), Bathsua Makin attacked the similarly condescending view that women "are so unstable and unconstant, born down upon all occasions with such a torrent of Fear, Love, Hatred, Lust, Pride, and all manner of exorbitant Passions, that they are uncapable to practise any Vertues, that require greatness of Spirit, or firmness of Resolution" (29).

52. See also Astell's remarks on inconstancy in *Serious Proposal*, 115–16.

53. Astell, *Serious Proposal*, 120. On another front, the problem of a "mechanical" view of life could also be said to have induced Astell to reject other important implications of Locke's empiricism, as in her argument in *The Christian Religion* that genuine spirituality required the contemplation of pure ideas, whose abstractness could lead the believer away from the body's limited senses to access to the immaterial Good. See Perry, *The Celebrated Mary Astell*, 87–97, for an account of Astell's disagreements with Locke's ideas; and Masham's published attempts in *Discourse Concerning the Love of God* and elsewhere to bolster Locke's position and attack Astell's.

54. Masham, *Occasional Thoughts*, 162–63.

55. Astell, *Serious Proposal*, 53.

56. Drake, 11–12. For some of the other instances where women's rational competency is claimed by female educationalists (some in Lockean terms), see Makin, 6–21; Woolley, 1; Astell, *Serious Proposal*, 23; Chudleigh, preface, sig. a2ʳ⁻ᵛ; and Masham, *Occasional Thoughts*, 161–62. For some of the men who also acknowledge women's rationality: Defoe, *An Essay upon Projects*, 284–85; Rollin, 38; and Wilkes, 73. Sheryl O'Donnell also discusses how Locke's empiricism had an important impact on other women writers of the period, including Lady Mary Wortley Montagu and Hannah More.

57. I am giving Bourdieu and Passeron's term *cultural capital* a gendered nuance. In *Reproduction in Education*, they argue that gaining cultural knowledge (re)produces in turn one's access to upper-class social power or position. See esp. 30, 32, 47.

For scholarly discussions of views about women's "learning" in the seventeenth and eighteenth centuries, see, e.g., Bremner; Ezell, *The Patriarch's Wife*, 5–6, 9–16, 43–44; Labalme; McMullen; Myers; Perry, *The Celebrated Mary Astell*, 98–119; Reynolds; and R. Watts.

58. More, 203; spelling standardized.

59. Chudleigh, 14.

60. Astell, *Serious Proposal Part II*, 286, 291.

61. For biographical accounts of Masham's personal and intensely intellectual relationship with Locke, see Cranston, 215–26, 236–38; and Aaron, 26, 37, 41–48.

62. Masham, *Occasional Thoughts*, 185–86.

63. See F. Smith, 104, 109–13, for a discussion of Masham's intellectual relationship to both Locke's and Astell's work. While Smith describes Masham's *Occasional Thoughts* as a text that "becomes to some extent Locke's *Thoughts on Education* feminized" (113), Masham's appropriation of Locke's pedagogical ideas proved to be more complicated than a mere extension or "translation" of their principles from one sex to the other (especially as Locke would have it), because her goals regarding both women and Christian faith introduced new problems to the educational process, including the fact that women's necessary, though unconventionally profound, understanding of biblical tenets would inevitably challenge men's traditional authority in the church (on this issue, see esp. Masham, *Occasional Thoughts*, 198–200).

64. This was particularly Locke's opinion of Masham: "The lady herself is so much occupied with study and reflection on theological and philosophical matters, that you could find few men with whom you might associate with greater profit and pleasure. Her judgement is singularly keen, and I know few men capable of discussing with such insight the most abstruse subjects" (*Correspondence of John Locke*, 4:237). See Nyland, 44–46, on this point; see Laslett for a more general discussion about Masham.

65. Astell, *Serious Proposal Part II*, 27. Astell did not believe, however, that individuals were born free in the state of nature. In "A Prefatory Discourse to Dr. D'Avenant," she refutes that idea, calling it "*a meer figment of Hobbs's Brain*" (xxxv, qtd. in Perry, *The Celebrated Mary Astell*, 201).

66. On this point, see Fraser, 333–34, 464; Hill, 18–24; Perry, *The Celebrated Mary Astell*, 71; and Thomas, "Women and the Civil War Sects." But cf. Ezell's dissenting view in *The Patriarch's Wife*, 5–17.

67. On this point with respect to Locke's political and pedagogical views, see Stone, 407. For Stone's other discussions of Locke's *Education*, see 20, 261, 264, 408, 440–41.

68. Astell, *Serious Proposal Part II*, 74–75.

69. Wilkes, 18.

70. For Locke's mention of educational "husbandry," see secs. 70, 90,

110; he discusses actually teaching young people husbandry in secs. 130, 194, 204. For a selection of related metaphors, see: "bowing" tender stems (sec. 34); "Cherry-stones" (sec. 110); "Fruit" (sec. 84); garden plots (secs. 66, 84); grafting (sec. 200); planting (secs. 64, 99, 126); ploughing and spading (sec. 84); "reaping" (sec. 212); ripeness (secs. 70, 80, 138, 140, 159, 172); "Roots" (secs. 35, 48, 67, 79, 100, 105, 110, 116); "Seeds" (secs. 37, 70, 84, 100); and "Weeds" (secs. 35, 64, 66, 84, 100, 110, 117, 147).

71. For Locke's mention of seasons, see secs. 34, 75, 84, 96, 105, 125, 160 ("seasonable"), 168, 186, 212. Another twist on this term is his occasional discussion of "seasoning" children's minds; see secs. 32, 78.

72. For these and other medical references, see: "contagion" (secs. 68, 70); "Cure" (secs. 67, 70, 113, 115, 123, 124, 127, 128, 131 ["work . . . the Cure"], 142, 145, 189); "Disease" (secs. 51, 55); "Distemper" (sec. 51); infection (secs. 68, 90); "Remedy" (secs. 78, 83, 85, 87, 109, 138, 139); and sickness (sec. 208).

73. See Locke, *Essay*, 2.23.12, 4.20.1; he also claims that "the Perception of the Mind [is] most aptly explained by Words relating to the Sight," and that "*Our Knowledge*, as in other Things, . . . has a great Conformity with our Sight" (2.29.2; 4.13.1). For a few of his references to light, see 4.2.1, 4, 6; 4.19.13–16.

74. See Locke, *Education*, secs. 85, 145, 94. "Observation" further specifies the mature ability of the child to perceive and adhere to rational and moral conduct; see, e.g., secs. 93, 143. See also Locke's reference to Indians' inclination to "observe much more Decency and Civility in their Discourses and Conversation" than European peoples (sec. 145).

75. See secs. 66, 45 (my emphasis); see also sec. 97, for being "*Under the Eye of a Father.*"

76. For other references to children's desirable obliviousness to being observed or pedagogically maneuvered, see secs. 102, 125, 129, 148, 149.

77. See Foucault, *DP*, esp. 195–228.

78. Locke, *Education*, sec. 148.

79. Locke, *Second Treatise*, sec. 107.

80. Locke, *Education*, sec. 37.

81. Foucault, *The History of Sexuality*, 101. Taking this tack amounts to my choosing one "version" of Foucault's disciplinary thesis over another, since I find more useful his stress in *The History of Sexuality* (which followed *Discipline and Punish*) on the heterogenous and sometimes even unstable relation of discourse to social power.

82. On this point, see Foucault, *DP*, 276–78.

83. Locke, *Education*, sec. 132.

84. Brathwaite, *The English Gentlewoman*, 182; and Woolley, 2. For other uses of garden imagery before 1688, see, e.g., Codington, 16;

Makin, 7, 26, 37; Walker, 4–5, 19, 31, 36, 48, 83; and Gailhard, pt. 1:4, 9, 12, 56, 61, 78, 100.

85. Brathwaite, *The English Gentlewoman*, 214; Walker, 4? For other instances of medical imagery in the mid-seventeenth century, see Walker, 4, 19, 65, 83, 93–94; and Gailhard, pt. 1:59, and preface to pt. 2:sig. A5ᵛ.

86. Brathwaite, *The English Gentlewoman*, 181.

87. Comenius, *The Great Didactic*, 192.

88. Woodward, *A Light to Grammar*, sig. a8ʳ.

89. Astell, *Serious Proposal*, 29–30.

90. Astell, *Serious Proposal*, 25–26; my emphasis. On Nature's double status, see also her distinction between "Animal Nature" and "Natural Motions" that "are easie and pleasant" (*Serious Proposal Part II*, 66). For some of her other gardening metaphors, see *Serious Proposal*, 12–13, 51–52, 92; and *Part II*, 23–24.

91. For a sampling of similar gardening tropes from the 1688 to the mid-eighteenth century, see *The Advice of a Father* (1688), 91, 123; Tillotson, *Six Sermons* (1694), 118–19; Hough, *Sermon* (1705), 16–17, 19; Loveling, *The Best Use of Riches* (1706), 22; King, *The Advantages of Education* (1706), 23; Fénelon, *Instructions* (1707), 24, 63, 64; Wilkes, *Letter* (1744), 78; and Sheridan, *British Education* (1756), xxxi, 62–64.

92. Masham, *Occasional Thoughts*, 4–5.

93. Sheridan, 4, 11, 25–26. For other examples of medical tropes from the 1690s to the mid-eighteenth century, see Astell, *Serious Proposal*, 103; Masham, *Occasional Thoughts*, 4–5, 28–29, 168, 193; Fénelon, *Instructions*, 50, 51, 68, 70, 72, 75, 183, 214, 252, 275; King, 6–7, 21; Loveling, 23; Clarke, 127; Essex, x, xxxii, xxxiv, 15; Wilkes, 8; Bourn, 54; and Sheridan, 1–2, 4, 12, 25, 493, 503, 504, 524. For a striking instance where, as in Locke's work, the metaphors of disease and plant life become meshed, see Astell, *Serious Proposal Part II*, 23–24.

94. Fénelon, *Instructions*, 207.

95. Trotter was a staunch defender of Locke's Christian orthodoxy, publishing several treatises on the subject, including *A Defence of Mr. Locke's Essay of Human Understanding, wherein Its Principles, with reference to Morality, Revealed Religion, and the Immortality of the Soul, are considered and justified* (1702) and *A Letter to Dr. Holdsworth, . . . Concerning the Resurrection of the Same Body* (1726). She refuted the notion of Locke's "Socinianism," including a supposedly heretical view on Original Sin, in a lengthy work published posthumously entitled *A Vindication of Mr. Locke's Christian Principles* (1751), esp. pt. 1:199–206. These works were all collected after her death in the volume *The Works of Mrs. Catharine Cockburn, Theological, Moral, Dramatic, and Poetical* (1751).

96. Astell, *Serious Proposal*, 102.

97. Masham, *Occasional Thoughts*, 176; Clarke, 5. For other similar references, see, e.g., Masham, *Occasional Thoughts*, 176–77; Fénelon, *Instructions*, 23, 47; and Peers, 4–5.

98. Fénelon, *Instructions*, 69. On Clarke's description of teaching Latin, see his *Essay*, esp. 11–16, 50–56.

99. Astell, *Serious Proposal*, 136, 140. For a sampling of men's views on fostering female friendship, see Fénelon, *Instructions*, 70; and Essex, xxi.

100. Astell, *Serious Proposal*, 15–16, 22. On this point, see also 4.

101. This peculiar story about Domitian (Titus Flavius Domitianus; Emperor A.D. 81–96) has been widely reported by historians. During the eighteenth century, for example, John Lemprière, in his *Classical Dictionary*, 3d ed., reports that Domitian "passed the greatest part of the day in catching flies and killing them with a bodkin, so that it was wittily answered by Vibius Crispus to a person who asked him who was with the emperor, 'Nobody, not even a fly'" (214). See also *Harper's Dictionary of Classical Literature and Antiquities*, 535.

102. Chudleigh, preface, sig. a2ᵛ; see also the exchange between Melissa and the parson on the issue of whether English women should follow the example of "The *Persian* Ladies" (11–15). These examples establish an early precedent for Mary Wollstonecraft's similar and more famous tack in *Vindication of the Rights of Women*, where she drew a detailed parallel between the plight of Persian women and the conditions for women in England.

In *Occasional Thoughts*, Masham also ends up endorsing the values of colonization, despite voicing reservations about Europeans' ability to corrupt foreign cultures. Without linking her argument directly to English women, she treats the Peruvians as an example of how Christianity can fully enlighten those who have previously benefited only from the light of natural reason (57–59).

103. Astell, *Serious Proposal Part II*, 9. For other references to the "tyranny" of the status quo (especially as "Custom") for women, see Astell, *Serious Proposal*, 46; *Part II*, 42; and Drake, 3. In 1703, Sarah Fyge Egerton would register a similar view in her poem "The Emulation":

> Say, tyrant Custom, why must we obey
> The impositions of thy haughty sway? . . .
> And shall we women now sit tamely by,
> Make no excursions in philosophy,
> Or grace our thoughts in tuneful poetry?
> We will our rights in learning's world maintain,
> Wit's empire now shall know a female reign. (ll. 1–2, 29–33)

104. Astell, *Serious Proposal*, 141–42. This sense of female (and imperial)

self-assertiveness, even given its inherent ambiguities, runs counter to Beth Kowaleski-Wallace's grim claim that the legacy of Locke's educational program for women in the eighteenth century—both authors and their fictional characters—is to establish a regime of paternalistic gentleness in which "rebellion becomes impossible . . . [because] there exist no obvious signs of tyranny or repression" (282). Writers such as Astell and Chudleigh deployed the language of "empire" with a very keen eye on transforming masculinist traditions, and they succeeded in changing, among other things, the terms in which women's status in early eighteenth-century England would be discussed.

105. Astell, *Serious Proposal*, 58, 97.

106. Astell, *Serious Proposal Part II*, 290–91.

Chapter 2

1. For a sampling of these narratives, see Locke, *Education*, secs. 78, 94, 115, 116, 130, 138, 145, 148, 151, 177, 178, 211.

2. Locke, *Education*, secs. 158, 215, 105. For other examples of Locke "think"ing, see secs. 107, 108, 115, 116, 136, 146, 152, 155, 156, 168; for another instance of "imagining," see sec. 110.

3. Locke, *Education*, sec. 70. For other examples of the reader's imagined interjections, see secs. 78, 115, 130, 168.

4. See the *Oxford English Dictionary* entry under "Thicken," notably its usage to denote: "To become more complex or intricate (esp. said of a plot); to increase in intensity." There is no conclusive evidence that Locke attended or was familiar with Buckingham's well-known play, although it is striking that their use of the phrase is contemporaneous.

5. Richetti, 46.

6. Locke, *Essay*, 4.16.12.

7. Locke, *Essay*, 4.17.4. See also Locke's comment that "wary Reasoning from Analogy leads us often into the discovery of Truths, . . . which would otherwise lie concealed" (4.16.12).

8. See also Locke's further characterization of the enthusiastic mindset, in which "Every Conceit that throughly warms our Fancies must pass for an Inspiration" (4.19.14).

9. Yolton, 5, 9. Reicyu, 59, 207, agrees that the *Education* is not a systematic enterprise intended to deduce pedagogical principles from Locke's epistemology.

10. Axtell, introduction, 51–52. See also Leites, who claims: "Locke believes his method of moral education is fit for all"; some of his methods "are particularly suited to gentlemen (or their betters), but the fundamental elements of moral training have wider application" (69).

11. Coste, preface to Locke, *De l'éducation des Enfans*, qtd. in Axtell, introduction, 52.

12. See Jameson, 242.

13. See de Man, "The Epistemology of Metaphor," 11–28. Similar arguments concerning Locke's characterization of language are made by Sitter and by Bennington. See Walmsley for a dissenting view, discussing Locke's "confidence in language as a medium of thought" (414).

14. I consider the theoretical aspects of this reorientation in a de Manian context in "Paul de Man and the Legacy of Suspicion," esp. 98–107.

15. Sedgwick, *Between Men*, 14–15.

16. See Pickering; also relevant is Summerfield's discussion, esp. 1–11. In *Artful Science* Barbara Stafford discusses eighteenth-century publishers' additional application of "Locke's illusionistic tactics" in the *Education* to the use of illustrations and scientific demonstrations in books intended to instruct children (49–67).

17. See Doody, *The Daring Muse*; and McKeon, *Origins*.

18. Shaftesbury, 2:217; 1:54; 2:158.

19. For a full discussion of Shaftesbury's relationship to Locke's empiricism, see Klein, 39–40, 64–69.

20. See Bakhtin's discussion of the carnivalesque in *Problems of Dostoevsky's Poetics*, 122–37; see also Terry Castle's application of this concept to eighteenth-century fiction in *Masquerade and Civilization*.

21. On this point, see Shaftesbury's discussion of dialogue in *Characteristics*, 1:48–53. In the context of Shaftesbury's relation to the eighteenth-century code of sentimentality, Robert Markley argues further that Shaftesbury represents natural human virtue as a celebration of "stability and harmony within a closed, paternalistic society" defined by staunch aristocratic privilege (214).

22. See Comenius, *The Labyrinth of the World*. In reflecting a similar seventeenth-century view regarding the task of teaching women, Richard Brathwaite refers to human experience as "the Maze or Labyrinth of this life" and as an "intricate Labyrinth of affliction" (*The English Gentlewoman*, 29, 213).

23. H. Fielding, *The Jacobite's Journal* no. 22 (30 Apr. 1748): 258, 259, 260. For discussion of Fielding's views on education, see Kropf. Martin Battestin, in an editorial note in H. Fielding's *Amelia* (167 n. 1), also comments on the connections among *Amelia*, Locke's pedagogy, and the sermons of Archbishop Tillotson.

24. Addison and Steele, *The Spectator* (no. 455) 4:104–5.

25. Addison and Steele, *The Spectator* (no. 1) 1:4–5.

26. Addison and Steele, *The Spectator* (no. 313) 3:132. Other references to the *Education* and its arguments are in 2:115 (on the harsh treatment of

children in schools); 2:396 (the drawbacks of teaching Greek); and 3:250 (on sacrificing children's innocence for the sake of inculcating Greek and Latin). Locke's other work was also frequently cited; see, e.g., 1:263–64, 399, 454; 3:403–4, 454, 547; 4:568, 575–76.

27. Addison and Steele, *The Spectator* (no. 418) 3:569–70.

28. Eagleton, 11.

29. Kroll, 56. See also his discussion of the process of epistemological observation, 73–74; on *The Spectator's* perceptual and critical orientation, see Ketcham, chaps. 1 and 2.

30. Collier, *A Short View*, sig. A2ʳ. He continues this argument in *A Defence of the Short View of the Profaneness and Immorality of the English Stage*.

31. The most comprehensive account of the history of antitheatrical sentiment in England is Jonas Barish's *The Antitheatrical Prejudice*; he discusses eighteenth-century views in chaps. 8 and 9. For a bibliography that lists nearly eighty contributions to the controversy about theater from 1698 to 1726, see Anthony, 300–7.

32. Rollin, 45. For one of the rare times Collier comments on the relevance of plays to young people or their education, see *A Short View*, 5–6.

33. Rollin, 45 n. A little later the translator adds this note: "What for instance, can contribute more to inspire Youth with a love for probity, and a Detestation of lewd women, than to see the Play of *George Barnwell* represented?" (45–46 n.). I will consider the gendered perceptions of the theater as polluting spectacle and/or reforming antidote in a moment.

34. Drake, 49.

35. Brathwaite, *The English Gentlewoman*, 25, 218.

36. Makin, 26; Astell, *Serious Proposal*, 37–38. Unlike Jeremy Collier, female educationalists of the period stressed the frivolousness of plays, rather than their drastic immorality. They also rejected Collier's tendency to characterize women as creatures whose modesty was not only "design'd by Providence" (*A Short View*, 11) but also so naturally delicate that they could not endure a play's potential improprieties. For Collier's discussion of plays and female audience members, see *A Short View*, esp. 7–11.

37. Chudleigh, *The Ladies Defence*, "Epistle Dedicatory," sig. a1ʳ. Chudleigh explains, "Tragedies fill the Mind with noble Ideas, and inspire us with great and generous Sentiments; Comedies show us our Faults in the clearest Lights; . . . and 'tis our selves alone we ought to blame, if we receive no Advantage from them, for they instruct at the same time they entertain" ("Epistle Dedicatory," sig. a1ʳ).

38. In *Timber: or, Discoveries*, Ben Jonson expressed an earlier version of this concern in terms that are probably the most famous in the seventeenth century:

I *have* considered, our whole life is like a *Play*: wherein every man, forgetfull of himselfe, is in travaile with expression of another. Nay, wee so insist in imitating others, as wee cannot (when it is necessary) returne to our selves: like Children, that imitate the vices of *Stammerers* so long, till at last they become such; and make the habit to another nature, as it is never forgotten. (597)

For late twentieth-century critics such as Jane Gallop, by contrast, this situation is less an undesirable predicament than a fundamental inevitability for both pedagogy and social relations in general; see her theoretical discussion of how teaching functions as a form of "impersonation" whose broader principles "can be understood as undergirding culture itself" (5).

39. Burgh, 6.

40. *The Advice of a Father*, dedication "To his Son," sig. A6^r. In *Of Education*, Obadiah Walker imagines a similar scenario of a young man's performance for an audience composed of both his family and the world at large:

[B]y his *Family* he is already placed upon the *Theatre*, where all his actions shall be observed, and praised, even more then they deserve; all mens eyes are upon him expecting somewhat extraordinary from him, and so he needs not some eminent action to introduce him into the good opinion of the World. (53)

41. Astell, *Serious Proposal Part II*, 273.

42. In *The English Gentlewoman*, Richard Brathwaite offers a much earlier example of reorienting women's sense of dramatic audience when he writes, "A Gentlewoman, is her owne *Tyrewoman*; one that wears her owne *face*; and whose *complexion* is her owne. . . . her Chamber is her Tyring-roome, where she bethinks her how she may play her part on the worlds Theatre; that shee [*sic*] may gaine applause of her heavenly Spectators" (concluding section on "Character," sig. Ff4^{r-v}). On the idea of staging a "real," rather than false, educational example for others, Jean Gailhard also writes in *The Compleat Gentleman*:

No man endued with Judgment and Reason, will believe him who acts the part of a Prince upon the Stage (though for a time he borrows Royal Ornaments, and assumes over his equals a Sovereign Authority) to be indeed what he seems and pretends to be; 'tis so but for a time, and to give delight to his Spectators: so will he off, who being a man of quality, is useless to those, who, because he is above them, have their eyes fixed upon him, and gives them neither good Precepts, Advises, nor Examples. There is no Star but hath its influences within her sphere, no good Tree but produces good Fruit; but he who is noble, and doth not *act his part*, is but a vain shadow. (pt. 1: sig. A4^i; my emphasis)

43. Astell, *Serious Proposal Part II*, 50–51. For other comments on novelty's dangers, see Behn, 61; and Essex, xi–xii, 17.

44. Marshall, *The Figure of Theater*, 5.

45. Other titles of full-volume dialogues include: *Astronomical Dialogues between a Gentleman and a Lady* (1719, 1725); J. Ferguson, *Young Gentleman and Lady's Astronomy, familiarly explained in Ten Dialogues between Neander and Eudosia* (1768); Martin, *Young Gentleman and Lady's Philosophy, in a Continued Survey of the Works of Nature and Art, by Way of Dialogue*, 2d ed. (1772); *Botanical Dialogues between Hortensia and her four Children* (1797); and *An Astronomical Catechism, or Dialogues between a Mother and her Daughter* (1818). For another example of staging educational scenes, in this case where parents and children converse, see Peers, *A Serious Call to Christianity*, esp. 6 ff.

46. Maidwell, 24–26, 27–32.

47. Penton, sig. A2^r.

48. George Hind has been the first critic to argue that Mandeville's *Fable of the Bees* is Menippean. On Bakhtin's discussion of Menippean satire's intermediary position between ancient literary forms and the novel, see *Problems of Dostoevsky's Poetics*, 93–97; he also briefly discusses Menippean satire in *Rabelais and His World*, 60–70, 386–88. For a history of Menippean satire from antiquity to the Middle Ages, see Relihan. For discussions of Mandeville's self-ironized positions regarding ethics, human nature, and virtue—all of which accompanied his Menippean bent—see, e.g., Chalk; Goldsmith, *Private Vices, Public Benefits* and "Public Virtue and Private Vices"; Monro; Scott-Taggart; and Primer. Kaye succinctly describes the *Fable's* textual history (1:xxxiv–xxxv) and the heated reactions to Mandeville's arguments by his contemporaries (2:401–17).

Women authors also adapted the conventions of Menippean satire— based on the classical examples of Varro's works and Lucian's *Icaro-menippea*—to novelistic narrative. Delarivière Manley, for instance, explains her collocation of diverse literary materials in *New Atalantis* this way: "*The* New Atalantis *seems . . . to be written like* Varonian *Satyrs, on* different Subjects, Tales, Stories *and* Characters *of Invention, after the Manner of* Lucian, *who copy'd from* Varro" (2:sig. A4^v).

49. See Rothstein, esp. 7–10. Rothstein also claims that eighteenth-century novelists were following Lockean cognitive premises by tracing the mind's function as "an acquisitive faculty" (246).

50. Rothstein, 6.   51. See Davis, 42–70.

52. See Bloom, introduction, 6.   53. Rousseau, *Emile*, 402, 50–51.

54. Manley, 1:29.

55. On aspects of Haywood's early career, see Ballaster, 153–95; Craft; and Schofield, "'Descending Angels'" and "Exposé of the Popular Heroine."

56. Haywood, *Life's Progress*, 3.

57. The twentieth-century portrait of the later Haywood as (quasi-) fallen feminist is the flip side of her image during the eighteenth century, when she was often characterized as an author who redeemed her work for feminine virtue in the last decades of her career. The author perhaps the most responsible for popularizing that image during the Enlightenment was Clara Reeve, who, in *The Progress of Romance*, claimed that "Mrs. *Heywood* had the singular fortune to recover a lost reputation, and the yet greater to atone for her errors" (1:121). By contrast, in characterizing Haywood's career as a case of making difficult social choices with offsetting advantages and disadvantages at every point, rather than as a matter of abandoning her earlier feminist interests, I agree with Pat Gill, who makes a similar argument about the overall history of women's fiction during the eighteenth and nineteenth centuries (471–76).

58. Haywood, *Female Spectator*, 1:2. On *The Female Spectator*'s relevance to Haywood's career, see Green, 22, 25, 39, 141; and Shevelow.

59. See Brissenden.

60. See Starr, "Sentimental De-education." In stressing that, since its earliest appearance, the novel of education has rested on the concept of profoundly reformable character, I am also tracking a different trajectory than that claimed by Eve Tavor Bannet, who argues that early examples of the female *Bildungsroman* concentrated on changing readers' moral constitution through the example of a "faultless, idealized heroine," before turning in the late eighteenth century to portraying a protagonist "who had faults that she had to learn to correct" ("Rewriting the Social Text," 219).

61. Jocelyn Harris, introduction, xviii. This point is confirmed by Marks's view of Richardson's novel as "the finest example" of the conduct book (22). For instances where Richardson also alludes to or explicitly cites Locke's *Education*, see *Grandison*, 1:55, 59, 261; 2:291, 316.

62. Richardson, letter to Thomas Edwards, 13 Feb. 1750/51, as quoted in Marks, 98. As Marks comments, "Harriet and Sir Charles are already good; the question is how should a good person respond to the difficult situations of life" (60).

63. See Joseph's argument with Parson Adams about the usefulness of schooling in H. Fielding, *Joseph Andrews*, 231.

64. H. Fielding, *The History of Tom Jones*, 43.

65. The definitive study of H. Fielding's views on charity and chastity is Battestin's *The Moral Basis of Fielding's Art*, esp. chaps. 2 and 3. For McKeon's commentary on this issue, see *Origins*, 398–409.

66. H. Fielding, *Amelia*, 114. For discussions of Fielding's views on Mandeville, see Battestin's comments in *Amelia*, 21 n. 1, 114 n. 1, 342 n. 1; and his essay "The Problem of *Amelia*," 626–28.

67. For a different assessment of the cross-gender dynamics in *Joseph Andrews* as a bipolar exchange, see Campbell, 61–130.

68. H. Fielding, *Amelia*, 295.

69. Rollin, 31–32. As a different version of the same idea, Benjamin Bourn, in *A Sure Guide to Hell*, adopts the persona of Satan in order to warn young women that, should they give in to vanity and allow a man's slightest sexual advances, an inevitable chain of events will bring them to ruin, so that by the end, "either entering into a Brothel, or being a kept Mistress, . . . you will never be able to return to the Paths of Virtue" (91).

70. Masham, *Occasional Thoughts*, 21–22.

71. Manley, 1:83.

72. Manley, 1:83. In *Rise of the Woman Novelist*, Spencer discusses this passage in the context of Manley's self-image as scandalous female author (58–59).

73. For a brief account of the *Télémaque*'s impact in France and England, see Patrick Riley's introduction to *Telemachus, Son of Ulysses*, xiii–xvii.

74. For McKeon's discussion of these ideologies, see, e.g., *Origins*, 21–22, 131–33, 205–11.

75. For McKeon's discussion of women's function in narratives employing all three of the ideological patterns, see *Origins*, 255–65.

Chapter 3

1. Locke, *Board of Trade Papers*, 2:378, 381.

2. Watt, 31.

3. See Armstrong, *Desire*, esp. chaps. 1–3.

4. Pocock, *The Machiavellian Moment*, 64 [hereafter cited as *MM* in notes].

5. Pocock also cites a third, more abstract meaning of virtue: "the essential property which made a personality or element what it was" (*MM*, 37). We might say that virtue's fundamental "virtue" or essence is constituted by the combination of power and morality.

6. Pocock briefly discusses the function of education in *MM*, 193, 195, 212, 245, 340, 432.

7. Locke, *Essay*, 2.28.7.

8. Pocock, *MM*, 424. Pocock concedes that deemphasizing Locke "is for the present a practical necessity," because Locke's influence has been widely exaggerated in the past (*MM*, 424). More recently, in *Virtue, Commerce, and History*, Pocock has provided a fuller account of how Lockean and liberal thought related—mainly as an antagonist—to seventeenth- and eighteenth-century republicanism (see esp. 45–52, 59–68, 160–91), although at the same time he claims that ultimately, "Locke's politics mark the end of one age rather than the beginning of another" (48). Other historians, however, have rejected that perspective. Among the earliest are Isaac Kramnick, who, in "Republican Revisionism Revisited," began to modify Pocock's dismissal of Locke's influence by arguing that the reform of Parliament in the 1760s relied heavily on Locke's political theories; he has developed this view further in *Republicanism and Bourgeois Radicalism*. Other scholars who have also challenged Pocock's position, in both American and British contexts, include Appleby in *Capitalism and a New Social Order* and *Liberalism and Republicanism in the Historical Imagination*; Diggins; Pangle; and Thomas in "Politics as Language."

9. My thanks to Steven Pincus for letting me read a draft version of his "Neither Machiavellian Moment Nor Possessive Individualism."

10. Burtt, 10, 13; see esp. chaps. 1 and 6.

11. Kloppenberg, 33. For other discussions of the ways in which a connection between liberal and republican tenets should be reconsidered, see also Isaac; Herzog; and Houston, 277–78; my views here have also been shaped by Michael McKeon's unpublished manuscript, "The Secret History of Domesticity: Public, Private, and the Division of Knowledge." For work that has recently revaluated the political climate of seventeenth-century England in more general terms, with some attention to literature, see, e.g., Pincus, *Protestantism and Patriotism*; N. Smith, *Literature and Revolution in England*; and the collections *Literature and the English Civil War* (ed. Healy and Sawday); *Culture and Politics in Early Stuart England* (ed. Sharpe and Lake); and *Republicanism, Liberty and Commercial Society, 1649–1776* (ed. Wootton).

12. I have selected this three-part historical perspective in order to offer a suggestively complex, though admittedly partial, picture of how the public and private spheres became conceived during the eighteenth century. There were of course a number of other social and discursive forces that played a part, including the articulation of a secularized, rational public space, as discussed by Habermas in *Structural Transformation of the Public Sphere*; the continuation of the process, begun at least a century before, of distinguishing the domain of the "state" from that of "society" (as McKeon outlines in his unpublished essay, "The Secret History of Domestic-

ity"); the cultivation of "sensibility" as a form of making private feelings reliably benevolent and publicly effectual; and the reconception of domestic space and proper femininity as described, for example, by Armstrong in *Desire and Domestic Fiction* and Poovey in *The Proper Lady*. For my purposes here, I have chosen texts and institutions with a notable emphasis on education, although a more comprehensive account would incorporate these and other relevant contexts.

13. Locke, *Education*, sec. 33.

14. Locke, *Education*, sec. 66. For other discussions of breeding's relation to virtue, see secs. 70 and 142–45.

15. In the hands of Shaftesbury, the emphasis is on the latter, innate sense of breeding's significance. On this point, see Markley.

16. See, e.g., Patey, esp. 84–87, for the Enlightenment distinction between natural and artificial signs. The concept of natural signs was substantially underwritten by the prevailing interest in calculating probability; for discussions of probability, see Foucault, *Order of Things*; Hacking; Kendall and Pearson; and Shapiro.

17. Locke, *Education*, sec. 110.   18. F. Ferguson, 73.

19. Locke, *Education*, sec. 148.   20. F. Ferguson, 74–75.

21. I use the phrase "nonpossessive education" to indicate how C. B. Macpherson's thesis about "possessive individualism" should be revised to include the educational process. In concentrating on the *Second Treatise*, Macpherson argues that Locke measures individual rationality by two distinct, and finally incompatible, conditions: first, individuals' success in gaining land and making it productive through their own labor; and second, the prospect of unlimited accumulation of property in a money-based political economy (Macpherson, esp. 232–38). The *Education*, however, indicates that the sensibility on which both kinds of propertied rationality are founded should be one trained, at least initially, to disown the unseemly appearance of selfishness or even materialistic self-interest, thereby ensuring all the more the ideological success of capitalist ownership.

22. Locke, *Education*, sec. 9.

23. Locke, *Education*, sec. 90. For other instances where Locke mentions the worthwhile value of paying a good tutor, see secs. 92, 94.

24. Locke, *Education*, sec. 122. For other instances of "Credit," see secs. 58, 129, 131, 200, and esp. 155: "Teach him to love Credit and Commendation."

25. Locke, *Education*, sec. 68. For other occasions when Locke discusses differing rank or class with regard to education, see secs. 89, 129, 142, 148, 151.

26. For one of the more recent analyses of how Locke's work made in-

dividual identity a broad topic for contemporary discussion, see Christopher Fox, *Locke and the Scriblerians*.

27. Isaac Watts, who drew heavily on Locke's pedagogical ideas, published *Logick: or, The Right Use of Reason* in 1725 and his chief educational text, *The Improvement of the Mind*, in 1741; for discussions of his work, see, e.g., Fliegelman, esp. 18–21; and Cremin, 506. William King published a sermon on education called *The Advantages of Education, Religious and Political* in 1706; for other examples of this common practice see Hoadly; Hough; and Loveling.

28. Stafford, *Body Criticism*, 89. For her general discussion of physiognomy's new self-image as a genuine science, see 84–129.

29. Locke, *Education*, sec. 101.

30. Saunders, 214.

31. La Chambre, sig. B1^v.

32. Indagine, "Of Physiognomy," in *The Book of Palmestry and Physiognomy*, sig. ^{2}G6^v. Indagine's use of the word *science* retains the older sense of a particular branch of knowledge or a trained skill, a fact not surprising given the long history of his book's publication. After appearing in Latin in 1522, *Chiromantia* was translated into English by Fabian Withers as *Brief Introductions . . . unto the Art of Chiromancy . . . and Physiognomy*, which was published first in 1558 and reissued in several versions under that title until the 1640s. From 1651 to the late 1690s, with Withers still listed as translator, the work was published in several more so-called "editions" with the title *The Book of Palmestry and Physiognomy*.

33. Stafford calls Lavater the "master eighteenth-century physiognomist" (*Body Criticism*, 84); as an indication of his popularity in England, there were fifty-five editions of Henry Hunter's translation of *Essays on Physiognomy* by 1810. See John Graham for a general account of how the book fared in England and France (61–74, 109–15), and a brief discussion of its relevance to the "English Romantic Novel" (75–84). For two useful histories of physiognomy during this period that link it to eighteenth- and nineteenth-century fiction, see Tytler, 3–81; and Rivers, 18–32.

34. La Chambre, sig. B7^{r-v}.

35. Lavater, *Essays on Physiognomy*, 1:20. Volume 1 was published in 1789, volumes 2 and 3 were published in 1792 and 1798, respectively; this volume series, translated by Henry Hunter, is cited as 1789–98. In the course of my discussion I will also refer to two other editions of this text: one translated by Thomas Holcroft and issued in 1789 (cited as 1789); and another translated by C. Moore, issued in 1797 (cited as 1797).

36. See, e.g., the dedication to La Chambre's book by John Davies, the English translator, who claims that if judgments of character based on physiognomical interpretation are generally useful,

how much more must they be, which are made by persons entrusted with the management of Embassies, and the most important Transactions of Crowns and Scepters, and consequently, oblig'd to treat with People of different Tempers and Climates? In these last it suffices not, to be guided by those common observations and characters of men, which are obvious to the Populace, and commonly mask'd and disguiz'd; but the grand secret is, to penetrate into the Closets, and insinuate into the very bosoms, of Princes and Favourites. (sig. A4^{r-v})

37. Bender, 128.

38. Both Paulson, in *Hogarth's Graphic Works*, 130, and Shesgreen, in *Engravings by Hogarth*, n.p., have identified this emblem as the mace of the Lord Mayor of London. For other discussions of the series in general, see: Gaunt, 12, 92–93; Lindsay, 137–44; Paulson, *Hogarth: His Life, Art, and Times*, 2:61–74, and "The Simplicity of Hogarth's *Industry and Idleness*."

39. Shesgreen, in *Engravings by Hogarth*, n.p., and Paulson, in *Hogarth's Graphic Works*, 130, for example, readily identify the man as the master. But despite his similar hairstyle, coat, and hat, the man's facial and bodily features in the first plate do not closely resemble Mr. West's in pl. 4: instead, his face appears younger and slimmer, and he also is without West's considerable girth.

40. See also Lindsay, who says: "the personal drama is fully enlarged in its social significance" (141).

41. See Paulson, *Emblem and Expression*, 58–78, and *Popular and Polite Art*, 9–23. For an alternate explanation of the series' ambiguities, see Shesgreen, "Hogarth's *Industry and Idleness*: A Reading," 596–98.

42. See also Paulson's discussion of Idle as a "generator of texts" in *Popular and Polite Art*, 14–15.

43. Hogarth himself identified the pedagogical purpose of *Industry and Idleness* and its corresponding design, explaining that the series was "calculated for the use & Instruction of youth wherein every thing necessary to be known was to be made as inteligible as possible. and as fine engraving was not necessary to the main design provided that which is infinitely more material viz that characters and Expressions were well preserved, the purchase of them became within the reach of those for whom they [were] cheifly intended" (qtd. in Paulson, *Hogarth: His Life, Art, and Times*, 2:63).

44. H. Fielding, *The Jacobite's Journal* no. 22 (30 Apr. 1748): 260.

45. Foucault, *DP*, 170.

46. Despite the increase of the poor and vagrants in London that Locke wrote about, according to Jack Goldstone in *Revolution and Rebellion*, 84–85, the general population growth in England from 1650 to 1750 was nearly stagnant in comparison to earlier periods: in contrast to the boom

of the sixteenth and early seventeenth centuries, the population increased less than 10 percent, from 5.2 million to 5.7 million. Similarly, London's growth rate also slowed to one-third its previous pace. Hence the increase in pauperism during the 1690s, especially in London, seems to have been caused by the financial strains and disruption of trade created by the Nine Years War (also called "King William's War") against France, which started in 1689. (For a brief account of the financial and political fallout of the war, see Brewer, 89, 119, 139, 148–54, 200.) In that case, Locke's proposal to the board of trade targeted the poor for conditions caused in large part by an unpopular war. But while they were conceived under those particular historical conditions, his ideas about working schools would later become applied to the general upturn in the population beginning around 1750.

47. Foucault, *DP*, 199.

48. Locke, *Trade Papers*, 2:383.

49. Locke, *Trade Papers*, 2:383. There is also a chilling moment when Locke says that the lazy but able-bodied poor "may be quickly reduced to a very small number, or quite *extirpated*" (2:382; my emphasis)—capturing in one word the double sense of thoroughly rooting out a social "weed," as well as destroying completely a noxious pest.

50. See Fox Bourne, 2:392–93; and Jones, 88.

51. Jones, 22–23.

52. In 1753, although he did not focus his proposal on children, Henry Fielding also contributed to public interest in and ultimate legislation for workhouses. Like those writers urging the usefulness of working schools, Fielding stressed the "amending" of morals and instruction in labor for the poor in his plan, entitled *A Proposal for Making an Effectual Provision for the Poor*. See his *An Enquiry into the Causes of the Late Increase of Robbers*, 219–78, esp. 247, 258, 269–72. In this context, see also Evans.

53. Society for Promoting Christian Knowledge, *Circular Letters* (1712), qtd. in Jones, 92.

54. Jones, 90.

55. *Pietas Corcagiensis*, 10–11. For a comparable account of the efforts in Ireland, see *Methods of Erecting, Supporting & Governing Charity-Schools . . . in Ireland*.

56. From *A Humble Proposal for Obtaining His Majesty's Royal Charter to Incorporate a Society for Promoting Christian Knowledge among the Poor Natives of the Kingdom of Ireland* (1730), qtd. in Jones, 234.

57. This phenomenon recalls Foucault's observation that the apparent "failure" of discipline leads to more—and more effective—forms of supervision and control. See *DP*, esp. 277; on a related point, see *The History of Sexuality: Volume 1*, 95.

58. Jones, 335.

59. Lancaster, *The British System of Education*, 45. See also Jones's discussion, 335.

60. Lancaster's comment on this illustration further emphasizes the cost effectiveness of his plan:

> Here are 56 boys represented as reading at eight lessons, only worth about two-pence each, exclusive of the mill-board they are pasted on; when they are done, and returned to their seats to practice writing on the slate, or to spell, by writing, or to write sentences from Scripture, another 56 may use the same lessons, and then another; so that above 300 boys may read or spell at eight lessons, in a single morning, and have the full advantage of 300 books, costing as many shillings; a fair, but very low average for an expense of paper and printing, not exceeding sixteen-pence. (55)

61. Bernard, *Of the Education of the Poor*, 35–36, qtd. in Jones, 337.

62. See Perry, *The Celebrated Mary Astell*, 100–1.

63. Astell, *Serious Proposal*, 60–61.

64. Even given Astell's aim that her academy be a temporary refuge, Defoe criticized her proposal because, he claimed, a religious retreat would restrain young women beyond their tolerance, and "nothing but the heighth of Bigotry can keep up a Nunnery" (*Essay on Projects*, 286). While acknowledging having "very great Esteem" for Astell's proposed school, and "a great Opinion of her Wit" (286), Defoe seems to have been smarting from the fact that her plan reached publication three years before his own did in 1697. He details his own ideas about an "Academy for Women" in his *Essay*, 282–303.

65. Astell, *Serious Proposal*, 9.

66. As another instance of the imagery of Eden that frequently appears in pt. I of the *Serious Proposal*, Astell remarks that her students' "affections [will] have daily regaled on those delicious Fruits of Paradice, which Religion presents them with, and are therefore too sublime and refin'd to relish the muddy Pleasures of sensual Delights" (142–43).

67. Fénelon, *Instructions*, 70. See also Essex: "this is a certain Tye to draw them to Goodness, by making or contracting a Virtuous Friendship one with the other" (xxi).

68. Astell, *Serious Proposal Part II*, 136.

69. Scott, *Millenium Hall*, 58; further references to the community's heavenly qualities can be found on 63, 69, 120.

70. Scott, 111. For the novel's frequent references to characters' countenances or physical appearance as a measure of their gradual self-improvement or ultimate accomplishments, see, e.g., 59–61, 80, 82, 91, 96, 132–33, 174.

71. Scott, 97. For other references to Louisa's self-scrutiny that have the tone of supervisory improvement, see 131, 139.

72. On the relevance of Astell's interest in friendship to the sponsoring of women's literacy and authorship, see Ezell, *The Patriarch's Wife*, 118–26. In "The Veil of Chastity: Mary Astell's Feminism," Ruth Perry discusses Astell's strong personal investment in cultivating feminine friendship (38). For a more general discussion of friendship in work by early modern women—including Charlotte Lennox and Eliza Haywood—see Todd, *Women's Friendship in Literature*, 305–19.

73. Astell, *Serious Proposal*, 86–87.

74. Makin, 15.

75. Bentham, *Panopticon*, 39; original emphasis removed. See also Foucault's discussion in *DP*, 207.

76. Foucault, *DP*, 222.

77. For Mandeville's use of Locke's work or concepts—especially Locke's idea of the tabula rasa and his limitation of parental power in the *Second Treatise*—see, e.g., *The Fable of the Bees*, 1:54 n. 1; 2:169, 204, 270, 280. See also Gunn. For Pocock's interpretation of Mandeville as part of the republican tradition see, e.g., *MM*, 465–66, 475, 487; and *Virtue, Commerce, and History*, 99, 114, 123.

78. Trenchard and Gordon, 1:142. See also Fliegelman, 16, for a discussion of this text's relevance to eighteenth-century educational theory.

79. Pocock, *MM*, 432.

80. Burgh, 13.

81. Burgh, 13–14. For Fliegelman's discussion of Burgh's views, see 22.

82. Sheridan, 1.

83. Sheridan, 25; for other references to England's social disease and potential cure, see, e.g., 4, 12, 25, 493, 503, 504, 524.

84. James Harris, *Discourse*, 91.

85. Foucault, *DP*, 193.

86. See Armstrong, *Desire*, esp. chaps. 1 and 2.

87. See Bender, esp. chaps. 1 and 2.

88. Richetti, 270 n. 3. Other critics who discuss this issue include Colie; and Aarsleff, 263.

89. Jones, 12.

90. See Sennett.

Chapter 4

1. Defoe, *Family Instructor*, 69.

2. As Paula R. Backscheider comments, using dialogues in a conduct book had already been introduced by William Darrell in *The Gentleman*

Instructed, although Defoe seemed apparently unaware of that work. See Backscheider, introduction to *Family Instructor*, 5.

3. Defoe, *Family Instructor*, 98. Though Defoe avoids satirizing particular parents, he does say earlier that his dialogues "are a Satyr upon their neglect of Duty, and a Reproof to them in Order to Amendment" (58). This momentary characterization of educational writing as satire is reminiscent of Locke's remark in *Some Thoughts concerning Education* that his attack on parents' indulgence of their children's appetites constitutes "a little Satyr" (sec. 37).

4. In part 3, Mary remarks she is religiously backward "having never been taught any thing, till I was almost 20 Years old" (349). Defoe never mentions her older brother's exact age.

5. Among Defoe's few references to Locke, for instance, is his calling him one of the "masters of science" in *The Compleat English Gentleman*, 69.

6. For Starr's remarks on the links between *The Family Instructor* and casuistry, see *Defoe and Casuistry*, 32–33, 35 n. 70, 39 n. 74, 43 n. 77.

7. Defoe, *Family Instructor*, 36. Defoe makes a similar observation in *The Compleat English Gentleman*, where he remarks that mothers

> have the particular power as well as opportunity of printing the most early ideas in the minds of their children, who are able to make the first impressions upon their imagination and perhaps the strongest and most durable; . . . these [mothers] have them in their arms and upon their knees at the very moments when the most early hints are to be given to the mind, when the genius, like a peice of soft wax, may be moulded up to what form, and to reciev what impressions, they please, and when, a few obstinacyes and meer incapacityes of nature excepted, a child may be form'd to be a man of sence or a brute which they please. (70–71)

See Leinster-Mackay, who in *The Educational World of Daniel Defoe*, 63–64, also briefly discusses Defoe's use of the wax-tablet metaphor.

8. Defoe, *Family Instructor*, 128. For other examples of metaphors of horticulture, see: 68 (children as green "Vegetables"); 69, 103 ("Roots"); and 204 ("Seed").

9. Defoe, *Family Instructor*, 109. For other examples of medical metaphors, see where the narrator cites the "Disease" and "Cure" of children's irreligion (73), and where in a related passage the prosperous master discusses his realization that his past errors are "a Wound no Surgeon can cure" (270–71). Leinster-Mackay, in *The Educational World of Daniel Defoe*, also cites this trope in the context of Defoe's advocation of strong punishment for wayward children (71–72).

10. Defoe, *Family Instructor*, 375. There is also a striking resemblance between Robinson Crusoe's experience and Mary's brother's dream of being dreadfully wounded in battle and relying inevitably on the sustenance of his still-alienated father. Unlike Crusoe, however, who in a feverish delirium heeds his dream's warning of impending disaster, reforms, and recovers his health, the brother goes headlong to his demise, fulfilling the dream to the last detail.

11. Another way of describing this problem could be to say that when brought into contact with Puritan pedagogy, the more secularized and liberal elements in supervisory education exacerbate a tension between self-determination and prohibition that is already an internal rift or fault line in the Puritan tradition itself. The task for Defoe and his fictional fathers, therefore, is to improvise ways to negotiate that newly difficult liaison.

12. Defoe, *Family Instructor*, 337; my emphasis. As Mary also says later, "*if we had been little Children*, it had been another Case" (338).

13. See Bakhtin, *The Dialogic Imagination*, esp. "Discourse in the Novel," 259–422.

14. Backscheider, introduction to *Family Instructor*, 7; she elaborates further in *Daniel Defoe: His Life*, 423–26. By contrast, in *The Reluctant Pilgrim*, J. Paul Hunter suggests several persuasive contact points between Defoe's conduct book and his novel, but remains undecided "whether or not *The Family Instructor* was his stepping stone to fictional form" (46). Bonamy Dobrée, however, in *English Literature in the Early Eighteenth Century*, would seem to agree with Backscheider in identifying the *Instructor* as a turning point in Defoe's success in combining dialogue and narrative effectively (403–44). In *Defoe and Casuistry*, Starr similarly claims that the *Instructor* is key in the "transmutation of traditional cases of conscience into the materials of prose fiction" (33). For a discussion of Hunter's argument, as well as additional points of comparison between Defoe's conduct books and *Robinson Crusoe*, see also Rogers, 51–58, 94, 131–32.

15. *Lives of the Poets of Great Britain and Ireland*, 4:322. See also the discussion in Rogers, 131–32. The authorship of the text has been variously attributed both to Theophilus Cibber and Robert Shiels.

16. Defoe, *Robinson Crusoe*, 1 [hereafter cited as *RC* in notes].

17. Defoe, *RC*, 62. For other instances of Crusoe's fitful "Despondency" (65), see also, e.g., 19, 35–36, 113, 163–64, 174–75, 184–85, 198.

18. In this sense, *Robinson Crusoe* marks an important exception to Defoe's position in novels such as *The Farther Adventures of Robinson Crusoe* or *Captain Singleton*, where his fascination with trade and entrepreneurial speculation produces an unqualified endorsement of seafaring travel.

19. Locke, *Essay*, 2.21.31.

20. See, e.g., Novak, "*Robinson Crusoe* and Economic Utopia"; and

Watt, 60–66, esp. 65, where Watt says that Crusoe's individualistic impulse for self-improvement is "the economic and social embodiment of the 'uneasiness' which Locke had made the centre of his system of motivation."
21. Tavor, *Scepticism*, 10.
22. Locke, *Essay*, 1.1.5.
23. Defoe, *RC*, 3.
24. Defoe, *RC*, 88, 131. In addition to spiritual ignorance, Crusoe confesses a reluctance to learn the value of the "middle Station" in life: "I would neither see it my self, or learn to know the Blessing of it from my Parents" (91).
25. See also Crusoe's rhapsodic remarks on "the great Lamp of Instruction, the Spirit of God" (209–10).
26. Hunter, *The Reluctant Pilgrim*, 45.
27. Locke, *Education*, secs. 66, 108, 94.
28. See Fliegelman, 67–83. More recently, in "Locke, Defoe, and the Politics of Childhood," Richard Braverman has examined how the relation between Locke's *Two Treatises* and the *Education* authorizes Crusoe's assertion of individual rights against any claims by arbitrary paternal authority. Drawing exclusively on the *Treatises*, Ian A. Bell arrives at a similar conclusion.
29. Locke, *Education*, sec. 85.
30. Defoe, *RC*, 131; my emphasis. Earlier, Crusoe makes a similar observation concerning the force of repeated action over prolonged periods of time: "I had alas! no divine Knowledge; what I had received by the good Instruction of my Father was then worn out by *an uninterrupted Series, for 8 years*, of Seafaring Wickedness" (88; my emphasis).
31. Locke, *Education*, sec. 46.
32. For discussions of the relation of Puritan autobiography to *Robinson Crusoe*, see, e.g., Hunter, *The Reluctant Pilgrim*; Starr, *Defoe and Spiritual Autobiography*; Novak, *Realism, Myth, and History in Defoe's Fiction*; McKeon, *Origins*, 317–23, 332, 336; Spacks, *Imagining a Self*, 28–29, 38–39; Flanders, "Autobiography and Memoir as Formal Modes," in his *Structures of Experience*, 51–78; Damrosch, 187–212; and Watt, 74–78, 90.
33. Defoe, *RC*, 99.
34. See Locke, *Second Treatise of Government*: "As much as any one can make use of to any advantage of life before it spoils; so much he may by his labour fix a Property in. Whatever is beyond this, is more than his share, and belongs to others" (sec. 31).
35. Defoe, *The Compleat English Gentleman*, 87–88.
36. See also Leinster-Mackay's discussion in *The Educational World of Daniel Defoe*, 70–72, concerning Defoe's pedagogical views in the context of original sin.

37. Defoe, *Family Instructor*, 312.

38. See Fliegelman, 67–83.

39. Cf. Fliegelman, e.g., who claims that "Lockean pedagogy of the eighteenth century was in large measure an adaptation and secularization of the Puritan narrative of the fortunate fall" (83).

40. Damrosch, 195.

41. Defoe, *RC*, 79.

42. In *An Epistle to Daniel Defoe* (1719), Defoe's contemporary Charles Gildon was particularly aggressive in attacking *Robinson Crusoe* as a "fable." For other discussions of this issue, see Davis, 154–73; and McKeon, *Origins*, 315–17.

43. I have consulted most of the editions of the novel issued from 1719 to 1790, all of which share the typographical and textual features I describe citing a modern version—including the initial "N.B." and the use of italics, and the later lack of such notation in instances such as "But I return to my journal."

44. My argument here approaches McKeon's claim that in *Robinson Crusoe*, "spiritual and secular motives are not only 'compatible'; they are inseparable, if ultimately contradictory, parts of a complex intellectual and behavioral system" (*Origins*, 319). But the very prominence of Crusoe's role as narrator attests to a generic and conceptual disjunction that may not be fully assimilable to the single system of what McKeon calls "progressive" ideology. Although Defoe's work obviously does promulgate progressive values, it does so provisionally, in the face of other competing social agendas—particularly those associated with the generic elements of Puritan and Lockean pedagogy.

45. Although some critics, such as Novak in his *Defoe and the Nature of Man* (see 121–23), have argued that Crusoe must ultimately embrace the natural law principle of obedience to parents, more recent arguments stress that Crusoe justifiably behaves according to Lockean, antipatriarchal principles. See, e.g., Bell; and Braverman.

46. Defoe, *Family Instructor*, 391.

47. Cf. Novak, who, in "Crusoe the King and the Political Evolution of His Island," trenchantly claims: "Crusoe's concept of himself as a monarch, whether absolute or patriarchal, is a delusion" (347).

48. Braverman, 47. For his part, Bell extends his analysis to *Robinson Crusoe*'s sequel, *The Farther Adventures*, to argue that Crusoe ultimately brings his colony from a natural to a genuinely political state in the terms Locke sets out in the *Second Treatise*.

49. Schonhorn, "Defoe: The Literature of Politics," 15–56; see also his *Defoe's Politics*, 141–64.

50. Defoe, *RC*, 210.

51. Braverman, 47, 39.

52. Defoe, *RC*, 217.

53. Regarding Crusoe's misrepresentation of himself as a form of "fiction" that solidifies his ability to "condemn" the mutineers to social reformation, see Bender, 55. Armstrong and Tennenhouse stress a similar point that Crusoe's fiction plays on the mutineers' irrational fears in a way that provides a general model for "the founding of the modern nation" (188).

54. Defoe, *Farther Adventures of Robinson Crusoe*, 166.

55. Defoe, *Farther Adventures*, 168. Crusoe confirms this scenario has the aura of a religious play when he reports that, although the priest persists in being unable to contain himself, "the Scene was not ended there" (168).

56. Defoe, *RC*, 14.

Chapter 5

1. Masham, *Occasional Thoughts*, 229–30.

2. Drake, 3.

3. Drake, 147. For a discussion of this idea in the context of English revaluations of the Don Quixote story during the Enlightenment, see Staves, esp. 195.

4. Warren, 371.

5. Paulson, *Satire and the Novel*, 276; see Doody, introduction to Lennox, *Female Quixote*, xxv–xxvi; Langbauer, 79–89; Ross, 462–64; Spacks, "Subtle Sophistries of Desire: *The Female Quixote*," chap. 1 in her *Desire and Truth*, 24, 29–30 (she is all the more emphatic on the issue of female power in the original essay on which this chapter is based: "The Subtle Sophistry of Desire: Dr. Johnson and *The Female Quixote*," 533, 540–41); and Spencer, 187–92.

6. Green, 47–48. In supporting this claim, Green cites other critics (see 171 n. 17) who agree about the deleterious effects of a woman's "heroinization," including Brownstein; Gilbert and Gubar; and Poovey.

7. Lennox, *Female Quixote*, 329.

8. Locke, *Some Thoughts concerning Education*, sec. 1.

9. Lennox, *Female Quixote*, 7.

10. Gailhard, 70; see Dufour, *Moral Instructions*, 33.

11. Fénelon, *Instructions*, 12–13.

12. Astell, *Serious Proposal*, 83–84, also 37–38. See also Makin, *An Essay To Revive the Antient Education of Gentlewomen*, 26; and a text attributed to Aphra Behn entitled *A Companion for the Ladies-Closets*, sig. A2^{r-v}.

13. Codington, *Second Part of Youths Behavior*, 2–3, 6.

14. Wilkes, 79.

15. Chudleigh, "The Epistle Dedicatory" to *The Ladies Defence*, sig. a1^r.

16. Woolley, *The Gentlewomans Companion*, 9.

17. Drake, 57. In *The Tea-Table*, Eliza Haywood similarly defends romances by claiming that their apparent superficiality is surpassed by an underlying pedagogical purpose. Invoking a process reminiscent of supervisory education's indirect methods, Philetus serves as Haywood's spokesman when he declares

> we cannot believe that the celebrated Madam D'Anois, Monsieurs Bandell, Scudery, Segrais, Bonaventure Des Perriers, and many other learned Writers, would have been at the Expence of so much Time and Pains, only for the Pleasure of inventing a Fiction, or relating a Tale —— No, they had other Views. —— They . . . knew that Morals, meerly as Morals, wou'd obtain but slight Regard: to inspire Notions, therefore, which are necessary to reform the Manners, they found it most proper to cloath Instruction with Delight. —— And 'tis most certain that when Precepts are convey'd this way, *they steal themselves into the Soul*, and work the wish'd Effect, *almost insensibly*, to the Person who receives them. (48; my emphasis)

18. For discussions of this development, see, e.g., Ballaster, *Seductive Forms*, 196–211; Doody, introduction, xv–xx; McKeon, *Origins*, 39–64; and Spencer, 181–87. In "Reading Shakespeare's Novels," Jonathan Kramnick also explores how the novel's putative generic ascendancy over romance played out in Lennox's and Johnson's competing interpretations of both Shakespeare's and eighteenth-century fiction's literary value.

19. H. Fielding, *The Covent-Garden Journal* no. 24 (24 Mar. 1752) 1: 282.

20. Doody, introduction, xix.

21. Penton, sig. A4^v, A5$^{r–v}$.

22. Penton, sig. A4^r; see also Penton's comment urging fathers to "Cure the Mother of the *Disease* called Fondness if you can" (65).

23. Lennox, *Female Quixote*, 279.

24. For Arabella's other references to her self-created "empire," see also 40, 43, 136, and 138.

25. Armstrong, *Desire*, 16.

26. In *Desire and Domestic Fiction*, Armstrong considers *Crusoe* only minimally significant, because Defoe's "masculine form of heroism" was ultimately incompatible with the new genre's emphasis on "the triumph of female virtue" (29). More recently, however, she has revised that conclusion in *The Imaginary Puritan*, where she and Leonard Tennenhouse argue that Defoe's novel is key in defining the modern, "disciplined" individual

as the conjunction of human irrationality and the rational techniques of social organization (184–95). In this new interpretation, Defoe's book provides an important link in the historical process beginning with Milton's earlier redefinition of writing as intellectual labor and Richardson's later differentiation of disciplined subjectivity according to gender.

27. Lennox, *Female Quixote*, 41; see also 6, 327.
28. See Watt, 32.
29. See McKeon, *Origins*, 21, 130–33, 150–59.
30. Lennox, *Female Quixote*, 138.
31. Lennox, *Female Quixote*, 197. For other occasions when "curing" Arabella is mentioned, see also 117, 320, 368.
32. Astell, *Serious Proposal*, 22.
33. H. Fielding, *The Covent-Garden Journal*, 1: 277, 276, 282.
34. H. Fielding, *Tom Jones*, 273, 275. For the problems generated by Jenny's "Erudition," including increased pride and self-isolation, see 48–50, 58, 85. For her, the only salvation is a complete personal transformation, in which she becomes the more circumspect Mrs. Waters in the later part of the novel. In *Amelia*, Fielding more thoroughly discredits the value of female learning, especially in satirizing the characters of Mrs. Bennet (see 255–59, 271–72, 281–85) and Mrs. Atkinson (407–10, 426–28). See also Battestin's note on the controversy about female learnedness in *Amelia*, 255–56 n. 1.
35. Lennox, *Female Quixote*, 320.
36. Ross, 458.
37. Brown, *The Ends of Empire*, 16; see also 135–69. As Brown indicates, most literary studies of early modern representations of the Amazon have been focused on the seventeenth century, such as Shepherd's *Amazons and Warrior Women: Varieties of Feminism in Seventeenth-Century Drama*; Orgel's "Jonson and the Amazons"; and Schwarz's "Missing the Breast." Two recent exceptions are Langbauer's brief discussion of Arabella's interest in Amazons in *Women and Romance*, 88–89; and Campbell's consideration of Amazons in the context of anti-Jacobite rhetoric in *Natural Masques*, 134–36, 137–45, 170.
38. Drake, 24–25.   39. Lennox, *Female Quixote*, 204.
40. Langbauer, 88.   41. Kristeva, 4.
42. See H. Fielding, *Tom Jones*, 89–90 (Mrs. Partridge); 174–75, 179–82 (Molly Seagrim); and 181–83 (Goody Brown). The narrator even reports that Goody Brown has a "great Advantage" over Molly in their mock-heroic battle because she has "no Breasts, her Bosom . . . exactly resembling an antient Piece of Parchment" (182).
43. The phrase "petticoat government" comes from a remark of Trapwit in H. Fielding's *Pasquin*. In *Natural Masques*, Jill Campbell discusses at

length Henry Fielding's concern with the inversion of sexual roles in mid-century England, citing especially a passage from *The Masquerade* where effeminate beaux are warned that "Your Empire shortly will be ended: / Breeches our brawny Thighs shall grace, / (Another *Amazonian* Race.) / For when Men Women turn—why then / May Women not be changed to Men?" (ll.5–6, qtd. in Campbell, 21).

44. Masham, *Occasional Thoughts*, 197, 198, 199, 200.

45. See, e.g., Lennox, 132, 136, 148, 164, 180, 315, 320.

46. See Marshall, "Writing Masters," 121–24.

47. Lennox, *Female Quixote*, 322–23.

48. Haywood, *Miss Betsy Thoughtless*, 8, 4.

49. See Doody, introduction, xxix; Ross, 461–62; and Spacks, *Desire and Truth*, 24.

50. Haywood, *Betsy Thoughtless*, 266.

51. Haywood, *Betsy Thoughtless*, 12. For a sampling of the many other times "reflection" is cited, see 8, 33, 69, 187, 206–7, 246, and 264. A related theme in the text is Betsy's development of thoughtful "penetration": see 70, 186, 464, 497, 558.

52. Haywood, *Betsy Thoughtless*, 450. For other references to her disposition, see 34, 114, 431; for examples regarding other characters, see 15, 45, 51, 190, 203, 213, 264, 424, 539.

53. See Woodward, who, in *A Light to Grammar*, proposes to "slip into a childs understanding before he be aware" (21).

54. Haywood, *Betsy Thoughtless*, 34.

55. Ellis, 291.

56. Haywood, *Betsy Thoughtless*, 172. For further mention of Betsy's unwillingness to dissemble, see 310, 467, 577, 578.

57. See Nestor, 587–88.

58. Haywood, *Betsy Thoughtless*, 58.

59. Lennox, *Female Quixote*, 370.

60. See Marshall, "Writing Masters," 111–15. For similar remarks by other critics on the problem of women telling their stories, see Doody, introduction, xxvii; Langbauer, 83–84; and Spacks, *Desire and Truth*, 31.

61. Lennox, *Female Quixote*, 327.

62. Small, 82.

63. John Mitford was the first to offer this view in print in a June 1843 letter to the *Gentleman's Magazine*, 132–33. Bate, 270; and McIntosh, 14, concur on this point.

64. Spacks, *Desire and Truth*, 15. Similarly, Langbauer comments, "it is impossible to know who really wrote the chapter—but whether Dr. Johnson wrote it or whether he influenced a most faithful pastiche is immaterial" (82).

65. Langbauer, 82–83.

66. In *Nobody's Story*, Catherine Gallagher provides a compelling account of Lennox as a "vanishing" female author at midcentury, arguing that Lennox's inclination for authorial collaboration, her lack of property rights in her published work, and her fiction's inducing a form of emotional divestment in her female readers all contributed to her enigmatic status as an example of "deserving, dispossessed authorship" (195). But while Gallagher therefore wants to see Lennox as "something of an emblematic figure for her male contemporaries" (195), my argument here stresses the crucial difference that gender difference made—and frequently still makes—in the interpretation of what kind of authorship could be genuinely successful.

67. For a thorough discussion of both Boswell's attribution and the peculiar structure of the dedication's signature, see Marshall, "Writing Masters," 117–20.

68. Richardson letter to Lennox, 13 Jan. 1752, qtd. in Isles, 424. See also Isles's discussion of Lennox's original plans on 424–26.

69. Lennox, *Female Quixote*, 377; the "Novel" is footnoted in the original text as *Clarissa*.

70. McKeon, *Origins*, 263. McKeon's example of such experimentation is William Congreve's much earlier *Incognita; or, Love and Duty Reconcil'd* (1692).

71. Haywood, *Betsy Thoughtless*, 51.

72. H. Fielding, *Joseph Andrews*, 46, 87. In the context of Richardson's agenda in *Pamela*, McKeon argues that this strategy serves "not to refute Richardson's progressive social ethics in the great contest between 'industrious virtue' and 'aristocratic corruption,' but to defuse its social volatility through the stealthy reversal of sexes" (*Origins*, 399–400). For Angela Smallwood, however, in *Fielding and the Woman Question*, the result is less equivocal, since she argues that Fielding's application of feminine virtues to men constitutes a qualified, though important, version of feminist arguments during the early eighteenth century (4–10). I am arguing by contrast that in the context of Haywood's and Lennox's work, Fielding's challenge to standard gender roles retains significantly masculinist assumptions.

73. Lennox, *Female Quixote*, 594. By interpreting Haywood's novel as a more successful implementation of supervisory narrative than *The Female Quixote*, my argument reverses the historical importance given them by Janet Todd in *The Sign of Angellica*, 146–60. She describes *Betsy Thoughtless* as marking the end of female novelists' "investigation of female masks, [and] the construction of woman by education and society," and *Female Quixote* as the beginning of the novel's "teaching the sentimental image of womanhood" (160). I argue instead that Haywood's novel represents an

important revision and ironization of her earlier interest in female "masks," an accomplishment that was far more important than Lennox's novel in influencing later authors such as Frances Burney and Jane Austen.

Conclusion

1. For McKeon, it should be noted, both the social and literary conventions that ultimately identified the novel as a "modern" discourse at midcentury remained thoroughly dialectical in their constitution of Enlightenment fiction. In that context, my claim for a provisional consolidation of generic features applies more specifically to the novel of education's distinct history as it was shaped by Lennox and especially Haywood.

2. Although her status as a commoner is clear, Betsy's socioeconomic standing is more ambiguous: after being displaced from the country gentry by the death of her parents when she was a child, she spends most of the novel living in London in middle- to upper-class conditions.

3. See Ellis, 281.

4. Rousseau, *Emile*, 184–85.

5. Bloom, introduction, 6.

6. Dilthey, 335, 336.

7. On this point, see Pickering; and Summerfield, 1–11. Summerfield also discusses Sarah Fielding in 86–93.

8. S. Fielding, *The Governess*, xi.

9. Haywood, *Betsy Thoughtless*, 567.

10. The resolution of Betsy's romantic desires as a significant, though ambivalent, success in feminine improvisation makes for a radically different pattern than the one April London perceives in Haywood's earlier fiction (including *Love in Excess*), in which women who encounter men in gardens become "in both senses 'natural' victims and, therefore, negative archetypes" (121). The difference may well lie in Haywood's later articulation of improvisational strategies whose subtleties and useful ironies could offer women better ways to approach genuine self-determination.

11. Brontë, *Jane Eyre*, 260.

12. See Sedgwick, "The Character in the Veil," 256, 267. Rather than follow Sedgwick's suggestion that psychological interiority is ultimately an effect of external impingement, I am here adapting her view to the particular dynamic of public privacy as it was portrayed by early eighteenth-century novelists.

13. Brontë, *Jane Eyre*, 260.

Works Cited

Aaron, Richard I. *John Locke.* Oxford: Clarendon Press, 1971.

Aarsleff, Hans. "Some Observations on Recent Locke Scholarship." In *John Locke: Problems and Perspectives,* ed. John W. Yolton, pp. 262–71. Cambridge: Cambridge University Press, 1969.

Adamson, John William. *Pioneers of Modern Education, 1600–1700.* Cambridge: Cambridge University Press, 1905.

Addison, Joseph, and Richard Steele. *The Spectator.* 5 vols. Ed. Donald F. Bond. Oxford: Clarendon Press, 1965.

The Advice of a Father: Or, Counsel to a Child. London, 1688.

Ainsworth, Oliver Morley. Introduction to *Milton on Education,* by John Milton. Ed. Oliver Morley Ainsworth. New Haven: Yale University Press, 1928.

Anthony, Rose. *The Jeremy Collier Stage Controversy 1698–1726.* 1937. Reprinted, New York: B. Blom, 1966.

Appleby, Joyce. *Capitalism and a New Social Order: The Republican Vision of the 1790s.* New York: New York University Press, 1984.

———. *Liberalism and Republicanism in the Historical Imagination.* Cambridge: Harvard University Press, 1992.

Ariès, Phillippe. *Centuries of Childhood: A Social History of Family Life.* Trans. Robert Baldick. New York: Vintage, 1962.

Armstrong, Nancy. *Desire and Domestic Fiction: A Political History of the Novel.* New York: Oxford University Press, 1987.

———. "The Rise of the Domestic Woman." In *The Ideology of Conduct:*

Essays in Literature and the History of Sexuality, ed. Nancy Armstrong and Leonard Tennenhouse, pp. 96–141. New York: Methuen, 1987.

Armstrong, Nancy, and Leonard Tennenhouse. *The Imaginary Puritan: Literature, Intellectual Labor, and the Origins of Personal Life.* Berkeley and Los Angeles: University of California Press, 1992.

Astell, Mary. *The Christian Religion, As Profess'd by a Daughter of the Church of England.* London, 1705.

———. "A Prefatory Discourse to Dr. D'Avenant." In *Moderation Truly Stated: Or, A Review of a Late Pamphlet Entitul'd Moderation a Vertue.* London, 1704.

———. *A Serious Proposal To the Ladies, For the Advancement of Their True and Greatest Interest.* London, 1694.

———. *A Serious Proposal to the Ladies. Part II.* London, 1697.

An Astronomical Catechism, or Dialogues between a Mother and her Daughter. London, 1818.

Astronomical Dialogues between a Gentleman and a Lady. London, 1719.

Axtell, James L. Introduction to *The Educational Writings of John Locke*, by John Locke. Ed. James L. Axtell. Cambridge: Cambridge University Press, 1968.

Backscheider, Paula R. *Daniel Defoe: Ambition and Innovation.* Lexington: University Press of Kentucky, 1986.

———. *Daniel Defoe: His Life.* Baltimore: Johns Hopkins University Press, 1989.

———. Introduction to *The Family Instructor*, by Daniel Defoe. 1715. Reprint, ed. Paula R. Backscheider, Delmar, N.Y.: Scholar's Facsimiles and Reprints, 1989.

Bakhtin, M. M. *The Dialogic Imagination: Four Essays.* Trans. Caryl Emerson and Michael Holquist. Austin: University of Texas Press, 1981.

———. *Problems of Dostoevsky's Poetics.* Trans. R. W. Rotsel. Ann Arbor, Mich.: Ardis, 1973.

———. *Rabelais and His World.* Trans. Helene Iswolsky. Cambridge: MIT Press, 1968.

Ballaster, Ros. *Seductive Forms: Women's Amatory Fiction from 1684 to 1740.* Oxford: Clarendon Press, 1992.

Bannet, Eve Tavor. "Rewriting the Social Text: The Female Bildungsroman in Eighteenth-Century England." In *Reflection and Action: Essays on the Bildungsroman*, ed. James Hardin, pp. 195–227. Columbia: University of South Carolina Press, 1991.

Barish, Jonah. *The Antitheatrical Prejudice.* Berkeley and Los Angeles: University of California Press, 1981.

Barney, Richard A. "Paul de Man and the Legacy of Suspicion." In *Liter-*

ary *Theory's Future(s)*, ed. Joseph Natoli, pp. 82–115. Urbana: University of Illinois Press, 1989.

———. "Subjectivity, the Novel, and the *Bildung* Blocks of Critical Theory." *Genre* 26 (1993): 359–75.

Barthes, Roland. *The Pleasure of the Text*. Trans. Richard Miller. New York: Hill and Wang, 1975.

Bate, Walter Jackson. *Samuel Johnson*. New York: Harcourt, 1977.

Battestin, Martin C. *The Moral Basis of Fielding's Art: A Study of Joseph Andrews*. Middletown, Conn.: Wesleyan University Press, 1959.

———. "The Problem of *Amelia*: Hume, Barrow, and the Conversion of Captain Booth." *English Literary History* 41 (1974): 613–48.

Bayne-Powell, Rosamond. *The English Child in the Eighteenth Century*. London: J. Murray, 1939.

Beddow, Michael. *The Fiction of Humanity: Studies in the Bildungsroman from Wieland to Thomas Mann*. Cambridge: Cambridge University Press, 1982.

Behn, Aphra. *A Companion for the Ladies-Closets: or, the Life and Death of the Most Excellent the Lady———*. London, 1712.

Bell, Ian A. "King Crusoe: Locke's Political Theory in *Robinson Crusoe*." *English Studies* 69 (1988): 27–36.

Bender, John. *Imagining the Penitentiary: Fiction and the Architecture of Mind in Eighteenth-Century England*. Chicago: University of Chicago Press, 1987.

Bennington, Geoff. "The Perfect Cheat: Locke and Empiricism's Rhetoric." In *The Figural and the Literal*, ed. A. E. Benjamin, G. N. Cantor, and J. R. R. Christie, pp. 103–23. Manchester, Eng.: University of Manchester Press, 1987.

Bentham, Jeremy. *Panopticon; or the Inspection-House*. 1791. In *Works*, vol. 2, by Jeremy Bentham. Edinburgh, 1838.

Bernard, Sir Thomas. *Of the Education of the Poor*. London, 1809.

Bloom. Allan. Introduction to *Emile, or On Education*, by Jean-Jacques Rousseau. Ed. and trans. Allan Bloom. New York: Basic Books, 1979.

Boas, George. *The Cult of Childhood*. Studies of the Warburg Institute, vol. 29. London: Warburg Institute, 1966.

Botanical Dialogues between Hortensia and her four Children. London, 1797.

Bourdieu, Pierre. *Outline of a Theory of Practice*. Trans. Richard Nice. Cambridge: Cambridge University Press, 1977.

Bourdieu, Pierre, and Jean-Claude Passeron. *Reproduction in Education, Society and Culture*. 2d ed. Trans. Richard Nice. London: Sage Publications, 1990.

Bourn, Benjamin. *A Sure Guide to Hell . . . Containing Directions I. To Parents in the Education of their Children. II. To Youth. . . .* London, ca. 1750.

Brathwaite, Richard. *The English Gentleman.* 1st ed. London, 1630.

———. *The English Gentlewoman.* 1st ed. London, 1631.

Braverman, Richard. "Locke, Defoe, and the Politics of Childhood." *English Language Notes* 24, no. 1 (1986): 36–48.

Bremner, Christina Sinclair. *The Education of Girls and Women in Great Britain.* London: Swan Sonnenschein & Co., 1897.

Brewer, John. *The Sinews of Power: War, Money and the English State, 1688–1783.* New York: Alfred A. Knopf, 1989.

Brissenden, R. F. *Virtue in Distress: Studies in the Novel of Sentiment from Richardson to Sade.* London: Macmillan, 1974.

Brontë, Charlotte. *Jane Eyre.* 1847. Ed. Margaret Smith. Oxford: Oxford University Press, 1993.

Brown, Laura. *The Ends of Empire: Women and Ideology in Early Eighteenth-Century Literature.* Ithaca, N.Y.: Cornell University Press, 1993.

Brownstein, Rachel. *Becoming a Heroine.* New York: Viking, 1982.

Buckley, Jerome Hamilton. *Season of Youth: The Bildungsroman from Dickens to Golding.* Cambridge: Harvard University Press, 1974.

Burgh, James. *Britain's Remembrancer: Or, The Danger Not Over.* London, 1746.

Burtt, Shelley. *Virtue Transformed: Political Argument in England, 1688–1740.* Cambridge: Cambridge University Press, 1992.

Butler, Judith. *Bodies That Matter: On the Discursive Limits of "Sex."* New York: Routledge, 1993.

———. *Gender Trouble: Feminism and the Subversion of Identity.* New York: Routledge, 1990.

Campbell, Jill. *Natural Masques: Gender and Identity in Fielding's Plays and Novels.* Stanford: Stanford University Press, 1995.

Carlyle, Thomas. *Sartor Resartus: The Life and Opinions of Herr Teufelsdröckh.* 1838. London: Oxford University Press, 1930.

Castle, Terry. *Masquerade and Civilization: The Carnivalesque in Eighteenth-Century English Culture and Fiction.* Stanford: Stanford University Press, 1986.

Chalk, Alfred. F. "Mandeville's *Fable of the Bees*: A Reappraisal." *The Southern Economic Journal* 33 (1966): 1–16.

Chévremont, Jean Baptiste de. *The Knowledge of the World: or, the Art of Well-Educating Youth, Through the Various Conditions of Life.* Trans. John Dunton. London, ca. 1695.

Chudleigh, Lady Mary. *The Ladies Defence: or, The Bride-Woman's Counsellor Answer'd.* London, 1701.

Clarke, John. *An Essay upon the Education of Youth in Grammar-Schools.* London, 1720.

Codington, Robert. *Second Part of Youths Behavior, or Decency in Conversation Amongst Women*. London, 1664.

Colie, Rosalie. "Locke and the Publication of the Private." *Philological Quarterly* 45 (1966): 24–45.

Collier, Jeremy. *A Defence of the Short View of the Profaneness and Immorality of the English Stage*. London, 1699.

————. *A Short View of the Immorality and the Profaneness of the English Stage*. London, 1698.

Comenius, John Amos. *The Great Didactic*. Ed. M. W. Keatinge. London: Adam and Charles Black, 1896.

————. *Janua linguarum reserata*. 1631. London, 1662.

————. *The Labyrinth of the World and the Paradise of the Heart*. 1631. Trans. Matthew Spinka. Ann Arbor: University of Michigan Press, 1972.

————. *Orbis sensualium pictus*. 1658. Ed. Charles Hoole. London, 1672.

————. *Pansophiae prodromus*. London, 1639.

————. *A Reformation of Schooles, Designed in Two Excellent Treatises*. London, 1642.

Coste, Pierre. Preface to *De l'éducation des Enfans*, by John Locke. Trans. Pierre Coste. Amsterdam, 1695.

Coveney, Peter. *The Image of Childhood: A Study of the Theme in English Literature*. Rev. ed. F. R. Leavis. Baltimore: Penguin, 1967.

Craft, Catherine A. "Reworking Male Models: Aphra Behn's *Fair Vow-Breaker*, Eliza Haywood's *Fantomina*, and Charlotte Lennox's *Female Quixote*." *Modern Language Review* 86 (1991): 821–38.

Cranston, Maurice. *John Locke*. London: Longman, Green, 1957.

Cremin, Lawrence. *American Education: The Colonial Experience*. New York: Harper & Row, 1970.

Damrosch, Leopold, Jr. *God's Plots and Man's Stories: Studies in the Fictional Imagination from Milton to Fielding*. Chicago: University of Chicago Press, 1985.

Darrell, William. *A Gentleman Instructed in the Conduct of a Virtuous and Happy Life*. London, 1704.

Davis, Lennard. *Factual Fictions: The Origins of the English Novel*. New York: Columbia University Press, 1983.

Davys, Mary. *The Reform'd Coquet*. London, 1724.

Defoe, Daniel. *The Compleat English Gentleman*. Ed. Karl D. Bülbring. London: David Nutt, 1890.

————. *The Complete English Tradesman*. 1726. In *The Novels and Miscellaneous Works of Daniel De Foe*, ed. Walter Scott. London, 1841. Reprint, New York: Guinn Co., n.d.

————. *An Essay upon Projects*. London, 1697.

———. *The Family Instructor.* 1715. Reprint, ed. Paula R. Backscheider, Delmar, N.Y.: Scholar's Facsimiles and Reprints, 1989.

———. *The Farther Adventures of Robinson Crusoe.* London, 1719

———. *The Life, Adventures, and Pyracies, of the Famous Captain Singleton.* London, 1720.

———. *The Life and Strange Surprizing Adventures of Robinson Crusoe.* 1719. Ed. J. Donald Crowley. Oxford: Oxford University Press, 1972.

———. *Of Royall Educacion: A Fragmentary Treatise.* Ed. Karl D. Bülbring. London: David Nutt, 1895.

de Man, Paul. "The Epistemology of Metaphor." In *On Metaphor*, ed. Sheldon Sacks, pp. 11–28. Chicago: University of Chicago Press, 1978.

———. "The Resistance to Theory." In *The Resistance to Theory*, by Paul de Man, pp. 3–20. Minneapolis: University of Minnesota Press, 1986.

DeMause, Lloyd, ed. *The History of Childhood.* New York: Psychohistory Press, 1975.

Diggins, John Patrick. *The Lost Soul of American Politics: Virtue, Self-Interest, and the Foundations of Liberalism.* New York: Basic Books, 1984.

Dilthey, Wilhelm. *Poetry and Experience.* 1906. Vol. 5 of *Selected Works*, by Wilhelm Dilthey. Ed. Rudolf A. Makkreel and Frithjof Rodi. Princeton: Princeton University Press, 1985.

Dobrée, Bonamy. *English Literature in the Early Eighteenth Century.* Oxford: Clarendon Press, 1959.

Doody, Margaret Anne. *The Daring Muse: Augustan Poetry Reconsidered.* Cambridge: Cambridge University Press, 1985.

———. Introduction to *The Female Quixote*, by Charlotte Lennox. Ed. Margaret Dalziel. New York: Oxford University Press, 1989.

Drake, Judith. *An Essay in Defence of the Female Sex. In which are Inserted the Characters of A Pedant, A Squire, A Beau, A Vertuoso, A Poetaster, A City-Critick, &c. in a Letter to a Lady.* London, 1696.

Dufour, Philippe. *Moral Instructions of a Father to his Son.* 1678. Edinburgh, 1743.

Eagleton, Terry. *The Function of Criticism: From "The Spectator" to Post-Structuralism.* London: Verso, 1984.

Egerton, Sarah Fyge. "The Emulation." 1703. In *The New Oxford Book of Eighteenth-Century Verse*, ed. Roger Lonsdale, p. 37. Oxford: Oxford University Press, 1987.

Ellis, Lorna Beth. "Engendering the *Bildungsroman*: The *Bildung* of Betsy Thoughtless." *Genre* 28 (1995): 279–301.

Essex, John. *The Young Ladies Conduct: or, Rules for Education.* London, 1722.

Evans, Robin. *The Fabrication of Virtue.* Cambridge: Cambridge University Press, 1982.

Ezell, Margaret J. M. "John Locke's Images of Childhood: Early Eighteenth Century Response to *Some Thoughts concerning Education*." *Eighteenth-Century Studies* 17 (1983–84): 139–55.

———. *The Patriarch's Wife: Literary Evidence and the History of the Family*. Chapel Hill: University of North Carolina Press, 1987.

———. *Writing Women's Literary History*. Baltimore: Johns Hopkins University Press, 1993.

Fénelon, François de Salignac de la Mothe-. *The Accomplish'd Governess: or, Short Instructions for the Education of the Fair Sex*. In *The Characters and Properties of True Charity Display'd*. London, 1752.

———. *The Education of Young Gentlewomen*. London, 1699.

———. *Instructions for the Education of a Daughter*. 1687. Trans. George Hickes. London, 1707.

———. *Telemachus, Son of Ulysses*. 1699. Ed. and trans. Patrick Riley. Cambridge: Cambridge University Press, 1994.

———. *Traité de l'Éducation des Filles*. Paris, 1687.

Ferguson, Frances. "Reading Morals: Locke and Rousseau on Education and Inequality." *Representations* 6 (1984): 66–84.

Ferguson, James. *The Young Gentleman and Lady's Astronomy, familiarly explained in Ten Dialogues between Neander and Eudosia*. London, 1768.

Fielding, Henry. *Amelia*. 1751. Ed. Martin C. Battestin. Middletown, Conn.: Wesleyan University Press, 1983.

———. *The Covent-Garden Journal*. 2 vols. Ed. Gerard Edward Jensen. New Haven: Yale University Press, 1915.

———. *The History of the Adventures of Joseph Andrews*. 1742. Ed. Martin C. Battestin. Middletown, Conn.: Wesleyan University Press, 1967.

———. *The History of Tom Jones, a Foundling*. 1749. Ed. Fredson Bowers. Middletown, Conn.: Wesleyan University Press, 1975.

———. The Jacobite's Journal *and Related Writings*. Ed. W. B. Coley. Oxford: Oxford University Press, 1975.

———. *Pasquin: A Dramatick Satire on the Times*. London, 1736.

———. *A Proposal for Making an Effectual Provision for the Poor*. 1753. In An Enquiry into the Causes of the Late Increase of Robbers *and Related Writings*, ed. Malvin R. Zirker, pp. 219–78. Middletown, Conn.: Wesleyan University Press, 1988.

Fielding, Sarah. *The Governess or, Little Female Academy*. 1749. London: Pandora, 1987.

Flanders, W. Austin. *Structures of Experience: History, Society, and Personal Life in the Eighteenth-Century Novel*. Columbia: University of North Carolina Press, 1984.

Fliegelman, Jay. *Prodigals and Pilgrims: The American Revolution Against Patri-*

archal Authority, 1750–1800. Cambridge: Cambridge University Press, 1982.

Foucault, Michel. *The Archaeology of Knowledge*. Trans. A. M. Sheridan Smith. New York: Pantheon, 1972.

———. *Discipline and Punish: The Birth of the Prison*. Trans. Alan Sheridan. New York: Vintage, 1979.

———. *The History of Sexuality. Volume 1: An Introduction*. Trans. Robert Hurley. New York: Vintage, 1980.

———. *The Order of Things: An Archaeology of the Human Sciences*. New York: Random House, 1970.

Fox, Christopher. *Locke and the Scriblerians: Identity and Consciousness in Early Eighteenth-Century Britain*. Berkeley and Los Angeles: University of California Press, 1989.

Fox Bourne, H. R. *Life of John Locke*. 2 vols. New York: Harper, 1876.

Fraiman, Susan. *Unbecoming Women: British Women Writers and the Novel of Development*. New York: Columbia University Press, 1993.

Fraser, Antonia. *The Weaker Vessel*. New York: Vintage, 1985.

Gailhard, Jean. *The Compleat Gentleman*. London, 1678.

Gallagher, Catherine. *Nobody's Story: The Vanishing Acts of Women Writers in the Marketplace, 1670–1820*. Berkeley and Los Angeles: University of California Press, 1995.

Gallop, Jane. "Im-Personation: A Reading in the Guise of an Introduction." In *Pedagogy: The Question of Impersonation*, ed. Jane Gallop. Bloomington: Indiana University Press, 1995.

Gaunt, William. *The World of William Hogarth*. London: Jonathan Cape, 1978.

Gay, Peter. *The Enlightenment: An Interpretation*. 2 vols. New York: Alfred A. Knopf, 1969.

Gilbert, Sandra M., and Susan Gubar. *The Madwoman in the Attic: The Woman Writer and the Nineteenth-Century Literary Imagination*. New Haven: Yale University Press, 1979.

Gildon, Charles. *An Epistle to Daniel Defoe*. 1719. London: J. M. Dent, 1923.

Gill, Pat. "The Conduct of Ideology: Musings on the Origin of the Bourgeois Self." *Genre* 26 (1993): 461–78.

Goldsmith, M. M. *Private Vices, Public Benefits: Bernard Mandeville's Social and Political Thought*. Cambridge: Cambridge University Press, 1985.

———. "Public Virtue and Private Vices: Bernard Mandeville and English Political Ideologies in the Early Eighteenth Century." *Eighteenth-Century Studies* 9 (1976): 477–510.

Goldstone, Jack A. *Revolution and Rebellion in the Early Modern World*. Berkeley and Los Angeles: University of California Press, 1991.

Graham, John. *Lavater's Essays on Physiognomy: A Study in the History of Ideas.* Berne, Switzerland: Peter Lang, 1979.

Green, Katherine Sobba. *The Courtship Novel, 1740–1820: A Feminized Genre.* Lexington: University Press of Kentucky, 1991.

Guillory, John. *Cultural Capital: The Problem of Literary Canon Formation.* Chicago: University of Chicago Press, 1993.

Gunn, J. A. W. "Mandeville and Wither: Individualism and the Workings of Providence." In *Mandeville Studies: New Explorations in the Art and Thought of Dr. Bernard Mandeville,* ed. Irwin Primer, pp. 98–118. The Hague: Martinus Nijhoff, 1975.

Habermas, Jürgen. *The Structural Transformation of the Public Sphere: An Inquiry into a Category of Bourgeois Society.* Trans. Thomas Burger. Cambridge: MIT Press, 1991.

Hacking, Ian. *The Emergence of Probability: A Philosophical Study of Early Ideas about Probability, Induction, and Statistical Inference.* Cambridge: Cambridge University Press, 1975.

Harper's Dictionary of Classical Literature and Antiquities. Ed. Harry Thurston Peck. New York: American Book Co., 1923.

Harrington, James. *The Common-wealth of Oceana.* London, 1656.

Harris, James. *Discourse on Music, Painting, and Poetry.* In *Three Treatises,* by James Harris. London, 1744.

Harris, Jocelyn. Introduction to *The History of Sir Charles Grandison,* by Samuel Richardson. 3 vols. Ed. Jocelyn Harris. London: Oxford University Press, 1972.

Harrison, John, and Peter Laslett. *The Library of John Locke.* Oxford: Oxford University Press, 1965.

Haywood, Eliza. *The Female Spectator.* 1744–46. 4 vols. London, 1775.

———. *The History of Miss Betsy Thoughtless.* 1751. London: Pandora, 1986.

———. *The Husband.* London, 1756.

———. *Life's Progress Through the Passions.* London, 1748.

———. *Love in Excess; Or, the Fatal Enquiry.* 1719–20. Ed. David Oakleaf. Orchard Park, N.Y.: Broadview Press, 1994.

———. *The Tea-Table: or, A Conversation between some Polite Persons of both Sexes, at a Lady's Visiting Day.* London, 1725.

———. *The Wife.* London, 1756.

Healy, Thomas, and Jonathan Sawday, eds. *Literature and the English Civil War.* Cambridge: Cambridge University Press, 1990.

Helvétius, Claude Adrian. *De l'esprit: Or, Essays on the Mind and its Several Faculties.* London, 1759.

Herzog, Don. "Some Questions for Republicans." *Political Theory* 14 (1986): 473–93.

Hill, Bridget. Introduction to *The First English Feminist: Reflections Upon Marriage and Other Writings by Mary Astell*, by Mary Astell. Ed. Bridget Hill. New York: St. Martin's Press, 1986.

Hind, George. "Mandeville's *Fable of the Bees* as Menippean Satire." *Genre* 1 (1968): 307–15.

Hoadly, Benjamin. *A Sermon Preach'd before the Right Honourable the Lord-Mayor, Aldermen, and Livery-Men of the Several Companies of London*. London, 1705.

Hough, John. *A Sermon Preach'd at the Church of St. Mary-le-Bow, Before the Societies for Reformation of Manners*. London, 1705.

Houston, Alan Craig. *Algernon Sidney and the Republican Heritage in England and America*. Princeton: Princeton University Press, 1991.

Howe, Susanne. *Wilhelm Meister and His English Kinsmen*. New York: AMS Press, 1930.

An Humble Attempt to Assist Parents and Masters In the Religious Instruction of Youth. London, 1744.

A Humble Proposal for Obtaining His Majesty's Royal Charter to Incorporate a Society for Promoting Christian Knowledge among the Poor Natives of the Kingdom of Ireland. London, 1730.

Hunter, J. Paul. *Before Novels: The Cultural Contexts of Eighteenth-Century English Fiction*. New York: W. W. Norton, 1990.

——. *The Reluctant Pilgrim: Defoe's Emblematic Method and Quest for Form in Robinson Crusoe*. Baltimore: Johns Hopkins University Press, 1966.

Indagine, John ab. *The Book of Palmestry and Physiognomy. Being Brief Introductions . . . unto the Art of Chiromancy, or Manual Divination, and Physiognomy; with Circumstances upon the Faces of the Signs*. 1651. 9th ed. Trans. Fabian Withers. London, 1697.

Isaac, Jeffrey C. "Republicanism vs. Liberalism? A Reconsideration." *History of Political Thought* 9 (1988): 349–77.

Isles, Duncan. "Johnson, Richardson, and *The Female Quixote*." Appendix to Charlotte Lennox, *The Female Quixote*, ed. Margaret Dalziel, pp. 419–28. New York: Oxford University Press, 1989.

Jameson, Fredric. *The Political Unconscious: Narrative as a Socially Symbolic Act*. Ithaca, N.Y.: Cornell University Press, 1981.

Jones, M. G. *The Charity School Movement: A Study of Eighteenth Century Puritanism in Action*. Cambridge: Cambridge University Press, 1938.

Jonson, Ben. *Timber: or, Discoveries*. 1640. In *Ben Jonson*, vol. 8, ed. C. H. Herford and Percy and Evelyn Simpson, pp. 560–649. Oxford: Clarendon Press, 1947.

Jost, François. "La Tradition du *Bildungsroman*." *Comparative Literature* 21 (1969): 97–115.

Kaye, F. B. Introduction to *The Fable of the Bees: Or, Private Vices, Publick Benefits*, 2 vols., by Bernard Mandville. Ed. F. B. Kaye. Oxford: Clarendon Press, 1924.

Kendall, M. G., and E. S. Pearson. *Studies in the History of Statistics and Probability*. 2 vols. London: Charles Griffin, 1970.

Ketcham, Michael G. *Transparent Designs: Reading, Performance, and Form in the* Spectator *Papers*. Athens: University of Georgia Press, 1985.

King, William. *The Advantages of Education, Religious and Political*. London, 1706.

Klein, Lawrence E. *Shaftesbury and the Culture of Politeness: Moral Discourse and Cultural Politics in Early Eighteenth-Century England*. Cambridge: Cambridge University Press, 1994.

Kloppenberg, James T. "The Virtues of Liberalism: Christianity, Republicanism, and Ethics in Early American Political Discourse." *Journal of American History* 74 (1987): 9–33.

Konigsberg, Ira. *Narrative Technique in the English Novel: Defoe to Austen*. Hamden, Conn.: Anchor, 1985.

Kowaleski-Wallace, Beth. "Milton's Daughters: The Education of Eighteenth-Century Women Writers." *Feminist Studies* 12 (1986): 275–93.

Kramnick, Isaac. "Republican Revisionism Revisited." *The American Historical Review* 87 (1982): 629–64.

——. *Republicanism and Bourgeois Radicalism: Political Ideology*. Ithaca, N.Y.: Cornell University Press, 1990.

Kramnick, Jonathan. "Reading Shakespeare's Novels: Literary History and Cultural Politics in the Lennox-Johnson Debate." *Modern Language Quarterly* 55 (1994): 429–53.

Kristeva, Julia. *Powers of Horror: An Essay on Abjection*. Trans. Leon S. Roudiez. New York: Columbia University Press, 1982.

Kroll, Richard. *The Material Word: Literate Culture in the Restoration and Early Eighteenth Century*. Baltimore: Johns Hopkins University Press, 1991.

Kropf, C. R. "Educational Theory and Human Nature in Fielding's Works." *PMLA* 89 (1974): 113–20.

Labalme, Patricia H., ed. *Beyond Their Sex: Learned Women of the European Past*. New York: New York University Press, 1980.

La Chambre, Marin Cureau de. *The Art How to Know Men*. London, 1665.

Lancaster, Joseph. *The British System of Education: Being a Complete Epitome of the Improvements and Inventions Practised at the Royal Free Schools, Borough-Road, Southwark*. London, 1810.

Langbauer, Laurie. *Women and Romance: The Consolations of Gender in the English Novel*. Ithaca, N.Y.: Cornell University Press, 1990.

Laslett, Peter. "Masham of Otes: The Rise and Fall of an English Family." *History Today* 3, no. 8 (1953): 535–43.

Lavater, John Caspar. *Essays on Physiognomy.* 4 vols. Trans. C. Moore. London, 1797.

———. *Essays on Physiognomy, Designed to Promote the Knowledge and the Love of Mankind.* 3 vols. Trans. Henry Hunter. London, 1789–98.

———. *Essays on Physiognomy, for the Promotion of the Knowledge and the Love of Mankind.* 3 vols. Trans. Thomas Holcroft. London, 1789.

Leinster-Mackay, D. P. *The Educational World of Daniel Defoe.* English Literary Studies Monograph. Victoria, B.C.: University of Victoria, 1981.

Leites, Edmund. "Locke's Liberal Theory of Parenthood." In *Ethnicity, Identity, and History,* ed. Joseph B. Maier and Chaim I. Waxman, pp. 61–79. New Brunswick, N.J.: Transaction Books, 1983.

Lemprière, John. *Lemprière's Classical Dictionary.* 1788. 3d ed. London: Routledge & Kegan Paul, 1984.

Lennox, Charlotte. *The Female Quixote, Or the Adventures of Arabella.* 1752. Ed. Margaret Dalziel. Oxford: Oxford University Press, 1989.

Lindsay, Jack. *Hogarth: His Art and His World.* New York: Taplinger, 1979.

Lives of the Poets of Great Britain and Ireland. 5 vols. London, 1753.

Locke, John. *Board of Trade Papers, Domestic.* Bundle B, no. 6. Reprinted in *Life of John Locke,* vol. 2, by H. R. Fox Bourne, 2:377–91, New York: Harper, 1876.

———. *The Correspondence of John Locke.* 8 vols. Ed. E. S. De Beer. Oxford: Clarendon Press, 1976–89.

———. *An Essay concerning Human Understanding.* 1690. Ed. Peter H. Nidditch. Oxford: Clarendon Press, 1975.

———. *Some Thoughts concerning Education.* 1693. In *The Educational Writings of John Locke,* ed. James L. Axtell, pp. 109–325. Cambridge: Cambridge University Press, 1968.

———. *Two Treatises of Government.* 1690. Ed. Peter Laslett. Cambridge: Cambridge University Press, 1988.

London, April. "Placing the Female: The Metonymic Garden in Amatory and Pious Narrative, *1700–1740*." In *Fetter'd or Free? British Women Novelists, 1670–1815,* ed. M. A. Schofield and C. Mackeski, pp. 101–23. Athens: Ohio University Press, 1986.

Loveling, Benjamin. *The Best Use of Riches.* London, 1706.

Lowe, Solomon. *The Occasional Critique: On Education. Proposing A New Scheme of Grammar, and Method of Instruction; By which the Grounds of Any Language May be Learn'd in a Few Hours, so as to Read an Author, and Write Intelligibly.* London, 1728.

MacLean, Kenneth. *John Locke and English Literature of the Eighteenth Century.* New Haven: Yale University Press, 1936.

Macpherson, C. B. *The Political Theory of Possessive Individualism: Hobbes to Locke.* Oxford: Oxford University Press, 1962.

Maidwell, Lewis. *An Essay Upon the Necessity and Excellency of Education.* London, 1705.

Makin, Bathsua. *An Essay To Revive the Antient Education of Gentlewomen, in Religion, Manners, Arts & Tongues.* 1673. Reprint, Los Angeles: William Andrews Clark Memorial Library, 1980.

Mandeville, Bernard. *The Fable of the Bees: Or, Private Vices, Publick Benefits.* 2 vols. 1728. Ed. F. B. Kaye. Oxford: Clarendon Press, 1924.

———. *Free Thoughts on Religion, the Church, and Natural Happiness.* London, 1720.

Manley, Delarivière. *Secret Memoirs and Manners of Several Persons of Quality, of Both Sexes. From the New Atalantis, an Island in the Mediteranean.* 1709. Reprint, Gainesville, Fl.: Scholar's Facsimiles and Reprints, 1971.

Marcus, Leah. *Childhood and Cultural Despair: A Theme and Variations in Seventeenth-Century Literature.* Pittsburgh: Pittsburgh University Press, 1978.

Markley, Robert. "Sentimentality as Performance: Shaftesbury, Sterne, and the Theatrics of Virtue." In *The New Eighteenth Century: Theory/Politics/English Literature,* ed. Felicity Nussbaum and Laura Brown, pp. 210–30. New York: Methuen, 1987.

Marks, Sylvia Kasey. *Sir Charles Grandison: The Compleat Conduct Book.* Lewisburg, Penn.: Bucknell University Press, 1986.

Marshall, David. *The Figure of Theater: Shaftesbury, Defoe, Adam Smith, and George Eliot.* New York: Columbia University Press, 1986.

———. "Writing Masters and 'Masculine Exercises' in *The Female Quixote.*" *Eighteenth-Century Fiction* 5 (1993): 105–35.

Martin, Benjamin. *Young Gentleman and Lady's Philosophy, in a Continued Survey of the Works of Nature and Art, by Way of Dialogue.* 2d. ed., 2 vols. London, 1772.

Masham, Damaris. *Discourse Concerning the Love of God.* London, 1696.

———. *Occasional Thoughts in Reference to a Vertuous or Christian Life.* London, 1705.

McGann, Jerome. *The Romantic Ideology.* Chicago: University of Chicago Press, 1983.

McIntosh, Carey. *The Choice of Life: Samuel Johnson and the World of Fiction.* New Haven: Yale University Press, 1973.

McKeon, Michael. "Generic Transformation and Social Change: Rethinking the Rise of the Novel." In *Modern Essays on Eighteenth-Century Literature,* ed. Leopold Damrosch, Jr., pp. 159–80. New York: Oxford University Press, 1988.

———. *The Origins of the English Novel, 1600–1740.* Baltimore: Johns Hopkins University Press, 1987.

McMullen, "The Education of English Gentlewomen 1540–1640." *History of Education* 6, no. 2 (1977): 87–101.

Methods of Erecting, Supporting & Governing Charity-Schools: with An Account of the Charity-Schools in Ireland. 3d ed. Dublin, 1721.

Milton, John. *Of Education.* 1644. In *Complete Prose Works of John Milton,* vol. 2, ed. Ernest Sirluck, pp. 357–415. New Haven: Yale University Press, 1959.

Mitford, John. "Dr. Johnson's Literary Intercourse with Mrs. Lennox." *Gentleman's Magazine* n.s. 20 (1843): 132.

Monro, Hector. *The Ambivalence of Bernard Mandeville.* Oxford: Clarendon Press, 1975.

Monroe, Will S. *Comenius and the Beginnings of Educational Reform.* New York: Charles Scribner's Sons, 1900.

More, Mary. "The Womans Right." ca. 1674. In *The Patriarch's Wife: Literary Evidence and the History of the Family,* by Margaret J. Ezell, Appendix II, pp. 191–203. Chapel Hill: University of North Carolina Press, 1987.

Moretti, Franco. *The Way of the World: The* Bildungsroman *in European Culture.* London: Verso, 1987.

Mücke, Dorothea E. von. *Virtue and the Veil of Illusion: Generic Innovation and the Pedagogical Project in Eighteenth-Century Literature.* Stanford: Stanford University Press, 1991.

Myers, Mitzi. "Domesticating Minerva: Bathsua Makin's 'Curious' Argument for Women's Education." *Studies in Eighteenth-Century Culture* 14 (1985): 173–92.

Nestor, Deborah. "Virtue Rarely Rewarded: Ideological Subversion and Narrative Form in Haywood's Later Fiction." *Studies in English Literature* 34 (1994): 579–98.

Novak, Maximillian E. "Crusoe the King and the Political Evolution of His Island." *Studies in English Literature* 2 (1962): 337–50.

———. *Defoe and the Nature of Man.* Oxford: Oxford University Press, 1963.

———. *Realism, Myth, and History in Defoe's Fiction.* Lincoln: University of Nebraska Press, 1983.

———. "*Robinson Crusoe* and Economic Utopia." *Kenyon Review* 80 (1963): 474–90.

Nyland, Chris. "John Locke and the Social Position of Women." *History of Political Economy* 25, no. 1 (1993): 39–63.

O'Donnell, Sheryl. "Mr. Locke and the Ladies: The Indelible Words on the *Tabula Rasa.*" *Studies in Eighteenth-Century Culture* 8 (1979): 151–64.

Orgel, Stephen. "Jonson and the Amazons." In *Soliciting Interpretation: Literary Theory and Seventeenth-Century English Poetry*, ed. Elizabeth D. Harvey and Katharine Eisaman, pp. 119–39. Chicago: University of Chicago Press, 1990.

Pangle, Thomas L. *The Spirit of Modern Republicanism: The Moral Vision of the American Founders and the Philosophy of Locke.* Chicago: University of Chicago Press, 1988.

Patey, Douglas Lane. *Probability and Literary Form: Philosophic Theory and Literary Practice in the Augustan Age.* Cambridge: Cambridge University Press, 1984.

Paulson, Ronald. *Emblem and Expression: Meaning in English Art of the Eighteenth Century.* Cambridge: Harvard University Press, 1975.

———. *Hogarth: His Life, Art, and Times.* 2 vols. New Haven: Yale University Press, 1971.

———. *Hogarth's Graphic Works.* New Haven: Yale University Press, 1965.

———. *Popular and Polite Art in the Age of Hogarth and Fielding.* Notre Dame, Ind.: University of Notre Dame Press, 1979.

———. *Satire and the Novel in Eighteenth-Century England.* New Haven: Yale University Press, 1967.

———. "The Simplicity of Hogarth's *Industry and Idleness.*" *English Literary History* 41 (1974): 1–30.

Peers, Richard. *A Serious Call to Christianity. Containing Some Directions, By which It may be More effectually Promoted, In the due Instruction of Children.* London, 1715.

Penton, Stephen. *The Guardian's Instruction, Or, The Gentleman's Romance. Written for the Diversion and Service of the Gentry.* London, 1688.

Perry, Ruth. *The Celebrated Mary Astell: An Early English Feminist.* Chicago: University of Chicago Press, 1986.

———. "The Veil of Chastity: Mary Astell's Feminism." *Studies in Eighteenth-Century Culture* 9 (1979): 25–43.

Pickering, Samuel F., Jr. *John Locke and Children's Books in Eighteenth-Century England.* Knoxville: University of Tennessee Press, 1981.

Pietas Corcagiensis. Or, A View of the Green-Coat Hospital: and other Charitable Foundations, In the Parish of St. Mary Shandon, Corke. Cork, 1721.

Pinchbeck, Ivy, and Margaret Hewitt. *Children in English Society: From Tudor Times to the Eighteenth Century.* 2 vols. London: Routledge & Kegan Paul, 1969–73.

Pincus, Steven C. A. "Neither Machiavellian Moment Nor Possessive Individualism: Commercial Society and the Defenders of the English Commonwealth." *The American Historical Review* 103 (1998): 705–36.

———. *Protestantism and Patriotism: Ideologies and the Making of English Foreign Policy, 1650–1668.* Cambridge: Cambridge University Press, 1996.

Plumb, J. H. "The New World of Children in Eighteenth-Century England." *Past and Present* 67 (1975): 64–95.

Pocock, J. G. A. *The Machiavellian Moment: Florentine Political Thought and the Atlantic Republican Tradition.* Princeton: Princeton University Press, 1975.

———. *Virtue, Commerce, and History: Essays on Political Thought and History, Chiefly in the Eighteenth Century.* Cambridge: Cambridge University Press, 1985.

Poovey, Mary. *The Proper Lady and the Woman Writer: Ideology as Style in the Works of Mary Wollstonecraft, Mary Shelley, and Jane Austen.* Chicago: University of Chicago Press, 1984.

Primer, Irwin, ed. *Mandeville Studies: New Explorations in the Art and Thought of Dr. Bernard Mandeville.* The Hague: Martinus Nijhoff, 1975.

Reeve, Clara. *The Progress of Romance.* 2 vols. 1785. Reprint, New York: Facsimile Text Society, 1930.

Reicyu, Nina. *La Pédagogie de John Locke: Actualités Scientifiques et Industrielles.* Paris: Hermann, 1941.

Relihan, Joel C. *Ancient Menippean Satire.* Baltimore: Johns Hopkins University Press, 1993.

Reynolds, Myra. *The Learned Lady in England, 1650–1760.* Boston: Houghton Mifflin, 1920.

Richardson, Samuel. *The History of Sir Charles Grandison.* 1753–54. 3 vols. Ed. Jocelyn Harris. London: Oxford University Press, 1972.

———. *Pamela Or, Virtue Rewarded.* 1740. Ed. Peter Sabor. New York: Penguin, 1980.

———. *Pamela II.* London, 1742.

Richetti, John J. *Philosophical Writing: Locke, Berkeley, Hume.* Cambridge: Harvard University Press, 1983.

Riley, Patrick. Introduction to *Telemachus, Son of Ulysses,* by François de Salignac de la Mothe-Fénelon, ed. and trans. Patrick Riley. Cambridge: Cambridge University Press, 1994.

Rivers, Christopher. *Face Value: Physiognomical Thought and the Legible Body in Marivaux, Lavater, Balzac, Gautier, and Zola.* Madison: University of Wisconsin Press, 1994.

Rogers, Pat. *Robinson Crusoe.* London: George Allen & Unwin, 1979.

Rollin, Charles. *New Thoughts concerning Education.* In *Some Thoughts concerning Education,* by John Locke. Dublin, 1738.

Ronksley, William. *The Child's Weeks-work: or, A Little Book, So nicely Suited to the Genius and Capacity of a Little Child, Both for Matter and Method, That it will infallibly Allure and Lead him on into a Way of Reading With all the Ease and Expedition that can be desired.* London, 1712.

Rorty, Richard. *Consequences of Pragmatism (Essays: 1972–1980)*. Minneapolis: University of Minnesota Press, 1982.

———. *Philosophy and the Mirror of Nature*. Princeton: Princeton University Press, 1979.

Ross, Deborah. "Mirror, Mirror: The Didactic Dilemma of *The Female Quixote*." *Studies in English Literature* 27 (1987): 455–73.

Rothstein, Eric. *Systems of Order and Inquiry in Later Eighteenth-Century Fiction*. Berkeley and Los Angeles: University of California Press, 1975.

Rousseau, Jean-Jacques. *Emile, or On Education*. 1762. Ed. and trans. Allan Bloom. New York: Basic Books, 1979.

Sadler, John Edward. *J. A. Comenius and the Concept of Universal Education*. London: George Allen & Unwin, 1966.

Said, Edward. *Beginnings: Intention and Method*. New York: Basic Books, 1975.

Saunders, Richard. *Physiognomie, and Chiromancie, Metoposcopie. The Symmetrical Proportions and Signal Moles of the Body, Fully and Accurately Explained; with their Natural Predictive Significations both to Men and Women*. 2d ed. London, 1671.

Schofield, Mary Anne. "'Descending Angels': Salubrious Sluts and Pretty Prostitutes in Haywood's Fiction." In *Fetter'd or Free? British Women Novelists, 1670–1815*, ed. M. A. Schofield and C. Mackeski, pp. 186–200. Athens: Ohio University Press, 1986.

———. "Exposé of the Popular Heroine: The Female Protagonists of Eliza Haywood." *Studies in Eighteenth-Century Culture* 12 (1983): 93–103.

Schofield, Mary Anne, and Cecilia Mackeski, eds. *Fetter'd or Free? British Women Novelists, 1670–1815*. Athens: Ohio University Press, 1986.

Schonhorn, Manuel. "Defoe: The Literature of Politics and the Politics of Some Fictions." In *English Literature in the Age of Disguise*, ed. Maximillian E. Novak, pp. 15–56. Berkeley and Los Angeles: University of California Press, 1977.

———. *Defoe's Politics: Parliament, Power, Kingship, and Robinson Crusoe*. Cambridge: Cambridge University Press, 1991.

Schwarz, Kathryn. "Missing the Breast: Desire, Disease, and the Singular Effect of Amazons." In *The Body in Parts: Fantasies of Corporeality in Early Modern Europe*, ed. David Hillman and Carla Mazzio, pp. 147–69. New York: Routledge, 1997.

Scott, Sarah. *A Description of Millenium Hall*. 1762. Ed. Gary Kelly. Orchard Park, N.Y.: Broadview Press, 1995.

Scott-Taggart, M. J. "Mandeville: Cynic or Fool?" *The Philosophical Quarterly* 16 (1966): 221–32.

Sedgwick, Eve Kosofsky. *Between Men: English Literature and Male Homosocial Desire*. New York: Columbia University Press, 1985.

————. "The Character in the Veil: Imagery of the Surface in the Gothic Novel." *PMLA* 96 (1981): 255–70.

Sennett, Richard. *The Fall of Public Man: On the Social Psychology of Capitalism*. New York: Vintage, 1978.

Shaftesbury, Anthony Ashley Cooper, Third Earl of. *Characteristics of Men, Manners, Opinions, Times*. 1711. 2 vols. Ed. John M. Robertson. Indianapolis: Bobbs-Merrill, 1964.

Shapiro, Barbara J. *Probability and Certainty in Seventeenth Century England: A Study of the Relationship between Natural Science, History, Law, and Literature*. Princeton: Princeton University Press, 1983.

Sharpe, Kevin, and Peter Lake, eds. *Culture and Politics in Early Stuart England*. Stanford: Stanford University Press, 1993.

Shepherd, Simon. *Amazons and Warrior Women: Varieties of Feminism in Seventeenth-Century Drama*. New York: St. Martin's Press, 1981.

Sheridan, Thomas. *British Education: Or, The Source of the Disorders of Great Britain*. London, 1756.

Shesgreen, Sean. *Engravings by Hogarth*. New York: Dover, 1973.

————. "Hogarth's *Industry and Idleness*: A Reading." *Eighteenth-Century Studies* 9 (1976): 569–98.

Shevelow, Kathryn. "Re-Writing the Moral Essay: Eliza Haywood's *Female Spectator*." *Reader: Essays in Reader-Oriented Theory, Criticism and Pedagogy* 13 (1985): 19–28.

Sitter, John. "About Wit: Locke, Addison, Prior, and the Order of Things." In *Rhetorics of Order/Ordering of Rhetorics in English Neoclassical Literature*, ed. J. Douglas Canfield and J. Paul Hunter, pp. 137–57. Newark: University of Delaware Press, 1990.

Small, Miriam Rossiter. *Charlotte Ramsay Lennox: An Eighteenth-Century Lady of Letters*. New Haven: Yale University Press, 1935.

Smallwood, Angela J. *Fielding and the Woman Question*. New York: St. Martin's Press, 1989.

Smith, Florence M. *Mary Astell*. New York: Columbia University Press, 1916.

Smith, Nigel. *Literature and Revolution in England, 1640–1660*. New Haven: Yale University Press, 1994.

Society for Promoting Christian Knowledge. *Circular Letters*. London, 1712.

Somerville, John C. "Towards a History of Childhood and Youth." *Journal of Interdisciplinary History* 3 (1972): 438–47.

Spacks, Patricia Meyer. *The Adolescent Idea: Myths of Youth and the Adult*

Imagination. New York: Basic Books, 1981.

———. *Desire and Truth: Functions of Plot in Eighteenth-Century Novels.* Chicago: University of Chicago Press, 1990.

———. *Imagining A Self: Autobiography and Novel in Eighteenth-Century England.* Cambridge: Harvard University Press, 1976.

———. "The Subtle Sophistry of Desire: Dr. Johnson and *The Female Quixote.*" *Modern Philology* 85 (1988): 532–42.

Spacks, Patricia Meyer, and W. B. Carnochan. *A Distant Prospect: Eighteenth-Century Views of Childhood.* Los Angeles: William Andrews Clark Memorial Library, 1982.

Spencer, Jane. *The Rise of the Woman Novelist: From Aphra Behn to Jane Austen.* New York: Basil Blackwell, 1986.

Spender, Dale. *Mothers of the Novel: One Hundred Good Women Writers Before Jane Austen.* London: Pandora, 1986.

Stafford, Barbara Maria. *Artful Science: Enlightenment Entertainment and the Eclipse of Visual Education.* Cambridge: MIT Press, 1994.

———. *Body Criticism: Imaging the Unseen in Enlightenment Art and Medicine.* Cambridge: MIT Press, 1991.

Starr, George A. *Defoe and Casuistry.* Princeton: Princeton University Press, 1971.

———. *Defoe and Spiritual Autobiography.* Princeton: Princeton University Press, 1965.

———. "Sentimental De-education." In *Augustan Studies: Essays in Honor of Irvin Ehrenpreis,* ed. Douglas Lane Patey and Timothy Keegan, pp. 253–62. Newark: University of Delaware Press, 1985.

Staves, Susan. "Don Quixote in Eighteenth-Century England." *Comparative Literature* 24 (1972): 193–215.

Sterne, Laurence. *The Life and Opinions of Tristram Shandy, Gentleman.* 1760–67. Ed. Ian Campbell Ross. Oxford: Oxford University Press, 1983.

Stone, Lawrence. *The Family, Sex and Marriage in England 1500–1800.* New York: Harper & Row, 1977.

Summerfield, Geoffrey. *Fantasy and Reason: Children's Literature in the Eighteenth Century.* Athens: University of Georgia Press, 1984.

Swales, Martin. *The German Bildungsroman from Wieland to Hesse.* Princeton: Princeton University Press, 1978.

Tarcov, Nathan. *Locke's Education for Liberty.* Chicago: University of Chicago Press, 1984.

Tavor, Eve. *Scepticism, Society, and the Eighteenth-Century Novel.* New York: St. Martin's Press, 1987. [See also Bannett entry.]

Tennyson, G. B. "The Bildungsroman in Nineteenth-Century English

Literature." In *Medieval Epic to the 'Epic Theater' of Brecht*, ed. Rosario P. Armato and John M. Spalek, pp. 135–46. Berkeley and Los Angeles: University of California Press, 1968.

Thomas, Keith. "Politics as Language." *New York Review of Books*, 27 Feb. 1986, 36–39.

———. "Women and the Civil War Sects." *Past and Present* 13 (1958): 42–62.

Thompson, James. *Models of Value: Eighteenth-Century Political Economy and the Novel*. Durham, N.C.: Duke University Press, 1996.

Tillotson, John. *Six Sermons*. 2d ed. London, 1694.

Todd, Janet. *The Sign of Angellica: Women, Writing and Fiction, 1660–1800*. London: Virago, 1989.

———. *Women's Friendship in Literature*. New York: Columbia University Press, 1980.

Trenchard, John, and Thomas Gordon. *Cato's Letters*. 1723. 2 vols. London, 1724.

Trotter, Catharine. *A Defence of Mr. Locke's Essay of Human Understanding, wherein Its Principles, with reference to Morality, Revealed Religion, and the Immortality of the Soul, are considered and justified*. London, 1702.

———. *A Letter to Dr. Holdsworth, occasioned by his Sermon Preached before the University of Oxford, On Easter-Monday, Concerning the Resurrection of the Same Body*. London, 1726.

———. *A Vindication of Mr. Locke's Christian Principles*. London, 1751.

———. *The Works of Mrs. Catharine Cockburn, Theological, Moral, Dramatic, and Poetical*. London, 1751.

Tytler, Graeme. *Physiognomy in the European Novel*. Princeton: Princeton University Press, 1982.

Walker, Obadiah. *Of Education Especially of Young Gentlemen*. London, 1673.

Walmsley, Peter. "Prince Maurice's Rational Parrot: Civil Discourse in Locke's *Essay*." *Eighteenth-Century Studies* 28 (1995): 413–25.

Warren, Leland E. "Of the Conversation of Women: *The Female Quixote* and the Dream of Perfection." *Studies in Eighteenth-Century Culture* 11 (1982): 367–80.

Watt, Ian. *The Rise of the Novel*. 1957. Reprint, Berkeley and Los Angeles: University of California Press, 1974.

Watts, Isaac. *The Improvement of the Mind*. London, 1741.

———. *Logick: or, The Right Use of Reason in the Inquiry after Truth*. London, 1725.

Watts, Ruth E. "The Unitarian Contribution to the Development of Female Education, 1790–1850." *History of Education* 9, no. 4 (1980): 273–86.

Webster, Charles. *The Great Instauration: Science, Medicine and Reform 1626–1660*. London: Duckworth, 1975.

———. Introduction to *Samuel Hartlib and the Advancement of Learning*, ed. Charles Webster. Cambridge: Cambridge University Press, 1970.

Wilkes, Wetenhall. *A Letter of Genteel and Moral Advice to a Young Lady. In a New and Familiar Method.* London, 1744.

Williams, Raymond. *Marxism and Literature.* Oxford: Oxford University Press, 1977.

Wilson, Milton. "Reading Locke and Newton as Literature." *University of Toronto Quarterly* 57 (1988): 471–83.

Winstanley, Gerrard. *The Law of Freedom in a Platform: Or, True Magistracy Restored.* London, 1652.

Wollstonecraft, Mary. *A Vindication of the Rights of Woman.* 1792. Ed. Carol H. Poston. New York: W. W. Norton, 1975.

Woodward, Hezekiah. *A Light to Grammar, and All other Arts and Sciences. Or, The Rule of Practise Proceeding by the Clue of Nature, and Conduct of right Reason.* London, 1641.

Woolley, Hannah. *The Gentlewomans Companion; or, A Guide to the Female Sex.* 1673. London, 1675.

Wootton, David, ed. *Republicanism, Liberty and Commercial Society, 1649–1776.* Stanford: Stanford University Press, 1994.

Wordsworth, William. Preface to *Lyrical Ballads.* 1800. In *English Romantic Writers*, ed. David Perkins, pp. 320–31. New York: Harcourt Brace Jovanovich, 1967.

Yolton, John W. *John Locke and Education.* New York: Random House, 1971.

Young, Robert Fitzgibbon. *Comenius in England.* New York: Arno Press and *The New York Times*, 1971.

Youths Behavior, or Decency in Conversation Amongst Men. Trans. Francis Hawkins. London, 1663.

Index

Library of Congress Cataloging-in-Publication Data

Barney, Richard A., 1955–
    Plots of enlightenment : education and the novel in eighteenth
-century England / Richard A. Barney.
        p.   cm.
    Includes bibliographical references and index.
    ISBN 0-8047-2978-6 (cloth : alk. paper)
        1. English fiction—18th century—History and criticism.
    2. Education in literature. 3. Psychological fiction. English—
    History and criticism. 4. Didactic fiction, English—History and
    criticism. 5. Education—England—History—18th century.
    6. Maturation (Psychology) in literature. 7. Knowledge, Theory of,
    in literature. 8. Enlightenment—England. 9. Bildungsroman.
    I. Title.
    PR858.E38B37 1999
        823'.509355—dc21   99-21524

⊛ This book is printed on acid-free, archival quality paper.

Original printing 1999
Last figure below indicates year of this printing:
08   07   06   05   04   03   02   01   00   99

Typeset by Robert C. Ehle in 10.5/12.5 Bembo